Cross-Cultural Communication

Cross-Cultural Communication

Theory and Practice

Brian J. Hurn and Barry Tomalin

First published 2013 by
PALGRAVE MACMILLAN

Palgrave Macmillan in the UK is an imprint of Macmillan Publishers Limited, registered in England, company number 785998, of Houndmills, Basingstoke, Hampshire RG21 6XS.

Palgrave Macmillan in the US is a division of St Martin's Press LLC, 175 Fifth Avenue, New York, NY 10010.

Palgrave Macmillan is the global academic imprint of the above companies and has companies and representatives throughout the world.

Palgrave® and Macmillan® are registered trademarks in the United States, the United Kingdom, Europe and other countries.

ISBN 978–0–230–39113–0

This book is printed on paper suitable for recycling and made from fully managed and sustained forest sources. Logging, pulping and manufacturing processes are expected to conform to the environmental regulations of the country of origin.

A catalogue record for this book is available from the British Library.

A catalog record for this book is available from the Library of Congress.

Contents

List of Figures		vi
Foreword by Professor Jack Spence, OBE		viii
Preface		xii
Acknowledgements		xiv
List of Abbreviations		xvi
About the Authors		xviii
1	What is Cross-Cultural Communication?	1
2	Key Thinkers in Cross-Cultural Communication (1)	20
3	Key Thinkers in Cross-Cultural Communication (2)	47
4	The International Use of English	62
5	Developing Cross-Cultural Communication Skills	78
6	Selection and Preparation for Foreign Assignments	98
7	Leadership Across Cultures	125
8	International Team Building and Teamworking	141
9	The Effect of Culture on International Negotiations	162
10	Multiculturalism and Diversity	191
11	Globalization and its Effect on Culture	208
12	Cultural Diplomacy and Nation Branding	224
13	Transfer of Skills, Technology and Knowledge	241
14	Cultural Profiling and Classification	259
15	Teaching Cross-Cultural Communication	274
Index		294

List of Figures

1.1	Culture – what is it?	4
1.2	Communication styles	7
1.3	A typical communication problem	11
1.4	Barriers to communication	12
1.5	Definitions of heaven and hell (mostly apocryphal!)	15
1.6	The STAR approach	17
2.1	Comparison of high-context and low-context communication	23
2.2	Summary of monochronic and polychronic cultures	27
2.3	High-context and low-context dimensions	29
2.4	Hofstede's four dimensions	31
2.5	Selected power distance scores	32
2.6	Selected individualism/collectivism scores	34
2.7	Selected masculinity and femininity scores	35
2.8	Selected uncertainty avoidance scores	37
2.9	Confucian dynamism values	39
2.10	LTO scores	40
2.11	Selected sixth dimension scores	41
3.1	The 'Mole Map'	55
3.2	The Lewis Cultural Model	57
3.3	Summary of Lewis' three types of culture	57
4.1	Examples of English 'borrowings' from foreign languages	63
4.2	The definition of 'lingua franca' from the *Collins English Dictionary* (2005)	64
4.3	Examples of Franglais	67
4.4	Examples of 'faux amis'	67
4.5	Examples of Hinglish	70
4.6	Examples of Strine	71
4.7	Examples of American English	72
5.1	Non-verbal communication	90
5.2	The culture gap	95

6.1	Main interest groups involved in foreign assignments	99
6.2	Development of cultural awareness	101
6.3	Likely 'stressors'	112
6.4	Full culture shock cycle	122
7.1	Challenges facing twenty-first-century leaders	126
7.2	Requirements of an international manager	128
7.3	Primary leadership dimensions	135
8.1	Summary descriptions of Belbin's Team Roles	144
8.2	Multicultural meetings – critical areas	150
9.1	Cultural aspects affecting negotiating	164
9.2	Assessment of cultural influences	170
9.3	Fundamentals of negotiating	172
9.4	Confucian loyalties	184
10.1	Characteristics of ethnicity	196
10.2	Problem areas facing immigrants	198
11.1	Globalization: driving forces	211
11.2	Top Fortune Global 500 2011 companies	213
11.3	'Glocalization'	219
12.1	Instruments of cultural diplomacy	228
12.2	Building national images	230
13.1	Profile of the effective aid adviser	245
13.2	Barriers to the transfer of skills and knowledge	247
13.3	Model of effective transfer	255
14.1	Types of cultural profiling	261
14.2	Framework analysis: UK/USA example	270
15.1	Learning outcomes	284
15.2	British proverbs	285
15.3	The 'young lady/old lady'	291

Foreword

A leading article in the *Financial Times* on 25 August 2012 neatly sums up a major theme of this timely and well-researched book – the potential for misunderstanding provoked by a failure to acknowledge subtle differences in interpretation in the way in which language is used as a mode of proficient communication across culture boundaries in business, politics and related fields. 'I was only trying to help' must be among the six words most feared in any language. The Japanese have a rather more refined phrase for unwelcome favours: *arigata meiwaku*. This literally means 'thank you for your trouble', but carries nuances along the lines of: 'I didn't want you to do that for me, in fact I tried to avoid having you do it, but you were determined to do me a favour and went ahead anyway, and now it's caused me a lot of trouble but social convention dictates that I express gratitude.'

This elementary but nonetheless revealing example is a product of 'culture shock', which the authors define as: 'When we enter a foreign culture and have difficulty in understanding or predicting why people in that culture behave in ways different from how we behave in our own culture, we feel cut off from familiar patterns of behaviour when all the nuances or shades of meaning are suddenly no longer there to give us support, the rules are unclear and we do not know what is appropriate or inappropriate.'

One of the many explanatory definitions of culture shock is: 'Culture shock is what happens when a traveller finds himself in a place where "yes" may mean "no", where a fixed price is negotiable, where to be kept waiting in an outer office is no cause of insult, where laughter may signify anger' (Alvin Toffler). Similarly, Kalvero Oberg, who coined the phrase during his field work in Brazil in 1958, stated: 'Culture shock is brought on by the anxiety that results from losing all our familiar signs and symbols of social behaviour when living in a foreign country' (Kalvero Oberg, 'Culture Shock: Adjustment to New Cultural Environments', 1960).

True, in the heyday of Western imperial penetration and economic dominance, colonial officers, corporate representatives, diplomats, explorers and missionaries (all examples of professionals who engaged with the outside world) were expected to cope as best they could. Plunged into societies profoundly different from their own, they nevertheless had the confidence (at least in public), indeed the arrogance, to believe that their particular beliefs, administrative systems and religious convictions were superior to the local version and they had a mission (in some cases God-given) to promote Western values and ways of doing things.

Ideological commitment allegedly made up for any private misgivings or difficulties of adjustment to unfamiliar circumstances. Culture shock there may well have been, but it was in many cases borne stoically. At least writers of the stature of E.M. Forster in *A Passage to India* and George Orwell in *Burmese Days* got it right by probing beneath the facade of ceremony, public duty and the 'stiff upper lip' to expose contradictions in the imperial mission. (Incidentally, Orwell's essay *Shooting an Elephant* is, in my view, perhaps the best comment on the contradictions between private doubt and public duty in imperial rule.)

I do not wish to denigrate the lives, indeed the achievements, of those who served in various outposts in remote parts of the Empire. Often, for example, a District Officer in the Colonial Service was responsible for single-handedly administering a territory the size of Wales. All he had to rely on was his legitimacy in the eyes of his subjects (although that proved to be a wasting asset) and administering a justice according to a local version of the rule of law. He was often lonely, cut off from base for long periods, but the great majority so placed coped with the 'shock of the new' with admirable fortitude. Some, such as those described so well in Philip Mason's monumental study *The Men Who Ruled India*, became authorities on the local culture, making a significant contribution to our understanding of distant societies.

Yet the retreat from Empire in the 1940s and 1950s meant that countries like Britain had no alternative but to rely on trade and investment in distant parts. Businessmen and diplomats alike had to do business with their newly independent and confident opposite numbers, although it took some time before the incentives and constraints governing success in this context were recognized. It was all too easy in the immediate post-war period to believe that those sent out on economic or political missions to African and Asian states would adapt without too much difficulty to life in a different culture, the social and economic mores of which might well have been alien in tone and substance. Those interested may well consult Ralph Furse's (aka Acuparius) account of his seemingly eccentric technique for picking likely candidates for the Colonial Service in the 1930s and 1940s.

In time, however, the impact of culture shock on those sent abroad on behalf of governments and major corporations was recognized, along with how best to cope with it, to manage its challenges and to create the appropriate responses to generate success rather than failure. To this end, how to survive, indeed how to prosper in an alien culture, had to rely less on an inherited tradition of behaviour or word of mouth, or – if they were fortunate – to sit, as some in the early post-war period did, at the feet of scholars such as Marjorie Perham at both Oxford and Cambridge where special courses were designed for would-be colonial civil servants. This would never do today in the world of psychometric tests and the like, but it seemed to work well enough. Subsequently, an academic industry developed in the 1960s and 1970s and thereafter designed to help those who went to work abroad and whose adjustment to local circumstances would not be easy.

The business schools have been crucial in this context, producing a body of teachers and scholarly researchers who recognize that those sent abroad by their companies or governments have to have some prior understanding of what to expect, how to behave without giving offence and how to bring the enterprise to a satisfactory outcome that is mutually acceptable to all parties, however different their varied cultural backgrounds.

What is especially impressive about this recognition of the difficulties of cross-cultural communication is the large body of relevant literature produced by scholars and practitioners on how best to cope with the uncertainties of expatriate life abroad in circumstances where professional past experience at home provides little if any guidance.

Few busy chief executives and their subordinates, few diplomats and few NGO expatriates have the time and the energy to navigate their way successfully through this vast literature, valuable as it is. This is precisely why this volume is so helpful. Both the authors have long experience as teachers and consultants in the field of cross-cultural communication. Both are deeply versed in the literature on this topic and well understand the impact of culture shock. Most importantly, their text provides a lucid and detailed account of what the expatriate and business traveller might expect and how best to cope successfully. The tone throughout is detached and free of jargon; the authors' commonsense prescriptions are easily understandable and the advice is always couched in practical terms. The substance of the text is based on careful and candid analysis of the pitfalls that await the unwary professional traveller. Case studies are provided and the analysis is informed by both wit and wisdom of a kind not easily available – if at all – in manageable form elsewhere. In short, the book clearly has intellectual depth based on a sound understanding of the complexity of cross-cultural communication. In addition, the difficulties of adjustment experienced by those returning home from their previous job are not neglected. The situation in the home culture will have changed: new colleagues will have been appointed and new structures and processes devised in the interim.

The authors are also sensitive to the changes that have occurred on the global scene since the end of the Cold War. Thus, they pay particular attention to the impact of globalization on corporations and governments alike. They rightly emphasize the 'shift towards a more integrated and interdependent world economy' (Charles Hill, *International Business*, 2003). Yet the overall theme of the book explicitly acknowledges the paradox that while 'national markets have been merged into one large marketplace', where the rules governing the economic process of buying and selling now enjoy well-nigh universal acceptance, individual professional responses often remain culture bound. Understanding what that constraint means in practice for sensible cross-cultural communication is crucial for successful negotiation, whether arising from orthodox diplomatic engagement or the signing of a trade or investment deal. By the same token, NGO representatives can profit from exposure to the arguments in this book.

What this study does – above all – is to offer helpful, carefully devised signposts of what the authors call 'coping strategies' to guide those who seek their fortunes – whether those of governments or corporations – in a world where cultural exceptionalism (some would say eccentricity) remains a potential source of division and profound misunderstanding. Any would-be travellers would be well advised to include this superb study in their briefcases along with the inevitable pile of business agendas, conference papers and all the accoutrements required for coping with both the 'near and far abroad'.

J.E. Spence OBE

Preface

We are all living in an increasingly globalized, diverse and multicultural world with different communication styles, attitudes, behaviour and cultural values. It is particularly important in international business management, marketing, human resource management and diplomacy that we are aware of the need for improved cross-cultural communication, for without it, the result may be the breakdown of cooperation, understanding and trust in business, diplomacy and international negotiations.

We need to be able to identify the complexities and consequences of cultural diversity in such areas as verbal and non-verbal communication, attitudes towards time, status, authority and the structure of organizations. We can then move on to understand more fully how to overcome the barriers to cross-cultural communication and become more effective in such areas as international negotiations, the transfer of skills and knowledge across cultures, building and working in multinational teams, and the use of cultural diplomacy as a form of 'soft power'. We also need to be able to assess the competencies and cultural awareness training required by those selected to live and operate in this challenging environment.

Cross-cultural awareness and the development of appropriate cross-cultural communication skills are a prerequisite for living harmoniously and working effectively with other members of the international community. The emergence of India and China as economic giants and the increasing influence of globalization have led to greater emphasis on the cultural dimensions of international business, diplomacy and international relations. As a result, many universities and colleges have either developed specific degrees or modules in cross-cultural awareness and cross-cultural/international communication or have made extensive reference to these areas in their undergraduate and postgraduate courses, both in the UK and overseas. The content of this book is therefore directly applicable to, for example, cultural studies, international business courses, international management, human resource management, international diplomacy and international studies. It is also aimed at those responsible for organizing courses for public bodies, NGOs and business enterprises.

As authors, we have extensive experience teaching these aspects to both UK and international students at undergraduate and postgraduate levels. We have also been extensively involved in cross-cultural training for business in the UK and abroad. Our challenge is to design a reference book to be used by both universities and training institutions as a practical guide to developing a deeper understanding of the need for cultural awareness and cross-cultural communication. The content is based on cross-cultural programmes developed by the authors and combines theory and practice through a series of real-life mini case studies and critical incident scenarios, and covers key concepts with a wide variety of examples, supported by a comprehensive reading list. In addition, each chapter can stand alone as the background material for developing a teaching module.

The book aims to achieve the following:

- develop a thorough understanding of the main theoretical and research background and concepts relevant to cross-cultural communication, comparing their value as well as their limitations and their application to contemporary situations;
- identify and apply strategies to overcome the barriers to effective cross-cultural communication;
- identify and evaluate the benefits of cultural diversity and the development of appropriate coping strategies to deal with culture shock encountered when living and working abroad and the subsequent repatriation to the home country;
- evaluate the role of cultural awareness in key international issues, such as globalization, multiculturalism, cultural branding and cultural diplomacy, along with the use of English as a major international language;
- identify the skills and competencies required for success in the international environment, including the personnel selection methods available and the options for pre-departure cultural training;
- assess how cultural issues affect international negotiations, leadership, decision making, the transfer of skills and knowledge across cultures and successful working in a multicultural team.

Acknowledgements

We should like to acknowledge the contribution, inspiration and the encouragement we have received from Professor Nabil Ayad and our colleagues at the Diplomatic Academy of London at the University of Westminster, and subsequently at the University of East Anglia's London campus.

Our book owes much to our discussions with our postgraduate students when we have both been module leaders, teaching Communicating across Cultures and Cultural Awareness. Our students have come from many countries and have included those from the diplomatic field, from embassies, High Commissions and international NGOs, as well as from multinational companies and government departments. They have all contributed to our knowledge through seminars, discussions and participation in conferences and we pay tribute to their influence and enthusiasm. We also acknowledge the contribution from our international business students, both at universities and during in-company training, to whom we have been emphasizing the importance of cross-cultural communication in the field of international business.

During this time, we have become increasingly aware of the need to attempt to produce an easy-to-read yet comprehensive book which encompasses the topics we have found to be the most significant. We hope to have included reference to those experts who have had the most impact through their research. These we have considered to be the 'cultural gurus' who have inspired us to take a lasting interest in the influence of culture on diplomacy and business in the increasingly globalized and interdependent world.

We have produced further reading lists for each chapter, as well as listing our references. Regarding the latter, we apologise in advance for any errors or omissions, and we have, wherever possible, sought permission for any lengthy quotations. If we have erred in this, it has not been by design and mistakes will be rectified in any future edition.

We acknowledge in particular permission to quote from the following: Geert Hofstede B.V. for material used in Figures 2.5–2.11; Nicholas Brealey Publishing for material in Figures 3.2 and 3.3 and for additional material published in R. Lewis in *When Cultures Collide* (2011), J. Mole, *Mind Your Manners* (2003) for Figure 3.1, F. Trompenaars with C. Hampden-Turner, *Riding the Waves of Culture* (2012) and M. Bennett, *Basic Concepts of Intercultural Communications* (2008); Sage Publications for material used in Figure 7.3 published in R. House *et al.*, *Cultures, Leadership and Organisations* (2004); the Belbin Institute for material used in Figure 8.1 and Thorogood Publishing for material used in Figure 14.2 and details of the RADAR profile in Chapter 4, originally published in B. Tomalin and M. Nicks, *The World's Business Cultures and How to Unlock Them* (2010). Our thanks are also due to Simon Anholt for his invaluable guidance and detailed comments on Chapter 12. Full details of all these publications can be found in the References and Further reading recommendations at the end of each chapter.

We wish to thank our publishers Palgrave Macmillan, Steven Kennedy for his initial advice and in particular Virginia Thorp, the Senior Commissioning Editor, and her assistant Keri Dickens for their guidance throughout the period in which we have been writing. We would also like to record our thanks to Jon Lloyd, our copy editor, for his detailed help in turning our manuscript into a book ready for publication. We also owe a debt of gratitude to Professor Jack Spence who has encouraged us in all our endeavours.

Finally, we should also put on record the support we have received from our families and, in particular, the invaluable work done by Sheila Hurn, who has typed our drafts, coordinated our contributions and critically proofread our work at the various stages. Any errors, of course, are our own.

Brian Hurn and Barry Tomalin
October 2012

List of Abbreviations

AOB	Any Other Business
APEC	Asia Pacific Economic Cooperation
ASEAN	Association of South East Asian Nations
BAA	British Airports Authority
BASIC	British American Scientific International Commercial
BRICs	Brazil, Russia, India and China
CARICOM	Caribbean Community and Common Market
CEO	Chief Executive Officer
CIDA	Canadian International Development Agency
CIPD	Chartered Institute of Personnel and Development
CNN	Cable News Network
CVS	Chinese Value Survey
DfID	Department for International Development (previously the ODA)
DISC	Drive, Influence, Steadiness, Caution profile model
DMIS	Developmental Model of Intercultural Sensitivity
FCO	Foreign and Commonwealth Office
FTSE 100	Financial Times Stock Exchange Top 100 listed companies
GATT	General Agreement on Tariffs and Trade
GDP	Gross Domestic Product
GLOBE	Global Leadership and Organizational Behaviour Effectiveness Project
GNI	Gross National Income
HRM	Human Resource Management
HSBC	Hong Kong and Shanghai Banking Corporation
IDV	Individualism Value (Hofstede)
IJV	International Joint Venture
IMF	International Monetary Fund
INCA	Intercultural Competence Assessment
LDCs	Less Developed Countries

LTO	Long-Term Orientation (Hofstede)
MAS	Masculinity Index (Hofstede)
MBA	Master in Business Administration
MBTI	Myers-Briggs Type Indicator – personality testing
MNC	Multinational company
MTV	Music TV, originally an American cable TV channel
NAFTA	North American Free Trade Agreement (comprising the USA, Canada and Mexico)
NATO	North Atlantic Treaty Organization
NGO	Non-Governmental Organization
NORAID	Norwegian Government Training Scheme
NVC	Non-Verbal Communication
OAI	Overseas Assignment Index
ODA	Overseas Development Agency (precursor of the DfID)
OECD	Organization for Economic Cooperation and Development
OPEC	Organization of Petroleum Exporting Countries
PDI	Power Distance Index (Hofstede)
PwC	PricewaterhouseCoopers
SMEs	Small and medium-size enterprises
SPM	Spony Profiling Model
STO	Short-Term Orientation (Hofstede)
UAI	Uncertainty Avoidance Index (Hofstede)
UNEC	Uniting Europe through Cultures project
USIS	United States Information Services
WHO	World Health Organization
WTO	World Trade Organization

About the Authors

Brian J. Hurn is Visiting Lecturer at the London Academy of Diplomacy at the University of East Anglia (London Campus), teaching Cultural Awareness. He also lectures on International HR and Doing Business in Asia for INSEEC in London and at a consortium of French universities. He was formerly Associate Professor at Schiller International University in London and Associate Lecturer at the University of Surrey School of Management.

A graduate in Modern Languages from the University of Exeter, he has an MA in Education Administration and Postgraduate Certificate in Education from the University of London.

He was a Lieutenant Colonel in the Royal Army Educational Corps and is a graduate of the Army Staff College, having held key appointments in education and training support at Sandhurst, in the Far East and at the Ministry of Defence. He was subsequently Director of Programmes at the Centre for International Briefing, Farnham, UK.

He is the author of numerous articles and international conference papers on cultural aspects of international relations and business.

Barry Tomalin is also Visiting Lecturer at the London Academy of Diplomacy, teaching Cultural Awareness and International Communication. In addition, he is Director of Cultural Training at International House, London.

He was formerly English Language Teaching Adviser to the government of Benin and was editor and producer of BBC English by Radio and TV at the BBC World Service. He was also Managing Director of Connect ELT Ltd.

He graduated from the School of Oriental and African Studies, University of London and has an MA in International Liaison and Communication from the University of Westminster. He is also a qualified teacher of English as a Foreign Language and is a member of the English Language Council of the English Speaking Union.

He has 30 years' experience in training in over 50 countries. His publications include *Key Business Skills* (2012), *The World's Business Cultures and How to Unlock Them* with Mike Nicks (2010) and *Diverse Europe at Work* with Jack Lonergan and Adam Duncan (2009).

1
What is Cross-Cultural Communication?

Summary

Influence of various disciplines on cultural studies
Language and thought debate
Semiotics
Definitions of culture
Corporate culture
Communication styles
Barriers to effective cross-cultural communication
Problems of cross-cultural communication
Perception, reality and stereotypes
What influences our cross-cultural effectiveness?

Introduction

This first chapter looks at the influence of other disciplines on cultural studies. It examines different definitions of 'culture' and 'communication' and looks at key areas of cultural diversity in visible behaviour and underlying values. It analyses strategies for optimizing successful communication with people of other cultures and overcoming the barriers to cross-cultural communication.

Many cross-cultural relationships break down because of failures in communication. This is not just due to speaking different languages, although that is certainly part of the problem; it is also due to different understandings of communication itself. In Chapter 4 we examine the role of the English language as arguably the prime medium of international communication worldwide. In this chapter we examine the role of communication itself in facilitating or hindering international exchange.

Cross-cultural communication is a multifaceted subject which has elements from a number of disciplines:

- anthropology;
- linguistics;
- philosophy;
- psychology.

Cross-cultural communication is about the way people from different cultures communicate when they deal with each other either at a distance or face to face. Communication can involve spoken and written language, body language and the language of etiquette and protocol.

In essence there are two main schools of research:

a) the Theory and Research (sociology and communications) school;
b) the Theory into Practice school (an interdisciplinary approach using psychology, anthropology, sociology and linguistics).

How linguistics influences communication

The key influences are the study of *semiotics*, the study of signs, and the study of the relationship between language and thought and language and culture.

There are three interrelated questions:

- Does the way we use language influence the way we think?
- Does the way we think influence the language we use?
- Does culture influence language or is it the other way round?

Semiotics

Semiotics was introduced by the Swiss linguist Ferdinand de Saussure (1857–1913). It is defined as 'the study of signs and symbols and their use in interpretation' (*Oxford English Dictionary*). Saussure put forward the idea that language is a cultural phenomenon and that it produces meaning in a special way. He developed the theory that any linguistic item such as a word represents a sign. A sign has three basic characteristics: it has a concrete form, it refers to something other than itself and it is recognized by other people as a sign. The physical form of a sign he called the 'signifier'. The mental association it refers to is the 'signified'.

To illustrate the concept, we can take the word 'friend'. A friend may mean someone who is not hostile to you, someone with whom you have a friendly association, a close lifelong buddy or someone who opposes the same things that you do. Similarly, the word 'boyfriend' or 'girlfriend' may signify a person you are going out with or in other countries simply a friend with no sexual connotation at all. The point is that 'friend' is a common word in all languages, but has very different connotations according to the society that uses it. Therefore, part of cultural study is to find out whether the same words mean the same thing in different cultures.

Language and thought

The first academic cultural studies were carried out by anthropologists in the mid-nineteenth and early twentieth centuries and were centred in the USA on the Native Americans. They wanted to understand the cultures of the rapidly disappearing Native-American tribes and, in particular, the study of their languages. They attempted to answer the question 'which came first, language or thought?'. Was it the cultural features which then gave rise to the language needed to express them or did the language itself condition how people thought about their society? If the language came first, did that limit how people thought about their society? Briefly summarized, the debate is whether language determines what we experience and how we see the world or whether our experience of the world determines how we think about it and how we then express it.

There has been much debate as to which comes first, that is, language or thought. This debate was continued by the American linguists and anthropologists Edward Sapir and his pupil Benjamin-Lee Whorf, who also had a special interest in American-Indian languages. They developed the Sapir-Whorf Hypothesis, which was based on linguistic determinism, in other words the proposition that language determines the way we think and speak. Sapir emphasized that the real world is, to a large extent, built upon the language habits of the group. We see, hear and otherwise experience as we do because of the language habits of our community, which predispose us towards certain choices of interpretation.

The cultural anthropologist and ethnologist Franz Boas established the link between language and behaviour from his studies of native American communities. He concluded that: 'The peculiar characteristics of languages are clearly reflected in the views and customs of the people of the world' (Boas, 1938: 31). He maintained that it was necessary to view the world around us through the eyes of other cultures if we really wanted to understand it.

However, Noam Chomsky (1975) supports the existence of linguistic universals (universal grammar), but rejects the existence of cultural universals. Chomsky is supported by Steven Pinker, who resists the idea that language shapes thought.

Modern linguists tend to put the emphasis on the potential for thinking to be influenced rather than unavoidably determined by language. The American researcher Lena Boroditsky (2001) also criticizes the polarization of thought which leads to thinking that one feature influences the other. She maintains that there is a symbiotic relationship between language and the way we think about culture, with each constantly influencing the other.

In the language versus culture debate, it is clear that sharing a language implies sharing a culture; for example, in Belgium, where Flemish and French are the main shared languages, the scores of the Flemish and French-speaking regions are on Hofstede's four dimensions of culture (see Chapter 2) very similar to each other, but different from those of the Netherlands.

Without knowing the language well, one misses a lot of the subtleties of a culture, for example, humour, and one is forced to remain a relative outsider. Therefore, in the cross-cultural encounter, experienced travellers recognize that it is prudent to avoid jokes and irony until they are sure of the other culture's perception of what represents acceptable humour: 'The essence of effective cross-cultural communication has more to do with releasing the right responses than sending the right message' (Hall and Hall, 1990: 4).

Definitions of culture

ART?	MUSIC?
LITERATURE?	HUMOUR?
FOOD?	LANGUAGE?
VALUES?	ATTITUDES?
CUSTOMS?	ETIQUETTE?

Figure 1.1   Culture – what is it?

As we might expect, there are many definitions of culture. Some of these include the following:

- 'Culture is man-made, confirmed by others, conventionalized ... It provides people with a meaningful context in which to meet, to think about themselves and face the other world' (Trompenaars, 2000: 3).
- 'A shared system of meanings. It dictates what we pay attention to, how we act and what we value' (Trompenaars, 1993: 13).
- 'Each cultural world operates according to its own internal dynamics, its own principles and its own laws – written and unwritten. Even time and space are unique to each culture. There are, however, some common threads that run through all cultures' (Hall and Hall, 1990: 3).

It would seem that a comprehensive workable definition of culture is based on the belief that its value systems lie at its core. These are what defines a particular culture. It includes its norms of behaviour, beliefs, aesthetic standards, patterns of thinking and styles of communication which a particular group of people have developed over time to ensure their survival.

Culture is therefore socially, and not biologically, constructed. Individuals are socialized into a particular culture and their individuality is developed within the overall context of that culture. All people carry within them patterns of thinking, feeling and behavioural responses which have been learned throughout their lifetime. Much of this is acquired during early childhood, when a person is most susceptible to learning and assimilating.

We can summarize these definitions to say that culture is a system of shared beliefs and values which are learned rather than inherited. It is composed of those values and beliefs, norms, symbols and ideologies that make up the total way of life of a people. Culture has also been defined as a form of 'map' which each of us has implanted in us by the society into which we are born. This 'map' defines reality, sets the guidelines for behaviour, thus developing our value system, and establishes the rules for problem solving or explaining events that are not normally encountered.

In most Western languages, 'culture' is taken to mean 'civilization', 'education', 'art'. This is culture in a narrow sense. However, culture is also a form of mental programming. As soon as certain patterns of thinking, feeling and behaviour have been established, for the individual to learn something different, the old patterns need to be unlearned. These patterns of thinking, feeling and behaviour can indeed be described as a form of mental programming, using a computer analogy, and have been called 'mental software', extending the analogy. Indeed, Hofstede describes culture as: 'The collective programming of the mind, which distinguishes the members of one group or category of people from another' (1994: 5). What we 'learn' is, in fact, modified by the influence of 'collective programming' (that is, culture) as well as by our own unique personal experiences throughout life.

A useful method is to divide culture into *implicit culture* – basic assumptions which produce norms and values which show in the *explicit culture* – observable reality which includes language, food, music, dress, literature, architecture, public emotion, work ethic, noise, physical contact and so on.

Oberg's iceberg analogy

The Danish writer Kalvero Oberg (1960) uses the analogy of an iceberg to describe visible and invisible culture. *Visible* culture is what appears above the waves, for example, the *explicit* culture referred to above. This can be relatively easily observed, even by those who have only a limited exposure to a new culture, for example, tourists and infrequent business travellers, although its significance may not be fully recognized. The *invisible* culture is what lies below the waves: the *implicit* culture. This includes assumptions, values, attitudes towards authority, risk taking, punctuality, communication patterns, how status is defined and how power is distributed in society. The assumptions, at the deepest level, are the most important levels of culture and the most difficult to understand. We can at least be aware of the differences that exist and can develop sensitivity so that we are prepared for any 'surprises' when they occur.

Corporate culture

Corporate culture is often described as 'the way we do things around here' or 'the glue that holds an organization together'. It is the collective behaviour of people in organizations where they share the same corporate vision, goals, values, customs and work procedures, a common working language and symbols. It is to be found in, for example, large multinational companies (such as Shell and Toyota), the Armed Forces and the Diplomatic Service. These common values are, in effect, a form of implicit control mechanism that permeates the ethos of the organization. Therefore, corporate culture is, to a large extent, how an organization exercises control over its members and how behaviour is regulated. A further example of corporate culture is found in professional life, codes of professional conduct and ethical standards, for example, those relating to lawyers, teachers and doctors.

Corporate culture within an organization includes the logo, advertising slogans and the common jargon used; for example, McDonald's employees are known as 'crew members'. Other corporate symbols can include the myths and stories about the founders, its particular successes, the annual office party and the company uniform. Corporate culture embodies a corporate ethos, with its own code of ethical conduct and social responsibility which is communicated to all employees and suppliers, and can cover such areas as human rights, employment practices and concern for the environment. Large multinationals further develop their corporate culture through the setting up of corporate universities, an early example being the McDonald's Hamburger University in Illinois, set up in the 1950s. Other large companies have followed this example and have set up branches of their corporate universities abroad to train their staff of various cultures in the corporate culture and strategy of the organization.

Communication styles

In modern cultural studies, the key issue is the way in which different cultures communicate. Communication is the process by which thoughts, information and instructions are passed between people. Communication breaks down into three broad areas:

- verbal communication;
- non-verbal communication (body language);
- written communication.

A fourth area, which is rapidly becoming even more influential, is the increased use of technology in communication. This covers the use of language on the Internet, as well as communication devices such as smartphones which many argue are changing the way we think and use language.

Tomalin and Nicks (2010) have developed a framework to help identify the key differentiating features in communication. In doing so, they represent the ideas put forward by Hall, Hofstede and Trompenaars (see Chapters 2 and 3) as they relate to communication. Their communication framework is summarized below. In the matrix, the key communication features are presented in opposition to each other. The contention is that if you, for example, understand your dominant style and compare it to your interlocutor's dominant style, you will be well placed to understand how your communication style might be misunderstood and therefore will adapt it accordingly.

Direct	Indirect
Details	Suggestions
What/why	Why/what
Formal	Informal
Emotional	Neutral
Fast	Slow

Figure 1.2 Communication styles

Direct/indirect

Direct communicators say what they think without adapting the message to the listener/reader. The result is transparent and clear, but may also be perceived as undiplomatic or even rude. Direct communicators, for example, North Americans, Scandinavians, Germans and the Dutch, have less sensitivity about causing offence. They have a reputation for expressing themselves in a direct manner and for being prepared to say frankly what they think. This approach may be misconstrued by indirect communicators, whose primary concern is to protect personal dignity and avoid causing offence. In extreme cases, this may even lead to the communication of wrong or misleading information to avoid the risk of upsetting the other person. Asian cultures are generally good examples of indirect communicators.

Details and suggestions communicators

Some societies, in particular the Chinese and the Japanese, believe that it is important to go into great detail so that everything is clearly understood and that there can be no misunderstanding. People in these societies will want high degrees of, for example, technical specifications and will ask many questions to gain clarification. Such an approach is often perceived by suggestions communicators as time-consuming and overly complicated. Suggestions communicators like to leave room for interpretation and initiative and may prefer to be more general in their approach. They may prefer to hint or make suggestions either to allow the recipient the opportunity to interpret what has been said in his or her own way or because they assume that the recipient will understand the context in which they are speaking. However, such an approach can be seen by detailed communicators as rather too general and lacking in clarity.

What/why – why/what

This is a re-statement of Edward T. Hall's concise/expressive communication paradigm, which is discussed in more detail in Chapter 2. A what/why culture corresponds to Hall's concise mode of expression. People say what they want and then why they want it. Tomalin and Nicks (2010) call this group 'the What/Why communicators'. The North European culture cluster will normally prefer this mode of communication. People tend to get to the point quickly and then provide explanations and context afterwards. A why/what culture corresponds to Hall's expressive mode and is exactly the opposite. An expressive communicator will prefer to provide the context and background before saying what he or she wants. He or she focuses on context first and comes to the point at the end. The rationale is: 'How can you possibly understand what I want unless I have explained the background first?'

Once again, perceptions play a part in miscommunication. What/why concise communicators tend to feel that why/what expressive communicators waste time in coming to the point. Why/what communicators become frustrated because they receive too little information from what/why communicators. They often feel they are being given orders and need more background information to understand what is required. Once again, simple linguistic strategies can resolve tensions. A why/what communicator who needs a little more patience from his or her counterpart simply has to say 'I'll answer your question, but I do need to give a bit of background first'.

Formal/informal communicators

This paradigm links into Hofstede's power distance index (see Chapter 2) as it indicates how power and status are reinforced by the communication style. As a rule, high power distance normally requires more formal language, for example, the use of titles such as Mr and Mrs or their equivalents, the use of professional titles such as Dr and, above all, a clear distinction between the familiar and the formal 'you', which does not exist in English.

Some societies prefer a relatively formal way of addressing you until they know you well. This is the case in many European cultures as well as in

Latin America, Africa and Asia. The more informal style of communication has, to a degree, been adopted in the predominantly English-speaking countries of the UK, the USA, Canada, Australia and New Zealand. In many other cultures, formality equates with respect. Formality may be interpreted in informal communities as a wish to maintain distance, whereas informality may be interpreted in formal communities as showing a lack of respect for age or status. The strategy is to find out what is the accepted way of addressing people and also the accepted way of communicating with them and to respond accordingly. Although the UK has a reputation for formality, the British can be as informal as the Americans when communicating with their peers and superiors, and this has been increasingly the case in recent years.

An example of the perceived inappropriateness of informality occurred when former US President George W. Bush welcomed Tony Blair, the former British Prime Minister, in public before the world's press in Washington with the ultra-familiar 'Yo Blair!' greeting.

Emotional/neutral communicators

An emotional society considers that an element of communication is to show one's emotions. Members of such a society believe that using their emotions is an important aspect of self-expression, so they use their voice, eyes and arms in a more demonstrative way. A neutral society is exactly the opposite because it believes that it is important to control your emotions, to keep a straight face devoid of expression and to restrict your body language while using neutral language. The most emotional societies are the Mediterranean and the Latin American cultures. Examples of neutral societies include those of Japan and Northern Europe, including the British with their supposedly famous 'stiff upper lip'. Once again, the style of communication you use can cause a number of different reactions. To a neutral communicator, an emotional communicator may possibly convey unreliability, while to an emotional communicator, a neutral communicator may run the risk of conveying a lack of clarity and even possible dishonesty.

When working with neutrals, a calm, measured approach is usually the most appropriate. You should keep your voice calm and your gestures minimal. If your counterpart does not smile, do not assume it is rudeness or anger. Similarly, if you are working with emotional communicators, be more expressive with your voice and gestures, be prepared to show your more human side and be ready to share personal stories about yourself and your family.

Fast/slow

This refers to whether the speed of communication is fast or slow and corresponds to Lewis' (2004) distinction between 'ping-pong' cultures (fast speaking, interrupting and tolerance of interruptions) and 'bowling' cultures (slower speaking, observing strict turn-taking in conversation and avoiding interruptions whenever possible). In a ping-pong culture, a conversation is like a game of table tennis, moving at a fast pace with people interrupting each other and not minding interruptions. Conversely, a conversation in a 'bowling' culture is like the game of bowls, where players roll a ball along the ground to see who can get closest to another ball thrown earlier. 'Bowlers' pause before speaking, give themselves time to consider and then speak. They may find interruptions offensive. 'Ping-pongers' can be seen as rather shallow and inconsiderate listeners.

Although all foreign speech probably sounds fast to a non-native speaker, the speed of delivery of languages like Spanish or Hindi has been found to be on average significantly faster than, for example, German or English. The pace of life in large cities, for example, in New York, Los Angeles or Chicago in the USA, may have an effect on the speed of speech delivery compared with that in surrounding areas, and the North of the USA is considered to have a faster speech rhythm than the Midwest or the South. The issue of speed of speech is probably less important than the significance given to interruptions. Some cultures accept interruptions called 'overlapping', but others consider it impolite.

Practical implications

The communication framework is a useful tool for identifying key verbal communication features, but it is important not to over-generalize. Clearly, the style of communication will vary according to the location, profession and lifestyle of the individual. The communication style may also vary between social groups. Nevertheless, it is a useful guide for applying theory to practice.

Barriers to effective communication

There is a Southeast Asian proverb that says: 'Misunderstandings don't exist; only the failure to communicate exists.' There is certainly a lot of truth in this. 'The essence of effective cross-cultural communication has more to do with releasing the "right" response than with sending the 'right' messages' (Hall and Hall, 1990: 4). Hall places communication at the heart of all cross-cultural interaction: 'Culture is communication – it may be seen as a continuous process of communicating and reinforcing group norms.' Communication involves transmitting messages (verbally or non-verbally) to another person, who decodes (that is, translates) these messages by giving them meaning. These messages may be sent by conscious intent or not and may include information about both the actual content of the message and the relationship between those involved in the communication process. The process is completed by coding, transmission, decoding and finally feedback.

However, misunderstanding often occurs in the transmission of the 'message' encoded by the sender and decoded by the receiver. 'Noise' or interference occurs along the way and the result can be distortion or misunderstanding which is shown in the feedback part of the loop, that is, in either the reply or the observed behaviour as a result of receiving the message. It may be dangerous to assume that others will necessarily decode our message in the way that we intended. It is therefore important to try to check how our message has been interpreted by the receiver. This is a typical sequence of events in which noise or interference can impact upon the correct delivery of the message sent.

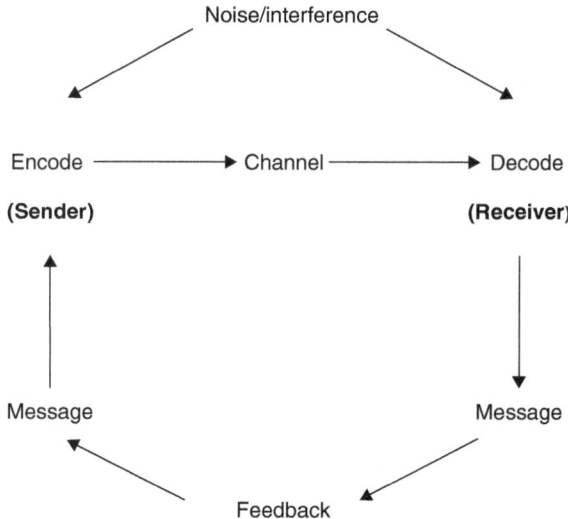

Figure 1.3   A typical communication problem

The problem is that whatever our message, we can be sure that it may often become distorted as it travels across cultures. Accepting this, we should:

- be aware of the distinct possibility of distortion or misinterpretation;
- understand how a message may, in fact, be misinterpreted;
- modify our behaviour to account for this in order to be prepared to correct any misinterpretation and, if necessary, remedy the situation.

Face-to face communication has the great advantage of providing instant feedback. In other forms of communication, particularly electronic communication, such as email, coding and decoding, problems occur when feedback is delayed.

When we wish to communicate internationally, we rarely see the whole context. The result is that we often have difficulty in fully understanding the situation. The outcomes are as follows:

- we have to make decisions about how to behave on the information we have, which is often incomplete;
- we choose to fill in or ignore contextual information in our attempts to make decisions;
- we use our own already pre-programmed expectations to do this.

As a result, we often make mistakes in perception, interpretation and evaluation.

Ideally, communication takes place in a continuous feedback loop: I communicate, you respond, I reply and so on until the communication is complete. However, in international conversations, misunderstandings are frequently liable to occur. We fail to evaluate the message properly, the result being that we do not give it appropriate importance.

Parochialism	Fear of embarrassment, conflict
Ethnocentrism	Ignorance of culture of others
Laziness	Stereotyping

Figure 1.4   Barriers to communication

Ethnocentrism

We tend to judge other cultures according to the beliefs, values and traditions of our own group or culture. We then categorize groups other than ours as bad, weak, immoral, stupid, crazy and so on. Ethnocentrism may be said to be almost universal. Members of nearly all the world's cultures regard their own way of life as being 'better' than even closely related neighbours. We often ascribe generalized, unfounded and negative attributes to other cultures. Our reactions can be summarized as follows:

- *Ignorance*: we are often very ignorant of other people's culture – their history, religion, art, customs, values and so on.
- *Fear and anxiety*: we are often afraid of novelty, embarrassment and conflict. We suffer anxiety and stress because we do not know what to do in certain situations.
- *Laziness*: we are often lazy, sometimes for good reasons, such as time pressures. This makes us reluctant to learn and practise tolerance and understanding. We also often prefer to take the easy way out by assuming similarity rather than attempting to understand actual cultural differences.

Our reactions to a cultural situation which differs from our own experience often follow the sequence given below:

- we observe what is happening;
- we try to communicate;
- we find it difficult to understand;
- we interpret the situation according to our own limited knowledge, our own values and possibly limited experience;
- we become judgmental and often in exasperation make our prejudices apparent.

Cultural diversity

Different cultures have different norms and expectations of behaviour in both formal and informal situations, for example, social interaction, meetings or negotiations. A lack of awareness and understanding of these differences can create misunderstandings and, in extreme cases, even offence.

Assuming similarity with one's own culture

There is often a tendency to assume similarities between the foreign culture and one's own, rather than understanding the differences. An example is the British and American perceptions that there are very few differences between their cultures, although in reality there are many subtle ways in which the two cultures differ, and this is only fully recognized when the two live and work in each other's culture.

Stereotyping

Stereotypes can be described as a group of beliefs and attitudes towards people who are members of another distinct group. People form pre-established expectations about how members of other groups are likely to behave and what they believe in. Experiences often do not fit into our preconceived categories and we are then faced with ambiguity. Our response is to try to force them into an inaccurate category, thus distorting our perception of reality, with the result that we feel insecure and uncertain. The danger is that categorizing can lead to stereotyping and we categorize people of other cultures in the simplest way possible. The end result is a tendency to often invest these categories with negative emotions because they constitute the unknown. Stereotyping provides a quick, simple way of classifying people, particularly those from other cultures, but it does not allow for variation and may be positive or negative. Stereotypes are usually harmless if used only as a general rule of thumb, but can be hurtful, dangerous and racist if taken to be the whole truth about another group of people. This is because all stereotypes contain value judgments. They are not based on personal experience but are often acquired from the media or the prejudices inherent in our own social group. For example, racial stereotypes reflect racial prejudices and when these are repeated in the media, there is the danger that they may become perpetuated and institutionalized. Another example is the way in which people are stereotyped or pigeon-holed due to their accent, dialect, physical appearance or social class and background. The result is the forming of often inaccurate opinions that have little factual basis and are grossly over-simplified. The socialization of people into particular cultures can give rise to distinct cultural values and associated perceptions, for example, views on poverty, immigrants, standards of economic development and so on. Our own group loyalty often encourages us to believe that our group is 'better' and more important than other groups.

Although national barriers are disappearing as a result of globalization and the Internet, national stereotyping persists. A moderate amount of stereotyping is inevitable, acceptable and at times even humorous, but displays of deep ignorance which cause offence are matters of concern. There is therefore a need for objective and informed knowledge about other cultures.

Common stereotypical categories may be labelled in terms of, for example, race, age, gender, social class and dress. The danger lies in the speed and intensity of these generalizations and assumptions about other people, which are usually based on very thin evidence and knowledge. Stereotyping can take two different forms:

- traits that we admire – ambition, modesty, cleverness, bravery;
- traits that we deplore or dislike – laziness, stupidity, lack of ambition.

However, there is a place for stereotypes, as our brain tries to sort into categories, and stereotypes become initially useful pigeon-holes until we learn more about other people and realize that within any group there are large individual differences. Stereotypes also play their part in providing a basis for possible further closer investigation.

Perception

Perception lies at the very heart of cross-cultural communication. We all tend to categorize our experiences in order to make sense of the world we live in. The problem is that when we encounter a new world we are not familiar with, we are faced with ambiguity, which in turn causes insecurity. Faced with insecurity, our natural tendency is to fall back on our own norms and values and perceive the person we are dealing with as alien and even hostile. Our negative emotions come to the fore and we stereotype the person we are dealing with, and these stereotypes are frequently negative. We assume quite incorrectly that we all think about and perceive the world in basically the same way. We have a tendency to see things not as they are but as we are.

Differences in culture are very often because of differences in perception. The problem is that when we communicate internationally, we often misunderstand the total context. We make mistakes in perception and we see things negatively that the speaker in his or her environment would consider totally non-confrontational. A good example is direct and indirect criticism. In China, Japan and, to a lesser extent, South Korea, it is important not to criticize anyone directly in order to save the 'face' of the person being criticized. The potential for communication failure is therefore greatly increased when the sender and receiver do not share the same cultural perceptions.

We often assume other people experience the same physical, intellectual and emotional reactions as we do. We believe that what is pleasing or distasteful to us is pleasing or distasteful to others. This is clearly not the case in reality. We therefore need to understand why this is so and at least to recognize our differences of perception. Some examples of attitudes regarding perception are as follows:

- 'Abroad is unutterably bloody and foreigners are fiends' (Nancy Mitford, 1945).
- 'Everybody has the right to pronounce foreign names as he chooses' (Winston Churchill).
- 'What is true on one side of the Pyrenees is not on the other' (Blaise Pascal, seventeeth-century French philosopher).

Whenever we go to live and work internationally, we all begin our time abroad with certain preconceived ideas, attitudes and prejudices. These are rooted in our experiences and our culture, and, as we have seen, they are coloured and often reinforced by what we read and are told. We look at

---

Heaven is where: The police are British
The cooks are French
The mechanics are German
The lovers are Italian
It is all organized by the Swiss

Hell is where: The police are German
The cooks are British
The mechanics are French
The lovers are Swiss
It is all organized by the Italians

Figure 1.5   Definitions of heaven and hell (mostly apocryphal!)

the world around us through the *filter* of our own values, prejudices and the stereotypes we have built up. The problems occur when we meet other people in other cultures who look at the same facts but come up with a different view. We may find this uncomfortable, even challenging, and perhaps at first sight somewhat intimidating. Other people's views may well be different but not necessarily wrong. If we are to understand their world, we need to understand their perceptions, including their perceived view of us in our culture.

Perception can often play tricks on us as things are not always as they seem. Perception is usually selective and culture-driven, and works on differences rather than similarities. Our perception of another culture is relative and comes from our own set of values in our own culture. Perception is, in fact, our reality; the 'facts' are almost irrelevant until we really understand the other culture.

The problem is often that, despite all our best efforts to suspend our judgment as we have been taught to do and to avoid stereotyping and be tolerant to differences in other cultures, when we are under pressure and stressed, we often revert to type and reveal our prejudices.

To overcome our perceptions of others, we need to recognize that other people are not better or worse, just different. To deal with others successfully and to control our own feelings when faced with ambiguity or insecurity, we need to do three things:

- *Accept difference*: we should accept that others are different from us.
- *Recognize ignorance*: we should recognize that we do not know precisely how others differ from us. We choose to fill in or ignore contextual information in attempting to make decisions and use our own pre-programmed cultural bias.
- *Take responsibility*: we should accept responsibility for our feelings and reactions when dealing with others.

One useful procedure for helping us to do this is to take the following five steps:

- **STOP**: in situations of ambiguity, our natural tendency is to speed up and extricate ourselves from the uncomfortable situation. In fact, we need to do the opposite, that is, slow down and reflect.
- **LOOK AND LISTEN**: look at the people and listen to how they speak. What does this tell you about their style and manner?
- **FEEL**: feel the atmosphere. Is it friendly, hostile or neutral?
- **DON'T ASSUME**: making assumptions is the most natural thing in the world, but can be the most dangerous.
- **ASK**: if you think something may be wrong, ask politely if there is anything you can do. This will not cause offence; in fact, people will be pleased that you are showing an interest (Tomalin and Nicks, 2010).

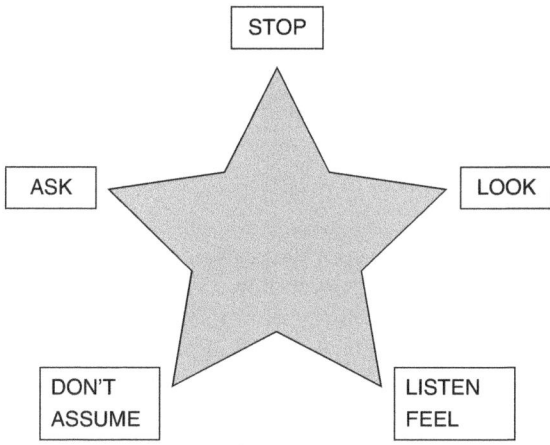

Figure 1.6 The STAR approach

Example

Mr Soto, a senior Japanese manager, was attending a presentation by a British company in Tokyo on its plans to open a large retail outlet there. The presenter, Mr Williams, spoke in English and included a number of jokes and what he thought were funny anecdotes about the culture shock he had encountered on his first visit to Japan. He noticed Mr Soto was not smiling, but sat straight upright with his arms tightly folded across his chest, a sure sign that the listener did not like what was going on. As soon as he had the opportunity, he asked Mr Soto whether everything was OK. Mr Soto looked uncomfortable and said he didn't understand English jokes. No doubt he was also surprised at Mr Williams' self-deprecating approach.

During the coffee break, having realized his approach was not working, Mr Williams resolved to continue the next stage of his presentation in a more formal manner. He had, of course, followed the STAR approach.

How then can we reduce these barriers to effective cross-cultural communication?:

• We can develop our listening skills. This will help us to avoid jumping to conclusions when we only hear 'words' rather than their intrinsic meaning.
• We should check our perceptions about what others say and do, realizing that our own perceptions tend to be rooted in our value system.

- We need to seek feedback to check whether other people understand our message. This may be difficult, for example, in many Asian cultures, where it is considered impolite to say 'no' or to disagree.
- We need at times to take risks in order to open up channels of communication.

Summary

- The study of cross-cultural communication is influenced by anthropology, linguistics, philosophy and psychology.
- The key influences are the study of semiotics, the study of signs and the relationship between language and thought.
- Culture can be divided into implicit and explicit culture.
- The basic obstacles to cross-cultural communication are ethnocentrism, ignorance, fear and laziness.
- Perception *is* reality – it is selective and culture-driven. We should check our perceptions about what others say and do and realize our own perceptions tend to be rooted in our value systems.
- Our cross-cultural effectiveness is influenced by our own individual personality, our national characteristics, our corporate culture and our professional training.
- We can reduce the barriers to effective cross-cultural communication by developing our listening skills to help us avoid jumping to conclusions when we only 'hear' words rather than their intrinsic meaning.

We can perhaps best summarize by formulating three basic rules to help us understand the importance of cross-cultural communication:

- We should accept that others are *different* from us.
- We should accept that we do not know precisely *how* others differ from us.
- We should accept *responsibility for our feelings and reactions* when dealing with people from other cultures.

In addition, we should remember that linguistic fluency does not necessarily equal conceptual fluency.

References

Boas, F. (1938) *General Anthropology* (Boston, MA: Heath).
Boroditsky, L. (2002) 'Linguistic Relativity', in *Galley Article 0056* (Cambridge, MA: Massachusetts Institute of Technology).
Chomsky, N. (1975) *Reflections on Language* (New York: Pantheon).
Hall, T. and Hall, M.R. (1990) *Understanding Cultural Differences* (Maine: Intercultural Press).

Hofstede, G. (1994) *Cultures and Organisations: Software of the Mind. Intercultural Cooperation and its Importance to Survival* (London: HarperCollins).

Lewis, R. (2002) *The Cultural Imperative* (London: Nicholas Brealey Publishing).

Lewis, R. (2004) *When Cultures Collide* (London: Nicholas Brealey Publishing).

Oberg, K. (1960) 'Culture Shock: Adjustment to New Cultural Environments', *Practical Anthropology* 7: 177–82.

Pinker, S. (1994) *The Language Instinct: How the Mind Creates Languages* (Harmondsworth: Penguin).

Sapir, E. (1966) *Culture, Language and Personality* (Berkeley, CA: University of California Press).

Tomalin, B. and Nicks, M. (2010) *The World's Business Cultures and How to Unlock Them* (London: Thorogood Publishing).

Trompenaars, F. (1993) *Riding the Waves of Culture* (London: Nicholas Brealey Publishing).

Trompenaars, F. (2000) *Riding the Waves of Culture*, 2nd edn (London: Nicholas Brealey Publishing).

Whorf, B. (1956) *Language, Thought and Reality* (Cambridge, MA: MIT Press).

Further reading

Axtell, R. (1993) *Do's and Taboos Around the World, A Guide to International Behaviour* (New York: John Wiley & Sons).

Bragg, M. (2003) *The Adventure of English* (London: Hodder & Stoughton).

Crystal, D. (2003) *How Language Works* (London: Penguin).

Harrison, B. (ed.) (1990) *Culture and the Language Classroom* (Oxford: Modern English Publications).

Mehrabian, A. (1981) *Silent Messages: Implicit Communication of Emotions and Attitudes* (Belmont, CA: Wadsworth).

Morris, D. (1977) *Manwatching: A Field Guide to Human Behaviour* (London: Jonathan Cape).

Morris, D. (1979) *Gestures: Their Origins and Distribution* (London: Book Club Associates).

Pease, A. and Pease, B. (2004) *The Definitive Book of Body Language* (London: Orion Books).

Spencer-Oatey, H. (2000) *Culturally Speaking: Managing Rapport through Talk Across Cultures* (London: Continuum).

Trompenaars, F. and Hampden-Turner, C. (2000) *Building Cross-Cultural Competence* (London: Nicholas Brealey Publishing).

Whorf, B. (1998) *Science and Linguistics – Basic Concepts of Communication: Selected Readings* (Maine: Intercultural Press).

2
Key Thinkers in Cross-Cultural Communication (1)

Summary

This chapter and Chapter 3 discuss the views of six selected researchers of cross-cultural communication and assess the value and application of their research. The key thinkers discussed are:

- Edward T. and Mildred R. Hall;
- Geert Hofstede;
- Fons Trompenaars;
- John Mole;
- Richard D. Lewis;
- M. Bennett.

These chapters survey their key theories, and discuss the advantages and limitations of each and their application to the understanding of the effects of culture. Examples are also provided to illustrate the discussion.

Introduction

Edward and Mildred Hall and Geert Hofstede are arguably among the most well-known leading researchers in the field of cross-cultural communication. They have developed much of the theoretical foundation on which cross-cultural analysis has been built. Their key ideas are in many cases complementary and provide a basic theoretical and methodological approach to a clearer understanding of the relationship between culture and communication. This chapter aims to assess their key research and to show how their findings can be applied.

Edward T. and Mildred R. Hall

Modern cross-cultural communication studies owe much to the work of the American psychologists Edward T. and Mildred R. Hall. US companies expanded into Europe after the Second World War and took advantage of the new European Common Market economy. The Halls analysed the cultural differences between US and European companies and employees, published their results in a book entitled *The Silent Language* in 1959 and expanded upon these results in *Understanding Cultural Differences* in 1990. In particular, they examined the different communication styles used and the impact of behaviour on the way in which people do business with those from different cultures. Their research helped establish cross-cultural communication as a research discipline.

The Halls introduced two key principles into the study of cross-cultural communication: one related to communication itself and the other related to the organization of time. These principles were later taken up and expanded in the work of Richard D. Lewis in *When Cultures Collide*.

The Halls identified two styles of communication in business, which they called high-context and low-context communication. The importance of *context* is emphasized as the name given to 'the quantity of information which surrounds any event' and is inextricably bound up with the meaning of that event. The elements that combine to produce a given meaning – events and context – are in different proportions, depending on the culture. In other words, context is everything which is not text (words written or said).

High-context and low-context communication

A *high-context* communicator is one who gives instructions and comments through suggestions rather than directly and in whose communication information is implicitly contained. High-context people tend to rely heavily on an elaborate system of symbols, body language, intonations of speech and hidden, culturally based meanings. More depends on the context in which communication takes place as most of the information is already in the person, while only little is in the coded, explicit, transmitted part of the message. In such cultures, people assume that everyone has most of the essential information they need. Because of this, there is little need for explicit rules and clarifying statements, and therefore communication can be economical, fast and efficient. There is a high degree of allusion and indirectness as well as politeness. This means that the person receiving the message or instructions has to read between the lines to work out the real meaning of the message. People in high-context cultures tend to be more accustomed to interpreting meaning in accordance with such factors as personality, rank and body language. Of course, this happens at a personal level, but the Halls contend that it is also a cultural feature. If you are a member of a particular cultural group, you understand the rules of communication and you are able to read between the lines. However, if you are an outsider or a foreigner, it can be very confusing. Examples of high-context communicators include the Japanese, Koreans, Arabs and, to some extent, Chinese, but also Italians and other Mediterranean people. These people usually have wide information systems, extensive family and social networks, and are accustomed to being involved in close personal relationships.

Relationships between individuals in a high-context culture are very often long-lasting. As a result, they are generally less in need in their day-to-day life of much indepth background. Their style of communication is 'indirect' or 'implicit', and more importance is given to the spoken than the written word. Non-verbal communication, particularly gestures and the use of silence, are important. Agreement tends to be oral rather than written and clear distinctions are evident between family or organization members ('insiders') and foreigners ('outsiders'). Westerners often complain that they find people from Eastern cultures 'inscrutable'. They are not, in fact, inscrutable to each other, merely to outsiders.

A *low-context* communicator does exactly the opposite of the high-context communicator. Here people do not assume that everyone has most of the information they require and communication therefore needs to be more explicit. The message itself carries meaning, so information and details must be spelt out as the context is less important. The message is clear, direct and detailed so that there can be no mistaking what is intended, as ambiguity is disliked. The Germans, Americans, Dutch, Scandinavians, British, Australians and Canadians set great store by low-context communication. They may not need the more elaborate socializing or personal rapport required in high-context cultures. Although marked by clarity, the low-context communicator is often seen as too direct, abrupt and at times even arrogant by high-context communicators. What you hear is what they mean. 'Insiders' and 'outsiders' are less clearly distinguished.

Written communication is considered important for low-context communicators. In business, great store is placed, for example, on contracts and minutes of meetings. Low-context people tend to view high-context people as rather evasive, even at times as somewhat secretive or distrustful. In addition, they have a tendency to compartmentalize their personal relationships, their time at work and many aspects of their social life. As a result, each time they meet, they tend to require more detailed background or 'context'. They have a general lack of extensive and well-developed information networks. As a result, they are more in need of detailed, background information, that is, context, for reassurance before making decisions. Communication is therefore more explicit, more formalized in the shape of memos, legal documents and written statements. Agreement is generally made in writing and contracts are treated as final once signed by all parties, and are as a result legally binding unless they are challenged or unless alterations are desired.

The challenge for management is to find the appropriate level of context required to deal with each situation. Too much information may make people feel you are patronizing them, whereas providing too little information or detail may make them feel unsure, anxious or confused.

The main points of comparison between high-context and low-context communication are summarized in Figure 2.1 below.

High context	Low context
Examples: Arabs, Japanese, Koreans	Examples: Americans, Germans, Dutch
Indirect style – can appear ambiguous	Direct style – can appear abrupt
High use of non-verbal communication	Less use of non-verbal communication
Comfortable with silence	Silence causes anxiety
Lower importance of written regulations	Greater reliance on written documents
Lower attention to detail	High attention to detail
Close personal relationships	Personal relationships less important
Importance of oral agreements	Oral agreements less important

Figure 2.1 Comparison of high-context and low-context communication

---

Example

A UK team member working in a Japanese company is given a high-context instruction he does not understand. The natural response for the UK team member is to ask the Japanese counterpart to explain or repeat. The Japanese find this request uncomfortable as it suggests he wasn't clear in the first place. Therefore, he loses 'face', or personal dignity, which is very important in Japan.

What the UK team member should have done was to 'take the shame' and to say that it was his/her misunderstanding that was to blame and not the Japanese manager's perceived lack of clarity. The Halls' point is that each side adopts its own style of communication without appreciating that there may be a difference which actually causes a communication breakdown.

Monochronic and polychronic cultures

The Halls' second conclusion about different cultures working together concerned the organization of time. When they talk of 'time', they mean 'the language of time'. Time can be either sequential, linear or monochronic, or synchronic or polychronic (Hall and Hall, 1990: 18).

There is often a danger that we project our own time system onto other cultures. If this occurs, we may not be able to read the hidden messages in the foreign time system. Different cultures have different views on the importance of time. A lack of appreciation of these differences by visitors, business people and those in the international community can often cause misunderstanding and, indeed, frustration. In many Western cultures, the importance of time is enshrined in such sayings as 'time waits for no man' and 'time is money', hence the development of courses in time management, the emphasis in the 1960s on time and motion studies, and the costing out of time spent by professionals such as lawyers and accountants. Surprisingly, a person's efficiency and importance are often measured by the number of hours worked, particularly in excess of the normal working hours. Timetables and punctuality can become almost an obsession. This is particularly the case with the Germans and the Swiss, although even the British, who are somewhat less time-sensitive, would be happier if their public transport did run on time.

Monochronic cultures

In predominantly monochronic cultures, for example, the English and Germanic-speaking cultures, time is expressed and used in a *linear* way, being divided into segments and compartmentalized. Time is almost tangible; it is seen as a valuable commodity and is given a monetary value, which can be 'saved' or 'spent' and which is not to be 'wasted' or 'lost'. It is seen as a scarce resource which cannot be retrieved and therefore must be used to the full and controlled, for example, through schedules and appointments. Monochronic people are perceived as active, at times even hyperactive, and often appear impatient, with an obvious dislike of being idle. They come to the point quickly with little introductory 'small talk' and tend to value quick responses in discussion. Spare time or having to wait is seen as time wasted or as frustrating. Time is used as a classification system for organizing both their working life and their social life. As a result, personal organizers, appointment diaries and the like are popular. The Halls distinguished between monochronic cultures (cultures ruled by the clock, in which everything takes place on time according to agreed schedules and with minimum slippage) and polychronic cultures (cultures in which the activity comes first and the organization of time is re-organized to fit around it). 'On time', (monochronic) cultures can run the danger of being in conflict with 'in time' (polychronic) cultures.

Polychronic cultures

Polychronic people see time very differently. For them, it is the simultaneous coming together of many things and they place more emphasis on the importance of human relationships than on keeping to deadlines. Time is therefore seen to be a commodity that can be manipulated, moulded, stretched or even done away with altogether. Arabs, Latin Americans, Africans, most Southern Europeans and most Asians tend to be polychronic, although the Chinese and, in particular, the Japanese are much less so. Plans are frequently changed and a lack of punctuality, delays and interruptions are considered commonplace. A time commitment is viewed as an objective to be achieved *if possible.*

Different attitudes towards the use of time are seen to be a fundamental cultural difference and are taken up by Hofstede, Trompenaars and, above all, Lewis. In the Halls' view, the leading monochronic cultures are the Germans, the Dutch, the Scandinavians and the British in Europe, the North Americans, the Japanese, the Australians and the New Zealanders. It may not be an accident that the monochronic cultures effectively created and dominated the industrial world in the nineteenth and twentieth centuries. It is also interesting to note that as polychronic countries industrialize, their business centres tend to become more monochronic. The other obvious factor is that when you run a multinational business across several continents and different time zones, the keeping to agreed times and schedules becomes extremely difficult if you adopt a polychronic approach to schedules.

Polychronic cultures use time to build personal relationships and to establish trust between the parties. Time is therefore something that does not always control one's activities, but can be used flexibly. Time spent in 'preliminaries', which Westerners often rather dismissively call 'small talk', is of enormous importance and is taken seriously in business before any indepth negotiation actually takes place. In this context, one is reminded of the Western businessman in Riyadh who did not appreciate that to an Arab, business is always personal and therefore time is well spent on building up personal relationships before any deal is discussed in detail, let alone agreed. He arrived with his return flight already booked and was not prepared to be flexible when discussions took longer than he expected. He did not win the contract in competition with those who were prepared to take more time building trust as a priority before detailed negotiations began.

Polychronic cultures tend to adopt an 'open door' policy, where interruptions and the arrival and departure of visitors are commonplace. Appointment times are often not strictly adhered to and business offices have large reception areas where informal discussions can take place, with precedence reserved for family or special clients.

Differences in attitudes towards time can often cause irritation, frustration, embarrassment and at times even hostility. These reactions can occur in comparatively simple ways, for example, when arranging appointments, deciding how long they should be fixed in advance and how long people should be kept waiting. They also occur when socializing, for example, deciding when one should arrive and when one should take one's leave.

Time spent on entertaining is also considered part of the process of building relationships when doing business. The authors remember only too well being advised not to suggest to some important southern French visitors that we should press on with our business and to save time by just having sandwiches for lunch in the conference room. This would have been construed as very impolite, especially as on our first visit to their firm in southern France, we had been taken out to lunch at an expensive restaurant, as this was considered by the company to be very much part of building relationships and mutual trust.

In Asia, time is usually seen as cyclical, with opportunities recurring and re-presenting themselves, not as 'once-only' situations. This cyclical approach permits contemplation and further consideration, as opposed to pressure for quick decisions, and owes much to the teachings of Confucius. However, the different attitudes towards time cannot simply be described as an East/West split. The Chinese, for example, although mainly monochronic, do have a flexible attitude towards time. They do not like to be rushed into making a decision, but prefer to spend time on reflection. They also have a keen sense of the importance of time to other people and place a high value on punctuality. The Japanese spend considerable time and effort in building up trust, forming relationships and considering all the implications of a business proposal. Time is allocated to a formal, almost ritualistic, series of actions, each of which forms an essential part of the traditional procedure, for example, the presentation of the business card, the 'meishi', the tea ceremony and the patient unfolding of negotiations step by step.

According to the Halls, the communication breakdown between monochronic and polychronic societies leads not just to misunderstandings but also to negative attitudes. Latin cultures are sometimes described as '*mañana*' ('do it tomorrow') cultures by their Northern counterparts, which are in turn described as impatient or at times arrogant by the Southerners.

The Halls link the ideas of time and context to form their concept of the 'action chain'. This chain is a sequence of events in which a number of people participate (Hall and Hall, 1990: 24) Each culture has a different representation of what constitutes a correct action chain. When one person's action chain does not correspond to that of another, the result is a conflict or misunderstanding, for example, arriving on time, being interrupted and attending meetings. There is thus a real need to read the hidden messages in the time system of other cultures if we are to avoid misunderstanding and possible friction. Perhaps an allegedly old Egyptian proverb sums it up very succinctly: 'God created time but man created the hurry.'

The common behaviour patterns identified by the Halls in monochronic and polychronic cultures can be summarized as follows.

Monochronic	Polychronic
Time seen in a linear way, almost tangible, sequential	Time seen as synchronic
One thing at a time – concentrate on the task in hand	Several things at a time
Time commitments strictly observed	Time commitments more relaxed
Dislike interruptions	Comfortable with interruptions
Appointments on time	Less emphasis on promptness
Low context – needs information	High context – already has the information
Closely follows plans and deadlines	Time commitments to be kept if possible
Committed to objectives and targets	More emphasis on personal relationships
Emphasize promptness; to be kept waiting is rude	Promptness based on relationships
More accustomed to short-term relationships	Place importance on long-term relationships

Figure 2.2 Summary of monochronic and polychronic cultures (adapted from Hall and Hall, 1990: 15)

The Halls also considered that cultures may be oriented towards different time dimensions:

- *Past-oriented cultures*: these are very much concerned with their past history and their traditions, which they revere and maintain. They show respect for their ancestors, predecessors and older people. Events are viewed in the context of their traditions and history. France and the UK are, to a large extent, examples of this type of culture, as are India and other Asian cultures.
- *Present-oriented cultures*: activities and enjoyment of the moment are considered to be of the greatest importance. There is less emphasis on future planning. Events are viewed in terms of their contemporary impact and the emphasis is on the 'here and now'. Australia is a good example of this type of culture.
- *Future-oriented cultures*: these focus on the future, with much planning and thinking about prospects and potential. They show great interest in youth and future potential. The present and past are used and exploited for future advantage. The USA is a good example.

Cultures such as the French and the British tend to place great emphasis on their traditions and cultural heritage. These cultures seek examples from the past to better understand the present and to make decisions about the future. Future-oriented cultures, such as the USA, are more likely to interpret present actions in terms of their future effects. The American view of the future, at least in the short term, is that it can be controlled by individuals through personal achievement and effort.

Territoriality (space)

We can talk about space and culture from two perspectives:

- space around people, that is, territoriality in general; and
- space between people – often called proxemics – our personal 'space bubble'.

This is a further area of cultural difference described by the Halls and is the name they give to those visible and invisible boundaries people place around themselves, at work and in their social life. This can, for example, be seen in the use of either private offices with closed doors (often preferred in Germany) or open-plan office layouts (as in Japan or China). In some cultures, senior personnel usually have their offices on the top floor.

Territoriality also concerns our own personal space, the 'space bubble' that surrounds us, in which we feel most comfortable and which we claim as our own, almost as if it were an extension of our own body. Human beings are essentially territorial; they tend to define their space and protect it. For example, in the UK, our home and garden are often bounded by fences and we have our favourite chair or seat at a conference table. We put up signs such as 'private, no trespassing', 'keep off the grass' and 'meeting in progress'. On a much larger scale, international examples have included the Great Wall of China, Hadrian's Wall and the Berlin Wall.

As a result of their research, the Halls discovered the following points:

- A high correlation between monochronic and low-context cultures, and polychronic and high-context cultures.
- The higher the context of either the culture or the organization, the more difficult the interface.
- The greater the cultural distance, the more difficult the interface.

The comparison can be further outlined as in Figure 2.3 below regarding how people think and behave.

Dimension	High	Low
Time	polychronic	monochronic
Space	shared	private
Communication	indirect	direct
Rewards	group	individual
Emotions	openly expressed	concealed
Information	hidden networks	open systems
Regulation	rituals, rites	written codes
Conflict	avoid	confront
Status and power	position, authoritarian	qualification, democratic

Figure 2.3   High-context and low-context dimensions

Example

A British firm was negotiating with an Italian supplier to tender for a Swedish client. The monochronic British and Swedish companies complained about late deliveries, laxity in responding to emails and written requests for information on the part of the Italians. The Italians complained that their British and Swedish counterparts were distant and unfriendly and that their communications were lacking in respect and courtesy; moreover, they always delivered 'in time' if not always at the scheduled time agreed. The result was confusion on the Swedish side and frustration on the part of the British and the Italians, eventually leading to a breakdown in the agreement. The situation could have been resolved if the Italians had paid more attention to acknowledging emails, making sure the 'paper trail' of correspondence was maintained and advising of any slippage in delivery ahead of time. The British, on the other hand, needed to work harder at creating a personal relationship with their supplier, use the phone more and explain the problems with the Swedish client to obtain the loyalty of the supplier and the commitment to timely delivery.

Geert Hofstede

Geert Hofstede's seminal research is the most commonly cited of all the cultural theorists in the field and has justifiably had the most influence on the understanding of the effects of culture on human activity. From 1967 to 1973, he conducted research as an industrial psychologist into national cultures at the Institute for Research on Intercultural Cooperation in Arnhem in the Netherlands. Using international employees from IBM, he collected data from a large sample (117,000) from 40 countries in which he compared the answers of the IBM employees to the same attitude survey research conducted in different countries. In 1983 he collected supplementary data on a further ten countries and three multi-country regions. He published his main findings in *Culture's Consequences: International Differences in Work-Related Values* (1980) and, with Gert Jan Hofstede and Michael Minkov, *Cultures and Organizations: Software of the Mind. Intercultural Cooperation and Importance for Survival* (1991), the revised third edition of which was published in paperback format in 2010. The latter title updated in detail his former work, building on the initial IBM study and analysing the data from other cross-national cultural studies which helped confirm and expand the results. This later research extended the results to a wider number of countries. This chapter includes references to the tables and text of this updated research.

Hofstede describes culture as the 'collective programming of the mind'. He maintains that the 'software' of the mind distinguishes the members of one group of people from another. It is built up by the family environment, schooling, the influence of the neighbourhood, the social environment of the local community and the workplace. All these influences add to one's life experiences and become part of one's cultural background.

Hofstede's work has developed a model of cultural differences used to compare the values of matched samples of the tasks of experienced workers and managers in a number of countries. Hofstede claims that the differences in values have important implications for managers and organizations which operate across national borders. He has put together a most comprehensive analysis of cultural differences between nationalities and has also asserted that one's own national cultural characteristics tend to prevail over other cultural characteristics acquired later, including those of a corporate culture.

Hofstede recognizes that there was previously no comparable scientific approach which could be used to provide cultural comparison, and his work aims to provide a systematic analysis and a common terminology to describe national cultures, rather than impressions and generalizations, which could lead to dangerous superficiality.

Hofstede emphasizes that describing a national culture does not mean that everyone in that culture will display the same cultural traits. In addition, his initial research does not allow for cultural differences between groups within a country, for example, regional differences, and differences in terms of social background, age, occupation or religion. His analysis uses national cultures to describe an *average* pattern of beliefs and values, but obviously individuals do not necessarily all conform to this average.

Through the analysis of the questionnaires he sent out, Hofstede identifies four key variables that characterized national differences between IBM employees of different nationalities. He describes these as four 'dimensions' and he scores the countries he analyses out of 100 in each dimension (although in a few cases his ratings exceed 100). His analysis shows that differences among his selected countries can be measured by these four different criteria. He aims to show that these dimensions play a significant role in determining people's behaviour, perceptions and values, as well as their subsequent impact on organizational life. He plots the position of the surveyed countries along the axes of these four dimensions of work-related value differences. These represent the relative, not absolute, positions of the countries and they concentrate only on measuring differences. His original first four dimensions are given in Figure 2.4 below.

PDI (power distance index) – attitudes towards authority, the extent to which power is autocratic
IDV (individualism index) – attitudes towards individualism and collectivism
MAS (masculinity index) – attitudes towards assertiveness and modesty
UAI (uncertainty avoidance index) – attitudes towards risk taking

---

Figure 2.4   Hofstede's four dimensions

Later, he adds a fifth dimension, based on research in the Far East, and only applied to a few countries which he called *LTO* (long-term orientation), which is contrasted with *STO* (short-term orientation). More recently, a sixth dimension has been added, which is called *Indulgence versus Restraint*. Both are explained later in this chapter.

The scoring allows us to make an instant comparison of countries in relation to our own. Countries higher up the scale may be considered to have a greater degree of whatever features are measured by the index and those lower down a correspondingly lesser degree. To clarify, let us take the IDV, where countries higher up the scale, such as the USA or Australia, are considered to display greater individualism than, say, Japan, which displays greater collectivism. People in cultures with LTO look to the future and put high value on thrift and perseverance. This is in contrast to a STO, which values the past and the present, respecting tradition, the cultural past and the importance of social cohesion.

PDI

This dimension explains how societies accept and deal with inequalities in power and wealth, and the extent to which the less powerful members of organizations and institutions like the family within a country accept this inequality as normal and desirable. Some societies play down these inequalities and some perpetuate them. Hofstede measured countries from small power distance to large power distance (0–100) using degrees of inequality to measure the gap between the most powerful and wealthy in society and the least powerful and wealthy. Countries with a high score have a high level of difference between levels of power, such as in parts of the Arab world (score: 80), Latin America and many Asian countries. Hierarchies are tall and respect should be shown to those above you in a company and in society, and power holders are entitled to receive privileges. Those with a low score make much less of the difference between power levels, such as Canada (score: 39) or Sweden (score: 31), and believe that the way to change a social system is primarily by redistributing power by evolution. The PDI which Hofstede defines concentrates on the way in which people perceive power differences.

The PDI is used in management to assess the degree to which management is centralized and hierarchy is imposed in a country's management culture. A culture with high power distance is likely to have a stronger 'top-down' managerial approach, with greater divisions between levels of hierarchy and a concentration of decision-making power at the top of the organization. Inequalities among the personnel in an organization are expected and accepted, as they are in society in general. Subordinates would expect their bosses to tell them what to do and would not expect to be consulted. Superiors are often not easily accessible. Latin and Asian countries tend to score higher on this scale. A culture with low power distance will have a greater level of delegated authority and decision making, and those at the top of the scale will attempt to diminish the extent of their power by consultation and by democratic processes of decision making. North American, Anglophone and Germanic countries tend to score lower on the PDI scale. In lower power distance countries, organizations are flatter and distinctions are less rigid or formal.

Example

A company seeking to source products from a Chinese company had to send two executives, rather than one, to negotiate the deal. The reason for this was that the manager who had operational and delegated decision-making responsibility was seen as too junior to negotiate with senior Chinese managers. As a result, the UK manager was accompanied by a senior manager, who was seen as having equivalent status and power to his Chinese counterpart, thus doubling the amount of time 'wasted' and the costs of the trip, in addition to the senior manager's salary.

Some examples of Hofstede's scores for this dimension are as follows.

Malaysia	104	Chile	63	UK	35
Russia	93	Greece	60	Switzerland	34
Venezuela	81	Spain	57	Sweden	31
Arab countries	80	Japan	54	Denmark	18
India	77	USA	40	New Zealand	18
Brazil	69	Canada	39	Israel	13
France	68	Germany	35	Austria	11

Figure 2.5   Selected power distance scores (Hofstede, Hofstede, and Minkov, 2010: 57–9, Table 3.1)

The scores show high power distance for most Asian, Eastern European, Latin American, Arabic-speaking and African countries. German-speaking and Nordic countries, Australia, Canada, Israel, the Netherlands, New Zealand, the UK and the USA display low values. Hofstede's further research in this dimension analyses power-distance differences by looking at the effect of social class, education and occupation.

IDV individualism/collectivism

This dimension represents a bipolar scale. It describes the relationships whereby an individual is integrated with other members of society. At the top end of the scale, individual self-interest predominates and personal time is important, as is freedom of association and expression in the workplace. Ties are loose and the emphasis is on individual freedom. The individual is seen as the core of the social unit, with group goals generally being subordinate to personal goals. People are supposed to look after themselves and their immediate families and to choose their own affiliations. Progress is straight-lined and upward, and change is inevitable. Self-esteem and personal success are closely linked. At the bottom end of the scale, people are born into strong, cohesive groups which are collective in their treatment of individuals. People belong to 'in-groups' (extended families, villages, clans, tribes) which are expected to protect them in exchange for loyalty. All are supposed to look after the interests of the group and actively promote the group's values and beliefs. There is respect for elders, status and hierarchy, while duty, harmony, politeness and modesty are important.

A highly individualistic country such as the USA (score: 91) can be compared with a highly collective society such as Japan (score: 46). In relation to business, the scale measures the degree to which managers feel empowered to make decisions individually or the degree to which they feel constrained to consult and implement a commonly agreed decision.

In management terms, the individualism versus collectivism scale illuminates how decision making takes place and how employees see themselves in relation to their company. In an individualist management culture, such as in North America, Anglophone countries and Northern Europe, managers tend to take their own decisions in relation to their job responsibilities and their budget. In a more collective management culture, decisions will be arrived at through a process of consultation and discussions, although the authority to make final decisions may still be vested at the top of the organization. Personnel would expect the possibility of career advancement to be based on an assessment of competence and laid down procedures for selection for promotion and regular appraisal. The job itself is generally more important than relationships with work colleagues. Hofstede regarded North American, Anglophone, Dutch and Nordic cultures as being more individualistic in approach, whereas Asian cultures tended to be more collectivist. The prime example of a collectivist management culture is Japan, where decision making is carried out through a consultative process, with everyone involved in the discussion and decision making.

The Japanese spend considerable time and effort in building trust and forming relationships, which they see as the key to success. In collectivist cultures, there is a strong moral relationship between employer and employee; relationships are based on trust and come before tasks. In business, relatives and close friends come before strangers and time is seen as being for relationship building.

Some examples of Hofstede's scores for this dimension are as follows.

USA	91	Sweden	71	Iran	41
Australia	90	France	71	Arab countries	38
UK	89	Germany	67	Greece	35
Canada	80	Israel	54	Mexico	30
Italy	76	Spain	51	Pakistan	14
Denmark	74	Japan	46	Venezuela	12

Figure 2.6 Selected individualism/collectivism scores (Hofstede, Hofstede and Minkov, 2010: 95–7, Table 4.1)

Example

A UK company found itself in danger of missing a deadline on an important merger and acquisition because its parent company in Japan delayed giving its approval to the deal. Only later did the UK subsidiary discover that the decision was delayed because of the consultative process, which meant that the Japanese staff were given the opportunity to discuss the proposal and approve the decision to go ahead. As a result, not all of them were able to do so in the time available. In this situation, the integrity of the collective decision-making process was considered more important to the Japanese than the rapid conclusion of the deal.

Hofstede widens his research in this dimension by considering the effect on individualism or collectivism within families and the influence of language, personality, behaviour and differences at school and in the workplace.

Masculinity and femininity index

This dimension examines gender roles in a society and concentrates on sociological aspects rather than biological aspects. It measures the importance a culture places on material wealth as opposed to the quality of life. Once again, Hofstede uses a bipolar scale and scores countries out of 100. Societies can be classified as to whether they try to maximize or minimize the social gender role divisions. On the *masculine* end of the scale, the dominant values in a society are success, ambition, money, recognition of achievement, decisiveness and performance, and the male is expected to take the dominant role. If we are working in a masculine environment, we would expect our bosses to be assertive and decisive. Ideas such as equity, competition and performance are considered important. The roles men and women play in society are seen as being distinct from each other.

At the *feminine* end of the scale, the dominant values are nurturing and caring, the importance of relationships, the concern for the quality of life, job satisfaction and support for the disadvantaged and the weak in society. Women will also tend to have greater concern for environmental and human values in the workplace. Cooperation and a search for consensus are considered important values in such a society. People generally work in order to live, whereas in masculine societies, people tend to live in order to work. In countries which score low on masculinity, such as the Scandinavian countries, cooperation and quality of life are highly valued.

In a 'feminine' society, men and women are expected to take the same social roles. In the workplace, men and women may assume similar roles, but men are not expected to be overly ambitious or competitive, whereas women put more emphasis on the quality of life rather than material success. Such societies tend to resolve conflict by dialogue. In a 'masculine' society, roles are more rigidly divided. According to Hofstede's analysis, Japan emerged as the most masculine society (score: 95), followed by German-speaking, North American and Anglophone countries. The most feminine societies are the Nordic countries, the Netherlands (score: 14), some Latin American countries, Portugal and France.

In management terms, the masculinity index clearly reflects the role of women in management and their position in the management hierarchy in relation to men. However, it also reflects the attitude of the country in relation to quality of working conditions, the management of relationships at work and concern about the environment.

Some examples of scores on this dimension are as follows.

Japan	95	Germany	66	France	43
Austria	79	USA	62	Russia	36
Venezuela	73	India	56	Finland	26
Italy	70	Arab countries	53	Denmark	16
Switzerland	70	Canada	52	Netherlands	14
UK	66	Brazil	49	Sweden	5

Figure 2.7 Selected masculinity and femininity scores (Hofstede, Hofstede and Minkov, 2010: 141–3, Table 5.1)

Example

The male managers of an Arabian Gulf organization, while showing immense social courtesy, consistently tried to ignore their Dutch female

> counterpart during the business meeting and addressed any business questions to her male subordinates. The Dutch executive felt she had to be uncharacteristically assertive simply in order to establish her authority and felt that it affected the tone of the negotiation. Nevertheless, she felt it wrong to absent herself or to underplay her responsibility.

Hofstede has expanded his research to include the degree of masculinity and femininity according to occupation, family influence, gender roles, education, shopping, working environment and the effect of religion.

Uncertainty avoidance index (UAI)

Hofstede's research identified countries as having strong or weak levels of uncertainty avoidance. The term 'uncertainty avoidance' describes the degree to which people feel threatened by ambiguity, unstructured or unpredictable situations and the extent to which society is able to tolerate uncertainty. As regards business, this index indicates the degree of acceptance of risk in the business culture concerned. A society with *high uncertainty avoidance* is more risk averse and will adopt beliefs and create institutions to avoid uncertainty. It will place emphasis on rules and regulations, concern for stability and a high value on the most efficient use of time and punctuality. Ideas that are unusual or deviant are likely to be resisted. People feel insecure in unstructured, unclear or unpredictable situations, which they therefore try to avoid by following strict codes of behaviour. They will try to 'beat the future' and avoid uncertainty by adopting particular technologies, such as dykes, dams and silos, by laws which aim to control uncertainties of behaviour and by beliefs and religious ideologies. Conflict and competition are seen as leading to unpredictability and are therefore seen as undesirable. Such societies see the need for consensus whenever possible.

A society with *low uncertainty avoidance* is more prepared to accept uncertain, unusual and innovative ideas and behaviour, to take conscious risks and to take each day as it comes. Uncertainty, risk, conflict and competition are seen as a normal part of life. People tend to become more pragmatic and more tolerant of change. Germany (score: 65) has reasonably high uncertainty avoidance, whereas neighbouring Denmark (score 23) has reasonably low uncertainty avoidance.

In management terms, a high uncertainty avoidance country will be more cautious in its decision making, more risk averse and more likely to adopt solutions that have been successful elsewhere. A low uncertainty avoidance country will be more likely to take risks, to seek radical alternatives and to accept a greater degree of uncertainty in its decision making. Competition is not seen as threatening and is considered to be fair play. Latin American countries, Central European countries, Japan and Korea tend to score more highly than most Asian, English-speaking and Nordic countries.

Example

A UK company was involved in an innovative but uncertain joint venture with a Japanese corporation. The UK executive team was concerned by the time the negotiations took, with seemingly trivial points being checked and rechecked and decisions being debated by committees at different levels of the company. At one point, the delays were so lengthy that the UK company believed the Japanese company was not serious and was on the point of pulling out. Fortunately, it realized that the Japanese by nature were extremely cautious and that the repeated checking and the committee agreement system were essential management tools employed by the company. The UK company therefore extended the time for further discussion and, as a result, was eventually successful in setting up the joint venture.

Some examples of scores on this dimension are as follows.

Greece	112	Venezuela	76	Netherlands	53
Portugal	104	Italy	75	Canada	48
Japan	92	Austria	70	USA	46
France	86	Arab countries	68	India	40
South Korea	86	Germany	65	UK	35
Israel	81	Switzerland	58	Sweden	29

Figure 2.8 Selected uncertainty avoidance scores (Hofstede, Hofstede and Minkov, 2010: 192–4, Table 6.1)

Hofstede has extended his research in this dimension to include uncertainty avoidance according to occupation, gender, age, influence of the family, health, happiness, schooling, in the workplace and motivation. He also includes the influence of xenophobia, nationalism and religion.

LTO versus STO

Michael Bond and his Chinese colleagues conducted a study among students in 23 countries, using a survey instrument developed with Chinese employees and managers. After Hofstede had formulated his four cultural dimensions, this work by Michael Bond convinced him of the need for a fifth dimension. It also had the added advantage of not possessing the Western bias that was present in the original IBM survey. This recognized the need to develop a new scale to take account of the emerging economic powers such as China. Bond composed a list of basic values believed to be held by Chinese people. This questionnaire, the Chinese Value Survey (CVS), discovered that there were three major dimensions very similar to those of Hofstede, but there was a lack of correlation with Hofstede's dimension of uncertainty avoidance.

This fifth dimension was added after the others to describe the difference in thinking between East and West. Historically, it can be traced to the teachings of Confucius and was initially referred to as 'Confucian Dynamism'. The CVS was distributed to 100 students in 23 countries, including the People's Republic of China, and was designed with a deliberately non-Western bias. It consisted of 40 items in both English and Chinese.

Hofstede identified a country with LTO as one which places more importance on the future and a concern with setting long-term goals and persistence or perseverance in achieving them. Relationships are structured according to status, and progress is made by displaying thrift and care in saving and controlling expenditure. Responsibility is taken for ensuring correct standards of behaviour.

Hofstede and Bond were influenced by those countries that shared the fundamental beliefs of Confucian philosophy, namely in essence a form of practical ethics without any religious content:

- A stable society requires the acceptance of certain unequal relations, for example, between ruler and ruled, with a strong sense of hierarchy.
- There is an emphasis on loyalty and reciprocal obligation between superiors and subordinates.
- The family is the bedrock of all social organizations. As a result, older people (parents) are entitled to exercise more authority than younger people and men are given more authority than women.
- There is strong respect for powerful and senior people, and consideration is also shown to colleagues.
- Virtuous behaviour to others means treating them as you would like to be treated.
- Virtuous behaviour in work means trying to acquire skills and education, working hard and being frugal, patient and persevering.

Western cultures are likely to promote equal relationships, emphasize individualism and focus on treating others as they would like to be treated, as well as finding fulfilment through creativity and self-actualization.

STO, on the other hand, means that people expect fairly rapid feedback from decisions, quick profits, frequent job evaluations and promotions. People are concerned with steadiness, stability, social pressure to 'keep up with one's neighbour' and self-gratification. The values of the past and present are emphasized, as are respect for tradition, fulfilling one's social obligations and concern for the preservation of one's 'face'.

There are claims of a correlation between certain Confucian values and recent Asian economic growth. However, this can be rather confusing, as both opposing poles of this dimension show some Confucian values. In contrast, a society with STO will think in terms of personal and short-term advantage, will set a high value on preserving status and position in the short term, will hold to traditions regardless of the need to change and will seek to undermine systems through the exchange of favours and gifts to gain personal advantage. Hofstede considers China (score: 118) as a supreme example of LTO and India (score: 61) and the African subcontinent (score: East Africa 25, West Africa 19) as examples of STO.

This new dimension of Confucian dynamism consisting of the following values is summarized below.

LTO	STO
Persistence/perseverance	Personal steadiness and stability
Ordering and respecting relationships by status	Protection of one's 'face'
Thrift, saving for investment	Respect for tradition
Having a sense of shame, concern with self-image	Reciprocity of greetings, gifts, favours
Pragmatic approach to life, acceptance of change	

Figure 2.9 Confucian dynamism values

The values for the LTO are directed more towards the future, especially thrift and perseverance, and are essentially more dynamic. The STO values are directed more towards the past and present and are essentially more static. The top five values for LTO are all taken by Southeast Asian cultures and include the Asian 'tiger' economies as well as China and Japan. Hofstede considers that the advance of the economies of Eastern Asia is likely to be due to their historical cultural past and the fact that the characteristics of LTO gave them a competitive economic advantage in the market conditions that existed in the post-Second World War years, which contributed to a large extent to their economic success and was assisted by the increasing development of a truly global marketplace.

When Bond and Hofstede developed a survey specifically for Asia and re-evaluated their earlier data, they found that LTO seemed to cancel out some of the effects of masculinity/femininity and uncertainty avoidance. The LTO scores of 22 countries are compared in Figure 2.10 below. The figures represent relative, not absolute, positions of the countries.

In management and social policy terms, this dimension describes the degree to which a society looks forward to planning for long-term growth and prosperity, as well as the degree to which it looks at short-term tactical positioning in order to take advantage of changing situations. Differences in international awareness of the need to take measures to protect the environment also exemplify this dimension.

China	118	Sweden	33
Hong Kong	96	Poland	32
Taiwan	87	Australia	31
Japan	80	Germany	31
South Korea	75	New Zealand	30
Brazil	65	USA	29
India	61	UK	25
Thailand	56	Zimbabwe	25
Singapore	48	Canada	23
Netherlands	44	Philippines	19
Bangladesh	43	Nigeria	16

Figure 2.10 LTO scores (Hofstede, Hofstede and Minkov, 2010: 240, Table 7.1)

Hofstede applied this dimension to assess the progress which emerging economies would take in relation to economic development. At the top of the scale are countries that institute policies that extend into the future, while at the bottom of the scale are countries which attempt to deal with or avoid current problems, but fail to think far enough ahead to deal with long-term needs. Unlike his other dimensions, Hofstede has not applied this index to all countries.

Example

In Hofstede's view, China has LTO due to its institution in 1979 of 'the one child policy' aimed at slowing China's massive population growth. Under this policy, a family was encouraged to have only one child and having more than one child might make the family subject to prosecution and a fine. Hofstede believed that China's population control released resources for economic development. By having smaller families, the Chinese could save more and invest more in their economic development. By contrast, Hofstede believed that India's failure to institute effective population control was an example of STO and led to resources being literally eaten up in the attempts to support and maintain large families.

Hofstede examines the implications of the LTO/STO differences from the point of view of family life, business, ways of thinking and school results.

Hofstede's sixth dimension

Following research by Michael Minkov, who extended the number of countries scored for the fifth dimension (LTO/STO), Hofstede identified a sixth dimension (Hofstede, Hofstede and Minkov, 2010). This he calls Indulgence versus Restraint (IVR). This dimension contends that people in societies that possess a high rate of indulgence are able to freely satisfy their basic needs and aspirations. However, people in societies which display restraint are less happy; they follow strict norms of social behaviour whereby the gratification of their desires and ambitions are suppressed by regulations and the resulting curbs on their freedom of action. They also have the perception that the enjoyment of leisure time and the ability to spend their earnings on whatever they wish can often be seen as unsociable and incorrect. Indulgence scores are found to be the highest in Latin America, parts of Africa, the Anglophone world and in Nordic Europe, whereas restraint is mostly evident in Southeast Asia and the Muslim world. Figure 2.11 lists selected scores for this dimension.

Venezuela	100	Nigeria	84	Ghana	72
UK	69	USA	68	South Africa	63
Norway	54	France	48	Zambia	42
Germany	40	Indonesia	38	Zimbabwe	28
India	26	Hong Kong	17	Egypt	4

Figure 2.11 Selected sixth dimension scores (Hofstede, Hofstede and Minkov, 2010: 282–4, Table 8.1)

This dimension is very much concerned with the degree of general well-being and happiness experienced by the people of a nation. This is called 'subjective well-being' (SWB). One of the perhaps surprising results is that countries with the highest percentage of happiness are in fact themselves not particularly wealthy. Examples include countries in West Africa and in some Latin American countries. It was also found that the extent of happiness is correlated with a high degree of individualism and low masculinity. No direct correlation, however, was found with the other dimensions, including LTO.

Hofstede widens his research in this new dimension by examining the key differences between indulgent and restrained societies in the private life of their citizens, their common behaviour, their attitudes towards sex and the influence of politics.

Manifestations of culture

Hofstede selects symbols, heroes, rituals and values as four key manifestations of culture. He likens these to the skins of an onion, with symbols representing the most superficial outer layer, values the innermost layer, and heroes and rituals in the middle. These are summarized below.

Symbols

These are specific to a particular culture and are important only to those who are part of that culture. They are often transitory (for example, national flags which may change, styles of dress and jargon in popular speech), although some are more permanent (for example, national anthems, memorials).

Heroes

These can be from the past or from more recent times and can include war heroes, nation builders and folk heroes who can be seen as role models for a particular culture. Examples include Churchill, Napoleon, William Tell, Gandhi and Nelson Mandela.

Rituals

These are mainly religious or social (for example, church services, funerals, weddings, styles of greeting, and Christmas and Thanksgiving celebrations) and are generally collectivist in practice.

Values

These comprise the fundamental mores of a culture. They are acquired at an early age and are passed down from generation to generation. They become instinctive and are seldom questioned. Examples include what is accepted as beautiful or ugly, evil or good, normal or abnormal behaviour and polite or impolite. Change in values in any society or culture happen only very slowly and with difficulty.

How is Hofstede's research viewed today?

Over 40 years after his original research was conducted, Hofstede's four dimensions remain the basic tool used in assessing national cultures and management styles. The main reason for this is that his initial research constitutes the most comprehensive analysis of cultural differences between nationalities conducted in the field using standardized questionnaires and, in addition, that it is validated according to scientific, psychological and statistical principles. He is seen as the pioneer in the field and has been a huge influence on management theorists and other researchers in the cross-cultural field. Hofstede himself recognizes that some cultural relativism is necessary, as it is difficult to establish specific criteria and there is no escaping some bias. He has over time used several versions of his questionnaire in analysing the IBM data.

However, inevitably there have been criticisms of his work. These can be divided into six areas.

1) Analysis needs further updating

Although Hofstede has reviewed and updated his work, his analysis has been criticized as being in need of an update in certain aspects. He has, however, negated much of this criticism by updating his own research and carrying out cross-analysis with other national surveys. However, the world continues to change, and as societies have become increasingly interconnected in a more globalized environment, their cultural styles have modified accordingly. In addition, countries such as Russia and China have come to prominence and are undergoing radical change. These, along with Eastern and Central European countries, were not included in the initial research project as IBM at the time did not operate in communist countries. The development of globalization and international cooperation, along with increased international mobility, has not been fully taken into account in terms of its effect on influencing a degree of cultural convergence. Hofstede's work also does not consider the influence of multiculturalism. It should be emphasized, however, that he defends the accusation that his findings are to some extent now out of date by arguing that cultural trends take a long time to change.

2) Too general

The mean score for a national culture is the average score of those who responded. Hofstede accepts there may indeed be wide variations within each national sample. Although he confines himself to national characteristics, many critics believe that the importance of regional differences within countries and especially ethnic and religious differences count for as much as national differences. Hofstede can be criticized for a tendency to treat national cultures as homogeneous entities when in fact they are made up of groups of different ethnicities with different characteristics.

3) Too Western-oriented

This criticism is aimed at the design of the research criteria and its application, its political and social orientation, and the narrowness of the population which provided the basis for the data collection. Although the total number of questionnaires analysed was large, the number of respondents from many of the countries was relatively limited. As a result, in some cases research conclusions have been based on statistically insignificant samples. In addition, although the results are mainly comparable, they do not represent the whole society or nation, but only one professional group.

The research criteria were set up and designed by Westerners. They were therefore biased towards Western values and may give insufficient recognition to alternative belief systems that might be based on other factors. In addition, the sample was mainly limited to middle-ranking employees, the majority of whom were male and mainly from the marketing and service divisions. However, the criticism of being too Western-biased has been reduced by the data obtained from the CVS.

4) Political orientation

By focusing on one successful multinational capitalist company, Hofstede could not effectively take account of the cultural values of socialist societies or of the developing world. However, to counter this, Hofstede says that a society's belief system goes beyond politics and he has attempted to deal with the developing world and emerging economies by his introduction of the LTO dimension as a follow-up to Bond's CVS.

5) Too few dimensions

It can be argued that more indicators are needed to adequately character-ize and contrast cultures. Hofstede agrees with this in principle, and to some extent the work of Lewis, Mole and Trompenaars helps to fill this gap. More recent research by Hofstede in cooperation with Michael Bond has produced the fifth dimension (LTO/STO), while his work with Michael Minkov and research colleagues has resulted in the formulation of the sixth dimension (IVR).

6) Methodology

Hofstede's original research was conducted on employees from a single American company, namely IBM, involving predominantly middle-class males and totalling about 117,000 responses. The strong IBM corporate cul-ture also has to be taken into account, and as a result, the questions in the survey were biased towards such a culture.

Hofstede's use of attitude surveys on which his research is based has been criticized as an inappropriate way of studying culture. However, it has also been contended that a survey-based approach is, in fact, highly efficient for the purposes of conducting cultural comparisons when a large number of countries are involved.

In addition, Hofstede conducted subsequent research into different but also limited populations, which he contends confirms his original conclusions.

After Hofstede

Those readers who are interested in examining how Hofstede's research has been further challenged are directed towards the collection of academic papers edited by Cheryl Nakata (2009). In summary, the main concerns expressed include the following:

- The need to challenge Hofstede's view that nations can be seen as cul-tures in their own right because of increasing cultural interpenetration, migration and multiculturalism.
- The fact that cultures are increasingly crossing national boundaries, becoming more hybrid and in conflict through the powerful influence of worldwide media, telecommunications, global trade and the power of information technology, especially social media sites.
- The powerful influence of the Internet, which has resulted in worldwide exposure to global brands and products across cultural boundaries.
- Hofstede's initial focus for his four dimensions was on values, to the exclusion of other aspects of culture. His further research has, however, widened the scope.
- Cultures can change more rapidly than Hofstede maintains. The support for cultural determinism relied heavily on the paradigm of cultural stabil-ity. However, large-scale economic and political changes have taken place,

for example, in India and China, as have changes in the levels of education in many countries. As a result, values themselves will have changed.

- The *Globe Leadership and Organization Behaviour Effectiveness Project* (GLOBE) commenced in 1993 under Robert House. It aims to build a framework for assessing culture by obtaining data from 17,000 managers in local, non-multinational organizations involved in food processing, financial services and telecommunication in 62 societies worldwide. The project expanded Hofstede's five dimensions to nine. House retained power distance and uncertainty avoidance, but divided collectivism into institutional collectivism and in-group collectivism, and masculinity/femininity into assertiveness and gender egalitarianism. He added two more dimensions, namely human orientation and performance orientation, derived from Hofstede's masculinity/femininity. The large amount of data collected in this ongoing project does not always correlate with Hofstede's research, but reflects the overall structure of the Hofstede model. The leadership aspect of the GLOBE project is referred to in Chapter 7.

Summary

- Edward and Mildred Hall identified two main styles of communication as high context and low context, and emphasized the need to find the appropriate level of context to deal with each cultural situation.
- They also drew attention to the two main differing attitudes towards time, namely monochronic and polychronic, as well as the different levels of importance attributed to the three phases of time (past, present and future).
- They also highlighted cultural differences experienced in defining the territoriality of space around people and space between people.
- Despite the limitations of Hofstede's work, many of which have been freely acknowledged by Hofstede himself, his research is of great value. The following points are of particular importance:
  - ○ it is an extensive study, the first of its kind. It has been widely used for further research and interpretation, and specifies a theoretical model which has been the basis for the development of his theories;
  - ○ the five identified dimensions are not considered in isolation. Their inter-correlation is most useful for business management;
  - ○ his work is interdisciplinary and, as a result, is cited by organizational psychologists, sociologists and management and communication researchers;
  - ○ he recognizes that not everyone in a society fits the cultural pattern precisely, but there is enough statistical regularity to identify trends and tendencies;
  - ○ the LTO/STO scores are of particular interest in explaining to some extent the reasons for the economic advancement of a number of East Asian countries;

○ cultural differences remain significantly valid despite the effects of increasing globalization. Diversity tends to increase cultural differences and the need for cross-cultural understanding remains essential if we are to be successful international communicators;
○ the scores for all the dimensions are listed separately in Hofsrede, Hofstede and Minkov (2010), which contains more research on LTO and the sixth dimension, IVR.

References

Hall, E.T. (1959) *The Silent Language* (New York: Random House).

Hall, E.T. (1976) *Beyond Culture* (New York: Random House).

Hall, E.T. and Hall, M.R. (1990) *Understanding Cultural Differences: German, French and Americans* (Yarmouth, ME: Intercultural Press).

Hofstede, G. (1980) *Culture's Consequences: International Differences in Work-Related Values* (Newbury Park, CA: Sage Publications).

Hofstede, G., Hofstede, G.J. and Minkov, M. (2010) *Cultures and Organizations. Software of the Mind. Intercultural Cooperation and its Importance for Survival*, 3rd edn (New York: McGraw-Hill).

House, R.J., Hanges, P.J., Javidan, M., Dorfman, P.W. and Gupta, V. (eds) (2004) *Culture, Leadership and Organizations: The GLOBE Study of 62 Societies* (Thousand Oaks, CA: Sage Publications).

Nakata, C. (ed.) (2001) *Beyond Hofstede: Culture Framework for Global Marketing and Management* (Basingstoke: Palgrave Macmillan).

Further reading

Bing, J. (2004) 'Hofstede's Consequences: The Impact of His Work on Consulting and Business Practices', *Academy of Management Executives* 18(1): 80–7.

Blodgett, J. and Gregory, C. (2009) 'A Test of the Validity of Hofstede's Cultural Dimensions', *Journal of Consumer Marketing* 25(6): 339–49.

Gudykunst, W.B. and Ting-Toomey, S. (1958) *Culture and Interpersonal Communication* (Newbury Park, CA: Sage Publications).

Hall, E.T. (1976) *Beyond Culture* (New York: Doubleday).

Hofstede, G. (1998) *Masculinity and Femininity: The Taboo Dimensions of National Cultures* (Thousand Oaks, CA: Sage Publications).

Hofstede, G. (2003) *Culture's Consequences, Comparing Values, Behaviour, Institutions and Organisations Across Nations* (Thousand Oaks, CA: Sage Publications).

Hofstede, G. and Bond, M.H. (1988) 'The Confucius Connection: From Cultural Routes to Economic Growth', *Organizational Dynamics* 16: 5–21.

Khan, H. (1979) *World Economic Development: 1979 and Beyond* (London: Croom Helm).

McSweeney, B. (2002) 'Hofstede's Model of National Cultural Differences and their Consequences: A Triumph of Faith – A Failure of Analysis' *Human Relations* 55(1): 89–118.

Soondergaard, M. (1994) 'Hofstede's Consequences: A Study of Reviews, Citations and Replications', *Organizational Studies* 15(3): 447–50.

3
Key Thinkers in Cross-Cultural Communication (2)

Summary

This chapter examines the views of four more selected key researchers in cross-cultural communication, all of whom develop findings which complement much of the work covered by Hofstede and Hall and Hall in Chapter 2:

- Fons Trompenaars
- John Mole
- Richard D. Lewis
- Milton Bennett

The chapter surveys their key theories, the advantages and limitations of their research, and their application to the understanding of the effects of culture on communication.

Fons Trompenaars

Fons Trompenaars and Charles Hampden-Turner were teachers at Pennsylvania's prestigious Wharton Business School, where they developed a series of continua based on their observation of management practices around the world. By placing countries at different points along a continuum, they avoided the rigidity of a scale of 100. This allowed for greater flexibility of interpretation, which can be seen to fit better the notion of intercultural awareness as a perceptual art rather than as a strict discipline.

Trompenaars' work was carried out over a ten-year period and was in many ways a similar study to that conducted by Hofstede, surveying 1,500 managers from 28 countries and drawing on key issues in organizational theory in his research methodology. After setting up his own consultancy, the Centre for International Business Studies, Trompenaars wrote a seminal book, *Riding the Waves of Culture*, in 1993 based on his 15 years of academic research. This was one of the first books to focus attention on managing cultural diversity and its aim was to dispel the notion that there is 'one best way' of managing and organizing. In it, Trompenaars shows how cultural differences affect business life and management, and emphasizes that we should be wary of the dangers of trying to force our own management style on other cultures. There are many examples of the problems that can result from doing this, particularly in the case of International Joint Ventures (IJVs) and Western involvement in developing nations.

Meaning of culture

A fish only discovers its need for water when it is no longer in it. Our own culture is like water to a fish. It sustains us. We live and breathe through it. What one culture may regard as essential, a certain level of material wealth, for example, may not be so vital to other cultures. (Trompenaars, 2012: 27)

Trompenaars looks at culture as an expression of our coming to terms with three eternal problems:

- our relationship with other people;
- our relationship with time;
- our relationship with nature.

He considers that we can distinguish our culture from others by the way we devise solutions to these eternal problems.

Relationships with other people

Trompenaars has identified five dimensions to describe how we relate to other people. These are particularly relevant to the conduct of international business and are summarized below.

Dimension 1: universalism versus particularism

This first dimension examines relationships with people. *Universalism* defines our relationship to society in terms of rules and regulations. Individuals from universalist cultures show respect and obedience towards rules and procedures and do not object to such things as standing in a queue or strictly obeying pedestrian crossing lights. Universalism refers to the belief that ideas and practices can be applied anywhere without modification.

Particularism defines our relationship to society in terms of family and friends. If we are from a particularist culture, we will be inclined to break or bend the rules if we believe they are getting in the way of other relationships. Particularism means that circumstances dictate how ideas and practices should be applied. These can be loosely associated with Hofstede's UAI as cultures with high universalism like formal sets of rules and customs to which they can adhere. Trompenaars, however, focuses on the degree to which a country/culture upholds accepted standards of behaviour, for example, national laws and regulations, and the degree to which people are prepared to bend the rules to suit family and friends. Countries such as Finland, Germany and the USA are likely to be more universalist, while South European countries, like Portugal, and Asian countries, such as China and Malaysia, are likely to be more particularist.

Dimension 2: individualism versus collectivism

Individualist cultures focus on individual performance and achievement. Collectivist cultures define an individual in terms of his or her relationship with a group and its goals, and how people adapt their actions in relation to the community. These two factors are the same as in Hofstede's work, with the notable exception that Trompenaars contends that in an individualist culture such as the USA, the individual chooses to avoid or adhere to the values of the group, whereas in a collectivist culture such as Japan, the individual is constrained by the group. Trompenaars, however, considers Hungary and the Czech Republic to be relatively individualistic, despite their communist past.

Dimension 3: affective versus neutral

Reason and emotion both play a role in our relationships with one another. The extent to which individuals allow their own reason or emotions to intervene in actions or decisions will determine whether they are from a neutral or affective culture.

If we are from a *neutral* culture, for example, Japan or the UK, where reason dominates, we are less likely to show our feelings or emotions, but are likely to keep them carefully under control. In a neutral culture, people are taught that it is incorrect to show excessive emotions. This does not mean they do not have feelings, it just means that the degree to which feelings may become apparent is limited. They accept and are aware of their feelings, but are in control of them. Neutral cultures may think the more explicit signals of an affective culture too excited and over-emotional.

However, if we are from an *affective* culture, for example, Latin American or Mediterranean cultures, where emotion is more overt, we are likely to show our feelings more openly by laughing, smiling and showing anger or frustration. Such displays of emotion are not objected to as it is not considered necessary to hide one's feelings or to keep them 'bottled up'. Our feelings will find an immediate outlet and are openly and naturally expressed. In such a culture, people do not object to an open display of emotions.

In the workplace, neutral managers therefore tend to contain their emotions and, for them, contractual concerns are more important than personal concerns. In contrast, emotional managers tend to show their feelings and emphasize personal relations. British managers tend to be more neutral and generally more distant, whereas Italian managers tend to be more emotional, since, for them, the expression of their feelings is important.

Dimension 4: diffuse versus specific

The *diffuse* and *specific* dimension describes whether we allow other people into multiple areas of our lives or only into specific areas. It therefore deals with our range of involvement. It also describes whether we are prepared to show other people more than one level of our personality or the specific level appropriate to a specific situation. An example would be our relationship with a superior. In a *specific* culture (for example, Germany), individuals have a large public space that they readily let others enter and share, and a smaller private, 'restricted' space that they guard closely and share with only close friends and associates. A *diffuse* culture (for example, the USA) is one in which both public and private space are relatively similar in size and individuals carefully guard their public space because entry into public space also affords entry into private space. In specific cultures, there is a strong separation of work life and private life, whereas in diffuse cultures, work life and private life are often closely linked. In developing countries, but also in Mediterranean and Latin American countries, work and social interaction go hand in hand and are seen as two sides of the same coin. In Spain or Mexico, for example, the working day is extended to allow for shopping, meeting friends, long working lunches and even siestas. This is a diffuse business culture where the work/life balance is mixed. In Scandinavia, however, the working day is shorter and work life and social life are usually kept separate. This is a good example of specific behaviour. Trompenaars' specific versus diffuse dimension is in many ways similar to the Halls' low-context versus high-context cultures.

Example

In a diffuse culture, you would accord your boss/superior as much respect because of his or her position or status outside the workplace as you do at work. In a specific culture, the amount of respect you give your boss will depend on the situation. For example, if you are a better bridge or tennis player, you would expect him or her to respect your advice because of your greater prowess or experience in those activities.

Dimension 5: achievement versus ascription

We accord different levels of *status* to different individuals. How we accord that status indicates whether we are from an *achievement-oriented* culture or an *ascriptive* culture. Ascriptive cultures attribute status according to such variables as age, social class, seniority, gender, wealth, education and connections. Achievement-oriented cultures (for example, the USA) attribute status according to an individual's personal achievement and performance. People in such cultures believe they have to prove themselves to achieve status on the merits of what they have accomplished through their own efforts and actions. This has important implications when we try to negotiate across cultures. The young go-ahead manager from an achievement-oriented culture such as the USA may be seen as brash and disrespectful by an older manager from an ascriptive culture such as Japan. Ascriptive managers tend to rise because of their personal loyalty or family position, whereas achievement managers rise through competitive promotion. This can be seen, for example, in Germany, which is more achievement-oriented, whereas Italy is more ascription-oriented.

Trompenaars also identified different systems of promotion and authority in the countries he surveyed. In many countries, particularly those dominated by small and medium-sized family-run enterprises, he noticed that family and personal ties were important sources of management promotion. Such business cultures put a subsidiary stress on efficiency and a stronger stress on personal loyalty. In such cultures, promotion could be said to be ascribed by the boss to a favoured person rather than to the impersonal process of recruitment, short-listing, interviewing and selection, which would be characteristic of an achievement-oriented business culture such as in Germany and the USA.

Relationship to time

In addition to the five 'relationship orientations', another major cultural difference identified by Trompenaars is the way people deal with the concept of *time*. In this sense, his research is very similar to that carried out by the Halls (see Chapter 2). This is summarized below:

- *Sequential or monochronic-oriented* cultures view activities as linear and as a sequence. People tend to do only one activity at a time, respecting punctuality and preferring to follow plans as laid down. Time is seen as being measurable and is often given a monetary value. Relationships tend to be subordinate to schedules. There is a preference for management techniques such as critical path analysis, and time management is a recognized skill. Tasks are broken down into predetermined units of time.
- *Synchronic or polychronic* cultures exist where people tend to do more than one activity at a time, appointments are approximate and relationships are given importance above schedules. Time is considered to be more flexible than in monochronic cultures.
- Trompenaars also describes time in three phases: past, present and future. We attribute different levels of importance to each. *Past-and-present-oriented*

cultures (for example, the UK, France and Japan) emphasize tradition, gradual evolution and continuity with the present. They may seek examples from the past in making decisions about the future. *Future-oriented* cultures (for example, the USA) are likely to interpret present actions in terms of their future effects and future opportunity, stressing radical change and continuous development as indicators of success.

Man's relationship with nature

In the first edition of *Riding the Waves of Culture* (1993), Trompenaars identifies two major attitudes to nature: the extent to which people in a culture feel they have control over nature and the extent to which they feel they can have an impact on their environment. This is based on the way we seek to have control over our own lives, destiny or fate and what impact we have on our surroundings. *Inner-directed people* believe they have the ability to control nature by imposing their will upon it. They see nature as a complex environment which can be controlled or managed if the right expertise or technology is used. Current examples are cultures that seek to exert some control over the perceived future effects of climate change and the preservation of endangered species. One's personal resolve is the starting point for action. Survival is taken to mean acting with or against nature. Such people do not believe in luck or predestination. They are inner-directed, that is, one's own personal resolution is the starting point for any action.

Outer-directed people believe that man is part of nature and must go along with its laws and forces. They should operate in harmony with the environment and show respect for the necessary ecological balance. They do not believe they can really shape their own destiny. Nature moves in mysterious ways and therefore it is impossible to predict what may happen, for example, earthquakes, tsunamis, droughts and floods.

Concept of culture in layers

To understand Trompenaars' concept as expounded in *Riding the Waves of Culture*, one has to think of an onion and to 'unpeel it layer by layer'. This is similar to Hofstede's concept, as seen in Chapter 2. The outer layer is explicit and includes aspects of culture which we can see, feel, hear, eat and communicate with, even if we are only visiting as a tourist. We should, however, realize that these are observable manifestations of a deeper level of culture. Prejudices mostly begin at this symbolic and observable layer. Each opinion we utter about explicit culture says more about where we come from than about the country or people we are judging. The middle layer is concerned with our norms and values, our sense of what is 'right and wrong', 'good and bad', as seen in a society's laws, system of government and institutions. At the core are our basic assumptions about our existence and our relationship with the environment. These are so deeply embedded that they are truly basic and unconscious. In the latest edition of *Riding the Waves of Culture* published in 2012, Trompenaars describes the model of culture as 'a series of nested spheres', which is very much the same concept.

Critique of Trompenaars' research

Hofstede and Trompenaars both remain acknowledged pioneers in cross-cultural communication theory. Hofstede's value dimensions have clearly influenced Trompenaars' research. Universalism versus particularism can be relatively associated with Hofstede's uncertainty avoidance, while Trompenaars' individualism versus collectivism reflects Hofstede's individualism and collectivism dimension.

Although Hofstede and Trompenaars share more similarities than differences, Trompenaars has extended his focus on culture by covering people's relationship with time and the environment, areas not researched by Hofstede, and these can be seen as innovative and unique to Trompenaars, as he places particular emphasis on these factors.

Overall, Trompenaars' research is more recent than Hofstede's and thus it reflects some of the important world changes, particularly the growth of globalization and concern for the environment.

However, Trompenaars' work can be criticized as there are a relatively limited number of responses from many of the countries surveyed, except from the UK and the Netherlands. Europe accounts for 57.3 per cent of respondents, whereas Africa provides only 4.5 per cent, with nine countries having so few respondents that they are statistically insufficient to develop a multidimensional model. In addition, 65 per cent of respondents are male and most are managers. Moreover, neither Hofstede nor Trompenaars deals in sufficient detail with the part gender plays in their examination of culture.

In addition, some of Trompenaars' cultural dimensions are more difficult to understand than those of Hofstede and appear to overlap each other. However, his use of continua rather than scored dimensions allows him greater flexibility in describing cultural differences as orientations rather than absolutes.

Trompenaars himself maintains that he has aimed to produce his research findings in a way that is easily understandable and of practical use in the training of staff for work in the international environment. In this he has been very successful. It can be argued that real-life cultures very often do not have strict physical boundaries like nation states. As a result, values and beliefs can assume different forms outside these artificial boundaries.

Therefore, the findings of both Hofstede and Trompenaars can be criticized on several grounds. However, it is important to realize that although they have generated controversy, this has been the spur for further research into attempts to evaluate differences in culture and their effect on international management. In both cases, the increasing effects of the contribution of globalization to cultural change had not been fully recognized at the time when they carried out their main research.

John Mole

After 15 years with a US bank in the USA, Middle East and Europe, John Mole became a consultant on human resource development. His thesis is that there are two dominant factors that determine differences from company to company and, indeed, from country to country. He looked at the values and attitudes related to *organization* and *leadership*. His views were first contained in *Mind Your Manners* (originally published in 1990, now in its third edition published in 2003), which concentrates on European cultures.

Organization

Mole examines the beliefs about an organization, the role of the individual within it and the extent to which it is believed that *rational* order should be imposed on human affairs. He considers organizations from two different perspectives, as summarized below:

a) *Systematic organizations.* Basic elements of an organization are *functions*, which are coordinated by *logical relationships*. Personal relationships are primarily determined by the function they carry out. The needs of an organization are more important than the needs of individuals; what you do is more important than what you are.

b) *Organic organizations.* Organizations are like living organisms growing out of the needs of members and their environment. Order is based on personal relationships and recognized social hierarchy. If there is conflict, the individual prevails or there is compromise.

Leadership

The leadership dimension is based on the extent to which it is believed that *power* is given by groups to individuals. Authority can be executed only with the consent of those being managed. There are two types of leadership:

a) *Individual leadership.* Power is a right to be exercised by superiors over subordinates. Examples of cultures where this exists include the USA and France. Emphasis is on individual accountability and responsibility.

b) *Group leadership.* Although individuals may be unequal in ability and performance, all have a right to be heard and to contribute to the decisions that affect them. Power tends to be shared and responsibilities allocated within the organization.

Mole sees the improvement of cross-cultural management communication being achieved by the development of an organizational culture and mode of communication acceptable to others.

The 'Mole Map'

Mole has developed a schema, the 'Mole Map'. The *relative* position on the map of various countries is more meaningful than their *absolute* position on the axes. Countries which are close together have such similar cultures that some organizations within each may be interchangeable on the map. The further away countries are from each other, the less likely it is that there will be this overlap. Mole contends that no position is better or worse than any other; the problems arise when two extremes meet and their cultures are significantly different.

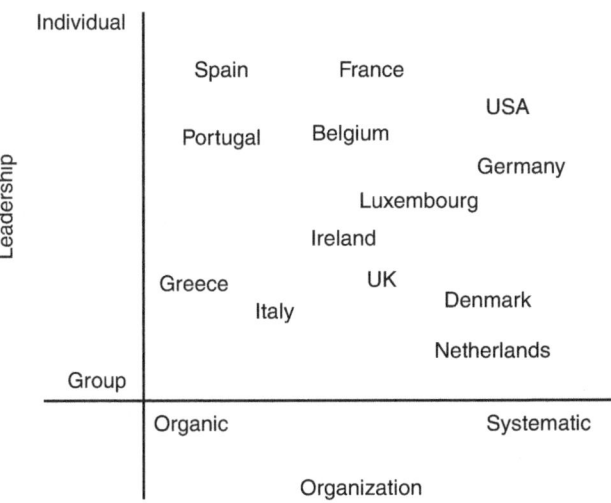

Figure 3.1   The 'Mole Map' (Mole, 2003: 39)

When working internationally, Mole advocates posing a number of questions:

- How does it affect me?
- Is there, in fact, a problem?
- If so, is it culture-related?
- Is it related to:
   a) *communication*: mainly language or non-verbal communication?;
   b) *leadership*: who has power? How is power obtained and exercised? What is authority based on and who takes decisions?;
   c) *organization*: how is work organized? How is information gathered and filtered down? How are forecasting and planning carried out and results assessed?

- If so, does it need:
  a) *cultural awareness*? If so, the time horizon is immediate;
  b) *tactical change*? If so, the time horizon is short term;
  c) *strategic change*? If so, the time horizon is long term.

With the fall of communism, the growing effects of globalization and the new independence of countries of Central and Eastern Europe who are now members of the EU, there is room for further research in this area.

Richard Lewis

Richard Lewis is the Chairman of Richard Lewis Communications, an international institute of cross-cultural and linguistic training in over 30 countries. His key work is *When Cultures Collide* (first published in 1996, now in its third edition, published in 2011). This builds on work by the Halls and Hofstede, and provides an essentially practical guide to understanding different cultures.

Lewis identifies three types of culture (Lewis, 2011: 33–4). These are summarized below:

- *Linear-active*: examples are the Germans, Americans, Swiss and Swedes, who tend to be highly organized, task-orientated and do one thing at a time. Time for them is clock-related as they are basically monochronic. Information is imparted in sequential blocks. Emphasis is placed on getting things done. Relationships are built through successful business rather than as a precursor to business itself.
- *Multi-active*: examples are the Arabs, Africans, Greeks, Italians and most Asians, who are characterized by flexible planning to deal with frequent change. They are polychronic and like to develop and acquire information polysynchronically. They are happy with interruptions and are less interested in schedules or punctuality. They build a network of contacts and often tend to handle information at a tangent, that is, one idea will spark another. They also tend to adapt to circumstances rather than appearing anxious about change. Most of the world's cultures tend to be multi-active and are seen by linear-active cultures as more disorganized, whereas the former see linear-active cultures as less flexible and, at times, verging on the arrogant.
- *Reactive*: examples are the Chinese, Japanese, Koreans and Finns, who prefer to listen first, make sure of the other person's position and then react. They do not speak in a direct way, but often prefer to 'beat about the bush'. As a result, they can be, to some extent, considered as a 'wait and see' culture. They often prefer to know their counterpart's position before exposing their own. They see events repeating themselves, and in these cultures, knowledge and wisdom are accumulated over time. These cultures are reflective

and introvert, and value silence and contemplation. They are skilled in non-verbal communication, using subtle body language. This approach can cause anxiety when they communicate with linear-active or multi-active cultures. They are more collective than proactive individualist cultures. In reactive cultures, communication is often a monologue, with pauses for reflection, as opposed to both linear-active and multi-active cultures, which prefer a dialogue mode of communication, with interruptions, comments and questions, all of which indicate interest in what is being said.

The *Lewis Cultural Model* is shown below in diagrammatic form.

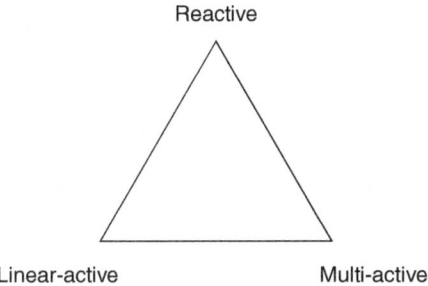

Figure 3.2   The Lewis Cultural Model (Lewis, 2011: 41)

Lewis' three types of culture can be summarized below.

Linear-active	Reactive	Multi-active
Schedules	Listens	Blocks of time
Introvert	Introvert	Extrovert
Punctual	Depends on circumstances	Unpunctual
High levels of pre-planning	Little feedback	Responds to circumstances
Medium to long term	Slow decisions	Short term
Formal agreement	Silence	Informal agreement
Facts important	Can be indirect	Relationships important
Likes privacy	Gregarious	Good listener
One thing at a time	Reacts to events	Several things at once
Follows plans	Makes small changes	Changes plans
Unemotional	Quietly caring	Emotional
Dislikes losing face	Avoids losing face	Has ready excuses
Limited body language	Subtle body language	Extensive use of body language
Rarely interrupts	Does not interrupt	Interrupts often
Job-oriented	People-oriented	People-oriented
Works fixed hours	Works flexible hours	Works any hours

Figure 3.3   Summary of Lewis' three types of culture (Lewis, 2011)

Culture and language

Lewis maintains that: 'The whole question of people using different speech styles and wielding their language in the national manner inevitably leads to misunderstanding, not only in expression but in intent' (Lewis, 2006: 66).

An example of this is the English, who may distrust the Italians because they wave their hands about and show much emotion. One could add to this example the often-held view of other Europeans that the Dutch style of communication can at times appear too direct and blunt.

Attitude to time

Lewis has similar views on cultural attitude to time as the Halls (see Chapter 2). He sees time from three different perspectives, which are summarized below (Lewis, 2006: 57–60):

- *Linear-active*: time is money, something to be saved and not wasted, as is evident in American and German culture.
- *Multi-active*: time is more flexible. Punctuality is less important. This approach to time is seen, for example, in Arab, Italian and Latin American cultures.
- *Cyclic time*: this view of time is apparent in some Eastern cultures. Here time is not a scarce commodity, as events and situations are seen as recurring. Many Asians, for example, the Thais, deal with problems not in a sequential way, but circle around them for a while before committing themselves to make a decision to act. Time is seen as a pool around which they walk. The Chinese tend to do the same, but notably they also show respect for the value of time.

Milton Bennett

Milton Bennett, when Director of the Cross-Cultural Institute in Portland, Oregon, explained his research in *Basic Concepts of Intercultural Communication* (1998). In this he explains the two concepts of ethnocentrism and ethnorelativism, which underpin his Developmental Model of Intercultural Sensitivity (DMIS). This provides an understanding of how people develop in their awareness of cultural differences. Bennett's views are summarized below:

- *Ethnocentrism*: we tend to judge other cultures according to the beliefs, values and traditions of our own group. Ethnocentrism may be said to be almost universal, as members of nearly all the world's cultures regard their own way of life as superior to those of even closely related neighbours. In ethnocentrism, people unconsciously experience their own culture as their only reality. They therefore regard the idea of the existence of cultural differences as a threat to the reality of their own cultural experience and often denigrate other cultures when compared to their own.

- *Ethnorelativism*: this is the opposite and involves judging other cultures by the values of the people you are dealing with. It attempts to be non-judgmental. Ethnorelativists recognize that all behaviour exists in a cultural context. They are prepared to attempt to understand other cultures as a means of enriching their own experience of reality.

Bennett's DMIS parallels the experience of culture shock. This is a model of six stages from ethnocentrism to ethnorelativism which have many similarities as regards the phenomenon of culture shock described by Oberg (1960) (see Chapter 6 below).

The stages are seen as a journey from ethnocentrism, being aware of one's own culture as the centre, through the honeymoon phase, the denial phase, defence and possible confrontation, the minimization of cultural differences to ethnorelativism with acceptance of difference, adaptation and finally integration. The cross-cultural learning progresses along a continuum which runs from ethnocentrism to some form of adaptation or integration.

At the *denial* stage, people are unable to interpret cultural differences in complex ways. They see differences but do not attribute them to culture. They are most likely to live in relative isolation from people who are different, either by chance or by choice. For these people, the world as they know it is their only experience and they remain ignorant of cultural issues. They rely on wide categories, such as 'foreigners', and often resort to ascribing stereotypes, without much thought, imposing their value judgments on what they see as good or bad in other people. They can stay in the denial stage so long as they have little contact with cultural differences.

At the *defence* stage, people are more able to recognize cultural differences through their own experience or through the influence of the media, but may still perceive them as a threat to their own identity and self-esteem. They defend against the threat of change by denigrating others with negative stereotypes and by having a positive and often superior evaluation of their own culture. This is, in effect, a way of defending their own system of values, dividing the world into 'us' and 'them'.

At the *minimization* stage, people try to over-generalize similarities between their own and other cultures. Differences are decreased, are considered inconsequential and are not viewed as threatening. There is a basically naïve belief that deep down, all people are essentially the same, are 'nice' and 'really very much like us'. They in fact lack cultural self-awareness and fail to realize that their perception of similarity is usually still based on their view of their own culture.

Ethnorelative stages

At the *acceptance* stage, people acknowledge that differences do indeed exist, are important and should be respected. This stage finally moves an individual from ethnocentrism to ethnorelativism. First comes a respect for cultural differences in behaviour, including an acceptance of verbal and non-verbal behaviour, and then a deeper respect for cultural differences in values, including an acceptance of various universal views that underlie most variations in behaviour. People begin to see their own behaviour in a cultural context with increased cross-cultural sensitivity.

At the *adaptation* stage, behavioural change is evident as people use their own knowledge of cultural differences to improve their relationships with people who are culturally different. They often choose to behave in a way that is more appropriate to cultures that differ from their own. They have by now acquired the ability to live and work effectively in the new cultural environment, to look at the world less judgmentally and have developed the ability and the skills to intentionally change their behaviour in order to communicate more effectively in another culture. They have become increasingly tolerant of the different views and values of other cultures, and begin to take an active interest in the benefits of cultural diversity.

At the *integration* stage, many people now see themselves as multiculturalist in behaviour and outlook. They tend to associate with new cultures that are different from those with which they are familiar and feel culturally competent in many different cultural environments. Organizations that have reached this stage are well able to succeed in a globalized environment.

Summary

- This chapter outlines the main cross-cultural research of Trompenaars, Mole, Lewis and Bennett, which assists the understanding of the concept of culture. The researchers chosen have mainly used empirical studies in an attempt to identify the specific key trends that can be used to compare and contrast various cultures.
- Trompenaars, like Hofstede, has concentrated on a 'dimensional' approach. Lewis has further examined the attitude of various cultures towards time, building on the research undertaken by the Halls.
- Mole concentrates on the European cultures, emphasizing the values and attitudes relating to organizations and leadership, and attempts to explain the differences by means of a schema, the 'Mole Map'.
- Both Mole and Lewis also build on research by the Halls and Hofstede and provide an essentially practical guide to understanding different cultures.
- Bennett compares and contrasts the two concepts of ethnocentrism and ethnorelativism. The various stages also have relevance to the understanding of culture shock (covered in Chapter 6).
- All these writers shed light on the way in which cultures vary between countries. The difficulty arises when one has to look at regional and ethnic differences within and between countries.
- Culture is undoubtedly a difficult concept to pin down. It is all too easy to deal in generalities and stereotypes, particularly in the modern world

of globalization, multiculturalism and the increased movement of people as a result of the growth of international trade and immigration.

- Although there is no universal acceptance of all their theories, the research writers selected have been the catalyst for further research in the attempt to evaluate differences in culture and their effect on international management.

- The main research theories have been discussed in this book, but teachers, trainers and students should refer to the important work carried out by other researchers such as Adler, Handy, Kluckhohn, Oberg, Schein and many others.

References

Bennett, M. (1998) *Basic Concepts of Intercultural Communication* (London: Nicholas Brealey Publishing).

Lewis, R. (2011) *When Cultures Collide*, 3rd edn (London: Nicholas Brealey Publishing).

Mole, J. (2003) *Mind Your Manners*, 3rd edn (London: Nicholas Brealey Publishing).

Trompenaars, F. with Hampden-Turner, C. (2012) *Riding the Waves of Culture: Understanding Cultural Diversity in Business*, 3rd edn (London: Nicholas Brealey Publishing).

Further reading

Adler, N. (1997) *International Dimensions of Organizational Behaviour*, 3rd edn (Cincinnati: South-Western College Press).

Bennett, M. (1993) 'Towards Ethnorelativism: A Developmental Model of Intercultural Sensitivity' in M. Paige (ed.), *Education for the Intercultural Experience* (Yarmouth, ME: Intercultural Press).

Magala, S. (1995) *Cross-Cultural Competence* (London: Routledge).

Mead, R. (1994) *International Management: Cross-Cultural Dimensions* (Oxford: Blackwell).

Mole, J. (1991) *When in Rome ... A Business Guide to Cultures and Customs in Twelve European Nations* (New York: AMACOM).

Richmond, Y. (1992) *From Nyet to Da: Understanding the Russians* (Yarmouth, ME: Intercultural Press).

Storti, C. (1990) *The Art of Crossing Cultures* (Yarmouth, ME: Intercultural Press).

Trompenaars, F. (2007) *The Whirlwind: Connecting People and Organisations in a Culture of Innovation* (Oxford: The Infinite Ideas Company Ltd.).

Trompenaars, F. with Hampden-Turner, C. (2010) *Riding the Waves of Innovation: Harness the Power of Global Culture to Drive Creativity and Growth* (London: Nicholas Brealey Publishing).

Victor, D. (1991) *International Business Communication* (New York: HarperCollins).

4

The International Use of English

Summary

The current position of English in the world
Lingua franca
Advantages of English as an international language
Disadvantages of English as an international language
Artificial languages
Opposition to choice of English
Variations of English
Off-shore English
Rivals to English
The decline in language teaching in the UK
The future of English as the international language

It can be argued that English has been called a world language for over 150 years, having enjoyed a dramatic growth from its early origins and influences. These included the Anglo-Saxons of Northern Europe, the Vikings and the Norman French, whose language was itself heavily derived from Latin. However, at the time of Shakespeare, there were only five million people who spoke English. In subsequent centuries, English has been influenced by 'borrowings' from other languages, consisting of words and phrases brought back from the countries of the Empire and by large-scale immigration into the UK itself. English is now well established in international organizations, such as the UN, where, along with French, Russian, Spanish, Chinese and Arabic, it is one of the official languages. The Organization of the Petroleum Exporting Countries (OPEC), the North American Free Trade Agreement (NAFTA), the academic world, popular music and culture, and increasingly international business in the globalized economy also use English as the main means of communication. In the world of science, papers are often first published in English before being reproduced in the author's mother tongue.

Source	Examples
Indian	bungalow, jodhpur, khaki, pariah
Dutch	yacht, deck, splinter, easel
Finnish	sauna
Inuit	kayak, igloo, anorak
Swedish	ombudsman, tungsten
Portuguese	albatross, marmalade, palaver
Russian	cosmonaut, vodka, tundra, tsar
Italian	pizza, volcano, fresco, villa, cameo
Arabic	sofa, algebra, cotton, mattress, arsenal
Malay	amok, bamboo, sarong

Figure 4.1   Examples of English 'borrowings' from foreign languages

Thousands of words have entered the English language from Greek, such as angel, alphabet, chorus, cycle, example, martyr and myth. There are also many from Latin, for example, altar, candle, circus, disciple, divine, essence, focus, literature, public, omnibus and referendum. Some are hybrids of both Latin and Greek, for example, television.

English is also spoken, albeit with many subtle differences, mainly in Australia, New Zealand, Canada, the USA, the Caribbean, the Indian subcontinent, and in parts of Africa and Southeast Asia. Differences manifest themselves mainly in terms of accent but also of syntax, style, spelling and vocabulary.

It is estimated that a quarter of the world's population speaks at least some English and this proportion is likely to increase in the near future, as English is being widely taught in China and in Eastern Europe, at schools and universities worldwide, and is frequently employed in international trade and commerce. Indeed, many performers in the Eurovision Song Contest sing in English, as English is recognized as the main language of pop culture.

English is spoken with some minor variations by over 350 million people worldwide as their mother tongue or first language. If the number of people who have learned English as their second or foreign language is included, Crystal considers that the estimated number of all English speakers in the world in 2005 could be somewhere between 1.5 and 2 billion. He emphasized that any further increase would mainly depend on how many people learned English in India and China (Crystal, 2005: 427–8).

In India alone, it is estimated that there are over 3,000 English-language newspapers. *The Times of India* is reputed to achieve sales three times those of *The Times* in the UK.

English is also the official language in nearly 50 countries and over 50 per cent of all scientific papers are in English. It is the language of air traffic control and Seaspeak (for maritime shipping), while over 50 per cent of international email and Internet traffic is conducted in English.

The British Council, which was set up in 1934, has the task of promoting British culture, interests, values and, importantly, the English language throughout the world by running language courses in many countries. This has become a very valuable and effective form of 'soft power'. English language teaching is one of the UK's major exports and in 2011 was estimated as having a value of £1 billion annually.

The expansion of the use of English in recent years can be attributed to the use of English as the major language on the Internet, Facebook and in data storage. Previously, the development of colonial possessions overseas and the subsequent Commonwealth expanded the use of English as the most convenient language for business, diplomacy and social communication. This expansion had been assisted by the large British Merchant Navy in the nineteenth century with its initial dominance of world trade, with the result that English was seen as the main language for commerce. As the UK's trading position declined, it was replaced by that of the predominantly English-speaking USA.

Lingua franca

1. Language used for communication among people of different mother tongues.
2. A hybrid language containing elements from several different languages used in this way.
3. Any system of communication providing mutual understanding.

Figure 4.2   The definition of 'lingua franca' from the *Collins English Dictionary* (2005)

There are at present some 6,000 recorded languages in the world, but many are fast disappearing with the death of their last native speakers, and it has been estimated that perhaps only 2,000 will survive by the end of this century. The main trend is perceived to be the spread of English, which has increasingly become the lingua franca, as we have already seen. The huge development of the Internet and electronic publication led Bill Gates in 1999 to publish Microsoft's new *Encarta World English Dictionary*, with the slogan 'One World: One Dictionary'. The next stage is perhaps 'One World, One Language'.

There have been several lingua franca throughout history in different parts of the world. One of the best known examples in recent times is Latin, which was recognized as the international language of the Church, education, diplomacy and learning in Europe from the eleventh century to the sixteenth century. After the Protestant Reformation of the 1530s and the development of local language printing with the invention of the printing press, the importance of Latin diminished, so that today many Roman Catholic Church ceremonies are conducted in the national language. From the seventeeth century to the nineteenth century, the international language of diplomacy was French, as well as at court and in polite society, for example, in Tsarist Russia. It began to be challenged, however, by the rise of English as the British Empire grew towards its peak at the end of the nineteenth century. German, the language of international science, research and publication, held sway in the nineteenth and early twentieth centuries, while Russian acted as the lingua franca of the Soviet bloc from 1917 to 1990.

In his book *Language Death*, David Crystal deplores the loss of many languages and puts this succinctly: 'If diversity is a pre-requisite for successful humanity, then the preservation of linguistic diversity is essential, for language lies at the heart of what it means to be human' (2002: 35). This is further emphasized by a Czech proverb which says: 'As long as the language lives, the nation is not dead.' Such concerns are seen in modern Britain with, for example, the successful attempt to retain a knowledge of Kernuak, the Cornish language, which was preserved from extinction by the government in 2002 when it was declared an official minority language in Britain. The Welsh language has also survived and is an official alternative to English in Welsh schools; it is also used extensively in the media, official documents and notices, particularly after the devolution of power to the Welsh Assembly. This is in contrast to the decline of the number of speakers of Scottish Gaelic, the ancient language used by a small minority in the Scottish Highlands and the Hebrides. By 1982, the number of fluent Gaelic speakers was only 80,000 and by 2002 the figure had declined to approximately 50,000.

The advantages of English as an international language

The main generally accepted advantages of using English are as follows:

- It has a wide, rich and cosmopolitan vocabulary that includes many foreign borrowings and assimilations and it is able to adapt easily to changes in social styles of communication. This ability to adapt is the chief strength of the English language.
- It also shares relatively similar structures and many common words with Germanic languages, in particular German and Dutch. In addition, it shares many words with other European languages derived from Latin, for example, French, Italian and Spanish.
- It has relatively simple inflections – simple plurals, verb forms and adjectives, uses natural rather than grammatical gender and has the additional advantage of not having cases.

- It is generally phonetic, although it does include a number of difficult pronunciations. It does not, however, have the difficulties associated with several-tone languages, such as Thai, Korean or Chinese.
- A number of English words have become universal, for example, airport, passport, hotel, telephone, tennis, golf, stop and jeans.
- Those who learn English acquire knowledge of British culture, literature, values and lifestyle. These have been actively promoted by the British Council and the BBC World Service.
- The dominance of English is reflected in the fact that the teaching of English in schools in non-English-speaking countries is increasingly seen as a 'lifestyle' subject, second only to the mother tongue, and is being introduced in primary schools for pupils as young as five.

In 2006, a British Council report predicted that the number of people learning English in the world would increase to two billion by 2020. English language tuition, including courses, teaching materials and books, is most likely to increase with China, Eastern Europe and Latin America being the main growth areas. The demand for online courses is also increasing with the development of digital programmes.

Disadvantages of English as an international language

English is a language with a very wide vocabulary. This is also a disadvantage, as it is rich in colourful and idiomatic expressions which can often cause mistranslations and incomprehension, as is exemplified in the following: 'We're in a bit of a spot. It's a tall order. We're pulling out all the stops, but bear with me.' This would undoubtedly cause some confusion with foreigners who are not familiar with colloquial English. It does of course mean: 'This is a difficult situation. You are asking a lot. We're making a special effort, but be patient.'

In addition, spelling is sometimes confusing, with many exceptions to the rules. There is also frequent lack of correlation between spelling and pronunciation, for example, 'rough', 'through' and 'thought'.

The very popularity of English has produced active resentment in other nations. This is particularly the case in France, where the former French President, Jacques Chirac, referred to the global spread of English as 'a major risk to humanity'. This attitude has been extended with the deliberate attempt to prevent the eclipse of *la langue diplomatique*, so much so that the French government has been very concerned that English would become the de facto official language of the EU at the expense of French. The very linguistic diversity of the EU is in itself a problem as there are over 20 official languages and, as a result, a huge number of documents need to be translated at great cost into all the official languages. This is despite the fact that, according to the European Commission, over 40 per cent of EU citizens have a good working knowledge of English, more than the combined totals of the next four languages (French, German, Spanish and Italian). The expansion of the EU has created an even larger group of people with English as their first choice of second language.

L'Académie Française was set up in 1635 by Louis XIII and Cardinal Richelieu to defend the French language against foreign influences and has been active ever since, in particular to prevent inroads being made by English. In 1994, Jacques Toubon, the then Minister of Culture, announced that the French government was seeking to protect the right of the French to be addressed in their own tongue. This was an additional move by the French to halt the increasing development of 'franglais', with the introduction of a law entitled 'Maintenance of the Purity of the French Language'. English has itself borrowed many French words and expressions which are still used today, for example, 'pièce de résistance', 'joie de vivre', 'tour de force', 'savoir faire', 'raison d'être', 'nom de plume', 'coup d'état' and 'carte blanche'. Some examples of English words that have been officially approved for use in the French language include 'le manager', 'le marketing', 'le weekend', 'le self' (self-service), 'le dancing', 'la cover-girl', 'le sandwich' and 'le parking'.

There are also a number of imported English words ('franglais') which have an official French version that should be used by all native French speakers. Examples are as follows.

Imported English	Official French
le welfare state	l'état-providence
le news-desk	la rédaction sedentaire
un disc-jockey	un animateur
l'élévateur	l'ascenseur
le job	l'emploi

Figure 4.3   Examples of Franglais

An additional problem in French for English speakers is the number of 'faux amis' (false friends), as shown in Figure 4.4.

French term	English translation
l'agenda	diary
intéressant	can mean 'profitable'
éventuellement	possibly
prétendre	to maintain, allege
assister à	to attend
avoir envie de	to desire
dramatique	disastrous
l'occasion	a hiring
les frites	chips
les chips	crisps

Figure 4.4   Examples of 'faux amis'

In 2003, a state commission which reported to the Académie Française, which was seen as the supreme arbiter of the linguistic purity of French, was set up to ensure that French words rather than English would be used when there is a perfectly good French word, particularly in the case of Internet and computer terminology, as well as on TV, radio and in the print media. This is part of an attempt to offset the encroachment of franglais.

Another problem which foreigners experience is the use of the English understatement. A classic example is the use by the English of 'rather good', which a foreigner may not realize is, in fact, a compliment. The use of the double negative is also confusing, as in the example 'I wouldn't disagree with that idea'.

Artificial languages

In endeavouring to simplify the problems posed by complex languages with wide vocabularies and the minefield of possible misunderstandings, there have been various attempts in the case of English to produce a relatively simple, standardized English devoid of colloquialisms, idioms and metaphors.

In the 1930s, Basic English (BASIC, the acronym standing for British American Scientific International Commercial) was promoted. It was a simple form of English which trimmed the excessive richness of English vocabulary and simplified some of the more complex areas of grammar. It had a basic vocabulary of 850 words selected to cover everyday needs.

Another later move in the 1970s was the Plain English Campaign in both the UK and the USA. This aimed to attack the use of unnecessarily complicated language, often used in particular by governments, business and the law, and replace the 'gobbledygook' with clearer forms of spoken and written English. This has had considerable success, notably in making the language used in government-issued forms and in legal documents more understandable. However, critics maintain that the simplification of vocabulary is often at the expense of more complex grammar and greater reliance on idiomatic constructions.

In the early part of the last century, attempts to develop a world language centred on the artificial language Esperanto, based on Romance language vocabulary and first invented in 1887. Although it had initial success, its adherents have dwindled in the face of competition by English, particularly after a UN proposal in 1966 for it to be accepted as an official international language failed. It is, however, a language choice offered by Google, Skype and Facebook, but the number of fluent Esperanto speakers has declined.

Within the EU there have been at least two attempts to develop a single European language. In 1999, Diego Marani, an EU translator, developed 'Europanto', a strange mixture of European languages as the linguistic answer to the single European currency. It did not really take off, nor did another attempt with a language called 'Globish', a simple, pragmatic form of English developed by Jean-Paul Nerriere, a former Vice President of IBM. His two books, *Don't Speak English, Parlez Globish* and *Découvrez le Globish*, sold well in France and were also published in Spain, Italy, Canada and even South Korea. Globish involves a limited vocabulary of 1,500 words, short sentences, no idiomatic expressions and a large number of hand gestures. It aims to replace the complexity of English and is also recommended for native English speakers.

Off-shore English

The colloquialisms and idioms frequently used by native English speakers often confuse their trading partners. As a result, there has been an increase in the development of a simplified form of English which can be acquired more easily for use in international business. This is called 'off-shore English' and for foreigners requires less investment in terms of time and effort than learning a complete foreign language. It concentrates on helping non-native English speakers make the most impact in English with a relatively limited vocabulary for practical use in business. At the same time, it aims to encourage native English speakers to modify their own use of the language to ensure greater understanding by foreigners. This approach is expanded in Guy and Mattock (1991). It has the additional advantage that it can continue to evolve and assimilate changes in usage and newly-coined words. Guy and Mattock (1991: 134–5) propose the following criteria for validating an international language:

- easy to learn;
- relatable to other mother tongues;
- contains a rich range of functions;
- is standardized.

Varieties of English

The dominance of English as a lingua franca masks the existence of many varieties of English in use around the world, for example, in the Indian subcontinent (and particularly in India itself), West Africa, the USA, Australia and Singapore, as well as in parts of the UK. In many countries, such as Sierra Leone, the Caribbean and Papua New Guinea, creole versions of English, or patois, have developed, a few of which have been recognized as indigenous languages in their own right. The Krio language of Sierra Leone is such an example.

Of greater significance is the variety of English spoken by non-native speakers. The term 'variety of English' was coined by the Indian linguist Professor Braj Kachru, who identified two circles of English usage, namely 'native speaker varieties of English', the so-called inner circle, and a 'non-native speaker varieties of English', the outer circle. Native speaker varieties of English are those spoken by citizens where English is the mother tongue. The outer circle of non-native speakers includes speakers of English in India and China, as well as speakers of English in countries such as Germany, France, Italy or Spain (Kachru, 1992).

The varieties of English mainly use words in the local language which have been assimilated into the English used in these countries. The following are some examples of this.

Hinglish

This consists of many English words used in Hindi. It is estimated that Indian English is spoken by 350 million people and has acquired a new, distinct vocabulary of words and usage. It is also influenced by Bollywood, the world's largest film industry. It is spoken mainly in urban areas in India, particularly among the young middle class and on college campuses. Hinglish includes many English-sounding words which have been specially adapted for use in Indian culture, such as those given in Figure 4.5.

Hinglish	English
Speed money	Money to expedite a transaction
Rail roke	Rail strike
Babu English	Flowery language
Snake juice	Illegally distilled liquor
How are you pulling in these days?	How are you getting on?
A fooding and lodging	A small hotel
Head bath	Hair washing
Badmash	Naughty
Glassy	In need of a drink

Figure 4.5   Examples of Hinglish

Singlish

This is a form of colloquial English used in Singapore and developed from a mixture of English, Malay, Tamil and the languages of Southern China, in particular Hokkien. There are no grammatical rules. The development of Singlish has been spurred on by the fact that English is one of the four official languages in Singapore and is the main language for administration, commerce and education. However, the use of Singlish is discouraged by the government and well-educated Singaporeans, and the government has created an annual Speak Good English Movement. Although its use is discouraged in the mass media and in schools, it often occurs in routine usage by ordinary working people on the street and on TV and radio, and has become an independent, English-based creole language with many colourful expressions. Examples include 'Ya ya papaya' (an arrogant person) and 'mugger toad' (a hard-working student who can regurgitate information).

It is interesting that although Hong Kong was a British-administered colony for many years, there has not been such a comparative development of a distinctive English form as the vast majority of the inhabitants there are Cantonese-speaking Chinese.

Strine

Strine is the Australian English vernacular which contains many colourful words and phrases, such as the following given in Figure 4.6.

Strine	English
Sickie	Day taken off work
Fair dinkum	Honest, genuine
Wowser	A kill joy, spoilsport
Mad as a cut snake	Very angry
Come the raw prawn	Attempt to deceive
Cobber-dobber	One who informs on a colleague
Daggy	Dirty, slovenly (meaning now is 'uncool')
Sheila	A single girl

Figure 4.6 Examples of Strine

American English

American English differs from Standard English in a number of ways. It was George Bernard Shaw who said that the UK and the USA are 'one people divided by a common language'. In particular, American English has a vocabulary which in many cases uses the same English word but with a different meaning. some examples of which are given in Figure 4.7.

There are also numerous differences in spelling, with American English preferring 'er' where standard English prefers 're', for example, 'theater' and 'center'. In addition, American English prefers 'or', whereas standard English prefers 'our', for example, 'favor', 'labor' and 'color'.

There are also many differences in the American English use of words compared to their usage in Standard English – for example, in English, if we say something is 'quite good', we mean that it is not great or outstanding but OK. However, in the USA, 'quite' is more a superlative, not a qualifier and means an emphatic 'very'.

American English is colourful, with metaphors and idioms that reflect their culture, including sporting references, such as those relating to baseball,

American English	English
Bad tempered	Mean
Yard	Garden
Elevator	Lift
Wrench	Spanner
Parking lot	Car park
Vacation	Holiday
Closet	Cupboard
Drapes	Curtains
Duplex	Semi-detached
Bathroom	Toilet
Trunk	Boot of a car

Figure 4.7 Examples of American English

whereas Standard English uses cricket analogies. John Major, when Prime Minister, used the term 'sticky wicket' (that is, something which is difficult), which caused much confusion among interpreters at an EU meeting. One of the main problems encountered by foreigners when taking part in meetings with Americans is understanding the 'management speak'. These expressions cause confusion with foreigners, particularly those who have been educated in Standard English.

Standard English

Standard English, or BBC English (also sometimes referred to as Oxford English), attempts to shape and refine the wide variety of the UK dialects and their accompanying vocabularies into a form of Received Pronunciation, a way of speaking that is not just national, but educated and correct. However, many dialect variations have resisted such a move. This is, for example, apparent in the development of the so-called 'Estuary English', which is Southern, urban, glottal and apparently classless.

Rivals to English as an international language

However, the perceived dominance of English may be facing competition. We mentioned earlier that the power of a lingua franca depends on the commercial power and political influence of the dominant native-speaker nation. In the nineteenth and twentieth centuries, first Britain and then the USA were the dominant powers, but in the early years of the twenty-first century, there are strong indications that this may be changing, especially with the increased influence of the BRIC nations (Brazil, Russia, India and China).

The dominance of English as the aspiring world language is, perhaps, only likely to be challenged in the near future by Spanish or Chinese. Spanish is already well established in all of South America, with the exception of Brazil, and most of Central America. With over 500 million Spanish speakers worldwide, it is now the third most widely spoken world language and, with English, is one of the world's fastest growing languages. The use of Spanish is certain to increase in North America, particularly in the USA, with many Southern states, especially Florida, Texas and California, becoming increasingly bilingual in Spanish and English. This trend has already been the subject of concern expressed by the Harvard Professor Samuel Huntington in *Who Are We? The Challenge to America's National Identity* (2004). This caused much controversy over his claim that Mexican immigration in particular will split America culturally, linguistically and economically. He maintained that the USA might transform in the future into two cultures, Anglo and Hispanic, and two languages, English and Spanish. Huntington believed that if Mexicans wanted to be part of the American dream, they would have to learn to speak English.

In Europe, however, English does not at present appear to face a serious challenge. The peoples of Eastern Europe are increasingly learning English at the expense of Russian. German has made little headway, although Austria and Germany, together with German speakers in Belgium, Luxembourg and Alsace, total 90 million, which makes German the most widely spoken first language in the EU.

Arabic is also increasing in importance as the lingua franca of the Middle East, while Hindi, the official language of India, is a lingua franca, spoken by about half a billion citizens. Finally, the most spoken first language in the world, but not yet the most widely spoken, is Chinese, with Mandarin Chinese as its common written form and increasingly dominant as a spoken form. This is perhaps the most likely challenge to the predominance of English in the future.

The decline in language teaching in the UK

However, the growing dominance of the English language as the most widespread international language has had a profound influence on the learning of foreign languages in the UK itself. There is a tendency for young people no longer to see the need to embark upon what is generally believed to be a more difficult option than some of the other subjects available on the school curriculum. The situation was exacerbated when in 2004 a foreign language at GCSE level was deemed by the government to be merely an optional rather than a compulsory subject. This has a knock-on effect on students' choice of 'A' Levels. In their turn, universities, in a climate of economic restraint, have closed a number of foreign language courses, with German being particularly badly affected. Independent schools on the whole continue to insist on a foreign language and some have introduced basic Mandarin, although attempts to introduce Russian and Japanese appear to have been less successful. All this is in marked contrast to schools abroad, where English is taught in many instances from primary school onwards, particularly in the EU.

The European Survey on Language Competence, conducted by the European Commission working unit in 2012, a consortium which included the English examination board Cambridge Assessment, reported that English pupils begin to learn a foreign language later than their other European counterparts. English pupils were reported to be among the least able in foreign languages, in particular regarding French, the first most commonly taught foreign language, and German, the second most commonly taught foreign language at school. Nick Gibb, the Schools Minister, said: 'For school leavers and graduates in England to be able to compete in the global jobs market, they need to be competent in at least one foreign language' (*The Times*, 22 June 2012). As a result, employment opportunities may be reduced. Relatively few British candidates gain positions in the EU for the same reason. In business too, without any knowledge of the local language, it is more difficult to engage in the niceties of polite 'small talk' which are often the prelude to establishing good relations before the serious business of negotiating a deal can commence.

British insularity runs the risk of having a detrimental effect on the UK's competitive edge in foreign trade and weakens its position as a major trading nation. Although business schools often offer a subsidiary language course as part of their first or second degree, the level of competence gained can be variable. It may be that the latest move by the government to introduce a new qualification, the English Baccalaureate, which includes a language, will improve matters, but it will take time before any discernible improvement becomes evident and overcomes the British complacency and lack of motivation to acquire fluency in foreign languages.

Learning the language of a foreign country, especially when it includes some of its literature, gives an insight into the thought processes and culture of that country. It also provides a deeper awareness and understanding of the mother tongue's grammar and flexibility. Without this extra dimension, it is not only success in business dealings which can be undermined; there is also the grave danger of developing insularity and becoming a culture of monolingualism. Language training should remain an important part of the National Curriculum for the majority of pupils and should be included in companies' business training plans.

Summary

In summary, the following trends are most likely to occur:

- In a report in 2006, the British Council estimated that the number of people learning English as a second language would increase substantially.

This figure may rise to over four billion by 2050, with nearly 50 per cent of the world's population having some competence in English.

- English will often be taught by second-language speakers, which will lead to more 'regional' forms of the language.
- Spanish and Chinese, and possibly Hindi, will also become more widespread and could be the main competitors to English as the chief global language.
- Minority languages will continue to disappear. The spread of English may marginalize local native languages and even threaten their survival.
- English may become more diglossic, as has already happened with German, Arabic and Greek, breaking up into mutually unintelligible dialects, but having an original English parentage. We might all speak varieties of English, but may have difficulty in fully understanding each other.
- There is already no longer a standard form of English throughout the world. The English language is becoming localized as it adapts to the needs of the local or regional community. Its vocabulary is being constantly enriched by local borrowings and inventions. To keep English as the main international language of business, it may become necessary for speakers to have to learn both Standard English and a local dialect.
- Artificial languages, on past evidence, will not be successful competitors.
- The resentment towards English will continue. The perceived dominance will still be seen by some as a form of linguistic imperialism, particularly in the case of the French.
- The continued attraction of learning English is not fundamentally cultural or linguistic, but mainly economic and utilitarian. It will continue to be increasingly taught by the top international universities and business schools.
- The current decline in modern language tuition in UK schools and universities is unlikely to be halted in the near future as regards European languages, but there is evidence of Chinese being the subject of increased attention.
- The use of English on the Internet will continue, with the majority of web pages written in English, but this may decrease in the future as a result of competition, particularly from Chinese.
- Learners of English now have a mainly instrumental requirement – namely they want to do business internationally, not just to talk to native English speakers. They are realizing the fact that the majority of English-language users are increasingly non-native speakers.
- In an increasingly competitive marketplace, fluency in the native language of potential customers will still remain an important factor in gaining a competitive advantage.

References

Crystal, D. (2002) *Language Death* (Cambridge University Press).
Crystal, D. (2005) *How Languages Work* (London: Penguin Books).
European Commission (2012) 'European Survey on Language Competence', available at: http://ec.europa.eu/languages/eslc/docs/en/final-report-escl_en.pdf (date accessed 22 December 2012).
Guy, V. and Mattock, J. (1991) *An Action Guide to Cross-Cultural Business* (London: Kogan Page).
Huntington, S. (2004) *Who Are We? The Challenge to America's National Identity* (New York: Free Press).
Kachru, B. (1992) *The Other Tongue* (Urbana: University of Illinois Press).
Woodcock, N. (2012) 'English Pupils at Bottom of Language Class', *The Times*, 22 June.

Further reading

Baugh, A. and Cable, T. (1993) *A History of the English Language* (London: Routledge).
Bhatt, R. (2001) 'World Englishes', *Annual Review of Anthropology* 30: 527–50.
Bragg, M. (2003) *The Adventure of English: A Biography of a Language* (London: Hodder & Stoughton).
Bryson, B. (1990) *Mother Tongue* (London: Hamish Hamilton).
Burridge, K. (2004) *Blooming English* (Cambridge University Press).
Cohen, R. (2001) 'Language and Conflict Resolution: The Limits of English', *International Studies Review* 33(1): 25–51.
Crystal, D. (1996) *The Cambridge Encyclopaedia of Languages* (Cambridge University Press).
Crystal, D. (1997) *English as a Global Language* (Cambridge University Press).
Crystal, D. (2004) *The Language Revolution* (Cambridge: Polity Press).
Graddol, D. (1997) *The Future of English?* (London: The British Council).
Graddol, D. (2006) *English Next: Why Global English May Mean the End of English as a Foreign Language* (London: The British Council).
Hogg, R. and Denison, D. (eds) (2006) *A History of the English Language* (Cambridge University Press).
Hurn, B.J. (2009) 'Will International Business Always Speak English?' *Industrial and Commercial Training* 41(6): 299–304.
Jenkins, J. (2009) *World Englishes* (London: Routledge).
Knowles, G. (1997) *A Cultural History of the English Language* (Oxford University Press).
Kramsch, C. (1998) *Language and Culture* (Oxford University Press).
Nettler, D. and Romaine, S. (2000) *Vanishing Languages* (Oxford University Press).
Ostler, N. (2010) *Futures of English* (London: Allen Lane).
Pennycook, A. (2008) *Global Englishes and Transcultural Flows* (London: Routledge).
Philipson, R. (2007) 'Linguistic Imperialaism', *Language Policy* 6: 377–83.
Pinker, S. *The Language Instinct* (London: Penguin Books).
Sapir, E. (1996) *Culture, Language and Personality* (Berkeley, CA: University of California Press).

Sewell, C. (2006) *Language Learning for Work in a Multilingual World* (London: CILT Publications).

Sharifran, F. (2009) *English as an International Language: Perspectives and Pedagogical Issues* (Bristol: Multilingual Matters).

Storti, C. (2001) *The Art of Crossing Cultures* (London: Nicholas Brealey Publishing).

Wardbaugh, R. (1993) *Investigating Language* (Oxford: Blackwell).

5
Developing Cross-Cultural Communication Skills

Summary

Key areas
Written and electronic communication
Presentations to international audiences
Development of listening skills
Networking
Uniting Europe through Cultures (UNEC)
Non-verbal communication
Recommendations for best practice

In Chapter 1, we examined barriers to effective cross-cultural communication. In this chapter, we look at how we can develop our cross-cultural skills in the key areas of:

- *language* – the words we use;
- *medium* – the medium by which we communicate (oral, written, aural, electronic);
- *behaviour* – the way we use language to convey formality and informality, power and status, and how we get things done. It also includes non-verbal communication.

To achieve effective communication across cultures, we need to consider all three aspects.

Language

Communication is much easier if we all speak the same language or have equal fluency in a lingua franca. It establishes a rapport, shows openness to the culture and increases our own self-esteem, confidence and self-reliance. It leads to better understanding, demonstrates commitment and, at times, gives the speaker a competitive edge.

As we saw in Chapter 4, English is becoming widely accepted as the world's lingua franca, but there are considerable differences between the English used by native speakers and the different varieties of English in use around the world. Even in our own languages, however, a number of features that we might consider normal or uncontroversial in our own national, regional or personal style may cause problems for others. These include speed, accent, volume, timing, silence and even our choice of words.

Speed

As measured by linguists, different languages are spoken at different speeds and with different degrees of inflection. For example, many people say that Indian national languages are spoken at speed and that this affects the speed of delivery of Indians when speaking English. In Europe, Spanish is generally accepted as the fastest language. The problem here is of non-understanding: 'I simply can't follow you. Slow down.'

Stress

Another important feature is stress. The stress in a word or sentence is where you place the most important emphasis. The issue is whether the stress carries meaning; for example, in English, we tend to stress the most important word in the sentence. However, in both French and Hindi, people tend to stress the end of the sentence. This means that if we speak a stress-timed language (in other words, stress carries meaning), the receivers need to adjust their antennae to focus on our message.

Intonation and volume

Intonation describes how the voice rises and falls in a sentence. We tend to assume stereotypically that great variations in intonation are a characteristic of Italians and that the further south you go, the stronger it becomes. We also tend to associate strong intonation with heightened emotion. In the same way, a loud voice tends to be associated with dominance and arrogance, both personally and nationally.

Silence and timing

Most Asian cultures and one European culture (the Finns) are much more comfortable with silence than most other nationalities. Sitting silently to reflect on what has been said and to consider one's response is particularly important for the Japanese, who say nothing but who are inwardly uncomfortable with the 'instant response' adopted by many Western nationalities. Alongside silence is timing. Linguists talk of 'conversational overlap', which describes the practice of interrupting or overlapping with another speaker before he or she has finished speaking. In countries like Japan, where strict turn-taking in conversation is observed, conversational overlap may be seen as very impolite.

Accent

In speech, accent can be a major source of misunderstanding. This is difficult to resolve, although much work has been done in Indian call and contact centres on 'accent neutralization' to make Indian accents more understandable to the overseas clients they are dealing with on the telephone. As a general rule, it is of course important, whatever your accent, to slow down and articulate clearly.

False friends

A further problem which influences language is the actual words we use. This includes 'false friends': the transposing of a word from one language to another, sometimes with embarrassing results. For example, a British colleague in Spain explained how she was 'embarrassada' to be late for a meeting, not realising that the Spanish word means to be pregnant. In the same way, a Spanish colleague who used the term 'constipated' during a conference call clearly did not realise that to be 'constipado' in Spanish ('having a cold') had a very different meaning in English!

There are a number of examples of 'faux amis' in French that cause problems (see Chapter 4 for more details on these).

Bad language

Other areas of misunderstanding include swearing and the use of insults. In many countries, particularly those with a strong religious sensitivity, swearing is strongly frowned upon, whereas in other cultures, it may be seen as the use of emphatic language. We are often insensitive to the shock value of a particular swear word we use in our mother tongue. What you may repeat in a foreign language almost as a joke may be a conversation stopper among your international colleagues and may reflect on your upbringing, education and general reputation in their eyes. If you are a user of 'colourful language', be especially careful, particularly in mixed company, when in a foreign cultural environment.

Written communication

It can be argued that written communication or 'snail mail' is perhaps out of date, but in business memoranda (memos), reports and contracts are still important. It is tempting to think that all written communication has a common format and style, but this is not the case. The style of written communication is affected by degrees of formality and informality. Written communication in the UK, the USA and, indeed, much of the Western world is brevity- and efficiency-driven. In addition, there is now a tendency for courteous greetings and sign-offs to be less frequently used.

A typical email communication might be as follows:

Brian

Am completing Chapter 5. Expect in one hour.

Barry

A more courteous and expansive form of communication might be more acceptable in Latin and Asian countries, so the communication to these cultures might read as follows:

Dear Brian

Hope everything is going OK. This is just to let you know that I am just completing Chapter 5 and will email it to you in about an hour.

Best wishes

Barry

The second communication does exactly the same job as the first, but is more personal and more courteous, although it takes longer to write and to read. The advice for such communication is first to be aware of your usual style and second to consider whether it is necessary to adapt to the other person's style. Above all, if you are used to a more courteous and lengthy style of expression, you should not be upset if you receive a communication that to you feels quite curt and abrupt. As with memos and messages, different conventions apply to reports. In Japan, for example, the preferred style for an executive summary is bullet points, with as much detail as possible attached as appendices. Other cultures and different companies have different conventions, so it is important to learn what these are and to observe them. Above all, you should not assume that your style works everywhere else.

Electronic communication

The dramatically rapid increase in electronic communication throughout the world has brought people of different cultures closer together. This is demonstrated, for example, in the growth of Facebook, which features over 100 billion entries a day, while in the case of Twitter, more than a billion tweets a week are generated. The use of mobile phones and text messaging has increased along with the huge number of emails sent daily, which is currently estimated at nearly 300 billion. These forms of communication drastically reduce the effect of time zone differences that used to complicate international telephone calls. Recipients can read and reply rapidly, and the transmission of information and decision making is speeded up.

Electronic communication includes written communication, email, voice communication and Skype, as well as the new social media communication methods. The latter are introducing new ways of expressing oneself, especially in Twitter (140-character messages) and using new forms of language such as texting or acronyms or initials, such as LOL (lots of love or laugh out loud). Since English still dominates the international media, most texting is done in English.

As communication channels, in particular those that are electronically based, are constantly changing, we need to keep up to date regarding the technological advances in computers, email, mobile phones, video conferencing and so on. The actual selection of the appropriate technology needs to be compatible with the culture with which we are communicating. We should bear in mind that high-context cultures which place high value on personal trust tend to prefer oral communication and oral agreements, whereas low-context cultures tend to place high value on forms of written communication.

Presentations

By definition, a presentation to a multicultural audience means dealing with local cultural expectations, avoiding embarrassment or offence being caused, and otherwise being disrespectful. It is important to discover in advance the expectations of the audience and the presentation style to which they are accustomed. Such preparation is essential in order to ensure success.

In Asia, Africa and Latin America, as well as the Middle East, respect for hierarchy and seniority is important. For example, a Westerner delivering a presentation with his or her sleeves rolled up and no jacket may be seen as disrespectful to an audience expecting more formal attire. Maintaining eye contact with the group may be less important than maintaining eye contact with the senior persons present and addressing the main points to them. British and American presenters are often less comfortable with the use of surnames and titles as they prefer greater informality. However, the correct use of surnames and professional titles in many cultures is necessary to show the minimum level of respect. The use of jokes in cultures, for example, in Germany, may suggest that your subject matter is lacking in gravity. In the UK, in contrast, humour is often used as an 'ice-breaker' to reduce formality and to relax the audience.

It is also important to be aware of the linguistic competence in English of your audience. Some of the participants may seem not to be paying attention to the lecture in English. This may be because they are referring to dictionaries to identify key words. They may also appear to be talking to each other, but this is usually not because they are bored but because they are attempting to translate for each other. When presenting in English, it is essential to keep sentences shorter, to speak clearly and slightly more slowly than with an all-native English-speaking audience, avoiding jargon and explaining any acronyms and initials. A strong local accent may also present a problem to non-native English speakers. Another consideration in presentations is their actual length. Those presenting to a multinational group should bear in mind that the concentration levels of the audience may be more limited because of their need to concentrate on the linguistic aspects as well as the actual information provided.

A common problem when using PowerPoint in presentations is the use of excessive detail. As a general rule, Western presenters advocate a maximum of seven-line slides with considerable white space and bold illustrative graphics. Many Asian presenters tend to fill their slides with a great deal of information and point to the parts they wish to emphasize. German audiences are known to prefer much more detail in presentations than American audiences, and Asian audiences will often comment in feedback that they would have preferred more slides with more information. In Muslim countries, cartoons and images tend to be less well received because their audiences are less used to representational art.

Any presentation needs to meet the expectations of the audience. It may be that they require facts and figures, a product pitch, a motivational speech, an analysis of the advantages and disadvantages, or to know how what they hear may benefit them or their country. A combination of several of these factors may of course be required. Lewis (2011) analyses these key needs and identifies them as part of the 'listening' habits of different cultures. One of his examples is the contrast between the needs of German and Scandinavian, and British and American audiences. He considers that German and Scandinavian audiences react adversely to a strong product pitch or 'hard sell' tactics and prefer to listen to a reasoned presentation of the advantages and disadvantages so that they can decide for themselves. British and American audiences, on the other hand, tend to respond to a 'qualities, costs, and benefits' approach and a strong 'what's in it for me?' outcome. Latin countries tend to focus less on the content of the presentation and the information provided, and more on the personality of the presenter. The essential question for them is to whether they can trust you. Latin audiences may prefer eloquence and charisma over information.

When presenting to multicultural audiences, it is important to structure carefully your address. Tomalin (2012: 33) offers the three S's approach to structuring a presentation: signposting, signalling and summarizing.

Signposting

- State what the main theme of the presentation is going to be.
- Indicate how long the presentation will last.
- Say what your main points will be.
- Say when you will take questions – any time or at the end.

If you imagine a presentation as a journey, the signposting stage will give the audience a route map, so they will know what is going to happen and how long the journey will last.

Signalling

- Indicate to the audience when you begin your first point.
- Summarize when you have completed it.
- Signal when you are about to begin the next point.

Summarizing

- When you reach the end of your last point, briefly summarize all the key points again. This allows your audience to remind themselves of the journey they have just undertaken and helps them identify any points they may have missed or of which they may not have fully appreciated the importance.
- At the end, reiterate the importance of the main theme.
- Finally, invite questions and remember to conclude by thanking the audience for its attention, thus indicating that the presentation has ended.

Chapter 15 provides further advice on preparing students to give effective presentations across cultural borders.

Listening skills

In this section we examine the importance of both *passive* and *active* listening skills. We look at the barriers to effective listening and how these can be overcome as part of our attempt to develop improved cross-cultural communication.

Listening has been described as a process of self-denial. It is a vital skill in assisting us to decode the messages we receive. When we listen, we are usually paying attention to the message and we attempt to make sense of what we hear. Research indicates that most of us listen in short 30-second spurts before our attention tends to wander. Listening tests have also indicated that, on average, people really remember only some 50 per cent of what they have heard immediately afterwards. As we saw in Chapter 1, unless we listen carefully to the message and understand its meaning, there is really little actual communication, only 'noise'. The listening process involves five related activities:

- *Receiving*: what we hear is often blocked out by external noise, distraction, our lack of concentration or lack of interest in the subject matter.
- *Interpreting*: the use of a different, unfamiliar frame of reference, values, concepts, attitudes and bias may also impede our understanding.
- *Remembering*: the process of storing for future reference, taking notes and summarizing.
- *Evaluating*: making a judgment regarding accuracy of facts, opinions, the quality of evidence and reliability of data.
- *Responding*: this involves various types of feedback as a result of what is heard, which may include verbal response, laughter, silence, applause and non-verbal responses such as nodding or shaking the head, frowning and smiling.

Passive listening is as important as active listening. It can show how we feel about what we are listening to, displaying such emotions ranging from pleasure and agreement to boredom or even hostility. We can reassure the speaker in subtle ways by showing empathy and appearing to concentrate closely, or we can show disagreement by looking angry or indignant.

Barriers to effective listening can include the following:

- Pre-judgment, which involves jumping to conclusions and allowing prejudice and preconceived ideas to dominate.
- Trying to take control of the conversation by 'jumping in' with interruptions. We believe that we should be the centre of attention and attempt to monopolize the situation. We are always trying to move the conversation round to a point where we can express our own point of view. We are, in effect, a 'shift responder'; the other speaker's conversation is simply a hook to allow us to interrupt and continue with our own train of thought: 'Funny you should say that. It reminds me of my own experience in ...!' This type of listener is sometimes called a 'marginal listener'.
- Listening selectively, concentrating only on what we want to hear and agree with.
- Competitive listening occurs when we are listening for what we do not agree with and we interrupt to correct, modify or criticize what the speaker is saying. Often described as 'judgmental listening', competitive listening is probably the most common type for professional people from all walks of life, but it can at times be seen as too aggressive and attempting to dominate.
- Reaction to emotive words, such as 'race' and 'stereotypes'.
- Interrupting – a tendency to 'over-talk' caused by our desire to put across our views.

- Attempting to take detailed notes and trying to establish what are the key points, a common mistake made by students.
- Day-dreaming – letting our attention wander to other more important or more interesting concerns.
- Judging the actual delivery rather than the content by concentrating on mannerisms, dress and accent.
- The delivery of the speaker – too fast, too complex, too long-winded, patronizing tone, poor preparation and unclear diction.
- Physical discomfort caused by the location – conditions which are too hot, too cold, too stuffy or subject to too much external noise. Below is a simple example encountered by one of the authors.

Example

Radoslaw, a Polish banker attending a top-level conference on the financial crisis in Europe, was fidgeting in his seat, clearly distracted and not concentrating on what was being discussed. Eventually, the presenter noticed him and wondered why he wasn't getting through to him. 'Perhaps', he thought, 'he disagrees with my argument or maybe I have offended him in some way.' When the presenter managed to enquire whether Radoslaw was feeling well, he was somewhat relieved at the answer. 'No', he replied, 'I am feeling too cold to concentrate.' Radoslaw was right. He was sitting right in front of the air-conditioning vent. Once it was turned off, he relaxed and paid full attention to the presentation.

Active listening is a training technique devised in 1977 by Thomas Gordon. It describes a way of focusing on the speaker so that the listener absorbs not only the meaning that the speaker wants to communicate, but also the meaning behind the meaning, that is, emotions and feelings. As a listening technique, it comprises three stages:

- *Repeating*: in the repeating stage, we listen and show interest. We may nod or make verbal signals to show we are listening. We pay attention and establish eye contact and we may show we are listening by giving feedback, using exactly the same words used by the speaker. Above all, we try not to interrupt the speaker's train of thought.
- *Paraphrasing*: when it comes to responding, we enter the paraphrase stage. This involves the same processes as repeating, but it is also important to give feedback by using similar phrases to the speaker. This shows that we have listened, have taken time to reflect and have reformulated what the speaker has said in a way that he or she can agree with.

- *Reflecting*: the final stage occurs when we give feedback to the speaker using our own words and approach.

Active listeners often complain about the strain of remaining silent while someone else talks. The speakers themselves often talk of the tension of speaking when the listener just concentrates and gives no response. There is therefore a need in networking to demonstrate active empathy. The way to do this is to use FACE, which stands for:

- Focus
- Acknowledge
- Clarify
- Empathize

First, you need to *focus* on the speaker by maintaining good eye contact, whilst always remembering that in some cultures strong eye contact may be seen as challenging. *Acknowledge* means using verbal or non-verbal cues to show you are listening, for example, nodding or saying 'uh huh'. *Clarify* means asking what happened next or repeating to the speaker what has been said. *Empathize* means showing appreciation or sympathy by using such phrases as 'great', 'that must have been difficult', etc.

Silence

What is immediately obvious about active listening is that it is a much more reflective, quieter and calmer process. It allows us to absorb how the speaker feels as well as the actual message. It allows time for us to reflect and to formulate in our turn a reasoned response which agrees common ground, but also allows us to state our own point of view. Silence is much more of a tradition in countries like Japan, China and Finland. For many of the rest of us, the urge to jump in and interrupt is too strong as we are uncomfortable with periods of silence.

All of us probably engage in many of these approaches to listening for different reasons and at different times. The challenge is to listen actively and to focus on the thoughts and feelings of the person we are listening to. In that way, we show interest, we acquire more cooperation and we learn more about the speaker.

Networking

In her book *Dinner with Churchill*, Cita Stelzer emphasizes how important meals were in Churchill's wartime diplomacy when he said in 1944: 'If only I could dine with Stalin [the Second World War Russian leader] once a week there would be no trouble at all.' Networking is a very useful way of gaining information, researching a problem and opinion making. It is often the key to successful business relationships, and the conversation around the water-cooler, the formal banquet and the coffee break are all networking opportunities to get to know people personally. One hedge fund manager once said that the best way to get to know his investment partners on brief visits to London was on the way to the lift after the meeting, so he always made a point of seeing his guests out himself.

Three qualities are essential to effective networking:

- the ability to listen, which we have covered earlier in this chapter;
- the ability to empathize;
- the ability to ask questions.

The ability to ask questions

There are two skills involved when networking: 'how to break the ice' and how to avoid embarrassing subjects, as the latter could be an 'ice-maker'. Many political subjects may be taboo, for example, comments on human rights, pollution or changes of government, all of which may be unwelcome, as may questions about wives, partners and families, which might be intrusive in some cultures but welcomed in others such as Latin cultures. In many parts of the world, the use of football as an ice-breaker may not go down well in countries whose national sport is ice-hockey or some other less widely played sport. Useful ice-breakers could include asking people where they come from, what they did in their previous job and whether they have travelled abroad much before. Such questions provide opportunities in a neutral, non-threatening way to find out more about people without touching on any controversial topics and giving them the opportunity to speak about themselves.

The UNEC project

In 2008, the EU Uniting Europe through Culture (UNEC) project provided a formula for analysing cultural differences. It identified five steps for dealing with cultural communication misunderstanding and behavioural differences by analysing cultural experience:

(1) Know your own culture. Understand what happens in your own culture. This can often happen only by confronting step 2.
(2) Identify difference. Examine what is different in the foreign culture from the expected communication style or behaviour in your own culture.
(3) Empathize. Attempt to understand why people in the foreign culture communicate or behave in different ways from what you expect. Try to ascertain what expectations and values these signify.

(4) Use your cross-cultural skills to manage the difference. Analyse what you need to do to adapt in order to achieve a successful outcome.
(5) Reflect on what you have learned from the experience and how it will influence future behaviour. Analyse what you will do, say and think when you next face a similar situation.

Non-verbal communication (NVC)

'We speak with our vocal organs, but we converse with our whole body' (Abercrombie, 1970). This quote gives a very apposite description of what we generally call body language. Albert Mehrabian, the Emeritus Professor of Linguistics at UCLA, has studied the communication of American high school students. From his studies, he concluded the following points (Mehrabian, 1981):

- Words account for seven per cent of a message as far as feelings and attitudes are concerned.
- NVC or body language account for 38 per cent of a message as far as feelings and attitudes are concerned.
- Facial expressions account for 55 per cent of a message.

In other words, the actual words we use are less important than the way in which we say things and our body language.

People convey meaning in NVC through their posture, gestures, eye contact, the physical distance they keep when communicating and how they dress. NVC is very often extremely subtle and subconscious. It is deeply embedded in one's own cultural background and when communicating with people of another culture, the wider the differences between the two cultures, the more difficult it is to read the meaning of the non-verbal messages.

NVC, often loosely called 'body language', should not be considered as something separate from speech, but rather as existing simultaneously with verbal communication. It gives out messages all the time. The verbal component of a face-to-face conversation is less than 35 per cent and over 65 per cent of communication is done non-verbally (Mehrabian, 1981). We communicate so much of our message non-verbally in conversation that, in many cases, the actual words we use are not so important. How we communicate (our tone, pitch, loudness, speed, dialect, etc.) is often more important than our NVC signals.

However, it should be emphasized that 'body language' is a rather loose term and is really inaccurate as an alternative to NVC, as the latter is more varied, covers a range of behaviour and often indicates the way we behave in response to the communication process.

NVC can be divided up as follows.

Gestures	Timing (chronemics)
Posture	Use of personal space (proxemics)
Facial expression (oculesics)	Manner (haptics)
Eye contact	Body movement (kinesics)
Appearance (including clothing)	Patterns of speech and silence
Use of colour (chromatics)	Use of smells (olfactics)

Figure 5.1   Non-verbal communication

It is often said that actions speak louder than words and often say all the wrong things. It is important to remember that with NVC, you need to maintain a high level of awareness as you cannot ask for it to be repeated. It is also less controllable than the spoken word and may therefore be more reliable as it is very often an instinctive reaction. Non-verbal signals will inevitably be interpreted by the receiver or an observer in the context of the situation and their own culture.

Gestures include any action that sends a visual signal to others. They are often described as 'talking with the hands' – in particular, the use of hand gestures aids understanding. In most cultures, the head nod signals agreement and reassurance to the speaker, and is used by good, attentive listeners. Gestures have three main functions – silent requests, expressing opinions and expressing moods or states of mind. The way in which the French stroke the face with one hand as if shaving is a signal saying 'I am bored'. Italians stroke the underside of their chin with the outstretched fingers to say 'I don't believe you'. There are several different ways of inviting someone to have a drink, from rocking one palm with outstretched fingers at mouth level, often used in the UK, to extending finger and thumb and bunching the middle fingers in Spain. For many cultures, gestures are an indispensable part of any conversation. For Arabs of all social levels, gestures are particularly important: 'To tie an Arab's hands while he is speaking is tantamount to tying his tongue' (Barakat, 1993).

Gestures vary not only between nationalities but also in the amount of gesturing employed. Italians, especially in the south of the country, are noted for the richness and variety of the gestures they use, whereas in Japan and China, gestures are much more restrained. In Southern Europe, gesturing is more marked than in Northern Europe, where people tend to be more reserved. In many African and Latin American countries, gestures are also more intense, with vivid facial expressions, hand gestures and often a display of emotions.

Some gestures in certain cultures have completely different meanings from those in others, such as the V sign, the nose tap and the eyebrow raise.

These can cause serious misunderstandings and need to be studied in order not to give inadvertent offence. For example, when President George Bush Sr. visited Australia in 1993, he intended to give the V for Victory sign from the back of his limousine, but unfortunately did it in reverse form. The result was that Australian newspapers reported that the US President had insulted Australia.

More examples of gestures and how they differ in their meaning are as follows:

- *Nose tap*: in the UK, this implies secrecy, confidentiality, 'keeping it dark'. In Italy, it means a friendly warning, 'take care'. In the Middle East, 'ala hashmi' (literally 'on my nose') means 'I will do the favour you ask'.
- *Head nod*: in Bulgaria and parts of Greece this means 'no'. In some states in southern India, it means simply 'I am listening', whereas in most other countries, it means 'yes'. In Japan, smiling and nodding imply understanding, but not necessarily agreement.
- *OK sign*: this must be used with caution. In many parts of Latin America, it is a sign of insult. In parts of southern France, people will consider it means 'zero', that something is worthless. In Japan, the thumb and forefinger are used for money, the fingers creating the round outline of a coin. In some Arab countries, it can mean a curse.

Facial expressions are the ones that we can best control and these can be deliberately false. The face is the most important source of non-verbal signalling. It is highly expressive and can send much information. The use and meaning of eye contact, for example, looking at people directly while you are speaking to them or not, varies between cultures. Eye movements can give powerful messages, which include showing interest, boredom or disbelief. In many cultures, make-up accentuates the impact of the eyes. There is an Arab saying that 'the eyes are the mirrors of the soul'. In some cultures, direct eye contact can be seen as intimidating, for example, in Thailand and South Korea. In Japan, a person who looks a subordinate in the eye can be felt to be judgmental, while someone who looks his or her superior in the eye is assumed to be hostile. As a result, the Japanese prefer to make glancing rather than direct eye contact. In most Western countries, eye contact is considered necessary and appropriate, and people are more likely to trust and like someone who looks them straight in the eye.

Another important facial expression is the way you smile, showing good humour, empathy, sincerity or sneering or sarcasm. 'Smile and the world smiles with you' is an English expression, but it is not necessarily true. Smiling at strangers on first meeting may be regarded as strange or inappropriate. In many Eastern cultures, smiling may often be used as a way to cover embarrassment.

Posture involves a number of potential pitfalls. How you stand can often have an influence on how you are perceived abroad. A common way of relaxing in North America for men is to stand legs apart and hands on hips. This is known as 'arms akimbo' and can be seen as a posture of defiance and even aggression in parts of Asia, especially in Japan. Standing up straight and 'walking tall' is a sign of confidence and self-respect in the West, but may be seen as a sign of arrogance and lack of respect in the East. In some cultures, such as Thailand and the Middle East, showing the soles of your shoes is considered disrespectful as they are seen as the lowest and dirtiest part of the body. An example of this was after the overthrow of Saddam Hussein: his statue in Baghdad was toppled in April 2003 and the mob beat the statue's face with the soles of their shoes as a sign of insult. Respect should be shown by sitting properly, not slouching or putting your feet up on a seat. The over-relaxed-looking Westerner who is trying to appear friendly is not respected, as in most cultures one's appearance reflects one's self-image. The issue of how we sit and who sits where, for example, at meetings is also different in different cultures. There are social conventions about posture and these can have symbolic meanings, for example, kneeling in church and bowing to senior people.

Handshakes vary in terms of their usage in different cultures. In some cultures, especially those involving Arab males, the handshake is prolonged and men may hold hands while walking together. The Japanese make a concession of shaking hands with Westerners, but many still prefer to bow. The degree of the bow shows the degree of seniority. The junior person may make a bow from the waist, whereas a more senior person may just give a nod of the head. Increasingly, young Westerners now greet each other with the 'high-five', but the firm handshake on meeting is still widely used. In most Latin cultures, the 'abrazo' (the hug) is as commonplace as the handshake, both between men and between women.

A classic example of confusion regarding the choice of greeting is given below.

Example

When President Obama made his first visit to Japan and met the Emperor Akhihito and his wife, he surprised the Western world by making a low bow before the Emperor, and commentators wondered how the most powerful man in the world could bow low before a Japanese emperor. However, the same body language impressed the Asian world by Obama's respect for etiquette and convention. In reality, Obama was using the occasion to affirm his commitment to building links between the USA and Asia. As he said at the time: 'I am a Pacific president.' Cultural commentators, however, were less impressed by his shaking hands and bowing at the same time. They felt he should do one or the other, but not both and certainly not at the same time.

Appearance/what we wear: it is often said that 'clothes maketh the man'. Clothes can signal a person's sense of self-esteem, status, group membership, socio-economic class and general character. In Italy, for example, 'fare la bella figura', that is, looking good and making a good impression, is very important, but in all cultures, dressing appropriately for meetings or for particular environments is also imperative. Jewellery often also conveys certain messages, as do spectacles, handbags, cigarettes, watches and pens, and the way they are handled also says something about their users. In Latin America, how you look is an important part of your self-presentation. Among the veil-wearing Tuareg, the veil covering the lower part of the face is raised or lowered slightly according to the seniority of the person joining the gathering. According to strict Islamic law and convention, Muslim women are expected to cover their ankles, their forearms and their hair. The dress code can vary from the full burqa (a full-length veil that covers the body with a mask that hides the face) to the niqab, a full veil or headscarf with a veil that hides the mouth but not the eyes, to the hijab, a much more common headscarf that covers the hair and neck but reveals the face. In Saudi Arabia, foreign women are expected to wear an abaya, a dress which covers their arms and ankles but leaves their face and hair uncovered. In all cultures, it is most important to wear the appropriate clothes when visiting a place of worship. When entering a mosque, it is important to remove your shoes or put on the provided cloth shoes. In a Christian church, it is considered respectful for men to remove their hat and in Roman Catholic countries for a woman to wear a head covering such as a scarf.

Haptics describes the amount of touching people do when they communicate. A knowledge of the accepted norms of behaviour in certain cultures is extremely important. How, when and where we touch others is sometimes the most misunderstood aspect of NVC. In some cultures, touching indicates a very intimate or personal relationship, while in others, it is just commonplace. Examples include Brazil, where people embrace each other spontaneously and cry together, or France and other Mediterranean countries, where young people kiss each other on the cheek when saying 'hello'. In the Middle East, it is very often the custom for men to shake hands on meeting, always with the right hand. One may shake hands several times with the same person during the course of the day. In Russia, it is not uncommon for men to embrace each other on meeting. However, the British are more reserved and tend to avoid intimate touching apart from the handshake, although this attitude is undergoing change as people experience other cultures. The Japanese generally have an aversion to any form of casual body contact, although most Japanese who come to the West make the concession of shaking hands rather than the traditional bow from the waist.

The most common area of touch is the handshake on greeting and leave taking. This is now regarded as an international gesture in business and diplomacy. However, the first-time visitor to another culture is still left with a number of questions. Do you shake hands when you first meet (France/ Germany) or only when you have been introduced (the UK)?

Kissing friends of the opposite sex on the cheek or both cheeks is increasingly common. Do you offer one kiss, two or even three? It is not uncommon in Spain to kiss complete strangers when you first meet them. Showing expressions of love, such as kissing in public, is considered inde- cent in Japan and can result in punishment in some Arab countries, but it is common in both Italy and France and, indeed, in many other Western countries.

As the recent HSBC TV advertisements graphically emphasize, 'never underestimate the importance of local knowledge'. Understanding the cul- ture of the country where you find yourself is so important and the best way to do this is to take local advice, as there is no global, universal behav- ioural etiquette. The style of handshake can be culturally misleading. In the Middle East and the Far East, a soft clasp of the hand is often preferred. This can be seen as 'weak' by West Europeans and Americans, who often prefer a strong, firm handshake. This in turn can be seen as dominant and even aggressive by 'soft hand-shakers'. In India and Thailand, for example, people greet each other by joining the hands together as if in prayer, either at chest level (India) or at forehead level (Thailand), often accompanied by a slight bow of the head.

Proxemics (distance): closely related to touching is distance, that is, how close people stand to each other, which will determine the degree of per- sonal comfort people have. In the Arab world, people prefer to stand closer together, as a sign of trust and friendship. This may be accompanied by arm or hand holding between men. In the USA, the UK or Japan, for example, where greater physical distance is preferred, a distance of about a metre (an arm's length) is acceptable. People from North European cultures prefer more personal space and touch each other less frequently to indicate agreement and friendship than, for example, Latin American and Mediterranean cultures. In Latin countries, people prefer to stand between 50 and 70 centimetres apart. This can seem very intimate and even threatening to many Westerners. At the same time, an 'arm's length' contact can be seen as far too distant and potentially unfriendly to a Latin. In most cultures, however, we are usually prepared to allow much greater close physical contact than normal when we are travelling with complete strangers in a crowded train or bus than we would do in a less congested situation.

Olfactics refer to smells. Different cultures have established different dimensions for olfactory communication. Various types of perfume, lotions, creams, powders and so on are accepted in most cultures. In some cultures, these fragrances are rather aggressive, while in others, they are more delicate and subtle. There are also societies that prefer natural human odours and even consider them attractive. Some examples of olfactics occur in American city streets with the smell of hamburgers, hotdogs and pizzas, and the use of anti-perspirants; in the UK, the smell of mown grass, fish and chips, and tea; and in France, coffee, fresh bread and garlic. In India, there is the very specific smell of fuel that comes from dried cows' dung competing with the smell of curry.

Use of silence: this is very often used, particularly in Japan, for inner reflection and to gain time, for example, in negotiations. It can also cover awkwardness, embarrassment and, at times, misunderstanding. In Greece, silence can be seen as refusal, whereas in Egypt, it can mean consent. In most Western countries, silence is considered awkward, possibly signifying a breakdown in communication and is therefore seen as a vacuum to be filled.

Paralinguistics includes elements of speech, such as pitch, tone, loudness, quality and rate of speaking. These interrupt or temporarily take the place of speech and affect the meaning of the message. We tend to pick up the meaning behind paralanguage rather than the actual meaning of the words spoken, for example, 'it is not what he says but the way he says it'. We are very often unaware of our own NVC signals, but we are usually very aware of the signals put out by others.

Chromatics refers to the significance of colours in a culture. In many Western cultures, for example, the UK and the USA, mourners wear black at funerals and brides wear white at weddings. In Japan, however, white is the colour of death. In Mexico, purple flowers are used at funerals and in Korea, red ink is used to record death.

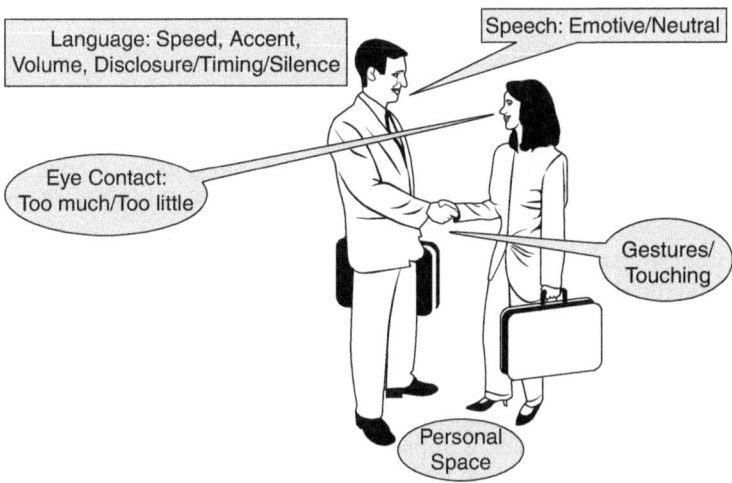

Figure 5.2 The culture gap

Best practice for successful cross-cultural communication

The following are suggested as examples of best practice when faced with the potential problems we have discussed so far:

- Suspend your judgment of the other culture despite your prejudices and stereotypical images; try to keep an open mind.
- Emphasize the positive aspects of the foreign culture and celebrate cultural diversity.
- Adapt your own English style and tone to the situation by avoiding complicated words or expressions, unfamiliar jargon and slang. Develop a simple, clear and unambiguous communication style with appropriate body language.
- Accept that your perception of other cultures and their perception of your culture are very often reality.
- Where necessary, use a skilled interpreter who is thoroughly briefed in advance. Allow the interpreter time to translate by building in appropriate pauses into your delivery.
- Develop your listening skills, both active and passive, and the appropriate reaction while attempting to understand the differences in the other culture.
- Prepare in advance by learning about the other culture with which you will be communicating.
- Develop your own confidence to discuss cultural issues and differences openly, and show that you are keen to learn more about the other culture.
- Above all, develop trust and personal relationships whenever possible.

Summary

- Communication provides one of the biggest pitfalls in cross-cultural dealings, as we are faced with differences between cultures not only in terms of what we say (words, choice of language), but also in the communication media we use (spoken, print, electronic) as well as in our behaviour and body language.
- One of the keys to successful development of cross-cultural communication skills is to show empathy by developing both effective active and passive listening skills. This requires awareness as to how the barriers to effective listening can be overcome.
- The widespread use of electronic means of communication has the advantages of speed, brevity and immediacy, but there still remains the need for a more personal approach in cultures where personal relationships are considered to be important.
- The EU UNEC project was designed to identify ways of improving cross-cultural communication by developing the appropriate ways of avoiding misunderstanding and potential conflict.

- In cross-cultural communication, one should always be careful to ensure that non-verbal clues are appropriate to the culture.

References

Abercrombie, D. (1970) *Problems and Principles in Language Study* (London: Longman Group Ltd.).

Barakat, H. (1993) *The Arab World: Society, Culture and the State* (Berkeley, CA: University of California Press).

Gordon, T. (1977) *Leader Effectiveness Training* (New York: Wyden Books).

Lewis, R. (2011) *When Cultures Collide* (London: Nicholas Brealey Publishing).

Mehrabian, A. (1981) *Silent Messages: Implicit Communication, Emotions and Attitudes* (Belmont, CA: Wadsworth).

Stelzer, C. (2011) *Dinner with Churchill* (London: Short Books).

Tomalin, B. (2012) *Key Business Skills* (London: HarperCollins).

Tomalin, B. and Nicks, M. (2010) *The World's Business Cultures and How to Unlock Them* (London: Thorogood Publishing).

Further reading

Axtell, R. (1991) *Gestures* (New York: John Wiley & Sons).

Axtell, R. (ed.) (1993) *Do's and Taboos Around the* World, 3rd edn (New York: John Wiley & Sons).

Hofstede, G. (1994) *Cultures and Organisations* (London: HarperCollins).

Hurn, B. (1998) 'Cultural Fluency for Business', *Corporate Structures, Business and the Management of Values* 4: 25–9.

Morris, D. (1967) *The Naked Ape* (London: Jonathan Cape).

Morris, D. (1977) *Man Watching: A Field Guide to Human Behaviour* (London: Jonathan Cape).

Pease, A. and Pease, B. (2004) *The Definitive Book of Body Language* (London: Orion Publishing).

Scheflen, A. (1981) *Body Language and the Social Order* (Upper Saddle River, NJ: Prentice Hall).

6
Selection and Preparation for Foreign Assignments

Summary

Required competencies for working abroad
Methods used for selection
Reasons for expatriate failure
Preparation for overseas assignments
Types of training available
Methodology of training
Culture shock: symptoms and stages, coping strategies
Specific culture-dependent business areas
Repatriation and 'reverse culture shock'

Introduction

This chapter covers the methods involved in selecting the appropriate personnel to live harmoniously and work effectively in foreign countries. It includes an examination of the cultural aspects of recruitment and the subsequent preparation for their assignments, in particular the various types of cross-cultural training and the agencies which provide the training. It also covers the repatriation of personnel after they have completed their assignment.

The main interest groups involved in foreign assignments are as follows:

- the organization or company involved;
- the individual concerned;
- the family concerned.

To some extent, all three have to be satisfied.

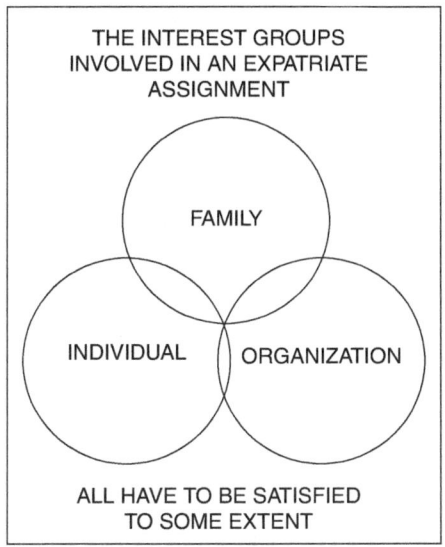

Figure 6.1 Main interest groups involved in foreign assignments

Those going to live and work abroad, be they diplomats, business people, teachers or members of non-governmental organizations (NGOs), are often insufficiently briefed on the differing cultural environments within which they will find themselves living and working, nor are they always made aware of the values, habits and customs of their host country. Failure to recognize, understand, accept and respond to these different cultural environments and the differing behaviour patterns to which they give rise can lead to a reduced ability to communicate, resulting in a reduction of the effectiveness of these people in terms of being able to apply their professional and technical skills. The result is often deep frustration and disillusionment, which can result in either premature repatriation or 'brown-out', that is, loss of enthusiasm and initiative. It is important for an individual's well-being to have a sense of belonging and not to feel a stranger in a new culture.

Those who work internationally are usually expensive, because of the associated, often enhanced, salaries, their air fares, accommodation, special allowances and children's school fees. It is therefore important that the learning time after arrival in the country is as short as possible. Failure to adapt, both on the part of the working partner and the accompanying family, can be both serious and expensive for the individual, the family and, of course, the organization itself. The international community is close-knit and any apparent failures are readily observable. The costs are not only of a financial but also of a psychological nature, with detrimental effects on the image of the company and the personnel concerned.

Clearly, therefore, it would be desirable to attempt to reduce such failure and increase effectiveness by some form of screening in the selection process and by specific preparatory training of those selected before their departure. There has been significant research into these areas, but where it has occurred, it has concentrated on the selection and preparation of the staff of mainly multinational companies (MNCs) who will be living and working overseas. However, many of the findings in the business area are transferable to those who work in the international community at large.

Selection for overseas assignment seldom fails because of a lack of professional or technical competence; failure is usually because of family and personal issues and a lack of cultural skills to enable people to adapt to their new cultural environment. This is exemplified by the following quote from an expatriate sent to work in Malaysia: 'Much more help was needed in explaining local cultural differences. On the surface it all appeared very Westernized and straightforward, but below the surface there is a complex society and rules which one has to learn and understand quickly in order to be fully effective.'

From the human resource management point of view, the key issues to be considered in the organization of foreign assignments are as follows:

- the selection process;
- terms and conditions and pensions;
- remuneration, cost of living allowances, foreign service allowances and other fringe benefits;
- incentives;
- pre-departure briefing and training;
- visas, work permits and driving licences;
- accommodation;
- issues relating to the family, including children's education;
- arrangements for repatriation at the end of the assignment.

Required competencies

An early survey in 1989–90 by Ashridge Business School highlighted a number of key characteristics considered to be desirable for international managers. The most important included, not surprisingly, strategic awareness, adaptability to new situations, the ability to work in international teams, international negotiating skills and linguistic ability. It is clear that these are all related to an awareness of the importance of culture in international business.

As we observed in Chapter 4, this cultural awareness should be manifested as follows.

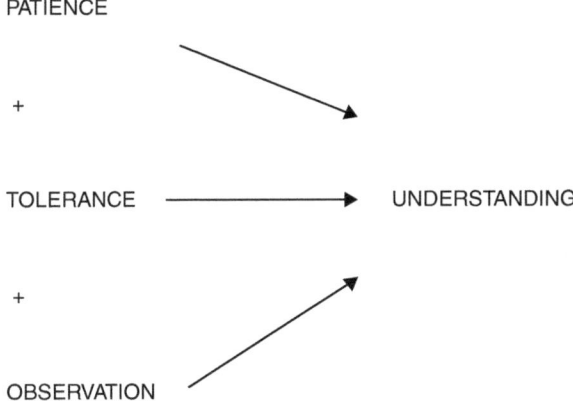

Figure 6.2 Development of cultural awareness

Criteria

One approach to selection is to have a clear set of criteria or competencies which are generally recognized as being required for international assignments. Apart from the prime requirement of technical competence and professional skill, the following competencies are highly desirable:

- cultural sensitivity, respect and empathy;
- flexibility;
- language skills;
- interpersonal skills;
- intercultural effectiveness;
- a stable family situation;
- experience of living and working in other cultures;
- the ability to deal with complexity, diversity and ambiguity;
- the ability to manage the work/family balance;
- curiosity to discover more about other cultures;
- maturity and emotional stability, and a strong sense of self-motivation;
- stamina, self-reliance and patience;
- a sense of humour.

The majority of the above competencies have strong cultural implications. This is demonstrated by a quotation from a major MNC on the training for senior executives which included the required competence to: 'Demonstrate cultural sensitivity, to match one's own style to the national culture ... without this a talented executive may do a good job; however, it is unlikely he will ever be outstanding.'

There is therefore a need for a 'new type of cosmopolitan, multinational, multifaceted executive who is operational across national borders' (Schneider and Barsoux, 2003: 185). Such an international manager who is to operate in Europe has been described as the 'Euromanager' (*The Economist*, 7 November 1992, p. 81) or 'The New Euro-Executive' (Hurn, 1999: 17–23). However, it can be still relatively rare for companies to judge their managers' ability to be effective in the international environment against any clearly defined criteria. One further problem is that previous overseas experience is not necessarily a reliable indicator of future successful performance in another culture.

Selection and pre-departure training need to be clearly planned in order to include, where possible, the employee, partner and the whole family. It should be designed to protect the investment in sending personnel to work overseas, but also to help them find a level of personal fulfilment in their new environment. The ultimate aim is to develop their cross-cultural awareness and cross-cultural skills in order to help them achieve this.

The changing role of international managers

The role of those who are in management positions in the international environment has widened considerably. Their responsibilities may now cover entire regions and therefore they have to be able to adapt quickly to operate in several different cultures. Many may be involved in relatively short-term assignments, often working without the support of their families or other colleagues, sometimes in isolated and potentially dangerous parts of the country. For these people, the importance of cross-cultural training is all the more urgent as they are often required to undertake visits at short notice. In addition, international managers are now younger and include more women amongst their number.

Methods used for selection for overseas assignments

Although there is a measure of general agreement as to the desired competencies of those living and working overseas, precise measurement during selection is much more difficult to carry out. In the commercial field, European companies have used the *Overseas Assignment Inventory* (OAI), one of the few validated screening methods specifically designed to assess the adjustment capability of an individual being considered for an international assignment. This instrument and the accompanying interview process can help identify individuals who may have difficulty in adapting to a foreign culture.

Occupational psychologists also claim to be able to provide information on a number of psychological stress factors, such as the ability to:

- adapt to life in different cultures;
- adapt to different working practices;

- interface effectively with colleagues in the host country;
- cope with living away from one's family or partner if unaccompanied or, if accompanied, to cope with spouse/partner's career or domestic conflicts;
- reduce lack of confidence and concern about the unknown.

Psychological assessments can be used to achieve a more comprehensive view of the ability to adapt to a new culture. These are useful predictors, but are not always infallible. Some of the standard psychological inventories, such as the *Jackson Personality Inventory*, are of limited use for screening for overseas assignments. They tend to show low coefficients of reliability and are predominantly culturally biased towards North Americans or West Europeans.

Another method that can be used is the *Myers-Briggs Type Indicator* (www.myersbriggs.org), which uses four dimensions to identify the ways in which people differ: introvert or extrovert people, those who gain information through the senses or by seeing relationships, those who make decisions either by logical deduction or because it 'feels right' and those who like to make definite conclusions or to seek further possibilities. These are helpful in establishing personality types and desired profiles for an overseas assignment.

Another method that can be used for assisting selection is the *Mendenhall and Oddou* model (1991). This attempts to link specific behavioural tendencies to probable international performance. The evaluation of a person's potential strengths and weaknesses helps focus attention on his or her cross-cultural ability, thus complementing any technical assessment. It also attempts to predict the ability to cope with the unfamiliarity of another culture.

Graphology

The study of handwriting is used in a number of countries, including both France and the UK, to assist the prediction of reliability and response to stress when selecting potential managers. It has also been included as part of the selection methods of some large companies, who claim it is a most effective and additional way of assessing the suitability of candidates. The science of graphoanalysis includes the examination of the slope of letters in writing and the spacing between words and letters.

Assessment centres

Many multinational companies, for example, Shell and HSBC, use their own internal assessment centres when recruiting future international managers, including internal and external candidates. Other large companies and a number of public sector organizations use independent assessment centres to assist in their recruitment. These have the advantage of providing a neutral venue with specialist staff with wide experience of assessment techniques and knowledge of the target cultures. However, they need to be fully aware of a company's corporate culture and detailed requirements.

Assessment centres run a series of structured interviews, in-tray exercises, group tasks and psychometric tests which are specifically designed to assess personality issues, cultural awareness and tolerance, as well as motivation and commitment. Discussions are held with those attending on the main problem areas and potential benefits involved with living and working in foreign cultures. These can include:

- the potentially nomadic lifestyle, with frequent moves;
- the loss of one's home/national ties;
- integrating with the local community;
- living with ambiguity;
- opportunities to develop new interests;
- the availability of support groups, particularly in an emergency;
- coping strategies to deal with culture shock;
- concern about career development, including the perception that 'out of sight is out of mind';
- opportunities presented by foreign assignments – new challenges, travel, acquisition of a new language and new friends;
- the assistance available to help with eventual repatriation.

There are, however, problems with some psychometric tests, in that they do not travel well across cultural boundaries.

Some detailed research was carried out in 1990 by the Canadian International Development Agency (CIDA) which clearly indicated that an individual possessing a high degree of professional and interpersonal skills has a much greater chance of becoming interculturally successful while abroad. Another interesting finding was that ease of adjustment overseas in one country does not necessarily mean that a person will necessarily be interculturally effective in another country. The assumption that 'management is management' anywhere in the world may be too simplistic. An effective manager in, say, New York may not do so well in Hong Kong or Tokyo. There is also the inherent danger in the belief that if the assignment overseas is only for a short period, 'he or she'll be fine. It's only two months anyway over there'.

The overall research findings highlight the need for improved procedures in the selection for international assignments. There is, however, a much clearer realization of the need for preparatory training and the development of cross-cultural sensitivity and communication as essential factors for successful and harmonious living and working overseas.

Expatriate failure

Despite all the warning signals about the frequent failure to adapt to a new culture, relatively few organizations send their staff on specific cultural awareness and orientation programmes before they go overseas, although profound culture shock, compounded by the inability to recognize it, to come to terms with it and to make the necessary cultural adaptations, has been identified as a major cause of the failure of many overseas assignments.

Expatriate failure can be defined as the premature return home before the period of the assignment is completed. It should be emphasized that expatriation is for many a major life change that puts individuals at risk of psychological difficulties. Three significant life events are involved: changing culture, changing jobs and changing accommodation. International assignment failures usually result more from an employee's or the family's failure to adjust to the new culture than from any business issues. Tung (1998) cites the following reasons for expatriate failure:

- The manager's inability to adapt to a different physical or cultural environment.
- The inability of the manager's spouse/family to adapt to a different physical or cultural environment.
- The manager's personality or emotional immaturity.
- The manager's inability to cope with the responsibilities presented by overseas work.
- The manager's lack of motivation to work overseas.

In 1993, the Shell Expatriate Survey 'Outlook' found that the major areas of concern related to the problems associated with moving overseas on assignment were:

- children's education and separation of families;
- partner/spouse's careers and employment;
- health and security;
- assistance and information regarding relocation on their return to the home country;
- recognition and involvement of spouses in pre-departure briefing.

As a result of the Survey, Shell introduced a number of 'mobility lubricants' to help ease some of these problem areas. These included:

- primary and/or secondary education of children in their own language in host country – setting up company schools or providing places in international schools;
- financial assistance with boarding education in the home country;
- provision of company medical facilities;
- assisted passages to the home country;
- assistance in finding suitable employment for the spouse/partner.

The Survey stated that: 'The aims of expatriation policies are to ensure that sufficient members of staff are fully mobile for international service and that satisfaction of staff and their families is maintained at a high level.'

The 1997/8 PricewaterhouseCooper Survey reported that cultural awareness training, although the most common form of pre-departure training, was still often offered on a voluntary basis rather than being mandatory. However, the Survey acknowledged that there was a gradual increasing awareness of the need to provide at least some basic cross-cultural training for the employee's acompanying partner and the rest of the family.

A further survey was made in 2002 of 400 European companies. A total of 50 per cent of these companies reported that they had experienced difficulties when trying to place staff in other countries in Europe regarding employment legislation, health care, taxation, education of children and knowledge of foreign languages. As a result, the company noticed an increase in the number of staff members who were prepared to commute back to the UK at weekends.

There are a range of other issues that may affect the non-working partner rather than the working partner. These include the following:

- partner/spouse's career, particularly dual career problems, namely the inability to continue with the career path which existed in the home country, as well as loss of income and status;
- coping with new domestic circumstances – servants, new school system, pressures of 'the social round';
- feeling of loneliness, a nomadic lifestyle, isolation, role change and homesickness, all resulting in low self-esteem;
- high expectations which have to be modified in the light of initial culture shock;
- separation while working partner is travelling;
- health and personal security concerns;
- children's education – disruption, language problems, etc.

Other contributing factors to expatriate failure

Other factors that may also play a role in causing expatriate failure are as follows:

- the length of the assignment;
- reluctance to move on the part of the employed partner;
- the international assignment not being seen as an important stage in career development;
- the need to move abroad without being able to take family members;
- the unwillingness of the spouse/partner to move;
- concern over being away from the perceived centre of power at head office.

The dual career problem

The issue of the dual career problem has become more significant. The human resource departments of multinational companies increasingly find that many of their employees have partners who have their own career and income which they do not want to leave behind. Apart from a potential loss of income, there is often the danger of a loss of self-esteem, identity crisis, frustration and psychological stress, all of which can impact on the employed partner. Unless these problems are recognized, there is the risk that dual career couples may present a barrier to international mobility. The resulting problems can include reduced availability of staff for overseas appointments, and further selection may be from a diminished pool of talent, as well as exerting a negative effect on performance and retention overseas.

The problem of the dual career is often of concern when families have relied on both partners working for economic and self-fulfilment reasons. There may be problems in obtaining work permits in some countries; in addition, the employment of expatriates, particularly women, may be discouraged. However, a company with a sound human resource policy has a duty of care to its personnel, particularly when they face the difficulties of coping with a new culture, and some companies will endeavour to find employment for the other partner, either in the company itself or elsewhere.

The costs of expatriate failure

The costs associated with expatriate failure can be high both to the company and the individuals concerned. They can be divided into the following categories.

Direct costs

Direct costs include air fares, foreign assignment salaries and allowances, training costs and costs of relocation.

Indirect costs

Indirect costs are more difficult to quantify but may include loss of goodwill, impact on company image, the effect on morale of local staff and on the individuals concerned and their families.

Methods of preparation

Methods of preparation can include the following:

- None at all, mainly because of urgency or crisis, for example, a natural disaster or a political coup in the country overseas.
- Shadowing one's predecessor in the job, which entails working with the current member of staff for a short period before he or she returns home.

- Working a short overlap period, that is, working in tandem with the person from whom the employee will be taking over.
- 'Look/see' orientation visit with or without one's partner to assess the conditions in the overseas country.
- Informal briefing and discussion with colleagues, in particular with those who have just returned.
- A formal, customized briefing course held within the company or at an external specialist organization. Such a course should, where appropriate, include the non-working partner and the rest of the family.

Pre-departure training

Types of courses can include:

- cross-cultural awareness;
- country-specific briefing;
- language courses;
- international negotiation skills;
- multinational team building;
- transfer of skills and knowledge across cultures;
- repatriation training.

Pre-departure training aims to provide cultural briefing for those going to live and work in foreign cultures. Specialist organizations involved in this field include the Centre for International Briefing in Farnham (UK), International House, London, the Clingendael Institute in The Hague, CIDA in Borden (Canada) and the Norwegian Government Training Scheme (NORAID). In addition, a number of university business schools also provide specialist short briefing courses tailored to a company's requirements. There are advantages in using outside agencies as they provide a supportive, neutral and residential venue away from the pressures of the office, with access to a wide network of specialists and a mix of delegates from different nationalities for discussion groups.

Business culture training can range from a one-day seminar or workshop to longer programmes that can include simulation exercises in which participants are immersed in another culture over several days. Courses can be scheduled on fixed dates or specially customized and tailored to specific needs. The latter are especially appropriate if the schedule dates are inconvenient, if there is an issue of commercial confidentiality or if a group from the same company is about to move to the same location.

Ideally, non-working partners and, where appropriate, teenage children should be involved in some aspects of the training. This is highly desirable, as life for them may often prove to be more difficult, at least initially, as they have to get to grips with a new routine in a new culture, whereas the working partner usually has the benefit of the familiarity and stability provided by the corporate culture of the working environment.

Training courses

Cross-cultural awareness

The sensitivity to cultural differences has become increasingly important with the development of globalization and the move towards strategic alliances, including IJVs. Training includes general cultural sensitization, during which those attending are encouraged to acknowledge their own personal cultural 'baggage', their false perceptions, the danger of stereotyping and ethnocentrism. They learn that their own behaviour is largely rooted in their own culture and thus acquire an understanding of how people in other cultures see them. Where appropriate, potential areas of conflict between local and Western values should be covered.

Country-specific briefings

These are usually the main core of preparatory training, covering geography, history, the current political and economic background as well as the cultural norms of the host country. The briefing could also cover such practical knowledge as the costs of living, local banking, socializing with hosts, children's education, local customs and taboos, personal security and health and hygiene. For the business partner, advice will be given on such aspects as local business law, business etiquette, communication skills, an overview of the country's society, economy and politics, local business practices, the extent of bureaucracy and, if applicable, corruption and relations with host nationals at work. This is mainly practical advice aimed at developing understanding and respect, and explaining why there are differences in the way in which business is conducted. A simple checklist of 'do's' and 'don'ts' is not enough.

Language training

This is an obvious but much-neglected area of training. It is often provided too late and for too short a time. Language has a symbiotic relationship with culture and a reasonable degree of fluency in the local language helps social intercourse, aids understanding of cultural nuances and signals a willingness to make the effort to integrate. If time is limited, emphasis prior to departure overseas should be on teaching 'survival' elements and building confidence to encourage further learning on arrival. Whenever possible, tuition should be given by native speakers and ideally both the employee and the spouse/partner should participate. Language is, however, more than words – it includes body language, tone and tempo, all of which have cultural nuances. These need to be explored and practised to avoid causing offence.

Negotiating skills

This specialized training develops skills in negotiating across cultures. Aspects such as setting agendas, organizing meetings, reaching agreement, the question of 'face' and the use of interpreters are covered. Westerners have much to learn in these areas as they tend to be relatively poor listeners, often appearing impatient and too direct. These characteristics can sometimes be offensive to other cultures. Negotiating training allows participants to practise and experiment with the communication style necessary for their new environment. A further development of such training is the building and sustaining of *multicultural teams* where the establishment of a climate of mutual trust and confidence across the cultures is essential. These aspects are considered in more detail in Chapter 9.

Transfer of skills and knowledge

Ensuring the effective transfer of skills and knowledge from one culture to another is of direct relevance to aid workers, project directors and those involved in 'turnkey' projects and joint ventures. Successful transfer relies on sensitive awareness of the host culture and the importance of building a relationship of trust, which involves understanding the local customs and traditions that may influence the ways in which skills are transferred. This aspect is covered in more detail in Chapter 13.

Training for specific business requirements

Language barriers, different working practices and the lack of cultural understanding are major obstacles to uniting the workforce behind a common vision ... in an increasingly competitive global market place, managing cultural differences has to be a corporate imperative, not a 'nice-to-have' option. (KPMG, *Mergers and Acquisitions Report*, 2000)

The above quotation emphasizes the need for business people to undergo preparatory training on business practices in the new culture, ideally before they begin their foreign assignment. The following are areas that need to be covered:

- attitude towards time, whether monochronic or polychronic;
- regard for authority, age and status;
- how decisions are made;
- communication styles (direct or indirect);
- ways of working (for example, the balance between task, effort and social interaction);
- notions of time and space (for example, meetings and personal space);
- managerial style (authoritarian, informal, formal);
- the balance between group demands and the needs of individuals;

- attitude towards class, gender and the position of women in business and in society in general;
- value systems (what is desirable or acceptable in terms of politics, economics and the environment);
- appropriate use of body language and what is taboo;
- importance of 'face' (both giving and receiving);
- socializing etiquette, gifts, greetings, etc.

Ideally, all preparation prior to departure for an international assignment should begin as early as a year or more before the commencement date, so that thinking about the new appointment becomes part of a continuous process.

Methodology

This should involve input by nationals of the cultures concerned, counselling, the use of simulation and role playing, with input on specific aspects being provided by specialists and discussion with recent returnees. Whenever possible, any training must be customized to meet individual requirements. More details on the methodology of cross-cultural training can be found in Chapter 15.

Culture shock

'Entering into a culture that is foreign to us is tantamount to knowing the words without knowing the music or without knowing the dance' (Adler, 1997: 203). This definition highlights vividly the main problem relating to culture shock.

Other definitions of culture shock are as follows:

(1) 'A state of distrust following the transfer of a person to an unfamiliar cultural environment which may be accompanied by physical symptoms' (Hofstede, 1994: 260).
(2) 'The frustration and confusion that result from being bombarded by too many new and uninterpretable cues' (Adler, 1997: 263).

Culture shock is experienced when we enter a foreign culture and have difficulty in understanding or predicting why people in that culture behave in ways different from those in which we behave in our own culture. In such situations, we may feel confused, inadequate or frustrated, and this has a negative effect on our self-confidence. We feel cut off from familiar patterns of behaviour, when all the nuances or shades of meaning which we understand and instinctively use to make sense of life are suddenly no longer there to give us support. We realize our own values can be challenged by people in the new culture and we often find ourselves in situations where the rules are unclear. As a result, we feel unsure what to do in this new environment, not knowing what is appropriate or inappropriate.

The term 'culture shock' is attributed to Kalvero Oberg, who first coined the phrase during his field work in Brazil in 1958. He later defined it as follows: 'When an individual enters a strange culture, all or most of the familiar cues are removed. He is like a fish out of water. No matter how broad-minded or full of goodwill he may be, a series of props have been knocked out from under him' (Oberg, 1960).

Culture-distance concept

The amount of distance or difference between one's own culture and the host culture is directly proportional to the amount of stress or difficulty experienced. One of the major problems with culture shock is coping with ambiguity in trying to make sense of why things are done differently. Despite our good intentions of listening, standing back to observe and avoiding quick decisions, we very often (and particularly in times of stress) fall into the trap of becoming judgmental. It then takes cross-cultural maturity to develop the culturally appropriate responses to the situations that confront us.

The stress of change

Many people experience stress and culture shock, even when moving within their own culture and country, particularly when there are geographical, climatic and social differences between regions. When people move to a different culture, these differences are emphasized and are therefore likely to cause greater stress.

As we have seen, the pressures are very often more intense for the frequent business traveller, whose lifestyle is likely to be characterized by a lack of adequate preparation and time for briefing, a disruptive family lifestyle, the frequent need to culturally 'change gear' and the need to 'hit the ground running'. Stressors in the expatriate environment are defined as: 'Uncertainties and demands in a foreign environment that are mismatched with an expatriate's personal resources' (Bhaskar-Shrinivas *et al.*, 2005: 257).

Cultural differences	Uncertainty over social role
Time differences	Feeling of isolation
Value conflicts	Role change – particularly for non-working partner
Security concerns	Inadequate public utilities
Ignorance of language	Non-availability of familiar food
Climatic differences	Poor after-sales service
Dealing with servants	Excessive bureaucracy
Finding accommodation	Children's education
Dealing with corruption	Long distance from support network

Figure 6.3   Likely 'stressors'

Many of the above are experienced in any international move and can cause the feeling of culture shock to be heightened, as culture shock arises when we find our values are brought into question and we are expected to function in the new culture where the rules of behaviour are unclear to us.

People find the ambiguity they experience when they go to live and work in another culture very difficult to cope with. They want all the answers quickly and often cannot seem to obtain them. This can cause a great deal of frustration and the typical response is: 'Why don't these people act in the same way as we do?' This feeling of frustration and confusion is very often because of uncertainty about the local conventions and how to act both socially and in business in certain situations.

Symptoms

According to Oberg (1960), the experience of culture shock is a quite normal and predictable phenomenon, and is not a sign of weakness, inadequacy or some form of illness. The symptoms of culture shock can appear at different times. Culture shock can manifest itself as:

- showing signs of strain, bad temper, lack of sleep, anxiety, fatigue, frequent illness, loss of appetite and hypochondria;
- a sense of loss and feeling of deprivation, homesickness and boredom;
- rejection, low self-esteem, depression, feelings of isolation, loss of status;
- confusion, challenged by constant ambiguity;
- surprise, even disgust, obsession with cleanliness;
- feelings of incompetence, lack of linguistic ability and apparent inability to establish local friendships;
- alcohol and drug abuse as a retreat from the effects of culture shock;
- a sense of loneliness, particularly for a single person in an international community that is family-oriented;
- an irrational fear of being robbed or cheated.

In addition, culture shock can manifest itself in behaviour, for example, by acting negatively and aggressively towards the host culture, and withdrawal into a form of 'little England', developing a ghetto mentality, which is compounded by a refusal to attempt to learn the local language and ascribing negative stereotypes to local nationals. A common reaction is to idealize the home country and take every opportunity to return on visits. Because of tension and conflict within the family and resulting marital stress, the employee is likely to have an ineffective attitude towards work, with resulting poor performance and lack of motivation.

Responses to culture shock

The responses to culture shock vary and can include displaying open hostility to the local culture, adapting a defensive attitude, frequently complaining and even becoming aggressive when one's ethnocentric impulse dominates. This is demonstrated by the following types of behaviour:

- Withdrawal from interaction with the local culture and people, and immersion in one's own cultural group while denigrating the local culture. Examples of this ghetto mentality include armed forces bases overseas, which can become self-contained with little interaction with the local community.
- Superficial acculturation, for example, adopting local dress and habits, which can often be seen as patronizing by people of the local culture.
- Adjustment to the new culture, understanding and respecting the differences, and yet affirming one's own individual and cultural identity.

Stages of culture shock

These have been described as a cycle of adjustment through which the newly arrived expatriate and family will pass. These stages are fairly predictable but may vary in length.

Honeymoon

This phase is usually characterized by initial positive reaction, even of enchantment and fascination with the new culture, enthusiasm and at least superficial relationships with its people. One stays in a good hotel, is introduced to colleagues and attends social functions. It is all rather exciting and one feels almost like a tourist. This stage is called 'euphoria' (Hofstede, 1994: 210).

Crisis

This is the stage when problems begin to emerge and culture shock kicks in. The cultural differences become apparent, with resulting feelings of frustration, disenchantment, impatience and even anger at the differences in language, values, familiar signs and behaviour. Problems may arise over such matters as children's schooling, accommodation, different consumer goods, poor public utilities, where and how to shop, obtaining a driving licence, coping with traffic and access to medical services. One asks oneself: 'Why on earth did I accept this assignment?' Minor nuisances can seem to be major problems and the newcomer shows increasing signs of pressure and disorientation, which affect both the job and the family. This is the critical stage where there is the need for considerable levels of support. The initial enthusiasm for the exciting 'newness' is often followed by a downswing in mood and increasing frustration.

Recovery

In this stage, there is at last light at the end of the tunnel, with the development of confidence and a positive attitude, characterized by an effort to learn the local language, enquire about the culture and make local friends. One begins to learn to adapt, finding better ways to deal with any residual negative feelings, and self-confidence begins to return.

Adjustment

This is the final stage where not only the employee but also the rest of the family are now enjoying the new experiences and are comfortable with the differences, whilst acknowledging that there may still be points of difference which can, from time to time, cause minor problems. One begins to feel at ease in the new culture and a sense of humour returns, friends are made and one actively explores the new culture. Ultimately, one becomes the 'expert' who gives positive advice to newcomers. Of course, what has happened is that the environment has not changed, but it is the employee who has changed and learned to adapt to the new culture. 'Motivation to adapt is perhaps the most important factor in determining the speed in which individuals pass through the stages' (Guirdham, 1999: 289).

Torbiorn (1982) developed as a model the traditional 'U curve', which shows the stages of culture shock and typical time for adaptation. Situations will, of course, vary, with much depending on the degree of pre-departure training, the support systems available on arriving and the level of cross-cultural skills of the individual. For many, the earlier phases can be the most critical time. Patience and realistic expectations play an important role. It may be necessary to allow up to six to eight months to really settle in. It helps to be able to recognize the indicators of culture shock and to talk about them, particularly with one's partner and the rest of the family, and, if possible, with local friends in order to try to understand why one feels the way one does.

Research by CIDA (1990) into identifying who were the most effective of their employees sent overseas came up with a clear statement that those who suffered initially the most from culture shock in many cases turned out to be the most effective expatriates. The most effective employees realized that experiencing culture shock was normal and, as a result, they made deliberate efforts to adjust as their pre-departure training had warned them what to expect. The CIDA study also found that those with previous overseas experience generally, but not always, adjusted to life in a new country more quickly and easily than those going overseas for the first time.

Although one can experience real anxiety and unhappiness as a result of culture shock, it does provide an opportunity for learning about new perspectives and developing a better understanding of oneself. It is important to stress the positive opportunities that are presented by living and working within an international community. These can include:

- broadening horizons for the whole family – travel, new culture, new experiences;
- learning a new language;

- establishing a new network of friends and local contacts;
- a possibly enhanced quality of life;
- possible career progression.

Some reasons for failure to adapt to a new culture

These may include some or all of the following:

- assuming that the practices followed in one's own country will be effective and acceptable in the new culture;
- a failure to recognize that one's presence in another culture may be perceived as a potential source of conflict;
- evaluating local conditions and habits against one's own values;
- adopting a patronizing or superior attitude, possibly as a personal defence mechanism;
- a failure to recognize the responsibility towards the development of local staff;
- neglecting one's own mental and physical well-being, as well as that of the rest of the family;
- believing that 'If I want something done properly, I had better do it myself';
- frustration on the part of the non-working partner who is unable to pursue his or her career in the host country;
- concern about aged relatives left behind in the home country.

The ideal expatriation should proceed as follows:

ADJUSTMENT
↓
ADAPTATION
↓
ACHIEVEMENT

Coping strategies

> To begin with, it helps enormously to know the stresses are coming. If we expect something of a rough ride, we aren't caught altogether off our guard. We may be still thrown by the experience, but being psychologically prepared diminishes the impact. (Storti, 1990: 9)

Coping strategies will, of course, vary between individuals. The following are some ways in which one can help the process of adaptation:

- Prepare in advance before departure. Learn as much as possible about the destination culture.

- Be aware that you are likely to pass through the four stages of culture shock, that this is a normal process and is not a sign of weakness or illness.
- Recognize and come to terms with your feelings when you feel lonely, unhappy and homesick, and discuss them with others.
- Begin with short-term realistic expectations and give yourself time to adapt.
- Establish as soon as possible a home base with some of your favourite possessions around you, for example, photographs, books, favourite toys for the children, etc.
- Make efforts to make new friends (both locals and other expatriates).
- Make efforts to learn and use the local language and explore the local culture.
- Keep in touch with friends and relatives in the home country and send them news of your experiences, as well as emails and videos.
- Develop new interests and hobbies. Keep yourself busy and look for positive opportunities, such as new challenges, the chance to broaden horizons and career progression.
- Develop a local support system as soon as possible with friends and membership of sports and social clubs.
- Write a diary or a blog for yourself, your friends and relatives.
- Help others with the cross-cultural adjustment process once you have adjusted.
- Above all, try to keep a sense of perspective, an open mind and a sense of humour.

The company or organization should also provide valuable support to reduce the effects of culture shock. This can include a welcome on arrival and providing a person to act as a link in order to help you and the family through the first few days and introduce you to local contacts.

Repatriation: the problems of return

Repatriation or re-entry is the transition from the foreign country back to one's own after living overseas for a significant period of time. This section covers the return of people who have been living and working overseas in the international community. Many suffer from what has been described as *reverse culture shock*. 'I never expected to feel like a stranger in my own country' is a cry that one often hears.

Research has indicated that one of the main problems encountered by international companies with their expatriates and their families is re-entry and re-adaptation back into the home country after a period overseas. The main concerns include the loss of autonomy, lesser status, lack of career direction and lack of recognition of expatriate experience.

The following two quotations sum up the problems experienced upon repatriation:

- 'The thing which gives expatriation a bad reputation faster than anything else is poor reintegration. Re-entry is the toughest assignment of all' (Tung, 1998).
- 'Returnees come back neither to the world they left nor to the world they are anticipating' (Adler, 1997).

Having established a home and a life in a new culture and made the necessary cultural adjustments, 'coming home' again is often viewed as presenting few difficulties. However, there are real problems encountered on return. Whereas pre-departure preparation and cultural orientation training are now recognized by many companies as important for both the employed partner and the family, in many cases little is done to prepare for return to the home country. In particular, a sudden imposed return to the home country because of a natural disaster or a change in the local political situation almost certainly heightens the need for support because of the organizational difficulties in reacting quickly to the situation and the pressure on those involved.

Typical scenario on return

The returning expatriate is often faced with the following situation on return to the home country:

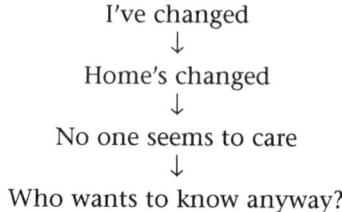

I've changed
↓
Home's changed
↓
No one seems to care
↓
Who wants to know anyway?

Reverse culture shock

When one goes to live and work overseas, there is usually an expectation that life will be different in the new culture and some form of pre-departure training or briefing may be organized prior to the commencement of the new assignment. Reverse culture shock experienced on repatriation is often unanticipated. It is accentuated by the fact that most people expect that life in the home country will be the same as before. They expect to be able to move back into the community, renew friendships, re-establish contacts and fit easily into their former lifestyle. However, reality may well be very different, for the following reasons:

- friends may have moved;
- people are not interested in what they have experienced overseas;

- some resentment or jealousy may be encountered at work about their time overseas;
- their new appointment may lack comparable status and scope with what they experienced overseas;
- few attempts may be made to debrief them on their overseas experience or contacts;
- family members (especially children) may encounter difficulties in re-adjusting.

Returnees are often surprised and disorientated when they find that their home country does not live up to their expectations and that the idealized home country of their memories is, in reality, very different. Reverse culture shock impacts on all members of the family and can result in the following behaviour patterns:

- *alienation*: negative feelings about the home culture;
- *reversion*: denial that important personal changes have taken place as a result of their period overseas;
- *integration*: difficulty experienced in fitting back into the home culture as a result of the changes in lifestyle and outlook experienced abroad.

Part of the problem is, of course, that those who have lived and worked abroad in another culture have developed as individuals because of their wider experiences. They have:

- often operated with more responsibility – being, in effect, a 'big fish in a small pond';
- developed wider interpersonal skills and hence confidence;
- widened their experiences in terms of travel, language, social interaction, etc.;
- in many cases enjoyed a higher standard of living – possibly a large house/apartment, servants, an official car and other fringe benefits.

The *challenges of repatriation* include:

- unrealistic expectations on returning to the home country;
- the extent of change in the home country (increased cost of living, taxation, inflation, etc.);
- a possible reduction in salary because of lack of overseas increments;
- a need for coping skills to deal with reverse culture shock;
- concerns about future professional career development after a period abroad.

Perhaps unrealistic expectations on return to the home country are the most difficult with which to come to terms. The following are some examples of common perceptions that help explain the reason for this lack of realism. Ideally, many of these issues should be addressed prior to return:

- I do not need professional help with repatriation: 'I'm going home, therefore there will be no problems!'
- My family will also find that returning home presents few problems.
- Everything will be basically the same as when I left, so I will easily fit back into my own culture.
- People back home are more efficient and courteous.
- Everything is cleaner, better organized, safer and easier at home.
- I will pick up my close friendships where I left off with them.
- I'll be better off financially when I return home.
- People will be very interested to hear about my exciting experiences.
- I expect some form of promotion on my return home because of my greater experience and my company will wish to apply what I have learned abroad.
- Because I have been successful in my job abroad, I have every reason to be equally successful on my return.
- My company will value my new skills and contacts highly and will wish to debrief me on these.
- While I have been overseas, my organization has kept me in touch with head office developments.

In fact, the following quotation from Somerset Maugham's *The Gentleman in the Parlour* still rings true for many who have spent substantial periods of time abroad: 'When I go back I know I shall be out of it. We fellows who have spent some time out here always are.'

Repatriation issues which affect the whole family include the following:

Professional

- Loss of status.
- Resentment by peers.
- Less autonomy.
- No recognition of new skills.
- Keeping abreast of organization and technological change.
- Job security – will there be a job on return?

Personal

- Reduced lifestyle.
- Role shift for spouse.
- Loss of friendships.
- Employment for spouse on return.

- Educational change for children.
- Reduced standard of living.

Faced with these concerns, the most important factor is the realization by those returning from overseas that the cultural experience of living abroad will have changed all members of the family and thus their expectations and perceptions.

Coping strategies

However, those returning home can do much themselves to assist reintegration. They should re-establish links with former contacts and friends. They also need to clarify and, perhaps, modify their own expectations and set themselves realistic goals. Wherever possible, they should seize opportunities to demonstrate the new skills they have acquired, for example, languages and knowledge of foreign cultures, by talks to local chambers of commerce and further education institutions. While still abroad, they should make every effort to brief themselves on any new changes in the organization in the home country. Their human resources department will appreciate the assistance and advice they can give on their return to other members of staff who may be visiting the region they have just left. Apart from these, there are usually a number of skills they have acquired as a result of their foreign experiences. These include experience of working in multinational teams, coping with ambiguity in changing situations, often under considerable stress, and increasing cross-cultural confidence whereby complex situations can be seen from a number of perspectives.

Organizations are now increasingly providing some form of repatriation training and assistance for both the employee and, where appropriate, the family, with the aim of providing a smoother transition. Training should be tailor-made for the individuals concerned and could include the following elements:

- recognition of reverse culture shock and advice on coping strategies;
- home country update (cost of living, health and social services, education, law and order, etc.);
- financial considerations (investments, insurance, taxation, etc.);
- employment opportunities (career development, re-training, counselling, etc.);
- changes in business practices.

Repatriation should not be regarded as an isolated event but as part of a continuous process of personal and career development for the individual, the family and the company: 'No-one goes home, rather we return to our native country and in due course we create a new home' (Storti, 1990).

The cycle of culture shock may well repeat itself on each new assignment. Most importantly, successful repatriation is crucial to a career development plan, which should aim to retain skilled, effective international managers (and, if applicable, their families) who wish to participate in future overseas assignments. However, they will in many cases experience the full cycle of culture shock once again. As a result, a typical cycle of expatriation and return to the home country will resemble a 'W curve' (Oberg, 1960), with peaks and troughs showing the stages experienced during culture shock, followed by those experienced on return to the home country. This pattern will be repeated in subsequent expatriation moves with varying degrees of intensity, depending on the new locations and previous ability to cope with new situations. This is represented below.

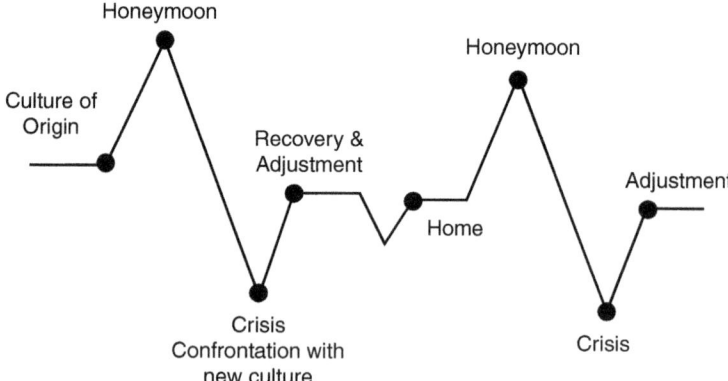

Figure 6.4   Full culture shock cycle

Summary

- Increasing globalization makes the need for careful selection and preparation for overseas assignments all the more important.
- The accompanying partner and the rest of the family should be involved, where appropriate, with the employee (the working partner) in pre-departure training.
- In the selection process, a variety of methods should be available both in-house and externally.
- The selection of suitable personnel for overseas assignments will need to take into account technical and professional skills and qualifications, cross-cultural skills and suitability, language skills, cultural requirements of the new location and family requirements, including children's education, accommodation, health and security.

- Pre-departure training should concentrate on cultural briefing and the business practices likely to be encountered in the foreign culture.
- Attention should be paid both to culture shock and the problems of return to the home country (reverse culture shock).
- Cultural briefing is important for the short-term overseas assignment and the business traveller.
- Culture shock is encountered by most people when they enter a foreign culture. It is a normal reaction and there are coping strategies to reduce its effect.
- No one is completely immune from culture shock, even after several international experiences.
- Recognition of the signs of culture shock will in itself help in progressing through the cycle of adjustment.
- Whenever possible, coping strategies should include all members of the family.
- The reasons for failure to adapt can be greatly reduced by careful preparation and support.
- Reverse culture shock is often experienced on return to the home country. Coping strategies can reduce this by advanced preparation during the overseas assignment and support from the company on return home.

References

Adler, N. (1997) *International Dimensions of Organisational Behaviour* (Cincinnati, OH: South Western College Publications).

Barham, K. (1990) *Making Managers International: Survey of Company Approaches to International Management Development* (Berkhampstead: Ashridge Management Research Group).

Bhaskar-Shrinivas, P., Harrison, D.A., Shaffer, M.A. and Luk, D.M. (2005) 'Input-Based and Time-Based Models in International Adjustment: Meta-analytical Evidence and Theoretical Extensions', *Academy of Management Journal* 48: 257–81.

Black, J., Mendenhall, M. and Oddou, G. (1991) 'Toward a Comprehensive Model of International Adjustment', *Academy of Management Review* 16(2): 291–317.

Canadian International Development Agency (CIDA) (1990) *Cross-Cultural Effectiveness: A Study of Canadian Technical Advisers Overseas* (Quebec, Gatineau: CIDA).

Guirdham, M. (1999) *Communication Across Cultures* (New York: Palgrave)

Hofstede, G. (1994) *Cultures and Organisations* (London: HarperCollins).

Hurn, B. (1999) 'The New Euro-Executive', *Industrial and Commercial Training* 3(1): 19–23.

KPMG (2000) *Mergers and Acquisitions Report*.

Oberg, K. (1960) 'Culture Shock: Adjustment to New Cultural Environments', *Practical Anthropology* 7: 177–82.

PricewaterhouseCoopers (1992) *Expatriate Survey*.

Schneider, S. and Barsoux, J. (2003) *Managing Across Cultures* (Upper Saddle River, NJ: Prentice Hall).

Shell International (1993) *Expatriate Survey: 'Outlook: Assessment, Selection and Preparation for Expatriate Assignment'*.

Storti, C. (1990) *The Art of Crossing Cultures* (Yarmouth, ME: Intercultural Press).

Torbiorn, I. (1982) *Living Abroad: Personal Adjustment and Personnel Policy in the Overseas Setting* (Chichester: John Wiley).

Tung, R. (1998) *Selection and Training of Personnel for Overseas Assignments* (Cambridge, MA: Bullinger).

Further reading

Bennett, M. (1998) *Basic Concepts of Intercultural Communication* (London: Nicholas Brealey Publishing).

Brewster, C. (1991) *The Management of Expatriates* (London: Kogan Page).

Chartered Institute of Personnel Development (2005) *Factsheets: Recruitment, Psychological Testing* (London: CIPD).

Dowling, P., Welch, D. and Schuler, R. (1999) *International Human Resource Management: Managing People in a Multinational Context* (Cincinnati, OH: South Western College Publications).

Hurn, B. (1999) 'Repatriation – The Toughest Assignment of All', *Industrial and Commercial Training* 31(6): 224–8.

Joynt, P. and Morton, B. (eds) (2000) *The Global Human Resource Manager* (London: CIPD).

Marx, E. (2001) *Breaking Through Culture Shock* (London: Nicholas Brealey Publishing).

Pilbeam, S. and Corbridge, M. (2006) *People Resourcing: Contemporary Human Resource Management in Practice* (Upper Saddle River, NJ: Prentice Hall).

Selmer, J. (2005) 'Expatriate Selection: Back to Basics?', *International Journal of Human Resource Management* 12(8): 68–84.

Weaver, G. (ed.) (1998) 'Culture Shock and the Problems of Adjustment in New Cultural Environments' in *Culture, Communication and Conflict Reading in International Relations*, 2nd edn (New York: Simon & Schuster), pp. 185–6.

7
Leadership Across Cultures

Summary

Definition: management and leadership
Challenges facing twenty-first-century leaders
Action-Centred Leadership
Situational leadership
Required competencies
The international manager
Leadership styles
Leadership development for women
Global leadership training
The GLOBE project
The Intercultural Competence Assessment (INCA) Project
Selection
Performance appraisal

Management and leadership: definition

Research in the field of leadership and management has not produced a universally accepted theory that can adequately explain the difference between the two terms. However, there is general agreement that leadership depends more on personality, even charisma, the ability to motivate and communicate with others, and vision. It is therefore more of an art, whereas the practice of management is more of a science, depending more on ascribed power and authority with the focus on decision making and administration.

Edgar Schein (1992) considers that: 'The unique function of leadership that distinguishes it from management and administration is concern for culture.'

Leadership across cultures

A monocultural approach to leadership is now less acceptable as an increasing amount of business is carried out beyond national boundaries. The ability to understand the fundamental values of other cultures is essential to avoid misunderstandings which may escalate into actual loss of business opportunities.

Business has become more interconnected, as is particularly evident in the increase of outsourced jobs, especially in IT and professional service industries. The increase in mergers and foreign acquisitions has also emphasized the need for leadership in managing corporate change and adjustment and in developing the ability to motivate a multicultural workforce. The result of this is the need for a truly global perspective. These changes, however, may well impose high levels of stress over sustained periods of time, which have an adverse effect on health and judgment, with the result that today's international leaders are more reliant on collaborative approaches. The heavy costs that may be incurred should they fail in their international assignments will impact not only on their family and themselves as individuals but also on their organization, its reputation and its position in an increasingly competitive global marketplace.

Challenges facing twenty-first-century leaders

Today's leaders must be prepared for the future as globalization intensifies the complex challenges due to the interdependent global economy and fast-changing political and economic events. Figure 7.1 outlines some of these challenges.

As a result of these challenges, the role of international managers has widened considerably. Their responsibilities may cover entire regions and they need the skills to adapt quickly to new challenges and operate effectively

- New technology and the increasing pace of change
- Increased shareholder expectations
- Increasing scarcity of raw materials with resulting international competition to secure available sources
- The development of regional trading blocs and the potential large market grouping being created in the Asia/Pacific region
- The repercussions of the financial and economic turmoil in the West, in contrast to large sovereign wealth funds held elsewhere
- New emerging markets (for example, the BRICs) and shifting competition bases
- Dealing with natural disasters, the effects of climate change and the awareness of the need for sustainable development

Figure 7.1   Challenges facing twenty-first-century leaders

in several different cultures. Traditionally, the international manager has been synonymous with the expatriate manager, but times have changed and the role has been extended. 'There is a demand for new types of cosmopolitan, multilingual, multifaceted executives who are operational across national borders, somewhat like James Bond' (Schneider and Barsoux, 2003: 185).

Global expansion has made business much more interdependent. As a result, the selection and training of those who will be the future leaders are of crucial importance. The challenges faced by businesses have demanded increasing reliance on strategic thinking, adaptability to fast-changing situations and the ability to interact with their counterparts in other cultures. As Levin states: 'Leadership is no longer a solo act. The concept of leadership is radically changing and the challenges that leaders are facing may well be beyond their individual capabilities' (Levin, 2007: 5).

Action-Centred Leadership

Adair (1982) introduced the concept of Action-Centred Leadership, which was included as part of the programme for all Officer Cadets at the Royal Military Academy, Sandhurst. This was based on the belief that a leader should take into account three inter-related areas of need, namely task needs, group needs and individual needs. The effective leader should be capable of re-adjusting the priorities of each of these three areas as situations change. Adair stressed the need for an effective leader to have certain personal qualities, such as determination, judgment, flexibility, empathy and resourcefulness. The relative importance of these attributes will vary according to the needs of the current situation. The performance of people as individuals and as members of teams is vitally affected by the actions the leader takes to support, clarify, challenge, guide, consult, plan and encourage. A leader needs to take action to enable the team to work together as a cohesive group, but at the same time actively to encourage the creative and innovative contribution of individuals towards the common objectives of the organization. To achieve all this, the leader needs to take action to:

- achieve the TASK;
- build the TEAM;
- develop the INDIVIDUAL.

A breakdown in or neglect of any one of these key areas will quickly impact on the other two. The leader's paramount role is therefore to take the appropriate action as the priorities of the situation change.

Situational leadership

Adair's concept of Action-Centred Leadership supports the current emphasis on situational leadership, that is, the need to re-define the priority of the key attributes of leaders, as the global situation is frequently subject to change.

Different leaders are required, for example, in times of war, large-scale national disasters and the current economic recession with its resulting austerity measures. However, appropriate leadership behaviour will still depend on personal power, with the focus on strong motivating ability and well-developed communication skills, and the capability to respond quickly to different changing situations.

Criteria for success

The cost of failure makes it imperative that organizations need to carefully select their potential leaders. The first step is to attempt to identify the competencies, motivational and personal attributes required in order to achieve success. Experience shows that technical competence, while highly desirable, does not in itself necessarily produce a successful international business leader. It is therefore important that organizations define the requisite criteria for success.

The development of an international elite of executives drawn from a company's operations worldwide is described by Schneider and Barsoux as: 'Members of a global commando or a SWAT team' (2003: 185). The 'global' manager can be seen as someone who pursues a 'borderless career' and whose corporate identity may even override that of his or her country of origin.

Heller described the requirements of an international manager which still hold good today as follows.

- The **stamina** of an Olympic runner
- The **mental agility** of an Einstein
- The **detachment** of a judge
- The **tact** of a diplomat
- The **perseverance** of an Egyptian pyramid builder

Figure 7.2   Requirements of an international manager (Heller, 1980: 48)

In addition, Heller listed the following as desirable attributes: 'The importance of sensitivity to other cultures, to show no sign of prejudice and the ability to merge with the local environment with chameleon-like ease' (1980: 48).

Research by Tung (1998) suggested that the following should be considered important criteria when selecting global managers:

- conflict resolution skills;
- social orientation;
- leadership style;
- flexibility and open-mindedness;
- effective communication style;
- the ability to cope with stress;
- interest in and willingness to try new things and ideas.

Tung's list of criteria remains essentially valid today. However, we should add to this list other criteria to emphasize the cultural implications related to living and working effectively in other cultures. These could include the ability to adapt to operating in different cultures, to work effectively in multinational teams and to be able to deal with increasing complexity, diversity and ambiguity in uncertain environments characterized by unpredicted change.

Marx (1999) claimed that the majority of companies base their selection of potential international leaders on their technical competence without paying much attention to their ability to operate successfully overseas. This situation has now changed, with more emphasis on what Marx describes as the 'soft issues'. There is clear evidence of this change in the following list of competencies in *A Handbook of Human Resource Management Practice* (Armstrong, 2006):

- cultural sensitivity;
- linguistic skills;
- the ability to manage ethical and cultural differences;
- resilience;
- adaptability;
- the ability to manage the work/family life balance;
- building, leading and sustaining multinational teams.

We could, perhaps, add to these the need for a sense of humour.

Apart from the obvious paramount requirements of technical and professional competency, the majority of the other competencies or requirements have strong cultural implications.

Leadership styles

Rugman and Collinson list leadership styles as: 'Ranging from individual-oriented, directive, autocratic, top-down, or authoritarian, to group-oriented, participative, democratic, bottom-up, or egalitarian' (Rugman and Collinson, 2006: 142).

In the globalized economy, cultural groupings may in fact exhibit both styles of leadership, but most tend to reflect one particularly predominant style. Potential conflict can occur when two cultures with different leadership styles are working together, as each of the two workforces is used to its own cultural leadership style. For example, a culture with high-power distance, for example, Spain, with individualistic and assertive characteristics, runs the risk of being considered somewhat aggressive and too directive by those cultures with low-power distance, such as Denmark.

Leadership style is defined by Mullins as: 'The way in which the functions of leadership are carried out, the way in which the manager typically behaves towards members of the group' (Mullins, 2005: 291). Mullins' three styles of leadership can be summarized as follows:

- *The authoritarian or autocratic style*: this is where the manager holds all the power, including policy and decision making. All action within the organization emanates from the manager.
- *The democratic style*: here the emphasis is on the group as a whole, where members should participate in policy and decision making. The leadership functions are shared within the group, with the leader being more part of the team.
- *The laissez-faire style*: here the manager tends to be more of an expert observer who stands back and allows members a high degree of freedom to act, while exercising a supportive and guidance role as required.

The second and third styles above challenge the old concept that superiors have the ultimate right to exercise power over their inferiors. This attitude has now been replaced in Western business style by the belief that although individuals may be unequal in their performance and ability, all have the right to express freely their views and to contribute to the decisions that affect both them personally and the business itself. In this context, leaders are accepted for as long as they continue to support the interests of those they represent, that is, the workforce, shareholders, investors and the wider community.

Schneider and Barsoux (2003) consider that, particularly in North America and Western Europe, with the move towards more participative management and individual empowerment, the role of leadership is changing, with the increasing emphasis on acting as a 'facilitator' or as a 'coach' rather than exercising direct control. This development is much less obvious in cultures where power is still retained at the top, individual initiative is less encouraged and workers are more prepared to defer to the authority of their leaders (Schneider and Barsoux, 2003: 111–12).

We have seen in Chapter 3 how Lewis (2011) groups cultures into three main clusters:

- *linear-active*: task-oriented, highly organized planning, do one thing at a time, monochronic (examples: Anglo-Saxon, Germanic and Scandinavian cultures);
- *multi-active*: people-oriented, emphasis on spoken word, flexible (examples: Southern Europeans and Arabs);
- *reactive*: introverted, good listener, respect for status, age and authority (examples: Japanese, Chinese and South Korean cultures).

Lewis deduces from the above main groups that the characteristics of managers in each will display certain cultural attributes. In summary, these are as follows:

- *linear-active managers*: managers who demonstrate and value high technical competence, emphasis on factual detail, logic before emotion, focus on immediate achievement and results;
- *multi-active managers*: managers who are more outgoing, flexible and able to deal with frequent change (essentially polychronic), who use their personality to inspire people;
- *reactive managers*: managers who possess good interpersonal skills and are exponents of the 'listening culture', who are respected for the positive and harmonious atmosphere they bring to multinational teams.

In the examination of the different styles of leadership, we should also consider what is described as charismatic or inspirational leadership. This is also equated with *transformational leadership*, which is concerned with motivation, inspiring commitment and having a clear vision of the future for an organization, which will produce a dramatic and beneficial change in the positioning of the organization in its sector in the marketplace. However, it has been argued that charisma alone is no guarantee of success.

Below are some examples of different cultural leadership styles:

- Germans seek strong and decisive leadership which engenders confidence in what they are talking about. Such leaders inspire respect, and their orders and instructions are obeyed because their functional competence is acknowledged. This is assisted by a clear chain of command, and instructions and information are passed down from the top. Considerable value is placed on gaining consensus.
- The French style tends to favour a more directive leader with a high degree of technical competence. The leaders are expected to give clear instructions to their subordinates and experience and qualifications are highly valued.
- The Italians tend to display the traditional leadership model from a family business. Authority is delegated personally to trusted individuals. Leaders are expected to be technically competent and to demonstrate creativity. Throughout Latin Europe, the management pattern is very similar, with employees in general willing to trust the decisions of their leaders.
- The Dutch tend to have less regard for hierarchy. Their leaders have an open relationship with employees and are seen as being the 'first among equals'.
- In Spain, the individual leader is seen more as a benevolent autocrat who is expected to be decisive and have authority derived from personal relationships with subordinates.
- In the UK, managers place considerable emphasis on establishing good relationships with their subordinates, with a flexible approach, yet ultimately reserving the right to take charge.
- The Swedish concept of leadership is essentially democratic, with senior staff being accessible to their subordinates and available for discussions.
- In Russia, there is generally a top-down hierarchy and individualism is not encouraged to the extent that it is in the West.

- Japanese leadership concentrates on getting the group to work together and there is a high degree of collective responsibility.
- American leaders are keen to achieve results for themselves, the company and the shareholders. They are given the authority and responsibility to act accordingly. Motivation is linked to a sense of achievement and the need to respond to challenges. Leadership is based on the belief in individual accountability, with the leader acting more as a 'coach' in the sporting sense.

When considering Hofstede's dimensions of culture (see Chapter 2), it is clear that one dimension in particular, namely that of power distance, is relevant to leadership styles in different cultures. One of the most important aspects is the balance of power in organizations between individuals and the group. This balance will vary between cultures with regard to whether:

- authority is vested in the leader or the group;
- the emphasis is on the structure and status of the hierarchy;
- women have equal opportunities in society to become leaders or whether there is a 'glass ceiling' to impede their career progression.

When we consider all four of Hofstede's main dimensions, leadership styles will vary in relation to what are considered by employees to be motivating factors:

High uncertainty avoidance: need for job security, less risk taking. Employees require strong direction and a clear framework of rules and regulations.
Low uncertainty avoidance: prefer more risky opportunities or variety and for fast-track advancement and the opportunity to contribute with suggestions.

High power distance: employees will expect their leaders to take charge and make decisions.
Low power distance: people are more motivated by employee participation, teamwork and relations with their peers.

High individualism: the focus is on need to motivate individuals by providing opportunities for personal advancement and autonomy.
Low individualism (collectivism): motivation is more likely to succeed through appealing to group goals and preserving group harmony.

High masculinity: employees tend to be more comfortable with the traditional divisions of work.
More feminine cultures: looser boundaries, motivating people through more flexible roles, equal opportunities and greater emphasis on compromise than conflict.

There is growing evidence in the EU of the increase in what has been called 'the multicultural executive' (Lewis, 2011) or 'the New Euro-executive' (Hurn, 1999), referred to in Chapter 6. The hallmark of this breed of European managers is extensive senior experience in the European market, backed by well-developed cross-cultural and linguistic fluency, as well as the ability to manage multicultural teams. These special leadership qualities are essential to meet the new challenges and opportunities presented in a fiercely competitive European market and the new fast-emerging markets in the BRIC nations.

Cross-cultural implications of leadership

The balance of power in organizations between individuals and the team varies between different cultures in the following main areas:

- Is authority vested in the leader or the group?
- Is the leader a facilitator or a supremo?
- Is the leader a coach?
- Is there an emphasis on hierarchy?
- Are age and seniority important or is status based on qualifications?
- What is the position of women in terms of opportunities and acceptance?

Leadership development for women

In Western Europe in particular, there has been much pressure on multinational companies, NGOs and both the public and private sectors to increase the opportunities for women to compete successfully for senior positions. This has been in addition to legislation in individual countries, such as the Equal Pay Act and the Sex Discrimination Act in the UK, as well as EU-wide legislation. Substantial progress has already been made in North European countries, such as in Norway, where 41 per cent of members of large company boards are now women; this figure is 27 per cent in Sweden. The French government has passed a law that sets minimum quotas for listed companies with the largest required to have a target of 40 per cent female board members by 2016. Spain, Italy, Belgium and the Netherlands already have quotas.

In the UK, the *Female FTSE 100 Board Report* of 2010 showed that the percentage of women on the boards of FTSE 100 companies had increased only from 9.4 per cent in 2004 to 15 per cent by 2010, and 13 large companies still had no female board members. The legal imposition of quotas for women is controversial and is opposed by many women themselves, as well as by companies and politicians. It has been criticized as a token gesture and companies argue that they have a duty of care first and foremost to their shareholders to appoint the best candidates, regardless of their sex.

There are a number of social and cultural factors that still inhibit women from wishing to pursue careers in senior positions and therefore break through the 'glass ceiling'. These include the cost of childcare when adequate state assistance is lacking, as well as the reluctance of many women to resume a full-time career while bringing up a family and afterwards. In addition, there are dual career problems in a family where the male partner is posted abroad and the female partner is unable to pursue her career if she accompanies him. Another factor is that some companies demand that all candidates from non-executive directorships must have first held executive positions in other companies in order to acquire suitable experience.

Despite these inhibitors, there are now more women at universities than men in many countries and more women are encouraged to apply for MBA and similar courses than in the past. However, this is not the case in some cultures, such as Japan, South Korea, many Muslim countries and in Latin cultures, where both social and cultural pressures mean that young women do not have the same opportunities as men or the encouragement to embark on professional careers.

In 2010, the Accenture International Women's Day Survey asked senior executives of medium-sized and large companies from 20 countries worldwide whether they were currently preparing more women for senior management roles than in 2009. A total of 60 per cent replied they were not, as opposed to 40 per cent that were. The Women's Matters Global Survey carried out by McKinsey in 2010 polled some 1,500 executives worldwide, enquiring what were considered the main barriers to increasing gender diversity within their top management structures. The most significant replies were the problems of balancing work and family responsibilities, the availability of childcare and its associated high cost. In addition, the Survey highlighted the problems of often being unable to respond to the need to move quickly, particularly abroad, the absence of sufficient female role models and, in many cases, the tendency not to promote themselves sufficiently when faced with competition from men.

In addition to the above inhibiting factors, those women who do reach executive positions may find it difficult to be accepted abroad, particularly in Japan, the Middle East and some Latin cultures. In China, where women make up 46 per cent of the workforce, it is still difficult to overcome the highly conservative attitude towards women in senior appointments. As a result, Chinese female high-flyers often find it easier to work for a multinational company (*The Economist*, 26 November 2011).

Cultural and social factors are slow to change despite equal opportunity legislation, but much can be done by career planning and training as well as integrating women's career development as a key function of human resource management. Other positive approaches include the provision of role models, mentoring and promoting the networking of women. Careers advice from school and universities can also play a part.

Considerable progress has also been made in promoting the development of leadership training and experience for women by such bodies as the Women's Global Leadership Forum, which has been instrumental in raising the awareness of the potential for women to hold senior management positions. The Women in Diplomatic Service Group has been set up to encourage women to achieve positions in the diplomatic service by opening up opportunities and providing training development.

It has been contended that women in senior management positions have a beneficial effect on the boards of companies as they are considered to have a calmer approach, tend not to make rash decisions and, in a crisis, are risk averse. In addition, they are usually less driven by power and ambition, and are keener to work towards compromise in many situations. There are, of course, strong examples of highly successful women in senior appointments in certain sectors, for example, retail, fashion and health care.

Global leadership training

In order to extend and develop the pool of available talent from which to select the global business leaders of the future, there has been an increase in global leadership programmes.

The GLOBE Research Project on Leadership Worldwide

The Global Leadership and Organizational Behaviour Effectiveness (GLOBE) Project began in 1992. It defined leadership as: 'The ability of an individual to influence, motivate and enable us to contribute towards the effectiveness and success of the organizations of which they are members.'

Developed by Robert J. House of the Wharton School, University of Pennsylvania, GLOBE involved 170 researchers, called 'country co-investigators', based in 62 of the world's cultures. Data was collected from 17,300 middle managers in 950 organizations, mainly in the telecommunications, food and banking sectors. Data was collected only from the corporate headquarters in the host cultures and not from foreign multinationals.

The research examined the extent to which the practices and values associated with leadership are universal, that is, similar worldwide, and the extent to which they are specific to a few societies. The project identified 21 *primary leadership dimensions* or *first-order factors* that in all cultures are seen, to some extent, as contributing to a leader's effectiveness or lack of it. These are as follows.

Administratively competent	Decisive	Non-participative
Autocratic	Diplomatic	Performance-orientated
Autonomous	Face-saving	Procedural
Charismatic	Human-orientated	Self-centred
Inspirational	High integrity	Status-conscious
Self-sacrificing	Malevolent	Team collaboration
Conflict-inducing	Modest	Team integration

Figure 7.3   Primary leadership dimensions (House *et al.*, 2004: 31)

From the results obtained, the research identified six culturally endorsed leadership dimensions:

- charismatic/values based;
- team-orientated;
- self-protective;
- participative;
- humane-oriented;
- autonomous (House *et al.*, 2004: 137).

These are intended to describe the ways in which people worldwide distinguish between effective and ineffective leaders.

The INCA Project

The INCA Project (www.incaproject.org) is a transnational interdisciplinary project funded by the EU under the Leonardo da Vinci programme in 2005. The project's full title is 'Intercultural Competence Assessment'. It arose out of the need to provide a suitable framework to assess the cultural skills required for management and is used as a basis for training. The main research was carried out by Professor Michael Byram of Durham University, who generated six qualities required by successful international managers, which he calibrated at the three levels of competence, namely: basic, intermediate and full.

According to the INCA Project, intercultural competence 'enables you to interact effectively and in a way that is acceptable to others when you are working in a group whose members have different cultural backgrounds'. 'Cultural' may denote all manner of features, including the values and beliefs you have grown up with, your national customs and, in particular, your attitudes and practices that affect the way you work.

The desirable cultural qualities are as follows:

- *tolerance of ambiguity*: coping positively with the unexpected and the unfamiliar;
- *behavioural flexibility*: the ability to adapt the way you work with others in order to avoid procedural conflicts;
- *communicative awareness*: the ways in which misunderstandings may occur due to cultural differences in speech and body language;
- *knowledge discovery*: a willingness to research and learn from intercultural encounters;
- *respect for otherness*: regard for values, customs and practices of other cultures;
- *empathy towards other cultures*: the ability to understand other people's thoughts and feelings; to see and feel a situation through their eyes.

The six characteristics of intercultural competence required for leaders are simplified by linking them with three strands of competence:

- *openness* includes *respect for otherness* and *tolerance of ambiguity*;
- *knowledge* includes *behavioural flexibility* and *communicative awareness*;
- *adaptability* includes *empathy towards other cultures* and *knowledge discovery*.

Global leadership competencies

In reality, knowledge and experience may vary greatly between individuals, but we can improve our intercultural competence as leaders as we acquire greater understanding of people from other cultures and experience their different value systems and beliefs.

There has also been increased emphasis on global leadership training with the introduction of specialist MBAs in business schools of universities, as well as by leading multinational companies and specialist leadership courses. Examples of these are organised by the Harvard Business School, the London Business School, the Henley Leadership Programme, the World Economic Forum Leadership Team based in Geneva, the International Institute for Global Leadership and many others. Much of this training consists of simulation and role playing, with the emphasis on experiential learning, involving managers from many cultures working together.

Brake (1997: 67–8) proposes the following three competency clusters required by global business leaders: business acumen, relationship management and personal effectiveness. In the relationship management cluster, he includes the importance of effective cross-cultural communication in a complex and diverse global business environment.

Edwards and Rees (2006) consider the myth of the international manager and question whether a select cadre of people who specialize in international management is being created, with the emphasis on selection less for their technical skills and more 'for such things as intercultural ability and global awareness'. If this is the case, they suggest that international human resource managers should place the emphasis on recruitment and selection, 'less on the particular national interest of the assignment and more on the international development of the manager' (Edwards and Rees, 2006: 212–13).

Selection methods

A number of selection methods were covered in Chapter 6, but here we briefly examine other methods that can be used to attract and select international managers with the potential for leadership in organizations. The first is selection from within the organization itself. This is often the first source, depending on the availability of tried-and-tested experienced personnel.

Joynt and Morton (2000: 100–3) refer to the following additional methods:

- *Head-hunters*: these employ executive search techniques to help identify high-quality candidates for senior level appointments. Their well-developed contacts enable them to operate internationally, often networking with large organizations and their extensive contacts in emerging markets.
- *Cross-national advertising*: this method involves the use of international advertising agencies and advertising consultants across the world.
- *Internet recruitment*: this is particularly effective in attracting internationally mobile managers for those firms requiring specialist skills, or multinational companies wishing to promote their presence and interest in a particular market. The use of the Internet has the advantages of lower costs, wider recruitment sourcing, websites, online application forms, job specifications and access to curriculum vitae/résumés.
- *International graduate programmes*: these can be useful in selecting 'high flyers' for future senior appointments, but organizations are wary of low retention rates and the possibility of a lack of long-term commitment from those recruited.

The cross-cultural implications of performance management and appraisal

In Western cultures, it is generally accepted that some form of performance appraisal is carried out both domestically and in an international context. In the latter case, it is considered even more important to assess whether managers in senior positions fulfil their potential, not only regarding their technical and specific professional functions but also 'in their cross-cultural skills, sensitivity to foreign norms and values, understanding differences in labour practices or customer relations and ease of adaptation to unfamiliar surroundings' (McKenna and Beech, 2008).

However, in many cultures, in particular Asian cultures such as Japan, China or South Korea, there are very real problems in implementing any form of direct performance appraisal. This is particularly the case when saving 'face' is a problem if managers provide feedback to their staff which draws attention to negative aspects of their performance. In addition, the focus on individual responsibility is seen as inappropriate in collectivist cultures.

The following are the key areas of cultural concern when considering the implementation of a performance appraisal system:

- the extent of the differences between national and corporate culture;
- the problems of giving feedback, in particular saving 'face';
- whether the focus on individual responsibility is seen as inappropriate in a collectivist culture;

- whether attainment goals can be measured and time-managed;
- power-distance differences;
- some cultures see organizations in terms of social relationships, with the focus on managing people, not tasks.

Summary

- There are a range of challenges facing twenty-first-century leaders.
- There is no one best form of leadership style as there are many variables. It is evident from the substantial research available that culture has an important effect on leadership styles.
- In the increasingly globalized world, those selected as the potential leaders in business need to have special competencies and skills to be effective across cultural borders.
- Different styles of leadership are appropriate in different cultures, and misunderstandings and even conflict can arise when these differences are not recognized and accommodated.
- Research has been undertaken to determine the important criteria in their recruitment and selection, and to collect data to identify the practices and values associated with different cultural leadership styles.
- Global leadership training has been widely developed to increase the pool of talent available for recruitment and selection of the global business leaders of the future.
- Research into leadership by the GLOBE and INCA Projects has identifed some desirable cultural qualities in potential leaders.
- There are strong social and cultural factors which still inhibit the progress of women in attaining senior leadership positions, but considerable recent progress has been made in both career development and the wider and now more accepted realization of the benefits and qualities that women can bring to senior appointments.

References

Adair, J. (1982) *Action-Centred Leadership* (Aldershot: Gower Publishing).

Armstrong, A. (2006) *A Handbook of Human Resource Management Practice*, 10th edn (London: Kogan Page).

Brake, T. (1997) *The Global Leader: Critical Factors for Creating the World Class Organizations* (Chicago: Irwin Publishing).

Edwards, T. and Rees, C. (2006) *International Human Resource Management: Globalization, National Systems and Multinational Companies* (Upper Saddle River, NJ: Prentice Hall).

Heller, J. (1980) 'Criteria for Selecting an International Manager', *Personnel* 57: 47–55.

Hofstede, G., Hofstede, G.J. and Minkov, M. (2010) *Cultures and Organizations. Software of the Mind. Intercultural Cooperation and its Importance for Survival*, 3rd edn (New York: McGraw-Hill).

House, R.J., Hanges, P.J., Javidan, M., Dorfman, P.W. and Gupta, V. (eds) (2004) *Culture, Leadership and Organizations: The GLOBE Study of 62 Societies* (Thousand Oaks, CA: Sage Publications).

Hurn, B. (1999) 'The New Euro-Executive', *Industrial and Commercial Training* 3(1): 19–23.

Joynt, P. and Morton, B. (eds) (2000) *The Global HR Manager* (London: CIPD).

Levin, A. (2007) 'The Future of Leadership: Where Do We Go from Here?', *Industrial and Commercial Training* 39(1): 5.

Lewis, R. (2011) *When Cultures Collide*, 3rd edn (London: Nicholas Brealey Publishing).

Marx, E. (1999) *Breaking Through Culture Shock* (London: Nicholas Brealey Publishing).

McKenna, E. and Beech, N. (2008) *Human Resource Management: A Concise Analysis*, 2nd edn (Upper Saddle River, NJ: Prentice Hall).

Mullins, L. (2005) *Management and Organisational Behaviour*, 7th edn (Upper Saddle River, NJ: Prentice Hall).

Rugman, A. and Collinson, S. (2006) *International Business*, 4th edn (Upper Saddle River, NJ: Prentice Hall).

Schein, E. (1992) *Organizational Culture and Leadership: A Dynamic View*, 2nd edn (San Francisco, CA: Jossey-Bass).

Schneider, S. and Barsoux, J. (2003). *Managing Across Cultures*, 2nd edn (Upper Saddle River, NJ: Prentice Hall).

'Special Report Women and Work' (2011) *The Economist*, 26 November.

Tung, R. (1998) *Selection and Training of Personnel for Overseas Assignments* (Cambridge MA: Bullinger).

Further reading

Beardwell, T. and Claydon, T. (2007) *Human Resource Management: A Contemporary Appraisal*, 5th edn (Upper Saddle River, NJ: Prentice Hall).

Culpan, O. and Wright G. (2002) 'Women Abroad: Getting the Best Results from Women Managers', *Journal of Human Resource Management* 13(5): 784–801.

Dowling, P., Welch, D. and Schuler, R. (1999) *International Human Resource Management* (Mason City, IA: South-Western College Publishing).

Evans, M. (2009) *S.K.I.R.T.S in the Board room: A Woman's Guide to Success in Business and Life* (New York: John Wiley & Sons).

Gordon, T. (1977) *Leader Effectiveness Training* (New York: Wyden Books).

Hurn, B. (2012) 'Removing the Boardroom Glass Ceiling', *Industrial and Commercial Training* 44(3): 126–31.

Mendenhall, M., Kuhlmann, T. and Stahl, G. (eds) (2000) *Developing Global Business Leaders: Policies, Processes and Innovations* (London: Quorum).

McGregor, D. (1969) *The Human Side of Enterprise* (New York: McGraw-Hill).

3i/Cranfield. European Enterprise Centre (1993) *The Euro-Manager Survey: Special Survey: Attitudes to Managers and Companies in Europe* (Bedford: Cranfield School of Management).

8
International Team Building and Teamworking

Summary

The challenge of building international teams
Selection of team members
Building trust
Cultural synergy
Problem areas
Language issues
Meetings
Virtual meetings
Advantages and disadvantages of multicultural groups
Training of international teams

Introduction

This chapter examines the cultural problems and organizational practicalities involved in building and sustaining effective multicultural teams in the international environment. Such teams are particularly important for those involved in International Joint Ventures (IJVs), international aid projects and diplomacy. They are also used in working groups, steering committees and task forces which transcend national boundaries, as well as in corporate and regional headquarters of large global companies.

In addition, the chapter looks into the key research in team building, including the pioneering work of Meredith Belbin at the former Administrative Staff College at Henley (now the Henley Management College), where the emphasis was on identifying the skills and competencies required by managers to work effectively as members of teams.

The aim is to encourage the development of an international team which is not dominated by any one national group and which seeks to encourage synergy and celebrate diversity. Dowling, Welch and Schuler emphasize that: 'Because international business involves the interaction and movement across national boundaries, an appreciation of cultural differences and when these differences are important is essential' (1999: 12). Companies operating internationally need to exploit the strength of cultural diversity if they are to be responsive to changes in their business environment. Being culture-rich is now considered essential for successful global business. Creating multinational teams is one of the main activities in the process of internationalization.

The requirement

There is a need for more staff to be trained to operate in multicultural teams as firms adopt global strategies with managers moving in and out of other cultures and working with colleagues from these cultures. Such participation requires a wide range of interpersonal skills, including tact, culture sensitivity, high motivation, confidence building and organizational skills, as well as a sound understanding of team-building techniques and international management styles.

The challenge

> Team building is a difficult exercise at the best of times, but doubly so when the team members are separated by language, culture and geography. (Davies, 1992: 100)

One of the main challenges when managing people from different cultures is to balance apparently opposite cultural values and practices. It is important to appreciate how much culture affects the way we do business. Even when speaking the same language, opportunities for misunderstanding and therefore mismanagement exist. It is a serious mistake to believe that because there are common business interests, there are necessarily common ways of achieving business aims. Multinational teams do not happen naturally – they have to be created and carefully nurtured. Gains from cultural diversity are not automatic; indeed, in order to achieve their full potential, multinational teams may often have to overcome barriers that single-culture teams may solve relatively quickly. 'The very richness of the cultural diversity makes the group dynamics much more complex' (Cox, 1991: 34). These differences can create interpersonal conflict and communication problems.

The challenge is to create a positive, dynamic and progressive climate where people work together harmoniously, recognizing their strengths and weaknesses and their cultural differences. The managerial skills are in harnessing their talents and energies to maximize their collective potential. It should be stressed that those involved must want to operate well in other cultures and be highly motivated by the challenge. This is important as there is inherently greater potential for frustration and dissatisfaction in multinational teams than in single-culture teams, often accompanied by a high turnover of team members. For teams to become effective, they need to be able to become integrated and balance both individual and collective efforts.

Team Roles

Meredith Belbin identified nine Team Roles that he considered were required for effective teamwork. He carried out research into team selection at the Henley Management College and at the Industrial Training Research Unit at University College London. To achieve this, he first used a Self-Perception Inventory Analysis in seven sections. For each section, respondents were asked to distribute a total of ten points among the given statements which they thought most accurately described their own behaviour. The results were then scored and discussed and a team profile emerged. Belbin has produced one of the most widely used questionnaires for team selection and team training, and his analysis forms the basis for much of the research in the field of selecting and building effective teams.

In his research, Belbin identified the key players who would be important to a team and who would provide the necessary balance and interaction within the group. Their roles and attributes are summarized below in Figure 8.1.

These roles ensure that a team consists of members with the appropriate skills and qualities required at the different stages of a project or programme from its planning stage through to its implementation. They also include the process skills to coordinate the diverse efforts. Belbin's research supported the general conclusion that individuals are seldom good at everything; they are dependent on the people they are working with and have more to contribute than their specific expertise. They are more motivated and happy working in a way that is natural to them. Team members should be selected both in terms of the team roles they can assume and also in relation to the team skills that are most needed for the purpose in hand. If the number of people in the team is small, it is possible for members to assume more than one role.

Belbin's research can be summarized as follows:

- Each individual has a *primary* role in which he or she tends to feel most comfortable. This is the dominant role and one to which the individual is best suited.
- Each individual may possibly have as many as one to four *back-up* roles which he or she is able to play but is less comfortable with.
- Team members have strong *diversity* roles and complement each other's different strengths. Teams with a mix of profiles and a balance of roles

TEAM ROLE	Contribution	Allowable Weaknesses
Plant	Creative, imaginative, free-thinking. Generates ideas and solves difficult problems	Ignores incidentals. Too preoccupied to communicate effectively
Resource Investigator	Outgoing, enthusiastic, communicative. Explores opportunities and develops contacts	Over-optimistic. Loses interest once initial enthusiasm has passed
Coordinator	Mature, confident, identifies talent. Clarifies goals. Delegates effectively	Can be seen as manipulative. Offloads own share of the work
Shaper	Challenging, dynamic, thrives on pressure. Has the drive and courage to overcome obstacles	Prone to provocation. Offends people's feelings
Monitor Evaluator	Sober, strategic and discerning. Sees all options and judges accurately	Lacks drive and ability to inspire others. Can be overly critical
Teamworker	Cooperative, perceptive and diplomatic. Listens and averts friction	Indecisive in crunch situations. Avoids confrontation
Implementor	Practical, reliable, efficient. Turns ideas into actions and organizes work that needs to be done	Somewhat inflexible. Slow to respond to new possibilities
Completer Finisher	Painstaking, conscientious, anxious. Searches out errors. Polishes and perfects	Inclined to worry unduly. Reluctant to delegate
Specialist	Single-minded, self-starting, dedicated. Provides knowledge and skills in rare supply	Contributes only on a narrow front. Dwells on technicalities

Figure 8.1 Summary descriptions of Belbin's Team Roles (www.belbin.com)

usually perform better. Too many members with the same type of role may cause tension in the team and reduce overall cohesion and effectiveness.
- Some cultures show more preference for certain roles – for example, the French are concerned with innovative ideas, the Germans concentrate on structuring the task, the Swedes are strong on obtaining the necessary resources and the Americans tend to be assertive and impatient to achieve results.

- Groups made up entirely of people with high intelligence tend to display the *Apollo Syndrome* and are actually less likely to be effective than a more balanced and diverse group. An example could be the management team of a hospital made up entirely of clinicians and consultants, which would be less effective than a more balanced team that would include finance, personnel and other departmental heads. Apollo Syndrome groups are often difficult to manage and have problems making decisions. Such groups are better suited to high-technology companies where there is a need to allow for quick turnover as newcomers enter to reinvigorate the technology.

Belbin stressed the value of selecting a *team* as opposed to concentrating on the search for the right *individual*. This was a different approach from the aims of previous research in which there was a natural tendency for organizations to recruit in their own image. Belbin's research remains a significant benchmark study. It emphasizes the ability of a team to:

- renew and regenerate itself by new recruitment;
- find within itself all the desired characteristics;
- build up a store of shared and collectively owned experiences.

Research undertaken at Cranfield University in association with 3i in 1992 highlighted the perceptions of managers from different European cultures and an awareness of their national prejudices by measuring 'perception distance', that is, the difference between the self-perception of one nation compared to the perception of it held by other nations. The larger the perception distance, the greater the difference between what that nation and other Europeans see as its managers' competences. High-perception distance indicates barriers of prejudice often based on national stereotypes; for instance, the British tended to have a higher opinion of themselves than their European colleagues, especially the Italians and the French. It was therefore considered likely that it would be those nationalities that they may well have most difficulty working with.

Apart from the essential prerequisites of technical and professional ability, those who will be working as members of international teams need strong self-motivation, cultural sensitivity and the ability to manage ethical and cultural differences.

Building trust

Creating an atmosphere of trust and building relationships is crucial to success in building multicultural teams. This is particularly important as the team may only meet infrequently. Gains from cultural diversity are not automatic, and training as well as time is necessary for multicultural teams to overcome cultural, organizational and procedural barriers that uniform, single-nation teams are often able to resolve quickly and instinctively. The biggest problem is a lack of trust due to the fact that members may find it difficult to overcome misunderstandings, deep-rooted prejudices and stereotypes.

Schutz (1960) developed a model of three levels of 'give and take' relationships in the trust-building process developed from his work with the US Navy:

Inclusion	example	Can you join me/us?
Control	example	Do it this way.
Affection	example	Did it go well?

He saw the trust-building process as three stages which tend to follow the same sequence in the development of a group of people into an effective team. In this process, people move from being just a member of a group into being a member of a team. Inclusion activity is followed by control issues and finally, if relationships are established, by affection. The initial inclusion phase is most important and requires special emphasis at the beginning of each meeting of the team. There are different views in different cultures as to how much time and effort should be directed towards relationship building prior to 'getting down to business':

- In many Asian countries, group cohesion is of primary importance. When Asian members are in an international team, they tend to place emphasis on maintaining harmony at the expense of expressing strong opinions, thus avoiding any potential conflict. In contrast, members from Western cultures will tend to show independence and self-expression, and will question and challenge the opinions of others. They may also display emotion, annoyance and frustration with their Asian team colleagues.
- The cultures of Southern Europe, the Middle East, Latin America and Japan are generally more relationship-oriented; people here may place more emphasis on the 'getting to know each other' phase and will feel pressurized if that phase is cut short. For them, business is personal and will develop only from the trust established by personal relationships.

Once created, trust is at all times fragile. It has to be nurtured slowly and can be destroyed by one thoughtless action. It is built up and sustained in different ways:

- In Germany, trust is heavily weighted towards an organization meeting its agreed commitments, including delivery on time, punctuality and integrity throughout the process. In other cultures, not meeting deadlines is less critical and will not in itself lead to a loss of trust if personal relationships remain strong.
- In the USA and Western Europe, trust is enhanced by looking people in the eye, which is considered a sign of respect and sincerity. In East Asia, for example, direct eye contact can be taken as intimidating and challenging.

Cultural synergy

The aim of synergy in teamworking is that once the right group of people is assembled, the resulting synergy is greater than the sum of their individual skills and talents.

When building a multicultural team, every effort should be made to preserve rather than neutralize the cultural differences in order to exploit their benefits. This approach can help produce cultural synergy, building on both the similarities and the differences. International teams tend to thrive on differing traditions and cultures, and if successful synergy is achieved, the team will make maximum use of all the participants' different cultural attitudes. Cultural synergy can be developed by a fusion of not only the home and host culture but also of the corporate culture.

Issues raised by multicultural teams working together

The following list covers some of the main issues that should be addressed with regard to teams working together:

- creating a focus, usually the agreed objectives, the common challenge, coupled with a sense of achievement;
- encouraging the dual process of empowerment and participation;
- establishing the transparency of the process which should be clear to all, unambiguous, with no hidden agenda and no surprises;
- monitoring and using the dynamics of the group;
- accounting for language, including the selection of the working language and the use of interpreters;
- developing trust as a continuing process as members leave the team and new ones join it;
- recognizing and making good use of differences, thus maximizing cultural synergy and celebrating diversity;
- allowing for added stress and fatigue because of the different cultural dimensions. This will require more organizational effort, more time and more consultation.

Language issues

The following list covers issues relating to language in teams working together:

- Use of English – it is advisable to use 'off-shore' or international English and it is important that tolerance is shown towards those who have English as their second language.
- Summarizing, both oral and written, as an aid to understanding involves extra time but avoids problems later.

- It is important to check understanding and agreement amongst team members; the importance of preserving 'face' in many cultures should also be considered at this stage.
- When planning language training, it is important to first carry out a needs analysis, to assess the time available and to decide on the standard of desired fluency.
- The use of interpreters and translators is necessary, as is the need for them to be familiar with a company's corporate culture and its objectives.

Use of humour

It was Victor Borge who said that: 'Humour is the shortest distance between two people.'

However, the main problem when trying to use humour in a multinational group is that it does not always translate well across the cultures. If that happens, there is always the possibility that some offence or frustration may be caused because of a lack of understanding. Different cultures also have different views on humour. In Germany, for example, there is less of a tradition of the daily banter one hears in the UK, where humour, including wry humour, is very much part of everyday life and the British often laugh at themselves. In France, there is often a preference for more clever or sophisticated humour, while in Asia, attempts to make fun of other people can cause a loss of 'face'. In the USA, humour is used in business meetings to act as an 'ice-breaker', but as soon as serious business starts, attempts at humour are curtailed.

The degree of humour displayed within a multinational team is itself a positive sign of trust and cooperation, particularly if the members can openly laugh and joke among themselves in a relaxed atmosphere. If used correctly, humour can help a team to bond. It can often aid in putting cultural differences on the table, but at times it can be a double-edged weapon. At best, it can be used to defuse a situation or to 'break the ice'. It is advisable to avoid sarcasm and cynicism, which is particularly inappropriate in relation to Asian cultures. Whenever possible, opportunities should be taken to develop 'shared humour', using culturally acceptable 'shared experiences', for example, interest in sport.

However, humour must always be used with care as it can fall flat, be misunderstood or, in the worst-case scenario, cause confusion or even offence. The following points provide examples of this:

- The British self-mocking, self-deprecation style of humour is not always appreciated and is scorned by the French and despised by the Japanese as it is beyond their comprehension or experience. The British use of humour at the beginning of presentations and meetings, usually with a joke intended as an 'ice-breaker', would not find favour with many German business people, who would consider excessive humour as potentially a cover for a lack of preparation or commitment.

- The Japanese use humour in after-work socializing. This is ignored the next day, when formality resumes.

Team training

Team members may require specialized training to support their work in different cultures with colleagues from different nationalities. Training can include conflict management, problem solving and time management, and is best carried out using scenarios which include role play and simulation.

Case study

In a workshop to develop the concept of multinational team building with Foseco, a leader in the foundry and metal treatment business at that time owned by Burmah Castrol, the emphasis was on developing a multinational approach as part of peer group development. It was concluded that top management commitment was an essential prerequisite, as was transparency in all stages in order to develop trust.

Problem areas raised by the participating managers included the need for a clear, agreed-upon specific agenda with no surprises. This aspect was particularly welcomed by the Japanese managers. The American and North European managers were introduced to polychronic attitudes to time which were very different from their own monochronic cultures. All managers agreed on the need for a skilful chairperson for multicultural meetings who could smooth out potential cultural misunderstandings. One major area of concern was the need to facilitate the inclusion of those who had difficulties with English and who as a result tended to feel culturally marginalized. Tactics to remedy this problem included the careful preparation of agendas issued in advance, with summaries of key points discussed at certain stages, backed up by translations and with the opportunity to pause in order to check understanding by all concerned at key stages in the meetings (Hurn and Jenkins, 2000).

Meetings

Meetings are an area where many potential problems may occur when operating a multinational team. They are also an area in which cultural sensitivity is essential. Meetings are seen by some (for example, the Americans and the Germans) as a decision-making forum and by others (for example, the British, the Italians and the Dutch) more as an exchange of ideas, to pool information and problems and then to resolve any conflict by consensus or compromise in order to obtain results. In all types of meetings, there is always a cost, in particular the expense of bringing people together, providing accommodation, setting up the venue and, of course, the salaries of the personnel, as well as the time involved. These factors, along with the concerns about security, have seen the increase in telephone and video conferencing, as well as online meetings and the use of virtual teams. However, businesses will still continue to organize meetings on traditional lines due to the advantages of face-to-face encounters, the benefits of socializing and the opportunities that meetings create for networking and informal discussions. It is important to allow time for such formal and informal socializing, building relationships and networking, as for some this is the most important aspect of meetings.

Critical areas

Preparation	Attendance
Clear objectives	Chairperson
Clarify expectations	Procedures and protocol
Layout and seating	Participation styles
Agenda	Gaining agreement
Timing	Socializing
Choice of language	Follow-up

Figure 8.2   Multicultural meetings – critical areas

Preparation

Good preparation is important for all meetings and for all cultures, but for some it assumes a greater degree of importance. This, for example, is the case with the Japanese, who call it 'nemawashi': preparing the ground. Germans put much emphasis on 'gute Vorbereitung' (good preparation), whereas the French often see a meeting as an intellectual exercise to test a hypothesis. The British, the Italians and the Spanish tend to do less preparation, in the worst-case scenario reading the brief on the aircraft. They will expect what is actually discussed at the meeting to be the most important aspect. With such a variety of approaches, it depends on the chairperson and the secretariat to issue the meeting papers well in advance, with requests for comments before the date of the meeting. In any case, it is most likely that at least twice as much time will be required for an international meeting as for a purely domestic meeting. At the beginning of the meeting, the reinforcement of the 'getting to know you' time is very important to help build relationships within the team.

Clear objectives

It is essential that the aims and objectives of any type of meeting, and particularly for multicultural meetings, are clear from the outset to avoid any confusion. There is a need to have a common sense of purpose. The main principle is to avoid any surprises on the actual day of the meeting. The Chinese and the Arabs, for example, in particular do not welcome any surprises regarding the finalized agenda. These cultures do their homework in advance of the meeting particularly carefully.

Expectations

In multinational meetings, expectations of outcomes can cause difficulty. It is important to understand the type of meeting and its anticipated outcome in order to ensure the right level of expectation and intervention. In British and American meetings, the aim is to obtain agreement on a range of actions, distributed after the meeting in minutes or a meeting report which lists action points, who is responsible and the dates when action has to be taken. In many Latin countries, on the other hand, the function of meetings is very often simply to gauge the mood of the group. Decisions may not be taken at the meeting, but the meeting's atmosphere may well be taken into account in the decision making undertaken elsewhere.

The French will differentiate clearly between meetings held to discuss policy, those to decide on a specific course of action and meetings to allocate functions and responsibilities. It is important for foreign participants to recognize these differences. In the first, the free discussion of ideas is welcomed, while in the second, it is the department directors who will decide how to proceed, and in the third they will allocate responsibilities and give instructions.

Meeting layout

The layout of the meeting should be as non-confrontational as possible, avoiding a strictly formal and hierarchical structure. A round-table layout is often the most suitable. There is a need for easy access to telephones, light refreshments and the entrance as some participants will come and go during proceedings. It should also be borne in mind that most Westerners require more personal space than other cultures, for example, Arabs and Africans, who will be happy to stand or sit closer together.

Agenda

The agenda is the most important organizing principle of the meeting, but attitudes to it can differ a great deal. For some cultures, an agenda is simply a list of things to discuss in no particular order and may even be created when the meeting actually convenes. In other countries, for example, the UK, the USA and Germany, the agenda is strictly followed as it is considered that a pre-agreed agenda circulated before the actual meeting should be adhered to in the meeting. The resulting action points which are circulated afterwards and followed up are considered the most efficient way of running a meeting. Such an approach may cause frustration among participants who need to have a more wide-ranging discussion at greater length and depth.

The agenda should be sent out in draft form well before the meeting and, once agreed, should contain no surprises on the day of the meeting.

The agenda must have a structure which includes the key points, but it must be flexible enough to allow time for discussion and summarizing. The agenda must be logical, with individual items as specific as possible. This is very important as some cultures (for example, Arabs) have a circular attitude towards an agenda with a tendency to jump from one item to another. Sufficient time should be left for summarizing and discussion of 'any other business', although care is needed if such discussion includes points which cause concern or surprise as they have not been included in the main agenda.

Timing

Apart from taking into account different time zones and travel time, multi-cultural meetings should avoid religious days. Misunderstandings about time can cause major problems, with participants having to leave early because of other commitments or arriving late. Other important considerations include different cultural views regarding punctuality and those cultures who consider it generally acceptable to leave a meeting to make telephone calls or to attend to other matters if the discussion is considered not immediately relevant to them. A possible solution is to have breaks at regular intervals for refreshments, informal discussion and telephone calls.

Another area to be considered is that of internal timing, particularly if it is decided on a 'timed agenda'. According to this area, a limited time is allotted to each topic. If this time is exceeded, the discussion is halted by the chair and the meeting moves on to the next point. This can be extremely frustrating for participants who feel the need for lengthier discussion. The scheduled end time can be equally controversial as, for example, the French believe that a meeting should continue until all items have been satisfactorily dealt with, whereas other cultures such as the Swiss and the Germans make a point of keeping to exact times.

Choice of language

The choice of the working language can be a major problem if the team is truly multicultural. The most likely choice will be English, but if other nationalities are present who are not native English speakers, they may be at a linguistic disadvantage and therefore there will be a need for interpreters. Some participants, particularly senior people, may bring their own interpreters who will act as 'chuchoteurs' (whisperers).

Organizations should carry out a regular language audit amongst their staff to ensure they have an up-to-date knowledge of those who are well qualified in foreign languages.

Apart from language fluency, patterns of language may vary between cultures. This includes the use of silence, which is skilfully used by the Japanese, who frequently consider matters in silence before making a contribution. In many Asian cultures, particularly in Southeast Asia, it is considered impolite to interrupt; indeed, individuals from such cultures often leave a respectful silence between utterances.

English for non-native speakers is often seen as complex, using a rich vocabulary and a host of metaphors and colloquialisms. If possible, it is advisable to use a form of international English or 'off-shore English', as already discussed in Chapter 4. This uses phrases and grammatical structures that are less likely to be misunderstood, avoiding acronyms, slang, jargon and complex structures. Preparatory papers and agenda issued before the meeting should wherever possible be translated to avoid any initial confusion. It is also important to realize how tiring it is for team members who are working in a second language, so more time should be allowed for questions and presentations. Multicultural teams can make adjustments to cope with one non-fluent member, but more members would most likely necessitate the use of interpreters. The lack of fluency in the working language is very often the major cause of exclusion and resulting feelings of frustration and isolation. This can be overcome to some extent by the use of relevant pictures and diagrams in presentations.

Attendance

Ideally, the aim is to get the 'right people', the decision makers, to attend, but this is not always possible. In some cultures, for example, the Arabs, it is not always predictable as to who and also how many will turn up. This may occur even though specific people have been notified as attending. However, with Arabs, the maturity and seniority of attendees are important if they are to have any credibility. In other cultures, for example, the British and the Dutch, junior managers may attend if the more senior designated representative is unable to take part. The Germans will usually try to send specialists to cover each area, whereas the British may well use generalists who have power to make decisions. In the case of the Japanese, if senior managers are present, junior managers will defer to them.

The chairperson

The appointment of the chairperson for a multicultural meeting is crucial to its success. The decision as to who is to be appointed needs to have the full support of all participants. The appointee should be a skilled facilitator, fluent in the working language chosen for the meeting and fully aware of the cultural sensitivities of the various participants. An increasing number of meetings in the West are on a need-to-know basis with a limited number of participants, usually for reasons of efficiency rather than confidentiality. In many Asian countries, notably Japan, a large number of participants are encouraged so that everyone is in the picture, even though they may not all actively participate in the meeting.

Whoever leads or runs the meeting in most cultures is the senior person in the room. The other members remain silent or contribute only when requested to do so. In many Western countries, participants are encouraged to interject when they have something to contribute. This can cause problems in multinational meetings, as such action may appear to show a lack of respect to the chairperson. In meetings in both the UK and the USA, the role of chair may be given to the person who is most in touch with the topic under discussion.

In Japan in particular, the senior person present may be responsible for overall strategy but may not actually deal with the tactical issues in running the meeting. It is not unknown for the senior person to be silent in deep concentration. In this situation, Westerners should be careful not to address all their remarks to possibly junior attendees who appear to be paying the most attention.

An indication of seniority and leadership in meetings is where people sit. In highly protocol-oriented business cultures, the most important person is traditionally seated furthest from the entrance, with more junior members of the meeting being nearer the door. Before taking your seat, you may need to check that your seat reflects your position in the company.

The chairperson should be able to summarize what has been agreed at various points and eventually to approve the minutes, as well as being able to deal sensitively with different cultural approaches to his or her authority:

- Some cultures, for example, the French, the Belgians and the Spanish, will consider it appropriate to challenge and even at times contradict the chair.
- The British, the Dutch, the Americans and the Germans will abide by the rules of procedure and channel their questions and contributions through the chair.
- The Italians, the Portuguese and the Greeks will be less constrained by the rules of procedure, with the Greeks seeing the chair as first among equals who is expected to compete with the other attendees to get points across.

Procedures and protocol

The procedures and protocol may be partly dependent on the national approach to meetings. In Japan, it is considered appropriate to focus in depth on a few issues. The French, however, favour a 360-degree approach in which a problem is discussed in all its aspects and from all angles. The British, the Americans and the Germans prefer a more linear approach with an organized series of points raised, discussed and actions agreed. These different approaches affect the duration of the meeting, with French meetings, for example, often lasting longer than those of the British or the Americans.

Participation styles

The chair has to cope with a wide variety of cultural styles, which include the following:

- The British usually adopt a realistic and pragmatic approach, and may offer opinions in areas outside their professional expertise or specialization.
- The Germans tend to be well prepared and make a contribution only when they feel well qualified and competent to do so. They do not appreciate interruption or contradiction.
- The French are models of rational thought and expect to win their points by logical argument.
- The Dutch are usually forthright, sometimes appearing blunt, but can use humour as the British do to reduce conflict or tension.
- The Americans often appear combative and assertive to other cultures. Anyone can speak but will defer to seniors at the point when decisions need to be made.

Gaining agreement

The chair will strive to achieve agreement, but needs to be aware that different cultures see the process of gaining consensus differently:

- Americans and most North Europeans will usually agree to what they feel committed to carry out.
- The British are more inclined to compromise in order to gain consensus.
- The French tend to favour adopting the best idea.
- High-context cultures have a different approach from low-context cultures.
- Decisions may be made either by a unanimous vote or by a majority – the method to be used should be made clear at the outset.

Socializing

Arrangements for both formal and informal occasions for socializing must be carefully made. The need to socialize, and particularly to network, is important to all cultures. Attention should be paid on formal occasions to seniority and status when arranging seating. There should also be agreement as to the amount of time devoted to socializing and whether spouses or partners should be involved.

Follow-up

As in all meetings, it is essential to maintain the momentum. Translations may be necessary regarding key decisions and action points. Minutes should be circulated for agreement by all concerned and then issued as soon as possible. If necessary, dates for future meetings should be decided and publicized, with dates fixed for further review if required.

Training methodology

The training of multicultural teams is an important requirement. Whenever possible, real teams should be involved in real-life scenarios. The first stage should include self-awareness training, understanding one's own culture and how it is perceived by others. This enables comparisons to be made and identifies how misunderstandings can arise and can be avoided. Training should include a significant degree of simulation and role playing, and can be consolidated by using experiential team-building exercises to allow team members to practise applying appropriate techniques, for example, management of meetings, consensus building, establishing trust, problem solving and conflict management.

Case study

A British company was concerned about working more effectively with its Italian IT colleagues as it had found that when both companies held international team meetings, things did not run smoothly. The senior management suspected that the problems were, to a large extent, likely to be based on cultural misunderstandings, different national procedures and a consequent lack of trust. Therefore, it was agreed to hold a cultural workshop to identify more closely the possible issues.

The workshop identified specific 'Italian' issues as seen by the British:

  (i) a tendency to deal with too many problems at the same time;
 (ii) insufficient analysis and a tendency to jump to conclusions;
(iii) a lack of 'discipline' in meetings – for example, members left meetings to make or take phone calls;
 (iv) a lack of commitment to the rules – for example, interrupting and speaking at the same time as others;
  (v) a preference for verbal rather than written instructions;
 (vi) a polychronic approach towards time.

The 'British' characteristics as seen by the Italians also caused concern:

  (i) an emphasis on procedures, rules and hierarchy;
 (ii) punctuality considered as a virtue;
(iii) a preference for the written word (agenda, minutes, etc.);
 (iv) a cautious, methodical approach;
  (v) at times coming across in an amateurish fashion – for example, using a style that was too informal, use of humour not appreciated, etc.;
 (vi) a monochronic approach towards time.

It was agreed that a further workshop would be held to brief both nationalities on each other's culture in order to assess style and perceptions of each other with a specific emphasis on their future meetings.

'Virtual' meetings

The attack on the Twin Towers in New York in September 2001 prompted an increase in the use of the 'virtual meeting'. It was considered cheaper, more cost-effective and, importantly, more secure to arrange conferences and meetings with people of different cultures in other companies and organizations around the world. With the increase in globalization for both diplomacy and business, more meetings are now becoming virtual conference calls. Such virtual meetings conducted via a telephone or video link have introduced stricter procedures to ensure maximum efficiency. Advances in technology now allow people to communicate by sharing information in real time. Such meetings can be arranged at relatively short notice, saving the expense of air travel and accommodation and the associated problems of jet lag. Immediacy is assured, but regard must be paid to differences in time zones when arranging virtual meetings, and in order for the meeting to be productive, an agenda should be agreed in advance. The conference call convener or moderator is the key figure in ensuring the smooth progression of the meeting. There is also a need for seriality, with participants ensuring they take turns to speak.

Many companies now use this facility regularly, in contrast to the 1990s, when technological problems, such as loss of signal, voice delay and relatively poor picture quality, acted as impediments to the use of such meetings. Security has been much improved by the use of private networks and picture quality has been greatly enhanced with the capability of using full wall displays and multimedia technology.

However, global virtual meetings present certain challenges, as team members need training to use the technology and in managing themselves. In a virtual meeting, the participants do not have any form of contact other than voice and/or visual and may not know each other personally. In addition, if English is used as the medium for the meeting, this can (as we have seen) disadvantage participants for whom English is not their mother tongue. This in turn puts added emphasis on clarity and brevity of contributions. Cultural differences must also be taken into account. There is a need to maximize the advantages of face-to-face meetings when sensitive and complex issues, privacy and confidentiality, and significant time differences are involved. The essential 'getting to know you' phase, small talk, informal contact and social interaction and networking, considered so important in some cultures, are in many cases best undertaken in face-to-face meetings, where the overall ambience is more conducive.

Tomalin (2012: 73) identifies the following key points regarding the successful running of virtual meetings and conference calls:

- greet everybody and check who is online;
- if necessary, do a quick round the table identification of each participant, which helps people become used to each other's voices;
- identify who will minute the discussion;

- ask speakers to identify themselves when they contribute;
- ask the chair to briefly summarize speakers' interventions in order to be clear that everything has been heard and understood and to ensure that the minutes reflect the conclusions accurately;
- at the end, summarize key action points to be undertaken by whom and when;
- say farewell and indicate when the conference is over.

Tomalin also identifies some of the key problems:

- extraneous noise – air conditioning, traffic, other people's conversations, jewellery knocking on the table or tapping on the keyboard can all cause distraction;
- silence – this is often out of respect for the seniority of other individuals taking part in the meeting or the speaker, but can cause problems, as the chair may wonder whether some participants have gone offline;
- speed and volume of delivery – too quiet, too loud or too fast can all cause problems of understanding.

In 'virtual' conferences, there are additional visual issues to consider:

- how you look – striped shirts, tops and ties may cause a strobing effect on the camera;
- the background – check that the wall behind the speakers sends the message you wish to convey; for example, does it display untidy or inappropriate images?;
- keep the conference table clear of unnecessary papers, cups and food;
- advanced video conference technology enables the camera to identify the voice of the speaker and to zoom in. However, the resulting shot may be of a number of people sitting close together, and in this situation it can be difficult to identify who is actually speaking. A simple hand gesture as the person begins to speak avoids this;
- people sitting on the periphery run the risk of being out of camera shot.

Summary

Below are key principles regarding the building and sustaining of multi-cultural teams:

- Agree a working structure from the outset.
- Select the most appropriate working language.
- Learn about the culture of the other members.
- Create a climate of trust.
- Draw on the strength of all members and develop cultural synergy.

- Recognize, accept and celebrate cultural diversity.
- Ensure top management support.
- Develop a sense of humour that is acceptable to all the team.
- Include members who have strengths in key functions following Belbin's research.

It is also important to recognize the advantages of multicultural groups:

- a greater spread of values and ideas and the potential for increased activity and innovation;
- more alternative points of view, new ways of looking at old problems;
- teaches patience, cultural sensitivity, humour and listening skills;
- provides excellent training in the need for clear verbal and non-verbal communication;
- reduces the likelihood of 'group think' because of cultural diversity and minimizes the risk of pressure for conformity;
- 'virtual' meetings offer the advantage of being more cost-effective if the circumstances are conducive to do so.

However, one must also recognize the disadvantages of multicultural groups:

- more time required to build trust and cultural understanding;
- the duration of meetings tends to be longer, with the resultant possibility of stress and fatigue;
- misunderstandings and frustration due to language problems;
- the need to maintain contact with members once the team has dispersed;
- more time needed for clarification; fine detail is harder to deal with in a second language;
- possible misunderstandings about the final agreement and future course of action;
- the richness of the diversity in the group can make the group dynamics more complex;
- can result in frustration, dissatisfaction and higher turnover of team members.

Regarding meetings, it is important not to assume that your way of running or participating is the same as in other cultures. It is advisable to find out in advance what the conventions are regarding the approach to the meeting, the use of agenda, procedures for decision making, recording agreement, taking the minutes and organizing follow-up measures.

The following are key factors for success in organizing intercultural meetings:

- detailed preparation;
- clear objectives;

- clarification of expectations;
- agenda – issued and agreed in advance to avoid surprises;
- timing – consider jet lag, different time zones and meal times;
- attendance – key players, senior observers;
- physical layout of the meeting room;
- language to be used, use of interpreters;
- selection of the chairperson;
- gaining consensus – unanimous or majority;
- socializing – breaks, formal and informal gatherings;
- follow-up – minutes, checking and evaluating progress.

References

Belbin, M. (1981) *Management Teams: Why They Succeed or Fail* (London: Butterworth Heinemann).

Cox, T. (1991) 'The Multicultural Organisation', *Academy of Management Executive* 5(2): 34–47.

Davies, G. (1992) 'Ganging-up. How to Build a Multinational Team', *Human Resources,* Spring: 40–3.

Dowling, P., Welch, D. and Schuler, R. (1999) *International Human Resource Management* (Cincinnati, OH: South Western College Publishing).

Hurn, B. and Jenkins, N. (2000) 'International Peer Group Development', *Industrial and Commercial Training* 32(4): 128–31.

Schutz, W. (1960) *The Interpersonal Underworld* (Palo Alto, CA: Science and Behaviour Books).

Tomalin, B. (2012) *Effective International Communication* (London: HarperCollins).

3i and Cranfield University (1992) *Special Survey 6: Attitudes to Managers and Companies in Europe* (Bedford: European Enterprise Centre, Cranfield School of Management).

Further reading

Belbin, M. (1996) *The Coming Shape of Organisation* (London: Butterworth Heinemann).

Brett, J., Behfar, K. and Ken, M. (2007 'Managing Multicultural Teams: Leadership and Managing People', *Harvard Business Review* 84(11): 84–91.

Claire, B. and Aqeel Timizi, S. (2008) *Effective Multicultural Teams: Theory and Practice* (New York: Springer).

Earley, P. and Gibson, C. (2002) *Multinational Work Teams: A New Perspective* (Mahwah, NJ: Lawrence Erlbaum Associates).

Gupta, S. (2008) 'Mine the Potential of Multicultural Teams', *Human Resource Magazine* (Society for Human Resource Management, October).

Guy, V. and Mattock, J. (1993) *The New International Manager: An Action Guide for Cross-Cultural Business* (London: Kogan Page).

Hill, C. (2009) *International Business: Competing in the Global Marketplace* (London: McGraw-Hill).

Jondt, F. (ed.) (2004) *Intercultural Communication: A Global Reader* (London: Sage Publications).

Joynt, P. and Morton, B. (2000) *The Global HR Manager* (London: CIPD).

Lewis, R. (2011) *When Cultures Collide* (London: Nicholas Brealey Publishing).

Melhman, A. and Trotman, T. (2005) *Training International Managers* (Farnham: Gower).

Mullins, J. (2005) *Management and Organizational Behaviour*, 7th edn (Upper Saddle River, NJ: Prentice Hall).

Phillips, N. (1992) *Managing International Teams* (London: Pearson Education).

Shapiro, L., Young, M. and Glinow, V. (2005) *Managing Multinational Teams: Global Perspectives* (Oxford: Elsevier).

9
The Effect of Culture on International Negotiations

Summary

Definitions
Cultural aspects
Protocol
Shared experiences
Use of humour
Choice of language
Use of interpreters and translators
Gift-giving and hospitality
Importance of 'face'
Assessment of cultural influences
Listening skills
Agents and mediators
Qualities of an international negotiator
Selected national negotiating styles
Training

Introduction

This chapter examines the impact of culture on the parties concerned in international negotiations, including diplomacy and business. Such negotiations can be heavily influenced by differing cultural conventions, values, assumptions and perceptions. The discussion here looks at the advantages to be gained by carrying out some form of cultural assessment of the parties involved as a vital part of pre-negotiation preparation, in particular assessing the importance of communicating style, choice of working language, decision making, etiquette and cultural values. Examples are included from international relations and the world of business.

The chapter also highlights the key cross-cultural skills required in international negotiations and international business, and provides examples of good practice from a range of cultures. People working in the international community, whether with multinational companies, in joint ventures, mergers, as members of trade missions, with the UN, the EU, NATO, the WHO and other regional organizations, with NGOs or in embassies, consulates or High Commissions, will inevitably be involved in some form of negotiation with people of other cultures.

Definitions

The Charter of the UN states that: 'All members should settle their international disputes by peaceful means in such a manner that international peace and security and justice are not endangered.'

A practical definition of international negotiating is the process whereby people of different nationalities resolve actual or potential conflicts or disputes by considered dialogue on an approved agenda. Parties with different interests are brought together in the hope of finding common ground.

Cohen refers to negotiations in international relations as: 'Diplomatic negotiations in its strictest sense consist of a process of communication between states seeking to arrive at a mutually acceptable outcome on some issue or issues of shared concern' (1999: 9). Regarding international relations, negotiation has been described as: 'Getting to "yes" without going to war' (Fisher and Ury, 2003: 21–2). This form of negotiation is a low-context problem-solving approach developed in the Harvard Program on Negotiation. Relationships tend to become entangled with the problem. Fisher and Ury advocate separating relationships from the problem and dealing directly with the people, focusing on interests, not positions and whenever possible going for a 'win/win' approach.

Negotiating across national borders differs greatly from negotiating within one's own culture in the domestic marketplace. A number of new factors have to be considered:

- different national negotiating styles influenced by culture;
- changes in ideology (for example, the collapse of the Soviet Union) and the moves from a command economy to a market economy in Eastern Europe;
- the reduction in trade barriers encouraged by the WTO and the expansion of regional groupings, in particular the EU;
- cross-border differences, including taxation, currency, labour relations and the conduct of business;
- changes of government, international terrorism and concern for security and the environment.

This chapter will concentrate mainly on the first point mentioned in the above list. In particular, negotiators need to be aware of the negotiating style of people of other cultures, while at the same time developing a style appropriate to their own personal strengths and those of their own culture.

Building relationships and trust	Communication styles
Gaining consensus	Decision making
Time sensitivity	Setting agenda
Face-saving issues	Power distance
Status and hierarchy	Level of participation

Figure 9.1   Cultural aspects affecting negotiating

Protocol

The observance of protocol and agreed procedures is an essential factor for successful meetings and negotiations. It gives a recognized structure to the proceedings and provides an agreed code of conduct which should help reduce intercultural friction and misunderstanding. Aspects of protocol can include correct seating arrangements with due respect for seniority, the presentation of business cards and appropriate dress. It also includes procedures such as methods of voting, addressing remarks through the chair, the composition of committees, any limitations on the times allotted to speakers and the production of the minutes at the conclusion, as well as any official *communiqués*.

Although there are generally recognized standards of official protocol in international meetings, for example, within the UN, there is no standardized international etiquette. In British culture, our traditions and values have produced an accepted code of behaviour. This is not, however, necessarily transferable to another culture, and cultural mistakes are inevitable for the culturally unwary. Such areas include degrees of punctuality, politeness, informality or formality and exchanging gifts, as the same occasion will require a different code of behaviour depending on the cultural situation. This is discussed later in the chapter.

Shared experiences

Cohen contends that cultural strangers cannot rely on shared experiences of family values, religion, education, national history, traditions or beliefs as: 'Cultural meanings are basically subjective meanings shared by members of a particular cultural group' (1999: 27). Shared experiences can include formal discussions at lunches, dinners, receptions and tour invitations, which provide opportunities for developing interpersonal relationships.

People who operate in the international community may have a number of shared interests or experiences, for example, hobbies, sport and children studying abroad. These can be researched as part of the preparation for negotiations and can be seen as a form of 'cultural shorthand'. They are extremely useful in preliminary, informal discussions, as 'small talk' or as an 'ice-breaker'. They can therefore be used to advantage, particularly in the 'getting to know you' phase, and are most suitable when dealing with cultures where business is considered personal.

In certain cultures where building relationships and mutual trust are initially more important in the early stages of a negotiating process than decisions about agreeing a deal or obtaining a satisfactory outcome, such experiences are invaluable in helping to develop good working relationships. However, the attempt to use shared experiences should be conducted with great care, as it is important to check the appropriateness and relevance of these experiences and whether they are fully understood. Once trust is established, it is easier to discuss openly if cultural differences might be affecting the issues.

The family and, indeed, the extended family are highly valued in many cultures (for example, in Africa and the Middle East), and therefore showing interest in the well-being of one's counterpart's family is important when developing successful relationships and mutual trust. These examples of the value of shared experiences are useful in high-context cultures where the emphasis is initially more on developing personal relationships and less on the detail of the desired agreement. In low-context cultures, in contrast, creating relationships is less important in the initial stages and only becomes more important when final agreement is made and contracts are signed.

Heads of state often meet in an informal, relaxed venue before the main negotiations commence. The President of the USA often takes VIP visitors to Camp David. In July 2004, when President Vladimir Putin visited George W. Bush at the Bush family compound in Kennebunkport, they went fishing, a sport enjoyed by both men. This was designed to help thaw relations between Russia and the USA over the US plans for a European missile shield. President Putin said that he had enjoyed 'the warm and homely atmosphere' at Kennebunkport that 'went way beyond' what he had expected.

Humour

The use of humour as an 'ice-breaker', particularly at the beginning of negotiations, can often be useful. It is designed to help people relax, but is effective only if it is clearly understood and does not cause any embarrassment or offence. It is therefore important to be fully aware of which subjects are taboo, particularly cultural and politically sensitive areas. Gaffes made in public at the beginning of a session can be difficult to overcome and their residual effect can be longlasting. It is therefore essential to research this area carefully and avoid any jokes that may not translate into the desired meaning or that are culturally unacceptable. It is always worth remembering the old adage that 'Humour is usually what gets lost in translation'.

As we have seen in Chapter 8, the use of humour in the more formal part of meetings is not always acceptable. There is a fine balance between making people laugh and relaxed and sharing the humour, and for all this to appear to some as lacking seriousness of purpose.

Language

> Language is a matter of custom, courtesy and taboo as well as meaning. A concept that appears simple to one mentality can cause confusion in another. (Binyon, 2001)

As discussed in Chapter 4, English is practically universally accepted as the foremost working international language, although it faces challenges in this respect from Mandarin and Spanish. Difficulties with language and interpretation can cause problems in negotiation – see, for example, the exchange between the former British Prime Minister Margaret Thatcher and the then President of France, Francois Mitterrand, who appeared not fully to understand a point, when Thatcher said at an EU meeting: 'We are using the same words, so why do we have so much misunderstanding?' The gist of Mitterrand's reply was that he was French, but that Thatcher always insisted on speaking English. Not everyone speaks English fluently or indeed necessarily wants to speak English.

Cohen (1999) emphasizes that cross-cultural differences occur in the meaning of such words as 'justice', 'sovereignty', 'leader', 'corruption', 'democracy' and 'intervention'. A word or phrase meaning one thing in one culture can mean something very different in another culture. A classic example is the emotive word 'crusade', used by many in the West without any historical significance – for example, 'a crusade against poverty'. In a very different context, namely the war in Iraq, the word 'crusade' was seen as extremely provocative because of its historical connotation by Arab countries. As Szaly states: 'The idea itself does not really travel, only the code – the meaning that a person attributes to the words received will come from his own mind. His interpretation is determined by his own frame of reference, his ideas, interests, past experiences, etc.' (1981: 135).

Michael Binyon (2001) quotes the case of a fast and essentially literal translation of the new use of an everyday word which has become a political cliché. He refers to the US proposal to use new 'smart sanctions' against Saddam Hussein. However, the Arabic translation was that 'smart' meant 'intelligent' and 'clever' rather than 'technically more accurately targeted'. This gave rise to the implication that the existing sanctions were stupid.

Diplomacy is said to be the art of linguistic invention. In diplomacy, language is sometimes referred to as 'diplomatspeak'. This is an international code of language perfected over centuries. It is very often deliberately opaque, using jargon and words such as 'appropriate', 'apposite', 'full and frank discussion', 'matters of mutual interest' and recently 'coalition of the willing'. Often 'yes' may mean 'perhaps' and 'perhaps' may mean 'no', but to say 'no' is undiplomatic.

The word 'sorry' is associated in some Eastern cultures with blame, loss of 'face' and even humiliation and guilt. As a result, the Japanese have found difficulty in finding a phrase that expresses an apology for some of the events in the Second World War which does not convey humiliation when used in Japanese.

It should be emphasized that when we are using English as native speakers, we should make every effort to use clear, simple and unambiguous English, remembering to:

- avoid slang, jargon, metaphors and acronyms;
- speak more slowly than usual without appearing patronizing;
- avoid complex sentence structure and the use of double negatives;
- use both verbal and written summaries as appropriate;
- use simple visual aids to reinforce key points and have copies available for distribution.

The use of interpreters and translators

As discussed in Chapter 8, in international meetings it may be necessary to use interpreters and translators. It is essential to use individuals who are well qualified, with experience in similar negotiations, particularly if the subject matter is highly technical. In all cases, the interpreters should be fully briefed in advance of the actual negotiations and given sufficient background information to help them 'read into the situation'. They should understand the business culture and, in particular, the corporate culture of the organization with which they are working. In addition, they must fully respect commercial confidentiality. Both interpreters and translators should also be fully familiar with regional dialects if they are used. In all cases when using interpreters, speakers should always address counterparts directly (that is, face to face) rather than the interpreter. Failure to do so shows disrespect.

When using interpreters, there is always the danger of mistranslation and loss of personal impact, particularly when the speaker has a high standard of rhetoric and personal charisma. Victor (1992: 141) cautions that as interpretation is often hard work, speakers should do all they can to lessen the burden on the interpreter by having frequent breaks in the proceedings, keeping the dialogue as simple as possible and injecting pauses at appropriate intervals.

Interpreters should also be available during both informal and formal social gatherings. Translators will be required as part of the negotiation's secretariat to prepare translations at key points during the negotiations, either as summaries of action taken at various points or to translate extracts from legal documents and technical data if this has not been done in advance. Cohen (1999) stresses the problems, both linguistic and cultural, that can arise when translating from one language to another, in particular in the case of subtle cultural nuances.

Gift-giving and hospitality

This area can be a cultural minefield. In the British culture, expensive gift-giving is less used than in many other cultures and there are often corporate company guidelines as to what is ethically acceptable. In many cases, companies require all gifts to be reported and approval must be given before acceptance if they are over a certain value. However, in many cultures, gift-giving is standard practice. Failure to either accept or reciprocate is considered at least as bad manners and at worst as an insult.

It is therefore essential to know the customs of a country, especially the social etiquette. In some countries, there are strict anti-corruption laws and to offer gifts to local nationals could potentially cause trouble for both parties. However, gifts that symbolize the status of your company and the importance of the impending deal, preferably an item characteristic of your local area or one that displays your logo, may well be permissible.

In certain cultures, before gifts are considered, it is necessary to check which are acceptable. This is particularly important if flowers are to be given because, for example, in France and Italy, chrysanthemums are given only for funerals. It is advisable not to give a clock in China as it gives the impression you wish to end the relationship. In cultures where 'face' is a sensitive issue, one should not give a lavish or expensive gift if it may cause a problem for the receiver to reciprocate in value. In Japan there are etiquette books that detail the suitable gifts for a variety of occasions. In any case, in Japan gifts are never opened in public. In other cultures, for example, Arab and many Western cultures, gifts can be opened in public, thus providing the opportunity for the recipient to graciously thank the giver. There are also social conventions as to whether gifts should be wrapped or unwrapped, and the colour of the wrapping paper can be significant.

Cultural sensitivities also apply to hospitality, although it is customary in all cultures to entertain business clients as part of the overall programme for the negotiations. This provides the opportunity to build closer relationships. Age and seniority should be taken into account when organizing social occasions, in particular the seating arrangements at formal meals.

The importance of 'face'

'Face' is a very important factor to be considered in international negotiations. Vic Feather, when General Secretary of the Trades Union Congress (TUC) in the UK, considered that a means of saving 'face' should be preserved in defeat. He is quoted as saying: 'Always leave the other fellow the bus fare home.'

'Face' is valued in all cultures, but its particular importance as a prime cause of cultural sensitivity has already been stressed. In many Eastern cultures, for example, Thai, Chinese and Japanese cultures, 'face' is the way in which one is regarded by others. It assumes central importance in Asian cultures and has a major effect on behaviour. In the case of the Chinese, 'face' ('mianzi') relates to a person's image and status within the social structure. 'Face' is also closely associated with trust, loyalty, reputation, competence and obligation issues. The Chinese have two dimensions of 'face'. The first, 'lien', is normally ascribed. Cardon and Scott (2003) state that a person who has no 'lien' is a social outcast. The second, 'mien tzu', is more achieved than ascribed. A person who lacks 'mien tzu' is considered to have low status.

Not giving 'face' to a person is seen by the Chinese as denying the person pride and dignity, and, as a result, the Chinese will usually refrain from an aggressive stance in negotiating. Indeed, the adoption of 'face-saving' or 'face-giving' behaviour in conflict situations is valued as an important means of maintaining group harmony. Restoring 'face' is very important in 'face'-related situations in order to restore a person's lost self-esteem. Fisher and Ury consider that: 'Face-saving reflects a person's need to reconcile the stand he takes on a negotiation or agreement with his principles and with his past words and deeds' (Fisher and Ury 2003: 29).

Those who have difficulty understanding the working language chosen for the negotiations may lose the sense of the point being dealt with, but will not admit this, nor will they ask for elucidation in order to retain 'face'. The situation can be compounded if other people think they have in fact understood and that their silence implies agreement.

In order to avoid cultural problems that involve 'face', the skilled international negotiator should follow these guidelines:

- check the importance of hierarchy and status in the other culture;
- use correct names, titles and formal greetings;
- remember one's obligations if acting as the host;
- always show pride in one's company and nationality, and extend this respect to one's counterpart;
- avoid backing the other party into a corner or situation from which it will lose 'face' by trying to extricate itself.

Assessment of cultural influences

Those preparing for international negotiations should carry out a cultural review (a form of cultural audit of the other cultures involved in negotiating) in order to help increase one's options. This aims to help avoid any pitfalls which might be caused by the lack of awareness of cultural sensitivities, customs and values, and improves the participant's ability to understand any cultural nuances in communication. Such an audit is useful in high-lighting potential areas of conflict or cultural misunderstanding and helps build up a picture of likely behaviour and reactions. It should consider the following from the viewpoint of one's own culture and those of the other people with whom one is negotiating.

Communication style – direct/indirect	Level of assertiveness
Chosen working language	Risk taking
Attitude towards time – punctuality	Relationship building – trust, confidence
Customs and habits	Work style – formal/informal
Non-verbal signals – gestures, silence	Socializing – food, drink, visits
Attitude towards status, age, hierarchy	Protocol – titles, greeting, seating, business cards, gift-giving
Decision-making style	'Face' – giving and receiving

Figure 9.2   Assessment of cultural influences

Listening skills

As discussed in Chapter 5, listening has been rightly described as a 'process of self-denial'. In international negotiations, good listening skills are of vital importance. The participants in complex negotiations, often in a foreign language, need to concentrate to detect the subtle nuances. This requires focusing on the speakers without interruption and interpreting the different frames of reference, as well as evaluating what is said. Careful listening and observation of the other party's views and body language require much patience and tolerance. It is important to adopt a non-judgmental approach and concentrate on any signals being passed by hand gesture, body move-ment or facial expression. If you have carried out your cultural assessment, you will be more able to understand their significance.

The Japanese listen very attentively and they use periods of controlled silence to good effect for both business and social interaction. Like the Chinese, the Japanese follow the virtues of silence: those who know do not speak – those who speak do not know. This silence is used for contem-plation, but it can be mistaken, particularly by Westerners, as showing a lack of understanding. This silence often makes Westerners feel uncomfortable and produces a tendency for them to break the silence and even unwittingly to make concessions. There is a Russian proverb that says that 'one should not hurry to reply, but hurry to listen'. This was discussed in detail in Chapter 8.

Use of agents and mediators

In some cultures (for example, Arab cultures), negotiations are very often conducted through agents or mediators. Arabs following Islamic traditions often use mediators to settle disputes. Mediation is also valued in the collectivist cultures of Southeast Asia, for example, in Singapore and Indonesia. The use of mediators helps protect the honour, dignity and self-respect of all parties and aims to avoid any direct confrontation between the parties. In addition, it avoids placing either party in a situation in which it has to show weakness, lose 'face' or admit defeat. When there is little familiarity with the other culture, negotiators may use an agent or advisor who is suitably familiar with the cultures of both parties involved in the negotiations.

Mediators may be most helpful when they are able to encourage one party in the negotiations to agree to adopt the cultural approach of the other party or (which can also be of mutual benefit) to follow the cultural approach of the mediator's own home culture. Mediation has the advantages of generally being less costly, less time-consuming and less adversarial than arbitration, and is more likely to produce greater satisfaction for both parties. It is based on procedural rules, requires the willingness of both parties to a dispute to receive help and may resolve the root causes of an ongoing dispute by focusing on basic issues rather than on positions. (Lewicki, 2008: 473–84).

The following list provides examples of mediation:

- The US Senator George Mitchell and the Canadian General Chatelaine mediated in the protracted discussions regarding the decommissioning of IRA weapons and the resulting peace process in Northern Ireland.
- The Dayton Peace Accords of 14 December 1995, signed after negotiations in Dayton, Ohio lasting almost a month, which created the Federation of Bosnia-Herzegovina and the Serbian Republic (Republika Srpska), an example of multitrack diplomacy with the USA acting as the mediator.
- The Camp David Accords in 1978 between Egypt and Israel, again with the USA acting as mediator.
- The warring political factions in Kenya in 2007 finally resolved their differences after Kofi Annan, the former UN Secretary-General, acted as the mediator assisted by the Centre for Humanitarian Dialogue (CHD), a Swiss-based organization of mediators.

The agenda

As in meetings, an agenda listing the points that have been agreed to be discussed should be issued to all concerned before the actual negotiations begin. This provides a structure to proceedings and helps signpost the stages in the negotiating process. It is also valuable when there are possible language difficulties and, above all, should contain no surprises if trust is to be maintained.

Qualities of an international negotiator

The fundamental requirement in an international negotiator remains proven technical and professional expertise. The following additional skills go across cultures. They include:

- listening skills – the need for patience, tolerance and a non-judgmental attitude;
- sensitivity to cultural differences – development of adaptability;
- orientation towards people – development of interpersonal skills;
- a willingness to use team assistance – team skills, consensus and synergy;
- high levels of self-esteem – professional competence, integrity and confidence;
- high aspirations and ethical standards (Adler, 1999: 197).

International negotiating fundamentals

If we are seeking fundamental guidelines for international negotiating, those given in Figure 9.3 below are considered highly desirable.

```
┌─────────────────────────────────────┐
│         Hard on issues               │
│         Soft on people               │
│   If possible, go for win/win result │
└─────────────────────────────────────┘
```

Figure 9.3   Fundamentals of negotiating

Characteristics of selected national negotiating styles

Much of the following is derived from the authors' own experiences in working with business people from the cultures concerned and from discussions with international business postgraduates and with colleagues from overseas.

The British negotiating style

British business culture is individualist, generally masculine and competitive. It often displays initial resistance to change and is by nature conservative in outlook, with a sense of restraint and dislike of the ostentatious. The British prefer to negotiate in English as the working language as relatively few managers are fluent in other languages. This may make them complacent and less inclined to make an effort to learn about other cultures, as many foreign business people speak English fluently.

Because English is an extremely flexible language, verbal subtlety has a high social value. Business communication relies on extensive use of email and the telephone, but discussions are often followed up by a written summary which becomes the record of the points agreed upon and of further action.

The British express a willingness to be flexible in negotiations and are prepared to make some compromises if necessary in an attempt to produce a mutually acceptable agreement. If meetings cannot reach agreement on a particular point, the task may be given to a specially formed committee to resolve matters. Indeed, the British liking for committees can appear in contrast to their undoubted individualist outlook. They are less comfortable with concepts, but prefer to be pragmatic doers, asking practical questions like 'how exactly are we going to do this?' rather than 'what should be our final objective?'.

The British generally show little emotion and often appear rather reserved, with relatively little use of body language, although they place importance on direct eye contact. However, experience in the global economy has changed their approach and they are now more expressive, although many of them are still uncomfortable with outward displays of emotion and value their personal space.

Despite the apparent reserve of the British, humour is widely used, both as a business and a social lubricant, and is employed as an 'ice-breaker' to reduce potential confrontation or to speed up discussion when excessive formality is in danger of slowing things down. Humour often includes self-deprecation, which is puzzling to many foreigners and is often specific to British society, and therefore does not translate well.

The British, although less impatient than the Americans, see meetings as a process whereby decisions can be made. All participants are free to express an opinion, even on matters outside their own particular sphere of knowledge. Negotiating team members are chosen as much for their ability to work as members of a team as for their specialist expertise. They often use deliberate understatement as a negotiating ploy. They may attempt to extend an agenda by adding 'any other business' (AOB) at the end, which is not always appreciated by other cultures, particularly those who are adverse to any surprises while a meeting is being conducted.

The British, although themselves law-abiding, dislike excessive regulations, central control and bureaucracy, and remain strong advocates of free trade. They have a strong sense of history and civic commitment. This is reflected in their negotiating style.

Business titles are often not used in conversation and first names are used frequently, although less so than by Americans. Business meetings begin and end with brief, light conversation and meetings are generally conducted in a relatively relaxed manner.

The British culture is still mainly masculine in most professions, although women do reach high positions in some sectors, for example, education, health care, fashion and social services. Legally women in business have equal opportunities, but there is still a 'glass ceiling' as a barrier to advancement in some professions.

Socializing in British business includes having an informal lunch together or, more formally, a dinner. It also includes corporate hospitality, often provided at sporting events, for example, the races at Ascot, tennis at Wimbledon and football at Wembley Stadium. Business discussions may also take place informally, such as on the golf course. The British tend to work longer hours than their European counterparts and often commute long distances to work. However, they usually try to have high levels of separation between their work and their private family life.

The American negotiating style

The USA is an example of the 'melting pot' of cultures, with its core culture rooted in Anglo-Saxon and predominantly North European cultures. However, there is an increasing Hispanic influence, particularly in the southern states. American culture is mainly monochronic, individualist and low context.

The USA remains a strong 'can-do' culture, which is action-orientated, dynamic, competitive and optimistic. The culture is backed by high technology and is risk taking in nature, where anything is considered possible and is accepted as a challenge to be overcome.

Communication style is direct, straightforward and to the point, all of which can at times be seen by others as blunt, abrupt and impolite. What has to be said is clearly stated – it is 'straight from the shoulder' and Americans do not 'beat about the bush'. They will disagree firmly and this can cause embarrassment to other cultures. American presentations are confident, highly focused and professionally delivered with the aim of making the maximum impact. Negotiators are well prepared and see meetings as a process whereby decisions are made.

Humour is often used by Americans as an 'ice-breaker' to reduce tension, but at times it is not always appreciated by other cultures as it is very much American culture-based. It is, however, direct and lighthearted, without the irony and innuendo so frequently encountered in British humour.

Negotiations are carried out in a relatively informal manner, with any member able to express a view, but when the time comes for decision making, such members will tend to defer to the senior members in their team. Americans see negotiations as an exercise in problem solving, usually through a process of 'give-and-take', based on respective strengths rather than as a process for sounding out views and gathering information. They are basically task-oriented, negotiate hard in the belief that there is always a solution and will explore all options in order to overcome an impasse. They do not show much emotion, but put a high value on direct eye contact. They show respect for deadlines and schedules, and performance is measured by 'getting the job done'. They see time as a resource to be maximized. As a result, they are often risk takers and are therefore more prepared to move early on a deal.

Americans prefer agreements to be confirmed in writing, although when negotiating, they will accept a 'yes in principle', providing there is a clear action plan to work out the details later. They are generally uncomfortable with lulls or silences during negotiations, often become impatient and do not have good listening skills themselves. They are also uncomfortable with ambiguity and at times lack cross-cultural awareness and sensitivity. However, with the spread of globalization, they have learned to develop their cross-cultural fluency.

'Americans usually attack a complex negotiation task sequentially – that is they separate the issues and settle them one at a time' (Graham and Herberger, 1983: 164). As a result, they are prone to make concessions at intermediate stages before the final agreement.

For Americans in business, entertaining and socializing are often informal. Unlike many cultures, they will invite their counterparts to their homes, but in general they tend to separate their work life and their social life.

The French negotiating style

The French business negotiating style is founded to a large extent on a strong, intellectual Cartesian tradition that prizes rational and logical thinking. The French thinking process is therefore often deductive, beginning with an idea or a theory and proceeding from the general to particular cases, in contrast to the opposite, inductive approach. This means that at times French negotiators appear to place too much emphasis on abstract concepts at the expense of facts and upon principles at the expense of interests. Intelligent discussion on issues is valued for its own sake. The French see no reason to compromise if their logic is undefeated.

French culture is individualistic, tending to be feminine by Hofstede's definition, with relatively strong power distance and fairly high uncertainty avoidance. They have a strong tendency to create hierarchies, bureaucracy and systems to help avoid uncertainty.

The education system places great store on higher education, the 'grandes écoles' and the 'polytechniques'. There is fierce competition for entry to these elite institutions and this elite membership provides the opportunity to gain authority and advantage in the bureaucratic hierarchies, particularly the civil service.

The French are always well briefed and prepared for meetings and negotiations. They consider that decision making should be concentrated in the hands of competent, professionally qualified individuals. They prefer a recognized hierarchy and see a team as a collection of specialists chosen for their proven competence in a certain area, under the overall direction of an accepted leader. They prefer to establish early on the underlying principles and structure and then proceed to the relevant facts. As regards coming to an agreement, the French will strive to adopt the best idea and will persist in upholding their views; as a result, they are unwilling to make major concessions. The use of humour is not actively encouraged in formal business meetings, unless it displays clever wit.

As regards language, French negotiators will often speak English well. It is important, however, to recognize that both English and French are truly international languages and both nations feel strongly about the importance of their own language. The French are particularly sensitive about the anglicizing of French words. If possible, foreigners should at least be prepared to conduct part of the proceedings in French, as this will be much appreciated and might help gain an advantage over English-only speakers. French business meetings are less frequent than in the UK. They are formal in nature, with strict rules of procedure and an established chairperson. At less formal meetings, it is quite usual for people to leave in the middle, make telephone calls and talk among themselves.

As regards business socializing, the French take meals in good-quality restaurants very seriously. If you are invited, it indicates that business is progressing well and should be similarly reciprocated. The British approach of coffee and sandwiches at the conference table and their apparent enthusiasm to press on with the meeting may give quite different signals compared to the French, for whom wining and dining are very much part of the business process. There is a clear distinction between personal and professional relationships and employees generally do not meet after work to socialize.

The German negotiating style

The Germans are meticulous in their preparation for meetings and negotiations. They are well briefed and expect the same from their counterparts. They also believe that objectives should be clear before the meeting. Business meetings run to a strict agenda agreed before the meeting with relatively little small talk. They are often scheduled well in advance in order to permit careful preparation. The Germans like to come straight to the point, rely on a structured approach and attempt to resolve, if possible, any differences before the actual meeting. Senior people will tend to dominate the proceedings and members are reluctant to make a contribution unless they are well prepared and well versed in the particular topic at hand. Their negotiators are well qualified in their area of expertise and expect the same status from those with whom they are negotiating. Most managers have degrees from a university or 'Fachschule' (technical high school) and many are qualified engineers who have higher professional status and visibility than, for example, their counterparts in the UK. Professional rank and status is usually based on an individual's achievement and expertise in a given field. Academic titles and background are important and should also be given due recognition. A Herr Doktor or Frau Doktor (not medical) is a person of distinction and should be formally addressed as such.

One of the most important values is order (*Ordnung*). The Germans have a very structured way of working, which is supported by rules and procedures. This approach does not always leave room for flexibility. They have a linear approach to work, with the aim of completing one set of actions before starting another. This marks them as much more monochronic than polychronic. Their business approach is cautious and they require detailed information and facts as a basis for decision making. These are critically and logically analysed before decisions are made. For a German, for an argument to be convincing, it must be *schlüssig*, that is, complete and logical. They are tough negotiators and will have thought in advance of counter-arguments and prepared second lines of attack.

The German business culture, like that of the Americans, is efficient and task-related, with the aim of achieving the task in the minimum amount of time possible. The adherence to timetables, schedules and deadlines is important. Personal networks assume a lesser role in German business culture than in some other cultures. The German communication style is direct, sometimes appearing rather blunt, and at times can be seen as confrontational. This is not intended to cause offence, but is basically an expression of their desire to solve problems relatively quickly and efficiently. They place more emphasis on written than oral communication, and information tends to be 'top-down', often on a 'need-to-know' basis.

The German attitude to time is certainly monochronic. Punctuality is considered an essential virtue and Germans will arrive well before a meeting in order to start on time. On arrival, Germans will shake hands with each other, and those attending from other countries should follow this approach.

Germans tend to work long hours and to separate their social life from their work life. It can therefore often take more time to build personal relationships than in other more open cultures. On the other hand, relationships that are made tend to be longlasting. Germans generally have a high regard for privacy and personal space. It is wrong to say that they do not have a sense of humour, as German humour can often be more subtle than, for example, British or American humour. However, they treat business seriously and humour is far less frequently used as an 'ice-breaker'. Germans do not appreciate self-deprecation and flippancy, but in social occasions after work is over, they enjoy humour as much as other cultures.

German culture is masculine and individualist with high uncertainty avoidance and is at the lower end of the power-distance scale. Their culture values reliability, dependability and quality. Theirs is a results-oriented approach, based to a large extent on a strong work ethic and good industrial relations. They operate within a well-defined hierarchy, with clear responsibilities and distinctions between personal positions and roles. Germany is a Technik-oriented culture; note the slogan 'Vorsprung durch Technik', which means advancement through technology, as befits the leading manufacturing country in Europe. A high value is therefore placed on technical skills, both at university and technical schools and in training. Managers, although appearing to be somewhat paternalistic, have good working relationships with their workers. As a result of good employee welfare and social responsibility, trust and cooperation are reciprocated.

Many German managers have a good grasp of English. However, German is the most widely spoken first language in the EU at present. It is also the official language in Austria and is widely used in Switzerland. Germans have great respect for foreigners who speak good German.

The Russian negotiating style

Churchill described Russia as: 'A riddle wrapped in a mystery inside an enigma.' To some extent, this remains true. Russia has a business culture that differs from the Western pattern and is, in some respects, more Asian in its origin than European, though since the collapse of communism and the Soviet Empire, it has been increasingly exposed to Western business influence. However, many of Russia's differences are rooted in its historical past and the wide diversity of its peoples. Although Russia has espoused some of the aspects of the market economy, central government and residual bureaucracy still retain a major influence on Russia's business practices.

'Dusha' or 'soul' still remains central to everyday behaviour, which means that personal relationships and mutual trust form a strong basis for successful business. However, in recent years, renewed national confidence and the economic strength of Russia's energy resources have given the Russians an increased economic advantage and have contributed to a tough negotiating stance that aims to gain concessions. This is particularly apparent in the negotiations over the exploitation of natural resources such as oil and gas reserves.

The Russian Federation remains a relatively collectivist rather than an individualist culture and this is still reflected in current business practices. There is a generally relaxed attitude towards time, although it is on balance more monochronic than polychronic, and a few minutes' delay or lateness is of relatively little importance. Business cards are essential, usually with one side in English and the other in Russian. Small talk and shared experiences, which normally involve talking about the family, personal matters and sport, are customary before getting down to business and are much appreciated. Gifts are exchanged and usually represent the status of the company and the importance of the impending business.

There is a definite hierarchical structure in Russian business practices, with the result that actual decision making is often made at a high level. Showing respect for seniority and acknowledging this hierarchical structure is vital for establishing and maintaining strong business relationships. Much value is placed on written documents, including memoranda of understanding, technical specifications and contracts. Presentations are well prepared and negotiating positions are carefully planned and orchestrated.

Russians favour good eye contact. They prefer to have a degree of informality in negotiations which aims to produce a relaxed atmosphere. Physical contact during business meetings, such as a hand on the arm, is taken as a positive sign. There is no word for 'privacy' in Russian, so Russians do not require so much social space. However, their communication style can at times appear rather blunt and direct. They have respect for counterparts who are well prepared and who show evidence of their professional experience. Meetings are often protracted and seating is usually hierarchical. They can be subject to interruptions and often do not keep strictly to time. Patience is important as Russians may vary their tactics in an attempt to win concessions before considering any form of compromise.

The Indian negotiating style

It must be emphasized that regionalism, religion, language and caste are all factors that must be taken into account when doing business in India. English is widely used as the main working language, although the government recognizes Hindi as the official language of India and, in addition, some states have different official languages. Translators are seldom required, but it can be very useful to have the support of an intermediary to ease a way through both local and government bureaucracy. Although there are many regional dialects, educated Indians mostly speak very good English. However, their use of English contains in places a mixture of English and Hindi, sometimes called 'Hinglish' (as discussed in Chapter 4), where words have different meanings. India is a multicultural, multiethnic and multilingual society, and its large cities are truly a 'melting pot' of cultures.

Building relationships is a vital part of Indian business culture as Indians prefer to deal with those they know and trust. It is therefore essential to form a good personal and working relationship with any prospective partner. Hindus themselves are very tolerant of diversity, both within their own traditions and outside them, as it is part of the Hindu belief that all religions are different paths towards the same goal. They are prepared to take risks in order to be innovative and display considerable business acumen, which have made them successful entrepreneurs both in Asia and in the European market, an example of the latter being the global giant Tata Group.

Hierarchy plays a key role in Indian business culture, as Indian society still operates within a framework of strict hierarchy that defines a person's role and status in the social order. Names indicate an Indian's background – for example, a Singh will always be a Sikh, while the suffix 'jee' (as in, for example, Banerjee) is a sign of a high caste. Although the caste system was officially abolished in 1947, it still exists at different levels. Women are now to be seen in more senior appointments in companies, although the position of women in the economy is still relatively weak. Indians like titles and status, and due deference is given to those in authority.

Punctuality is expected, although Indians are not truly monochronic. However, the responsibilities of the extended family may take precedence, so last-minute changes of personnel are possible. Meetings should be arranged well in advance and, if possible, should avoid the heat by scheduling between October and March. Excessive bureaucracy can make life difficult for business, particularly regarding taxation and labour laws. Business negotiations are often protracted and decisions may have to be made at the highest level.

Indians dislike high-pressure negotiating tactics and usually try to avoid any form of confrontation. Wherever possible, they seek outcomes which will please all parties and therefore will often be prepared to accept compromises. Criticism and disagreement should always be expressed only in the most diplomatic language. Indians have a dislike of saying 'no' as it may be considered impolite and cause offence. However, it is always important to listen to their response to your question. If expressions such as 'we'll see' or 'I will try' are used, it may be that they are actually saying 'no'. Indian negotiators exercise control over their outward emotions and show respect for the other party. However, they are patient but tenacious negotiators and are prepared to put their position both eloquently and persistently.

When doing business in India, etiquette at meetings requires a handshake, although many Indians themselves use the 'namaste'. This occurs when the palms of the hand are brought together at chest level with a slight bow of the head. Using the 'namaste' is a sign that a foreigner is making an attempt to show an understanding of Indian etiquette. Business cards are exchanged at the first meeting and should be translated on one side into Hindi, more as a sign of respect than of linguistic necessity. One should receive and give a business card with the right hand.

The Japanese negotiating style

The Japanese are a high-context culture, with many specific rules for social and business situations. They depend on extensive information networks and place high value on close personal relationships. In Hofstede's definition, they are collectivist, with the emphasis on group values rather than the individual. Their culture is high in masculinity and uncertainty avoidance, and medium in power distance terms. Women are usually only minor members of a negotiating team, if at all. The Japanese may at times appear to ignore women in Western negotiating teams, irrespective of their seniority. Japan is an essentially masculine society and it is therefore rare to see women in high positions in business, and the traditional nature of their culture does not encourage them to have the power to negotiate.

Many older and senior Japanese managers may not speak fluent English and will therefore need the aid of an interpreter. In general, the Japanese see their own language as creating the right mood and atmosphere for business, whereas they see English as more direct and used mainly to exchange information.

Relationships are more formally negotiated rather than spontaneous or casual and once established are assumed to be longstanding, with considerable ongoing personal involvement. The Japanese want to be certain that by doing business with someone, their network of contacts will be reinforced and not impaired in any way.

The Japanese are cautious negotiators with a long-term perspective. They are always well prepared and spend time on building relationships and mutual trust. Business is therefore personal. The Japanese see relationships as a constant process of interpersonal discussion that builds trust with their counterparts. In the early stages, there may be several preliminary meetings, lunches and dinners at which relatively little business is discussed. Foreigners must be prepared for every stage of the negotiating process to be longer than that to which they are accustomed. Loyalty, a strong work ethic, respect for seniority and effective teamwork are traditional Japanese values.

As a high-context culture, there is much emphasis on non-verbal, implicit and indirect communication and less on written, legalistic contracts. The Japanese negotiating style can appear to be impersonal and unemotional, but in fact emotion is important for the Japanese as logical and intellectual argument cannot alone convince them. Japanese negotiators often exploit 'haragei' (literally 'belly talk'), the value of silence in meetings and negotiations. Silence that creates a 'verbal vacuum' is considered as a time for reflection and is not seen as showing a lack of understanding or rudeness. Westerners often find such silence embarrassing and feel obliged to say something to reduce the perceived tension. If the silence arises from some difficulty in solving a particular problem, the Japanese may postpone proceedings to give everyone the opportunity for further discussion in an attempt to reach agreement. Body language clues are very important, particularly regarding eye contact. Smiling can at times be a cover for embarrassment. The Japanese do not traditionally shake hands, but have become accustomed to doing this. It is still normal, particularly for the older generation, for many Japanese to bow.

Japan is an ascriptive culture according to Trompenaars' definition. It is therefore important to bear in mind that achievement cultures such as the USA and the Netherlands would often have younger members in their negotiating team. The Japanese, however, may have more senior people briefed by a number of subordinates and may be surprised at the comparatively younger representatives of achievement-oriented cultures (Trompenaars, 1994: 98).

The Japanese are sensitive regarding status and seniority, in line with Confucian principles. Senior managers attend negotiations, but leave their juniors to do most of the talking while they listen carefully. They may consult at all levels within a group before they reach the decision-making stage. Decision making is therefore usually undertaken by consensus after many questions are posed in order to gain more information. However strong their negotiating team is, the Japanese may feel obliged to refer back to their headquarters for approval of any agreement. As such, it is often unlikely that decisions will be made at the first or even the second meeting. The second meeting may cover similar ground to the first, but the questions are likely to be more searching as the Japanese are anxious to achieve clarity, thereby avoiding later misunderstandings. However, once they have made a decision, their negotiating team expects quick action.

In an attempt to avoid controversy, Japanese negotiators are also anxious to save 'face' and dislike being pushed into a corner with little apparent escape or alternative options. The Japanese 'hai' ('yes') does not always mean 'I agree with you'; it can often mean 'I hear what you say'. They are reluctant directly to say 'no' as it may cause embarrassment and a loss of 'face', and will strive for harmony throughout negotiations. They hesitate to challenge arguments entirely or break off the negotiations while the harmony exists. There is a tradition ('naniwabushi') of being flexible to cope with changed circumstances and Japanese negotiators may appeal to outsiders to work with them in order to change a deal after it has been formally approved.

Negotiations and meetings are formally conducted and formal introductions are of great importance. This etiquette is part of a strict ritual ('jikoshokai') and the Japanese place great significance on both verbal introductions and the presentation and receiving of the business card ('meishi'), which is presented with much formality and respect. It should be offered with both hands with the Japanese translation side upwards. Their card should also be received with both hands and it shows respect to take a few moments to peruse it carefully. Foreigners should be aware of this ritual and should be seen to reciprocate and show they understand the Japanese etiquette.

The Japanese are always patient and polite, but do not always readily appreciate the informal Western approach. They also do not appreciate the British sense of humour, particularly self-deprecation, which they feel is misplaced, even demeaning, and is not understood. The use of humour may well give the wrong impression and indicate a lack of seriousness about the business in hand. However, on informal and private occasions, when everyone knows each other, there can be a great deal of joking and humour. Examples of this are karaoke sessions, which are normally for men only and are held after work.

As regards their attitude towards time, the Japanese are basically monochronic and punctual. However, they do not like to be rushed and need considerable time to weigh up all the implications of a business proposal. There is a long consultation process both upwards and downwards within their organizations. It is also important not to introduce deadlines in the early stages of negotiations.

Gift-giving and hospitality play an important part in Japanese business and follow a strict etiquette. Indeed, most business and social life in Japan is to a large extent ritualistic and is an expression of the Japanese need to consider carefully by observing you to decide whether you and your company show signs of potential for a long and fruitful business based on a strong enduring friendship. The appearance of a gift is very important; indeed, the container in which the gift comes and its packaging are considered almost as important as the gift itself. The Japanese avoid using black or bright colours for wrapping paper. Black and white are reserved for funerals.

Case study: who shall be sent to Japan?

A European multinational company is about to select a manager to lead the negotiations for a new joint venture in Japan. The nominee will have to be acceptable to the Japanese partners.

The obvious choice for the position is Deborah Ransome, an able colleague with many years' experience and a proven track record as a project manager. There are two other male possibilities for the post, but neither is ideally suited. One of the men is considered too young and the other does not have sufficient experience with the product intended for the Japanese market. As the senior management European selection committee meets to discuss and then confirm who will represent the company in Japan, one member of the committee points out that, given certain cultural features of the Japanese business scene, sending a woman to Tokyo might present some difficulties. The selection committee now has to decide what to do.

The following points should be considered:

(1) What are the known features of the Japanese business scene with respect to women as a member of a negotiating team?
(2) Should the chairman advise the committee to take account of the cultural concerns of the Japanese or just do what is best for the company?
(3) Should the company send Deborah Ransome?

The Chinese negotiating style

Chinese culture is essentially collectivist, with cultural attitudes and values greatly influenced by Confucianism. Confucius was a moral philosopher whose aim was to establish a practical philosophy based on criteria for the right way to live. He was concerned with conformity to the values and behaviour which underpinned the stability of the established order and moral behaviour. In the ideal world, everyone knows his or her place. The duty of humans in Confucian ethics may be summed up as *reciprocity*. This is closely associated with loyalty to others and this principle is exemplified in the five relationships of the family and the state in society.

```
Ruler – Subject
Father – Son
Husband – Wife
Elder Brother – Younger Brother
Elder Friend – Younger Friend
```

Figure 9.4   Confucian loyalties

These five basic relationships ('wu lun') are based on mutual and complementary obligations – for example, the senior owes the junior protection, guidance and consideration, and the junior owes the senior respect and obedience. Confucianism symbolizes social stability, national decorum and retention of the 'status quo' (Stockman, 2000: 71).

These characteristics have survived for centuries and have withstood the actions of the communist government since 1948. Despite greatly increased contact with other cultures in recent years and the spread of globalization, they still have a considerable effect on Chinese business. For the Chinese, Hofstede's power distance is large because of many years of centralized control, which has promoted a tradition of obedience in which inequalities are more readily expected and accepted.

Hofstede (1994: 165–8) refers to a fifth dimension, which he calls 'Confucian dynamism', in his subsequent study of Chinese culture, identified in the CVS. He suggests that there is a correlation between certain Confucian values and the economic growth of Asia in recent years. In particular, the CVS results indicate the value of a long-term perspective in business, supported by hard work and perseverance. This was discussed in more detail in Chapter 2.

The other influence on Chinese behaviour is Taoism, created by Lao Tzu (born in 604 BC). Its main philosophy is described in the book *Tao Te Ching*, meaning 'The Way and the Power'. Taoism has three main teachings, which overlap each other. The first can only be understood through mystical insight, while the second refers to the principle of order behind the universe and represents the rhythm and driving force of nature. The third advocates that people should live their lives in order to be in balance and harmony with the universe. For many Chinese, Taoism, Confucianism and Buddhism are seen as being complementary and are considered to be 'the three faiths in one'. As a result, many Chinese accept Confucianism as a guide to the way in which they should conduct their daily life. They also often use Taoist practitioners for ritual purification and employ Buddhist priest for funerals.

Chinese negotiations are formal, highly structured and often protracted, with frequent breaks in the proceedings. They usually begin with 'small talk' and put great value on including 'shared experiences' between themselves and the other nationalities involved in the negotiations. They begin the negotiating process by gathering information and assessing trustworthiness. They are anxious to obtain as much technical and commercial data about the company's product as possible (Mead, 1998: 236).

The Chinese place an initial emphasis on detailed technical aspects before price and terms of the contract, and they prefer to receive detailed background information in advance. Chinese negotiators look for a commitment to work together rather than a water-tight contract. The signing of a contract is often not the end of the negotiations, but simply a continuation of the negotiating process.

By nature, the Chinese seek to avoid confrontation in negotiations. They are pragmatists and, whenever possible, prefer to 'bend with the wind'. They believe that patience is a virtue in negotiating and do not openly show frustration, anger or impatience. Patience is also considered a demonstration of superior inner strength and the preservation of dignity or 'face', that is, self-respect, particularly in the eyes of others. They are reluctant to say 'no', but will hint at various difficulties. In this case, 'yes' may mean 'I hear you', but not necessarily 'I agree'. They are likely to delegate only limited authority to their negotiators and may well require them to refer to higher authority for important decisions. Their tactics are often to extract as many concessions as possible from their counterparts before making any themselves. They dislike surprises and will insist on an agreed agenda before the start of negotiations.

The Chinese are basically monochronic, but do not like being rushed in negotiations. They value time for reflection and further consideration. However, they do appreciate the value of time and are punctual both for business and social occasions.

The Chinese place great store on the importance of 'face', as it is of significance to a person's image and status in the eyes of business associates. They use various communication strategies in order to save 'face' and to give 'face', including indirectness and the use of intermediaries. Counterparts should avoid wherever possible backing a Chinese negotiator into a situation which provides little room for manoeuvre. The Chinese conceptualization of 'face' is much more complex than that of Westerners and is viewed as an essential component of communication (Cardon and Scott, 2003).

Names are very important to the Chinese. They are seldom called by their given names except by close relatives or friends. Surnames come first. They place importance on titles and these should be used if known. The Chinese are far more comfortable with silence than Westerners are. What is left unsaid can be as important as what is expressed directly. Silence can be a sign of politeness or a ploy to find out more information.

Chinese negotiations are often lengthy and a signed agreement is seen as only an important milestone on a long journey. Their negotiating team will include a number of specialists (for example, in finance or technology) and their input will often lead to long, drawn-out negotiations. One of the important ways of reaching agreement is the use of 'guanxi' (connections), the importance of knowing people in high places or simply in the right place and motivating them to help you by granting a favour. The Chinese will often deliberately cultivate such people in the anticipation that a favour might be needed in the future. The right connections do much to help lubricate the Chinese system, providing access and clearing the path through bureaucracy.

'Feng shui' (literally 'fire and water') plays an important part in Chinese business and social life. It is concerned with the importance of preserving harmony between people and the environment. Good 'feng shui' is synonymous with good luck and involves harnessing the natural energy of the environment to bring good fortune. This ancient philosophy is based on the benefits of the positive influences of life forces and is concerned, for example, with the correct positioning of buildings, office design and positioning of plants, favouring those with rounded rather than pointed leaves. All this is an attempt to enhance the chance of successful business. 'Feng shui' experts, who have a combination of the skills of the geomancer, astrologer and soothsayer, are regularly consulted.

The Arab negotiating style

The Arab world extends from Mauritania on the Atlantic coast to Oman on the Indian Ocean and includes Sudan and Somalia. It is the dominant culture of the Middle East and the Mahgreb. It contains the heartland of Islam and its culture and customs are built upon Islamic teachings. Islam is both a religion and a way of life, and provides an ethical framework for business. Negotiations are therefore greatly influenced by Islamic teachings and traditions. Unlike most Western cultures, there is no separation of state and religion.

Being an Arab has less to do with ethnic origins and more to do with language, thought systems, values and, above all, a sense of pride in Arab history. Islam is shaped both by history and Arab thought. The Arab language is spoken throughout the Arab world, providing a unified concept, although there are regional variations. Some attempt by foreigners to use Arabic, however faltering, is usually much appreciated, even if one gets no further than the ritual greetings.

In the Arab world, all business negotiations develop from personal relationships and meeting the 'right people'. The first meeting with an Arab businessman is used to build trust and subsequently to establish a working personal relationship before getting down to the real business. Time spent on developing close personal relationships and mutual trust is therefore a prerequisite for success. Foreigners should, for their part, always adopt a dignified approach and not press hard for quick decisions. Personal introductions and networking play a large part in business. Once close relations are established, the expectation is that the parties will continue to nurture these relationships. Care should be taken when shaking hands as it is considered disrespectful for a man to offer his hand to a woman unless she extends hers first.

Arabs are a high-context culture; they communicate less directly and are less adversarial. Combative, confrontational negotiations are not tactics followed by Arabs out of choice as they prefer to place emphasis on harmony and the avoidance of confrontation. Their style of communication is more circular than the Western linear approach. They prefer face-to-face communication, followed by telephoning, followed by email and then written documentation. Many Arabs tend to develop their business alongside social relationships, so socializing with clients and agents after working hours is common practice.

Arab culture is essentially a polite culture, but it is usually advisable not to discuss religion or politics unless encouraged to do so. When negotiating, one should expect verbal interruptions by the other party, but rudeness is not intended as interruption. To an Arab, it indicates the interaction of ideas and evidence of a continuous exchange of information.

Silence is not welcomed during negotiations and is perceived as an awkward sign that may indicate that communication has, for some reason, broken down and that therefore the relationship must be rebuilt. Arabs welcome eye contact during negotiations, but too much eye contact may cause them some discomfort. Note-taking at meetings is seen as interfering with personal contact and should therefore, where possible, be delegated to junior personnel, thus raising the profile of senior negotiators.

Emphasizing common ground ('shared experiences') is particularly effective in the Arab world. This is well liked by Arabs as it assists in getting to know the members of the other negotiating team, thus establishing trust and helping to break the ice. When approaching a potential problem in negotiations, it is considered advantageous to emphasize the mutual benefits that are likely to result from working together to achieve a solution. The Arab management style is paternalistic and visiting business people need to demonstrate they have the appropriate level of authority if they are to be given any credibility.

Prayers are said five times a day, and in some parts of the Arab world, especially in Saudi Arabia, meetings will often stop and businesses will close during the time of prayer. During the month of Ramadan, government offices and businesses may close their offices at midday. It is therefore preferable to avoid business visits if at all possible during Ramadan. If non-Muslims do visit during that time, they should, out of respect, refrain from eating, drinking and smoking in public. Friday is the weekly day of rest. Care must be taken about gift-giving. All alcohol is strictly forbidden and gifts should always be presented using the right hand. It is common practice in the Arab world to exchange small gifts to establish an initial bond of friendship. Failure to do so would be considered bad manners.

It is important to understand the expression 'Inshallah' (if God wills), which is much misunderstood by Westerners. Intentions may not readily materialize into acts, so the expression can mean several things:

- I should like this to happen.
- I will try my best.
- I cannot be sure about this proposal/plan.
- I need time to think about this.
- I don't really want to respond to your proposal.
- The answer will be 'no', but let us observe the normal courtesies.

'Ma fi mushkilleh' is another Arab phrase which may cause problems for foreigners. Literally translated, it means 'there is no problem'. However, this phrase may actually hide the fact that there is an obstacle. Effective communication derived from personal relationships with your Arab counterparts will usually help indicate which of these meanings applies to the current situation.

Arabs will strive to avoid breaking off negotiations and will attempt, wherever possible, to build long-term relationships for future business. In many negotiating situations, Arabs, following Islamic teaching and traditions, may decide to use a mediator to settle situations where there is real or potential conflict. The mediator is considered neutral, has the trust of both parties, understands their respective positions and will strive to bring about an honourable solution for all parties involved.

Training

Training for the cross-cultural aspects of international negotiations should follow much of that suggested for building and sustaining multicultural teams. It should include cultural sensitivity training and briefing as part of the preparation phase. In addition, simulation exercises using role play based on real-life scenarios should be used. The use of cultural assimilators which develop critical incidents in a particular culture provide another training alternative. Critical incident scenarios are best written by nationals or by expatriates with wide experience of the particular culture, and the responses are first tested among others with similar experience to ensure that the solutions are valid. Such training, apart from being of value to individuals, helps develop the group dynamics.

Language training, as has been emphasized earlier, is effective only if it is begun early enough and should, if at all possible, involve time in the relevant country. It should always involve nationals, preferably with business experience. Language training is best undertaken intensively on a one-to-one basis, with the main emphasis on oral fluency and a gradual build-up of vocabulary to acquire sufficient fluency to take part in negotiations. If circumstances permit, language training should be continued in the country where negotiations are likely to take place.

Summary

International negotiators need to:

- attempt to establish personal relationships before negotiations begin;
- appreciate the importance of building mutual trust;
- prepare well in advance and study the culture and history of the other nationality;
- establish what is to be the working language and, if necessary, decide whether translators are required;
- build on 'shared experiences';
- appreciate that the other party will interpret your input in the light of their own cultural and linguistic background;
- be alert to non-verbal gestures and the use of silence;
- keep emotions under control and show patience and tolerance;
- avoid anything that might lead to loss of 'face';
- appreciate the importance attached to status and seniority;
- be prepared for negotiations to continue beyond the apparent conclusion of an agreement.

A word of caution is necessary when attempting to comment on the key characteristics of the negotiation style of different cultures. As the world becomes increasingly globalized, interdependent and interconnected, there is inevitably a degree of cultural convergence. As a result, these characteristics will modify and we must be careful not to ascribe stereotypical values to individual cultures.

References

Adler, N. (1991) *International Dimensions of Organizational Behaviour* (Boston, MA: PWS-Kent Publishing Company).

Binyon, M. (2001) 'A Sorry Business', *The Times*, 13 August.

Cardon, P. and Scott, J. (2003) 'Chinese Business Face: Communication, Behaviour and Teaching Approaches', *Business Communication Quarterly* 66(4): 9–22.

Cohen, R. (1999) *Negotiating Across Cultures: International Communication in the Independent World* (Washington DC: US Institute of Peace Press).

Fisher, R. and Ury, W. (2003) *Getting to Yes* (London: Random House).

Graham, J. and Herberger Jr., R. (1983) 'Negotiations Abroad – Don't Shoot from the Hip', *Harvard Business Review*: 160–8.

Hofstede, G. (1994) *Cultures and Organisations. Software of the Mind. Intercultural Organisation and its Importance for Survival* (London: HarperCollins).

Hofstede, G., Hofstede, G.J. and Minkov, M. (2010) *Cultures and Organizations. Software of the Mind. Intercultural Organization and its Importance for Survival* (New York: McGraw-Hill).

Lewicki, R. (2008) *Negotiation* (New York: McGraw-Hill).

Mead, R. (1998) *International Management* (Oxford: Blackwell).

Stockman, N. (2000) *Understanding Chinese Society* (Oxford: Blackwell).

Szaly, L. (1981) 'Intercultural Communication: A Process Model', *International Journal of International Relations* 5: 133–46.

Trompenaars, F. (1994) *Riding the Waves of Culture: Understanding Cultural Diversity in Business* (London: Nicholas Brealey Publishing).

Victor, D. (1992) *International Business Communication* (London: HarperCollins).

Further reading

Axtell, R. (ed.) (1985) *Do's and Taboos Around the World* (New York: John Wiley & Sons).

Brown, P. and Levinson, S. (1987) *Politeness: Some Universals in Language Use* (Cambridge University Press).

Buttery, E. and Leung, T. (1998) 'The Difference between Chinese and Western Negotiation', *European Journal of Marketing* 32(3/4): 374–89.

Daniels, J., Radebaugh, L. and Sullivan, D. (2007) *International Business: Environments and Orientations*, 11th edn (Upper Saddle River, NJ: Prentice Hall).

Davies, P. (2004) *What's This India Business?* (London: Nicholas Brealey Publishing).

Fowler, A. (1999) *Negotiation Skills and Strategies*, 2nd edn (London: Institute of Personal Development).

Hall, E. and Hall, M. (1990) *Understanding Cultural Differences: Germans, French and Americans* (Yarmouth, ME: Intercultural Press).

Harris, P. and Moran, R. (2000) *Managing Cultural Differences*, 5th edn (Houston, TX: Gulf Publishing).

Hurn, B. (2007) 'The Influence of Culture on International Business Negotiations', *Industrial and Commercial Training* 39(7): 354–60.

Lewis, R. (2011) *When Cultures Collide*, 3rd edn (London: Nicholas Brealey Publishing).

Marshall, Sir Peter (1997) *Positive Diplomacy* (Basingstoke: Macmillan).

Richmond, Y. (1992) *From Nyet to Da: Understanding the Russians* (Yarmouth, ME: Intercultural Press).

Richmond, Y. (1995) *From Da to Yes: Understanding the East Europeans* (Yarmouth, ME: Intercultural Press).

Tan, T. (1992) *Culture Shock! Britain* (London: Kuperard).

Tomalin, B. and Nicks, M. (2010) *The World's Business Cultures and How to Unlock Them* (London: Thorogood Publishing).

10
Multiculturalism and Diversity

Summary

Definitions
Multiculturalism/pluralism
Cultural diversity
'Melting pot' or 'salad bowl'
Integration or adaptation
Legislation
Gender issues
The UK, Switzerland, Canada, the USA, France, the Nertherlands, Belgium and Australia
Immigration
The Diverse Europe at Work Project

Definitions

There is general agreement on the enrichment that cultural diversity adds to society. The 1991 Nobel Peace Prize winner Aung San Suu Kyi praised cultural diversity as follows: 'It is precisely because of the cultural diversity of the world that it is necessary for different nations and people to agree on those basic human values which will act as a unifying factor.' This theme is continued by Felipe Fernandez-Armesto (2000), who champions the value to society of migration: 'All history is the history of migration. All of us get to where we are because we or our ancestors moved there.' He argues that migration has enriched recipient cultures, brought new ideas, challenged traditional assumptions and, apart from being generally beneficial, has, in many cases, been of vital importance to their future development, emphasizing that: 'Societies with high rates of immigration find that newcomers do more good than harm.'

However, when we come to the concept of multiculturalism, there is less of a consensus. Multiculturalism has become one of the most controversial intellectual and political concepts in contemporary Western democracies. The term does not always enjoy universal recognition, particularly when it is considered as an official response to coping with diversity. This approach is based on the theory that it is beneficial to a society to maintain more than one culture within its structure. Ravitch defined multiculturalism as: 'The public policy for managing cultural diversity in a multi-ethnic society, officially stressing mutual respect and tolerance for cultural differences within national borders' (1990: 337).

The meaning and interpretation of the term 'multiculturalism' was critically examined in the light of the terrorist attacks in London in 2005. As a sociological concept, it is taken to refer to diverse ethnocultural minorities who each define themselves as culturally different and express their desire to remain so. It is designed to engender respect for people of different faiths who follow different lifestyles. It observes and respects diversity as an essential and valued component of society, and recognizes the contribution of minorities. It can also be seen as a society in which people from a range of cultures live together in the same area, sharing equal rights and opportunities, where diversity is valued and individual differences are celebrated. Brahm Levey defines multiculturalism as: 'A set of practical policies aimed variously at improving the absorption of minorities and harmoniously integrating a culturally diverse society around liberal, democratic values' (Brahm Levey, 2007: 199).

Barry (2001) believes that by treating people differently in response to their different culturally based beliefs and practices, one is actually treating them equally. He explains how such public policies can be classified into one of two types. He sees positive policies providing advantages to certain cultural groups, for example, the proportion of reserved places in education and the workforce. Negative policies, however, are those that provide individual exemptions from generally applicable laws, for example, the controversy that arose in the UK regarding the wearing of turbans and crash helmets by Sikhs, as well as the wearing of the hijab by Muslims in France.

Gamble and Heywood (2003) contend that multiculturalism can be used as both a descriptive and a normative term. The former refers to the cultural diversity which occurs when two or more ethnic groups within a society have beliefs and traditions which in sum produce a sense of collective identity. In the normative sense, multiculturalism is seen as 'positively endorsing communal diversity based upon the right of different cultural groups to recognition and respect. In this sense it acknowledges the importance of beliefs, values and ways of life in establishing a sense of self-worth for individuals and groups alike'.

Watson (2000) attempts to clarify further the terms 'multicultural' and 'multiculturalism':

The former points to the visible and universally accessible products of cultural diversity, namely food, clothes, music, theatre and sometimes special occupations, and, on the whole, it has a very positive response. Multiculturalism, on the other hand, directs our attention away from these purely visible acts of diversity to the deeper philosophical and political implications of different cultures and to engagement with the world, and the way in which these differences jostle for recognition within national and global boundaries, sometimes in relative harmony with each other and sometimes in real conflict.

Multiculturalism is generally taken to mean that different cultural communities should live their own way of life in an essentially self-contained way. In this sense, multiculturalism requires that all cultures should be open, self-critical and interactive in their relations with each other. Multi-ethnicity does not simply mean multiculturalism, but it relies on multiculturalism to keep its vibrancy. This is seen by the opponents of multiculturalism as a narrow and inherently in the long run potentially dangerous approach, which does not help create a common sense of values, hopes and aspirations that unite all people within a society, but runs the risk of establishing a form of tribal society with no apparent common identity. Preserving their original culture can often lead to more isolation of immigrants and minorities. Their resistance has the potential to strengthen racism and, in times of tension, cause social instability.

However, multiculturalism can be interpreted in a different way. It can be seen from a liberal standpoint as the right of every culture to live side by side with other different cultures and to pursue their differences in cultural values and beliefs, while being treated as politically equal. This view can be extended to include the belief that cultures benefit from close proximity with other cultures. A third view is that cultures are constantly changing and adapting, and therefore multiculturalism is no different in this respect as it is inherently dynamic, open to the influences of other cultures, and, as a result, constantly evolving.

Cultural pluralism

The term 'cultural pluralism' is often used interchangeably with 'multiculturalism'. In a pluralistic society, recognition of the diverse cultures within it is generally accepted to be based on three principles: that all people are considered equal, that all cultures deserve respect and that the concept of cultural pluralism is given support under the law. As a result, cultural pluralism implies that various ethnocultural groups coexist under a single government within a multilingual framework.

In the UK, we tend to look upon our society as essentially pluralistic, a society in which all are considered equal in law and in society, where tolerance is encouraged and all cultures deserve respect. Critics have said that this approach does not necessarily encourage integration, or indeed assimilation, or a set of values, hopes and expectations that unite all in a sense of identity that is 'Britishness'. They criticize the concept that encourages different cultural communities to live their own way of life in an essentially self-contained way. Such concerns led the British Home Office to introduce the citizenship test to be taken by any immigrant seeking naturalization. Successful candidates are also required to take an oath of allegiance.

Ravitch (1990) describes both the 'melting pot' of the USA and the Australian 'cultural mosaic' as being different forms of multiculturalism, describing them as 'pluralistic' and 'particularist'. She considers pluralistic multiculturalism as viewing each culture or sub-culture as contributing unique and valuable aspects to the whole culture. Where multiculturalism has been implemented as an official government policy, it is seen as a 'particularist' form of multiculturalism that is more concerned with preserving the distinction between cultures.

Assimilation or integration?

Governments which represent multicultural groups within their national boundaries have two main policy options towards multiculturalism:

- *Assimilation*: this is the process whereby minority cultures are absorbed into the culture of the majority and the official recognition of any differences is discouraged. This option, called the 'melting pot' approach, has been chosen by the French and the US governments in an attempt to develop a cohesive national identity.
- *Integration*: this is the alternative approach, which encourages support for cultural diversity and a pluralistic, multicultural society. This option is the policy pursued by the Canadian government. In Canada, the different cultures are encouraged to exist under the laws of the Canadian government, but allowances are made for the different cultures, in particular the French speakers, to exist with their cultural differences being respected. This is known as the 'salad bowl' approach.

Affirmative action

This approach is also known as positive discrimination. It involves the use of quotas to ensure equal rights and representation for particular minorities, for example, in education, employment and promotion, as well as quotas for political representation, such as for women and ethnic minorities, and where there are specific skill shortages.

Diversity

> Let us not be blind to our differences – but let us direct our attention to our common interests and the means by which those differences can be resolved. And, if we cannot end our differences, at least we can help make the world safe for diversity. (John F. Kennedy)

Diversity is about promoting equality in society in general and in the workplace in particular. Cultural diversity includes both visible and non-visible differences, that is, different genders, age groups, ethnic origins, physical appearance, educational background, parental status, religious beliefs, sexual orientation and work style. It should produce equality of opportunity, better working conditions and labour relations, thus achieving enhanced productivity and work performance, with increased staff motivation and employee involvement. It prevents dissatisfaction by providing greater job security and safer working conditions, with fair remuneration and equal opportunities for men and women for job selection, training and promotion.

'Cultural diversity presents major opportunities for synergy – the output of two or more individuals or groups working in cooperation is greater than would be the combined output of their working separately' (Mead, 1998: 14). Culturally, synergy builds on a fusion of home and host cultures, and on their similarities and differences. Good examples of this are the inclusion of many immigrants in the cultures of such countries as the UK, the USA, Canada and Australia. Cultural diversity is a concept that extends beyond language, religion, race and ethnicity to include sexual orientation, gender and age.

Ethnocentrism

Ethnic groups encounter ethnocentrism whereby the main host's predominant culture tends to judge all other cultures according to its own beliefs, values and traditions. This also tends to reinforce *stereotyping*, often as a result of feeling insecure and uncertain when faced with people who are different, with the result that people from other cultures are categorized in the simplest way possible. There is a tendency to invest these categories, because they constitute the unknown, with negative emotions. This point was examined in more detail in Chapter 1.

Monocultural peoples tend to be insensitive to other people's cultures and are therefore usually unaware of potential points of conflict and misunderstanding. They tend to be basically ethnocentric in their outlook and unable to see the other culture's point of view; as a result, they are themselves often unable to communicate effectively with people from other cultures. They tend to resort to the 'blame game', saying 'it's all their fault ... they don't understand'. As such, they rarely acknowledge that the breakdown in communication that occurs is really due to their own lack of cultural awareness and sensitivity.

Multicultural people, on the other hand, will be aware of their own behavioural patterns and those of the different cultures they encounter. They are more likely to understand the impact of their own behaviour on others and, where necessary, will be able to moderate their own behaviour accordingly. In effect, they will 'listen and learn'.

Ethnicity

Ethnicity is defined as applying to a distinct group that shares all (or the majority) of the essential characteristics outlined in Figure 10.1.

Cultural tradition of its own, not necessarily closely associated with religion
Common geographical origin or descent from a small number of common ancestors
Common literature
Long history, of which the group is conscious, that distinguishes it from other groups
Common religion which is different from that of the general community surrounding it
Being a minority, oppressed or dominant group within a larger community

---

Figure 10.1   Characteristics of ethnicity

It should be noted that the term 'ethnic group' is often applied to groups which have a minority status in the larger group.

Legislation

Much legislation has been introduced both by individual countries and the EU to provide protection within the law to promote equality. This includes in the UK:

- the 1975 Sex Discrimination Act;
- the 1975 Equal Pay Act;
- the 1976 Race Relations Act;
- the 1995 Disability Discrimination Act;
- the 2000 Race Relations (Amendment) Act, which places a duty on public authorities to promote racial equality in employment, service delivery and procurement;
- the Equalities Act 2010, which codifies anti-discrimination laws in the UK and covers equal pay, sex discrimination, race relations, disability discrimination and discrimination in employment on grounds of religion or belief, sexual orientation and age;

- the setting up of the Equal Opportunities Commission and the Commission for Racial Equality to oversee much of the legislation. Both publish codes of practice advising employers on how to avoid discriminatory practices. The two have now merged to form the Equality and Human Rights Commission.

Member States of the EU are primarily responsible for their own labour laws, but the following have EU-wide application:

- *The 1989 EU Charter of Fundamental Rights*: under Article 31, all workers have the right to working conditions that respect their health, safety and dignity. Every worker has the right to limitation of maximum working hours, daily and weekly rest periods and an annual period of paid leave.
- *The 1999 Amsterdam Treaty*: this treaty made employment and social policy a true European concern. It includes regulations to combat discrimination. Key points are:
  (i) freedom of movement of workers within the EU;
  (ii) health and safety at work;
  (iii) a maximum working week of 48 hours and four weeks' holiday a year;
  (iv) non-discrimination applicable to part-time as well as full-time employees.
- *The Schengen Agreement*: this enabled the passport-free movement of people between participating European countries. Members may temporarily reintroduce border controls for reasons of national security. The UK opted not to join Schengen for these reasons.

National policies towards multiculturalism and diversity

The UK

London is one of the most culturally and linguistically diverse cities of the world, its inhabitants from many cultural backgrounds making it a unique world city. More than a third of the approximately 8.2 million London residents were born abroad and almost a quarter are not British citizens. The Office of National Statistics' figures in 2006 show that Bangladeshis, Indians, Russians, Brazilians, South Africans, Ghanaians, Poles and Australians were currently leading the globalization of the capital. These are the 'new Londoners', adding to the large number of immigrants from the Indian subcontinent, Africa and the Caribbean who in many cases have been resident for much longer. It is estimated that over 40 per cent of all immigrants in the UK live in the Greater London area. The UK itself is becoming more of a 'rainbow nation' with 'mixed race' being the fastest growing ethnic minority – one in ten children is now living in a mixed-race family.

'Multilingual Capital', the first survey, in 2001, of modern London's languages, found that there were 307 clearly identified languages spoken by school children in London, with only two-thirds of these children speaking English at home. This phenomenon causes many problems for teachers in London schools, requiring innovative and culturally sensitive methods of teaching English and building confidence among their pupils. This is a particularly serious problem in a number of inner-city London primary schools, where it is estimated that 55 per cent of primary school children do not have English as their mother tongue (Migration Watch Report, 2010). The Migration Watch Report anticipates that by 2018, 23 per cent of pupils in UK schools will not have English as their mother tongue.

In 2004, Trevor Phillips, the Chairman of the Commission for Racial Equality in the UK, which was founded to promote multiculturalism, criticized multiculturalism for: 'Defining people as different and then treating them differently.' He believed that a policy of multiculturalism, attempting to promote the culture and values of ethnic minorities, can in fact produce the very opposite result. Instead of uniting the peoples of the UK in a recognizable common citizenship and national identity, it would increase their differences, which in turn ran the risk of leading to a widespread sense of alienation from the rest of society. He wanted to rehabilitate the term 'integration' as he believed that: 'Multiculturalism does not mean that anybody can do anything they like in the name of their culture.' He recommended in the Commission for Racial Equality Report 2004 that all citizens should: 'Assert a core of Britishness ... We need to remind people that we are all equally British regardless of race or religion. Our claim for equality is founded on the certainty of our citizenship, on what we have in common, not our differences.' He also advocated establishing a set of 'British' values to which all groups should subscribe.

Citizenship training has now been officially introduced by the British government to facilitate integration and help overcome the problems outlined in Figure 10.2.

Lack of English language proficiency	Employment opportunities
Coping with local regulations	Coping with family separation
Understanding the social welfare system	Having realistic expectations

Figure 10.2   Problem areas facing immigrants

Special courses are organized to prepare those who wish to apply for citizenship, including increasing understanding in such areas as:

- a basic competence in English;
- the history and society of the UK;
- national institutions – roles of the monarch, the prime minister, Parliament, the Cabinet and local government;
- the role of elective representatives and political parties;

- the concepts of freedom of speech of the press and open government;
- the law: what the police can and cannot do, rights and duties of a citizen, basic obligations under the law, reporting crime and the role of the courts;
- employment: how to get a job, the National Insurance system, the role of trade unions, employment laws;
- sources of assistance: Citizens Advice Bureaux, councils and councillors, public libraries, access to health care and the taxation system;
- everyday needs: housing, banks, post offices, entertainment and leisure facilities, national holidays and the etiquette of everyday life.

At the same time, state secondary schools are now required to include citizenship in the compulsory curriculum.

Such a course for training for would-be citizens aims to provide a test of 'Britishness' before they are granted UK citizenship after a residential qualification. There is also a requirement to take an oath of allegiance to the Queen and an oath of loyalty to the UK with respect for its rights and freedoms, as well as to uphold democratic values, observe UK laws and fulfil the duties and obligations as a British citizen. The first citizenship ceremony was completed in London in February 2004. In 2009, the UK government introduced the citizenship test for foreigners who wished to become British. They have to study a special booklet, *Life in the UK*, to help prepare them for the test. The test itself has been criticized for its emphasis on knowledge of factual information.

Switzerland and Canada

A good example of multiculturalism in practice is Switzerland, which has the canton system in which separate cultures and languages are preserved, yet all citizens consider themselves Swiss. To a large extent, this is also true of Canada, with the French culture and language preserved in Quebec, although all citizens are considered to be Canadian. Canada is generally recognized as the first country after Switzerland to use the term 'multiculturalism'. It first became publicized after it was recommended in the 1965 report of Canada's Royal Commission on bilingualism and biculturalism, a government body set up to respond to the pressures of Canada's French-speaking minority. In 1985, the Canadian government passed the Canadian Multiculturalism Act, which came into effect in 1988, which stated that it:

> Recognizes the diversity of Canadians as regards race, natural or ethnic origin, colour and religion as a fundamental characteristic of Canadian society and is committed to a policy of multiculturalism designed to preserve and enhance the multicultural heritage of Canadians, while working to achieve equality of all Canadians in the economic, social, cultural and political life of Canada.

The Canadian approach to multiculturalism is often called the 'salad bowl', in which each culture maintains its own characteristics, while living side by side with other cultures. Canadian multiculturalism is based on the belief that all its citizens are equal and can retain their identities, taking pride in their cultural roots, yet having a sense of belonging as being Canadian. The Canadian experience recognizes the potential of all Canadians and encourages its citizens to play an active part in the full range of Canadian life. Multiculturalism, therefore, from the Canadian point of view, is seen as positively encouraging racial and ethnic harmony, while discouraging discrimination, intolerance and violence.

To become a Canadian citizen, one must show proof of residence in Canada and pass a test on the country's history, geography and politics and on the rights and responsibilities of a Canadian citizen. In addition, applicants have to appear before a citizen judge who asks general questions about Canada. If successful, applicants then take the citizenship oath. Canada's current multiculturalism policy illustrates that diversity has been maintained, but cultural clusters have become the result. Canadian national identity can therefore be loosely described as a function of all of its main cultural clusters where national identity has been described as an 'embedded mosaic', presenting distinct opportunities for integration. However, in order to ensure that the integration does not lead into assimilation in any one distinct cultural cluster, the evolution has been gradual. In effect, this has been advanced by means of formal intra-state diplomatic representation of the main cultural clusters.

The USA

The former American President Theodore Roosevelt warned in 1915 against the dangers of what he called 'hyphenated Americans' when he said: 'There is no room in this country for hyphenated Americanism ... the one absolute certain way of bringing this nation to ruin, of preventing all possibility of its continuing to be a nation at all, would be to permit it to become a tangle of squabbling nationalities.' In the USA today, multiculturalism is widely considered as both a social and a political concept in which the differences between individuals and groups are seen as a source of strength rather than of conflict. It is intended to work on a basis of synergy, celebrating the diversity of cultural origins and emphasizing the ideals of equality and freedom on which the US Constitution is based. Multiculturalism in the USA has developed as a result of the Civil Rights Movement and as resistance to the earlier approach of monocultural assimilation. The USA attempts to mix all immigrant cultures in a form of 'melting pot' without any direct state intervention. The former President Jimmy Carter saw it differently: 'We become not a melting pot, but a beautiful mosaic. Different people, different beliefs, different yearnings, different hopes, different dreams.' This approach shows respect for all individuals and groups and is recognized as a main component of the success and growth of the USA.

The USA is coming to terms with the fact that its population is expanding, its growth fuelled by mass immigration, much of which is illegal, from across the Mexican border. In the USA, applicants for American citizenship undergo the complicated and expensive process of acquiring a Green Card. They then attend an interview where their knowledge of American history and government, as well as their ability to speak English, is examined. They are also required to swear an oath of allegiance to the American flag.

France

The French have attempted to pursue a policy of integration whereby immigrants are expected to be assimilated into the French culture. For them, France is an ideal, embodied both in the French language and culture which all citizens should be urged to pursue and admire. The principle of 'laïcité', that is, secularism, the separation of the church and state, the belief that religion should have no place in civil affairs is enshrined in the French Constitution. All citizens are considered equal and the same, the very foundation on which democracy has evolved in France over the last 200 years. In France, there is no real policy of multiculturalism as all inhabitants are considered French with no overt recognition of ethnic minorities, although a significant majority of French immigrants come from the former French colonies, in particular from North Africa. Article 2 of the Constitution in fact avoids recognizing the existence of national or linguistic minorities within France's borders. This approach is characterized by a civic concept of citizenship, namely that French citizens, whatever their ethnic origin, enjoy equal civic, cultural and linguistic rights as individuals, but not collectively as minority groups. This integrationist approach to cultural diversity assumes that the non-recognition of minority groups is a way of preserving state unity and social cohesion. Therefore, one is in essence either French or a foreigner.

In February 2004, a bill was introduced in France banning the wearing of religious symbols in state schools. In practice, this meant that Muslim pupils should not wear the hijab, Jews the yarmulke, and Christians large crucifixes, in effect banning 'signs and clothes that conspicuously manifest the religious affiliations of the peoples'. The bill was subsequently passed with a large majority in the French National Assembly, although there was strong opposition from some of France's over five million Muslims, mostly from North Africa.

The hijab ban was supported by most teachers in French schools, who hoped it would halt the move towards multiculturalism, which was seen as separating pupils along ethnic and religious lines. They supported the ban on the grounds that it enabled Muslim girls to integrate more easily into mainstream French life. Opponents, however, claimed that the new law was really an attempt to find another way of improving integration policies that have often been considered as a failure, as evidenced by the concentration of many immigrants in poor outer city suburbs, which often resemble ghettos. These conditions in turn have caused resentment and provide fertile grounds for those who wish to preach extremism.

Since January 2012, candidates for nationalization have to pass a new citizenship test in which they have to demonstrate knowledge of French history, culture and even French cuisine. The former President Nicolas Sarkozy emphasized the importance of cultural assimilation and an appreciation of the philosophical basis of 'liberté, égalité et fraternité', together with some knowledge of France's cultural heritage and its contemporary culture. Those wishing to become French citizens are required to sign a Charter of Rights and Duties of the Citizen, which emphasizes the symbols of the French Republic. They are also tested on the French language and culture as above. The then Interior Minister Claude Guéant stated that: 'Assimilation is totally necessary and involves the language and adhering to the essential values of our democracy.' The Charter stresses that: 'France is an indivisible, secular, democratic and social Republic.' France, like the UK, has experienced some difficulty in designing the questions of such tests and has found that many of its own citizens are ignorant of some of the answers. Many questions have been criticized as appearing somewhat irrelevant to real life. More important is the requirement for French immigrants desiring citizenship to have an acceptable level of language proficiency. Applicants will need to be able to 'produce a simple and coherent speech on familiar subjects', as it is felt that 'assimilation is totally necessary and involves the language and adhering to the essential values of our democracy'.

The Netherlands

The Netherlands has been a long-time champion of cultural tolerance, but the Dutch liberal attitude as a tolerant and welcoming country was severely challenged by the murder of Pim Fortuyn, who set up the Livable Rotterdam Party, which was based on policies against immigration and multiculturalism. He believed that the country could not cope with more immigrants. 'Holland is full', he said and emphasized the growing potential problem of assimilation in the large cities. Growing concern has arisen over the number of people of ethnic minority origin, mostly from Turkey or Morocco, or the former colonies, particularly in Amsterdam, Rotterdam and The Hague, where newcomers already outnumber the native Dutch among the under twenties. The Dutch, like the Germans, had welcomed 'guest workers' into their country to meet the need for labour and had allowed them to remain even after the slump that followed the 1973 oil crisis. The Dutch policy was to create a tolerant, multicultural society where cultural differences were accepted and, indeed, appreciated. The Dutch government helped to fund mosques, religious schools and language courses, as well as providing generous housing assistance.

The situation in the Netherlands has now changed, with increased opposition to the policy of multiculturalism, and there is the danger of a clash of cultures. This is accentuated by the fact that ethnic minorities account for 40 per cent of social security aid and make up a larger proportion of the unemployed. In October 2005, the Dutch government issued proposals to ban the wearing of the burqa, worn by only a minority of Dutch Muslims. The government had already introduced Dutch language and culture classes for immigrants, who were encouraged to observe the country's liberal values. Many Dutch people have become concerned that a small country of 16 million inhabitants now has over 1.5 million immigrants amongst its population.

Belgium

Modern Belgium inherited a form of multicultural society from its colonial days. The state has now reformed itself by granting greater regional and community autonomy. However, in effect, a linguistic border still exists between Flanders and Wallonia, with Brussels as the autonomous, bilingual capital. The main problem still remains, namely the recurrent polarization of issues between the two communities and their lack of cultural exchange in the past. Some argue that the emphasis of multiculturalism on the promotion of each community's differences actually impedes social interaction between them, thus causing a degree of alienation.

Australia

Up until the 1960s, Australia maintained an essentially 'white Australia policy', with limits on immigration and relatively little regard for the culture of the nation's indigenous minority, the Aboriginees. However, under pressure for change and a wider realization and political acceptance of the need to respect all human rights, the government's policy changed from one of assimilation to one of integration.

The key statement of the Australian government's present multicultural policy is *Multicultural Australia: United in Diversity*, published in May 2003. This updated the 1999 *A New Agenda for Multicultural Australia*, which set strategic directions for multicultural policy with a specific emphasis on community harmony. This policy aims to ensure that all Australians have the opportunity to be active and equal participants in Australian society, and are free to live their lives and maintain their cultural traditions. This is further reinforced by legislation at Commonwealth, State and Territory levels. The fundamental principle of Australian multiculturalism is to preserve a 'cultural mosaic' of separate ethnic groups. The four key principles underlying multiculturalism in Australia are as follows:

- freedom for all Australians to practise their culture and religion;
- equal opportunity to participate fully in economic, social, cultural and political life within Australia;

- the responsibility to commit to the democratic system and respect the rights of all individuals;
- maximization of the economic benefits derived from multiculturalism.

In 2007, the Australian government drew up plans to promote Australian values among immigrants. Applicants for citizenship are now required to pass a test which examines their knowledge of Australian history, culture and government.

Immigration

Immigration is a sensitive issue in many countries. In April 2011, the UK put in place an annual cap of 21,700 skilled workers allowed into the country from outside the European Economic Area in an attempt to reduce the number of immigrants by 2015. Immigration from within the EU remains open. According to the Office of National Statistics, net long-term migration to the UK in 2010 was 226,000. Such figures have been considered unsustainable, mainly because of increased pressure on the social services, housing, health and education facilities, and opportunities for employment.

Legal immigration consists of the movement of people between countries to acquire eventual citizenship as well as those seeking long-term permanent residence. Short-term visitors and tourists are not considered to be immigrants. Many people who wish to come to another country are essentially economic migrants seeking better employment opportunities and many will remit their wages back to their home country. The downside is that there can be an increased burden on the state, especially on welfare services, if immigrants are unable to obtain work. In times of recession, large-scale immigration can cause resentment if immigrants compete for job vacancies.

Illegal immigration involves crossing international borders without the required documentation, passports or visas, thereby violating the immigration laws of the destination country. It often involves people-trafficking and the over-staying of work or student visas in order to continue working in the host country. Illegal immigrants run the danger of experiencing racism and exploitation of their labour, including low wages, long hours and poor conditions. They tend to live in social isolation, often in ghettos, with no legal access to social welfare, and may turn to crime if excluded from opportunities to find work. Many illegal immigrants are trying to escape from poverty and unemployment in their home country, from political and social unrest and from the results of national disasters, as well as attempting to avoid criminal justice in their country of origin. The UK has set up the Border Control Agency to check for illegal immigration and to vet asylum seekers.

Despite the negative perception of immigration, there are many positive advantages. Immigration enriches the culture of the host nation and provides additional skills and labour, filling existing skills gaps and counterbalancing those countries with an ageing population. The resulting religious and cultural diversity also enriches society.

However, we need to realize that there is often opposition to immigration – mainly the fear of job losses and erosion of the host culture. We need to recognize that this is often expressed by people of the receiving culture as hostility towards ethnic minorities. Nevertheless, immigrants often wish to retain key aspects of their original culture, for example, religion, language and social customs. A British Asian explained this as follows: 'I am British, but I am also Asian. It is not a matter of forsaking one culture for another, but of having the space to express them both, individually or together. However Western my lifestyle may appear, I will always enter social situations thinking and feeling like an Asian.'

The Diverse Europe at Work Project

This is a five-year project, funded by the EU, consisting of a ten-country consortium with the aim of helping migrant workers and host country workers to harmonize relations at work. It is a research programme covering six industries (catering, construction, education, health, retail and transport) in each of the ten partner countries. The project consists of DVD scenarios which develop a range of intercultural skills:

- understanding one's own cultural style;
- comparing it with another's cultural style;
- developing empathy – putting oneself in the other person's position;
- developing cultural knowledge and skills to deal with the situation;
- developing the ability to reflect and review how one feels and what one will do.

The series covers ageism, authority, body language, cultural sensitivity, disability, dress, food, gender issues, punctuality, sexual orientation, talking to foreigners and understanding foreigners and work relationships. These aspects are covered by the 16-unit training course, which aims to improve understanding of the people you work with who come from other cultures and to harmonize working relationships within society (Diverse Europe at Work, 2010).

Summary

- The debate about multiculturalism is likely to continue as there is no one model which can be applied universally. The often conflicting demands of multicultural policy are difficult to reconcile. The aim to create a sense of unity among people of different cultures also needs to protect the differences between the various cultural groups within a country. Ethnic minorities must believe that their cultures are respected and that their people can succeed in society.

- It is important to establish a set of values, hopes and aspirations to which all cultural groups in a society should subscribe, embracing freedom of speech and association, tolerance and respect for different religions and equality of opportunity in both social and public life. This may well require educational programmes designed to improve language skills in the main national language, as well as programmes to cover institutions and values of the society in which immigrants wish to become citizens.
- There are advantages and disadvantages of immigration, in particular the advantages of cultural diversity, including increased skills, new ideas and creativity and the disadvantages of pressure on the existing welfare services, housing and education.
- Mahatma Gandhi perhaps expressed the concept of cultural diversity particularly well: 'I want all the cultures of all lands to be blown about my house as freely as possible, but I refuse to be blown off my feet by any.'

References

Australian government (2003) *Multilateral Australia: United in Diversity.*
Baker, P. and Eversley, J. (2001) *Multilingual Capital* (London: Battlebridge Publications).
Barry, B. (2001) *Culture and Equality: An Egalitarian Critique of Multiculturalism* (London: Polity Press).
Brahm Levey, G. (2007) 'The Antidote of Multiculturalism', *Griffith Review* 15: 197–208.
Canadian government (1985) Canadian Multicultural Act (asserted 21 July 1988).
Diverse Europe at Work (2010) Lifelong Learning Programme. Sponsored by the EU under the Leonardo da Vinci Programme.
Fernandez-Armesto, F. (2000) *Civilisations* (London: Macmillan).
Gamble, A. and Heywood, A. (2003) *Political Ideologies: An Introduction* (Basingstoke: Palgrave Macmillan).
Green, A. Sir (2010) *Migration Watch UK Report.* November.
Haselden, L. (2004) *The Minority Report.* Office for National Statistics, 7 January.
Mead, R. (1998) *International Management* (London: Blackwell).
Office of National Statistics (2011) *Census Report.*
Phillips, T. (2004) *Commission for Racial Equality Report.*
Ravitch, D. (1990) *Multiculturalism: E Pluribus Plures* (London: Polity Press).
Ravitch, D. (2001) *Culture and Equity: An Egalitarian Critique of Multiculturalism* (London: Polity Press).
Roosevelt, T., President (1915) Speech in New York, 15 October.
Watson, C. (2000) *Multiculturalism* (Milton Keynes: Open University Press).

Further reading

Baker, P. and Eversley, J. (2001) *Multilingual Capital* (London: Battlebridge Publications).
Cable, V. (2005) *Multiple Identities: Living with the New Politics of Identities* (London: Demos).

The Economist (2008) 'A Special Report on Migration', 5 January.

The Economist (2011) 'Briefing: Migration and Business: Weaving the World Together', 19 November.

Fowler, S. (2005) 'Training Across Cultures: What Intercultural Trainers Bring to Diversity Training', *International Journal of Intercultural Relations* 30(2): 401–11.

Glazer, N. (1997) *We are all Multiculturalists Now* (Cambridge, MA: Harvard University Press).

Human Rights and Equal Opportunity Commission of Australia (HREOC) (2007) *Multiculturalism – A Position Paper*.

Huntington, S. (1993) *The Clash of Civilizations and the Remaking of the World Order* (New York: Free Press).

Macpherson, W., Sir (1999) *The Stephen Lawrence Inquiry Report* (London: Stationery Office).

Malik, K. (2005) 'Multiculturalism has Fanned the Flames of Islamic Extremism', *The Times*, 16 July.

Parekh, B. (2000) *Rethinking Multiculturalism: Cultural Diversity and Political Theory* (London: Macmillan).

Paxman, J. (1998) *The English: Portrait of a People* (London: Penguin Books).

Rushdie, S. (1995) *The Satanic Verses* (London: Vintage Publications).

11
Globalization and its Effect on Culture

Summary

Definitions
The components of globalization
The driving forces behind globalization
Global corporations
Is globalization a myth?
The reaction to globalization
Advantages and disadvantages
Opposition to globalization
Cultural convergence/divergence
Future trends

Introduction

This chapter looks at the spread of globalization, its effect on culture, society and economic development, and its advantages and disadvantages. It considers the opposition to globalization and whether globalization has an effect on cultural convergence or divergence. The driving forces behind globalization are examined and the future trends in globalization are suggested, particularly with relevance to the BRICs:

> Globalization is not incidental to our lives today. It is a shift in our very life circumstance. It's the way we now live. (Giddens, 1999: 19)

The conduct of international business and diplomacy has been transformed by the emphasis on global interdependence and the continuing erosion of traditional boundaries. International business has increased global interactivity, with greater participation, for example, by shareholders interested in ethical standards, the spread of the fast-growing influence of the social media (for example, Facebook and Twitter) and the influence of international NGOs, for example, Médecins sans Frontières and the humanitarian relief agencies and international charities. There is also global concern for the environment, global warming and the possible countermeasures such as control of emissions, as seen at the Davos meetings and the increasing demand for the development of renewable energy technology.

We have seen the impact of austerity measures, the shock waves of the banking crisis and the recent worldwide recession, the continuing crisis in the Eurozone and the impact of natural disasters. Against this background, there has been the rise in the economies of the BRICs, the Arab Spring, which has still to run its full course, the continued uncertainty about the nuclear weapons aspirations of both Iran and North Korea, and the concern over 'failed states' such as Somalia. All these events have their effect on the interdependence of nations in the increasing globalized economy of the twenty-first century and hence on traditional cultural values.

Definitions of globalization

Globalization has been described as: 'The production and distribution of goods and services of a homogeneous type and quality worldwide ... the operation of dispersed organizations with sales and production units close to markets' (Rugman and Collinson, 2006: 454). It is the interlinking of national and regional cultures economically, politically and culturally under the impact of international trade and international trade organizations, such as the World Trade Organization (WTO), the International Monetary Fund (IMF) and regional groupings such as the EU, NAFTA, Asia-Pacific Economic Cooperation (APEC) and the Caribbean Community (CARICOM).

If we take the fashion industry as an example of globalization's effect on working practices and cultural convergence, multinationals such as Marks & Spencer, Gap, Next and Sainsbury's 'Tu' brand source their materials and outsource their production all over the world. Raw materials such as cotton, wool and silk provide employment for workers in less developed countries (LDCs). Alpaca wool comes from South America, cotton comes from Egypt, wool comes from New Zealand and silk traditionally comes from China and Thailand. Their manufacturing process is equally international, as, for example, Marks & Spencer's products are made in a wide range of countries where local labour is cheaper than in the UK, such as Indonesia, Madagascar, Turkey, Sri Lanka and Bangladesh. A pair of jeans will often be the product of several countries, with the design in the USA, cotton from Benin, the pockets from Pakistan, the material being dyed in Spain, France making the zips and Germany the buttons. As a result, a typical teenager's wardrobe may contain jeans, shirts and belts from China, T-shirts from Peru, a hoodie from Pakistan, other shirts from the United Arab Emirates, Turkey and Vietnam, and other jeans from Egypt. After China, Bangladesh is now the world's second largest manufacturer of clothing.

A global village

'By 2010 we shall be truly living in a global village and cyberspace will be the town square' (Snyder, 2004: 22). The expression 'global village' was originally coined to illustrate that through the advancement of electronic communications, the peoples of the world can now be as closely linked as the people in a traditional village. This notion has now been enlarged to include religion, trade and migration, and the whole world is now seen by many as a single community. Roger Byers, the diplomatic editor writing in *The Times* on 23 June 2012 about the need for greater understanding and trust among nations in Europe, says that: 'The continent of Europe is the sum of its regions.' He cites as an example: 'An inhabitant of Nuremberg is a Nuremberger first, a Franconian second, a Bavarian third, then a German and a European.'

The components of globalization

Hill (2005) maintains that globalization refers to a shift towards a more integrated and independent world economy with three main components. His views can be summarized as follows:

- *Globalization of markets*: national markets have been merged into one larger marketplace. The emergence of a global norm in terms of customer expectations has made it possible to sell standardized goods all over the world, for example, the acceptance of Coca Cola, Levi jeans, McDonald's hamburgers, and Honda and BMW cars. Other examples include the sheer size and reach of companies like Wal-Mart, the world's largest retailer, ExxonMobil, the largest oil company, the merger of major airlines such as British Airways and Iberia to form the International Airline Group, and the acquisition of Cadbury's by the American food giant Kraft.
- *Globalization of production*: companies spread different parts of their production processes to different locations around the globe to take advantage of national and cultural differences in the cost and quality of the factors of production. They aim to base their individual productive activities at the most favourable locations. This can have the advantage of stimulating growth in the local economy, particularly in terms of providing local jobs and increased spending power.
- *Emergence of global institutions*: partly as a result of institutions such as the WTO and the IMF, global trade has grown faster than global output and foreign direct investment has greatly increased. Imports have penetrated industrialized nations and competition has increased in many industries. National economies are no longer self-contained as trade barriers

have come down as a result of the increase in cross-border trade and technological advances.

Globalization has helped accentuate international cooperation, such as in the expansion of the G8 group of countries to the G20. Greater diversity is seen as a major benefit to global problem solving. The EU is considering the development of a diplomatic service to represent all of its Member States.

The *IMF*, a multi-governmental organization, was formed in 1944 with the aim of preserving global financial stability and assisting the World Bank and other organizations in the global war on poverty. It also aims to facilitate the international flow of currencies. The current Chief Executive, Christine Lagarde, was appointed to succeed Dominique Strauss-Kahn. Min Zhu from China has been appointed as Deputy Managing Director, in recognition of the significance of the new emerging nations and especially the BRICs.

The *World Bank*, also formed in 1944, is a multilateral institution set up to provide investment capital for countries.

The *WTO* is a voluntary organization through which groups of countries negotiate trading agreements. It is the successor to the General Agreement on Tariffs and Trade (GATT) in which over 140 nations negotiated tariff reductions and made progress regulating such issues as intellectual property and trade in services. It is primarily responsible for policing the world's trading systems and has the authority to ensure that nation states adhere to the regulations laid down in trade treaties and to oversee trade disputes and the enforcement of trade laws. China was admitted to the WTO in 2002 and as a result of its membership is expected to reform its business environment with increased transparency, to abide by the WTO's global trading rules and to begin to increase the liberalization of its economy.

The driving forces behind globalization

Before we attempt to examine the advantages and disadvantages of globalization, it is helpful to summarize the main influences that have been the driving forces behind it. It must be stressed that there is no firm agreement about how to measure the increase in globalization accurately. However, those listed in Figure 11.1 are generally accepted as the main driving forces.

Decline in trade barriers – deregulation
Increased access to markets
Drive to secure competitive advantage
Access to different markets
Increased diversity and greater distributive risk
Expansion of English as an international language
Developments in electronic communication

Figure 11.1   Globalization: driving forces

- The *decline in trade barriers* and the deregulation of markets, with the resultant liberalization of trade and reduction of cross-border regulations with less bureaucracy, have made it easier to move goods, services, labour and finance across borders. International boundaries have therefore become less relevant as regional groupings have been set up to promote trade, such as the EU and NAFTA. There is also the possibility of the establishment of a large free-trade zone of 21 Asia-Pacific countries, to include China and Japan, by 2020.
- The *increased access to markets* involves increased competition, together with consumer pressure and greater consumer spending power. Access to new and wider markets offers the opportunity to trade a wider range of products. Firms can locate facilities wherever it is most advantageous, coordinate activities between facilities and transport their products to customers worldwide.
- The *desire to gain competitive advantage*: in the current globalized marketplace, there is intense pressure to find cheaper labour and establish control over scarce resources, particularly raw materials required for production, including rare earth metals such as lithium, lanthanum and cerium used in fibre optics, mobile phones and laptops.
- *Access to different markets* offering the opportunity to sell a wider range of goods. Economies of scale have been achieved by the rationalization and standardization of product ranges. Countries have specialized in the production of goods and services that are produced most efficiently.
- *Advances in technology*, for example, the increased use of automation, robotics and containerization, have improved both production and distribution. Improved communications have included electronic financial transactions, computer networks, the rapid interchange of information and ideas, and speedier decision making.
- *Greater distributed risk*, especially increased international diversity, as financial risk can be distributed across different markets with a wider range of products.
- The *spread of English* as the major international language, especially in advertising, the media and on the Internet.
- *IT developments*, including expansion of the Internet, e-commerce and social media sites, which have spread awareness of global brands and products. Developments in information processing and communication have reduced the costs of managing a global production system.

As a result of these, the traditional barriers to cross-border trade and investment, including time zones, distance, language, different national government regulations and business practices, have become much less significant.

Global corporations

The Fortune Global 500 is a ranking of the top 500 corporations worldwide as measured by revenue. The list is compiled and published annually by *Fortune* magazine. The USA still dominates the Fortune 500 list of the world's top-performing companies with 133. It has been estimated that over 50 per cent of US trade is carried out by global companies. Of the world's 500 largest companies, 40 per cent have their headquarters in the USA, 30 per cent are based in Europe and the rest are mostly in China, India and Japan.

Rank	Company	Country	Field
1	Wal-Mart Stores	USA	Retail
2	Royal Dutch Shell	UK/Netherlands	Petroleum
3	ExxonMobil	USA	Petroleum
4	BP	UK	Petroleum
5	Sinopec Group	China	Petroleum
6	China National Petroleum	China	Petroleum
7	State Grid	China	Petroleum
8	Toyota Motors	Japan	Automobiles
9	Japan Post Holdings	Japan	Diverse
10	Chevron	USA	Petroleum

Figure 11.2 Top Fortune Global 500 2011 companies (adapted from Fortune Global 500, 2011: http://money.cnn.com/magazines/fortune/fortune500/2011/full_list [date accessed 14 December 2012])

Wal-Mart was the largest company on the list in 2007 and 2008. ExxonMobil was in second place in 2007 and 2008, but overtook Wal-Mart in 2009. Wal-Mart regained the top spot in 2010.

An increasing number of global companies from emerging markets, in particular from the BRICs, are now appearing in the list. They include, for example, Gazprom (Russia), Petrobus (Brazil), Indian Oil and Tata Group (India) and Permex (Mexico). However, the G20 nations still represent 80 per cent of the world's economic output.

Below is a ranking of the top eight countries with the most Global 500 companies in 2011:

1. The USA   133 (165 in 2001)
2. Japan   68

3. China   61 (12 in 2001)
4. France   39
5. Germany   37
6. The UK   29
7. Switzerland   15
8. The Netherlands 13
(Fortune Global 500, 2011)

Is globalization a myth?

The debate over whether globalization actually exists still continues. Rugman and Collinson (2006) claim that many multinational companies are not making their profits from trade with LDCs, but rather from countries that are already affluent. Much of the argument depends on the definition of a global business. Rugman maintains that this is 'generally accepted as a firm with major operations (at least 20 per cent of its total sales) in each of the three regions of the broad "triad" of [the] EU, North America and Asia' (Rugman and Collinson, 2006: 80).

Much therefore depends on the definition itself. There is strong evidence that there has been a significant growth in trade within the three regions mentioned above. This fits the definition of regional business, where a firm has the majority of its sales inside one of the three triad regions, usually the home region. In practice, the debate between globalization and regionalization is really one of degree.

LDCs in a number of cases have been marginalized, receiving a declining share of trade and investment, and suffering from a high rate of debt and debt servicing. The net result is that there is still unequal distribution of income and an increasing gap between the rich and the poor.

The failure of the Doha Conference to gain full consensus for a free trade agreement and the pressure on Western Europe, the USA and China to consider at least a limited return to protectionist policies during the global recession have been a cause for concern. In his State of the Union address in January 2012, President Obama warned of the need for further measures to encourage US companies to reverse the shift of manufacturing off-shore because of the loss of jobs and the stagnation of wages in the USA.

The reaction to globalization

The downside of globalization is the outsourcing of manufacturing from the West, where factories have been forced to close as multinationals have found cheaper sources of production, in particular with significantly reduced labour costs, and raw materials in LDCs.

There is concern that global inequality is growing, with the result that in many countries there is increasing political instability and the widening of the gap in incomes between the minority privileged elite and the rest of the population. This trend is compounded by lower wages, poor health and safety in the workplace and corrupt business practices. These all contribute to a feeling of resentment and envy. The demonstrators against globalization, such as the Occupy movement, are part of a protest that sees globalization concerned more with making profits at the expense of social concerns and doing little to remove inequality. They maintain that they are forced to act outside legitimate politics because mainstream politicians do not appear to recognize the root causes of their dissatisfaction.

There are two very different ways of analysing the effects of globalization. One approach is to see the working of the market economy bringing about a world in which the gap between rich and poor increases. The second (and more optimistic) view is that a market economy will enable countries to converge towards a more equal state of prosperity as global trade liberalizes the world economy. If poverty persists, it will be because we have failed to allow the market to operate freely.

Workers, factory owners and those involved in the setting-up and financing of international operations gain in terms of wages. The transportation of the products is a further source of economic advantage to the countries concerned. Their finances in general benefit from the increased spending power of those employed as well as the psychological advantages to workers of having a job. Even where working conditions are relatively poor and the wages are low, many would say this is preferable to being unemployed without any source of income.

In *Globalization and its Discontents* (2002), Joseph Stiglitz, former Chief Economist of the World Bank and a noted academic economist, was a strong critic of globalization because its benefits are spread unevenly throughout the world. This is particularly the case in LDCs, where many people remain in poverty, notably in Africa, mainly because of a lack of resources in education to take advantage of the new technologies that have begun to make a difference to living standards in India and China. Stiglitz (2007) also contends that market reforms have been pushed forward too quickly, whereas individual countries should be free to experiment with alternatives and develop ways that are best suited to their cultures and their needs. He does, however, contend that globalization has some benefits: 'Opening up international trade has helped many countries grow far more quickly than they would otherwise have done ... Because of globalization, many people in the world live longer than before and their standard of living is far better.'

Writing in *The Times* on 19 February 2007, Stiglitz maintained that India and China have taken full advantage of the globalization of knowledge and markets to move hundreds of millions out of poverty, but in other parts of the world, the gap between rich and poor nations has increased, mainly due to the large subsidies in the North, which have depressed the incomes of those in the South and have increased their levels of poverty. He sounds a warning that unless globalization has 'more winners and fewer losers, there can be a backlash against globalization'.

Tony Blair, the former British Prime Minister, stated that: 'If globalisation only works for the benefit of the few, it will fail. The West must follow the principles that power, wealth and opportunity must be in the hands of the many, not the few. The global economy must be a force for good and an international movement' (*The Times*, 2 October 2001). In the foreword to a report on globalization for the Institute of Public Policy Research in January 2012, Peter Mandelson reiterates this view: 'There is growing evidence that global economic integration brings rising inequality within economies if the balance between those who benefit from globalization and those who bear the burden of the adaptation is not actively addressed.' This was a view that Professor Samuel Huntington had already expressed in his *The Clash of Civilizations* in 1993, when he emphasized that: 'The new global civilization is in fact a very narrow one, consisting only of the assumptions and values held by most people in the West, but worldwide this culture is shared by very few outside the West.' He went on to argue that because the world is modernizing its way of doing business and its communication systems, it does not necessarily mean that it is becoming more Westernized: 'The impact of urbanization and the mass communication, coupled with poverty and ethnic divisions, will not lead to people everywhere thinking as we do.'

However, despite Huntington's prediction, the so-called 'triad of the rich', namely North America, Western Europe and Japan, is now being increasingly challenged by the growing spending power of an affluent class emerging in the BRICs.

Opposition to globalization

The main arguments against globalization can be summarized as follows:

- Individual cultures are under threat of becoming more like each other because of the pressure of perceived cultural imperialism.
- Global companies do not always observe the minimum standards of health and safety for their workforce, with unfair wages and no trade union representation. These concerns are seen in the employment of children, poor safety at work, particularly in mines, such as in South America and China, and the exploitation of migrant workers, including people trafficking.
- The pervasive inroads of 'global soft power', as exemplified by the global branding of products, aggressive advertising by the media and their influence, particularly on the younger generation.
- Advanced economies move their manufacturing to LDCs for cheaper labour, thus causing employment problems in the home country, particularly for unskilled workers.

- The increased danger of protectionism because of the loss of manufacturing jobs and the stagnation of lower- and middle-class wage levels.
- Global companies should pay taxes in those countries where they make their profits. Instead of repatriating them to their home country, they should invest in the country where they are based.
- Global companies that pollute the environment should be made to pay for the clean-up costs. The principle of 'the polluter pays' should be enforced, as has been the case with BP following the huge oil spill in the Gulf of Mexico.
- Globalization is often used as an excuse for the transfer of moral responsibility and inertia in the face of social and economic deprivation.
- Global companies can be seen as a threat to the independence of the nation state, which appears to be subordinate to their power and influence.
- The outsourcing of employment, particularly in IT and the financial services sectors, to overseas countries can have negative effects on the home country economy.
- The demise of local languages caused by the widespread use of English.

Cultural convergence

Globalization has been compared to the process of cultural diffusion whereby elements of one environment permeate another and bring about significant change. Lower airfares, the media (particularly stations like MTV and CNN), the Internet and greater opportunities to travel are seen to bring about a certain degree of cultural convergence. Companies like Apple, Sony, Nokia and IKEA have aimed to drive the market and educate their customers to accept their products worldwide, and to consider them as 'must-have' products that are obtainable across national and cultural boundaries. This trend is defined as: 'The growing similarity between national cultures, including the beliefs, the values, aspirations and the preferences of consumers which are partly driven by global brands, the media and common global icons' (Rugman and Collinson, 2006: 132).

Theodore Levitt, an earlier supporter of the concept of the cultural convergence of trade in consumer goods across cultures, maintained in his 'The Globalization of Markets' that: 'Different cultural practices, national tastes and standards are vestiges of the past.' He sees the homogenization of tastes and preferences increasing, and national differences becoming less apparent, with global companies seeking to gain economies of scale and competitive advantage (Levitt, 1983: 92–101).

Globalization is open to the charge of cultural imperialism, which has been defined as: 'Replacement of one's culture, traditions, folk heroes and artefacts with substitutes from another' (Wild, Wild and Han, 2006: 56). Examples include the growth of the McDonald's franchises and theme parks such as Disneyland. The signs of an emerging global culture are often seen by some as predominantly Western and American, as in the teenage market for clothing, popular music and Western films. These trends arouse fears that the widespread standardization and availability of many global products will destroy the rich diversity of individual cultures. In business, there is evidence of a common 'global management culture', with the emphasis on global markets, global production and global communications producing common working practices. In Western Europe, North America and the BRICs, the more affluent and middle-class professionals continue to become more similar in terms of income, lifestyle, educational background and, most significantly, their aspirations.

Cultural divergence

However, Samuel Huntington (1993) believes that: 'Culture consciousness is getting stronger, not weaker. Nations will work closely together because of their similar cultural roots, rather than because of any ideological reasons.' He warns of the impending reaction against Western culture by other civilizations and maintains that the world after the Cold War still had its divisions, the most important being cultural, not ideological, political or economic. He saw the world fragmenting into different civilizations, including Western, Islamic, Hindu, Orthodox, Latin American, Chinese and possibly African.

Changes in the process of cultural convergence are generally very slow and there is considerable resistance to and evidence of actual cultural divergence. Cultures often force companies to adjust their business policies and practices, for example, in labour relations and the motivation of the labour force. Cultural differences still matter and may result in the need to launch local products to meet local requirements and tastes. The term *glocalization* has been coined to express the 'need to think global, act local' as the spread of globalization is increased by cultural diversity.

We now live in a more interconnected, less nationalistic world which promotes innovation, international trade and economic growth, the exchange of ideas, social interaction and cultural interchange. As a result, there is enhanced capacity to produce both local and national products. Consumer goods have become more focused on the preferences of individuals, with the result that consumer demand is less for uniformity but more for diversity. Multinationals are under continuous pressure to respond to local markets, local tastes and preferences. They employ local managers who better understand the local consumers and encourage them to take up positions in other parts of the world to broaden their cultural understanding and experience.

As such, cultural change in the modern world involves two contrasting and often conflicting processes, as outlined in Figure 11.3.

GLOBALIZATION **OR** LOCALIZATION

Companies resolve this conflict by meeting local preferences and adapting to local cultures by a process of 'GLOCALIZATION', which is:

GLOBAL INTEGRATION + LOCAL RESPONSIVENESS

Figure 11.3 'Glocalization'

People tend to pick and choose what to accept and reject, based on their views of their needs in relation to the culture in which they live. The supporters of cultural divergence believe that only superficial aspects of culture provide evidence of cultural convergence. In contrast, deeper moral norms that affect how people interact are less influenced by globalization. From the late twentieth century onwards, there are clear signs that consumer goods are more focused on the individual demands for diversity and not conformity. We are said now to live in a 'global village', but national cultures and cultural differences still persist: 'Nations have their own identities – spiritual, intellectual, cultural and political – which they reveal to each other through their actions' (Vaclav Havel, former President of the Czech Republic).

Future trends

Global trade depends on a stable financial climate and security to build business confidence. The financial turmoil in 2008–9 and the subsequent crisis in the Eurozone from 2011 slowed down the pace of globalization and the amount of foreign direct investment. The threats of international terrorism, including cyber-terrorism, piracy off Somalia and continued financial instability have contributed to a decline in the amount of international aid being given to the LDCs. In addition, there is the problem of the high rate of debt and debt servicing affecting many countries.

The Fairtrade Foundation was set up to increase the sales of Fairtrade products. It is an example of the increased pressure to obtain a fairer price for the workers' crops in LDCs. The Fairtrade organization aims to provide producers in LDCs with a basic price to cover production costs, everyday expenses and a small premium to be used to invest in community products such as building schools, health centres and improving the water supply. The lives of cotton farmers and their families have in this way been improved, particularly as more companies are buying Fairtrade cotton as part of their ethical trading policies.

Attempts by Fairtrade to improve the living standards of producers (mostly farmers) in LDCs have had some (albeit relatively limited) success. A total of 49 countries participate in the scheme to sell Fairtrade products that give a better deal to producers with the premium customers pay, for example, in coffee shops such as Costa and Starbucks. Café Direct is a non-profit coffee-making organization which attempts to guarantee a fair price to coffee growers. The principle behind Fairtrade ventures is to assist trade and reduce the reliance on direct aid as the best way of getting people out of poverty. However, the West continues to subsidize its own agriculture – for example, the USA has subsidized its own cotton, keeping the cost down in competition with African producers.

Environmental issues will continue to assume importance as the world is faced with a growing shortage of raw materials, fresh water and increasing energy requirements. Large global companies will continue to invest in new areas in the search for resources both under the ocean and in remote parts of the world. Even developing the technology to harvest rare metals from outer space is under consideration. Measures to reduce the effects of predicted global warming are being considered, despite resistance because of cost and, in some quarters, scientific scepticism about the reality of the effects of climate change. Plans to reduce carbon emissions already in place will be further developed, as will more research into renewable sources of energy. Pharmaceutical development will continue its efforts to eradicate diseases such as malaria and HIV/AIDS. With the world's population now having reached seven billion, there will be more research into and development of genetically modified crops.

In the twenty-first century, there has been a significant increase in global maritime trade, particularly in petroleum, natural gas and manufactured goods, including much use of containerization. As a result, there has been an increase of 40 per cent in the global maritime container fleet between 2008 and 2011, with more than 80 per cent of the world's trade being carried by sea. This has meant that the potential 'choke points', such as the Malacca Straits, through which pass three times as much trade as through the Panama Canal and twice that through the Suez Canal, are of vital importance to global trade. In addition, the Straits of Hormuz are the conduit for a quarter of the global oil production. Their security is threatened by piracy, international terrorism and hostile neighbouring states. As a result, there is active consideration of opening up an alternative northern route for much of global trade, in effect a new Northwest Passage.

The interdependence of global business means that any disruption to the global supply chain will have serious economic consequences. This is borne out by the results of the earthquake and subsequent tsunami and nuclear disaster in Japan in 2011. This caused disruption to the supply of components from Japanese plants, which affected car production in other countries and caused, for example, the temporary closure of General Motors' production lines. Global supply chains are threatened not only by natural disasters but also by local political turbulence and conflict, local corruption and international terrorism, as well as sudden fluctuations in demand, price volatility and failures in the transport infrastructure.

The drive to exploit scarce resources worldwide is another aspect of globalization which increases competition between those countries who are seeking new reserves of oil, gas and precious metals outside their own national boundaries. This drive is at its most intense in Africa, where China is investing heavily in the search for rare earth metals. As a result, prices have risen significantly and China has been accused of following a policy of 'economic imperialism'. However, both Chinese investment and that of other foreign nations have helped improve local economies, raising the standard of living and providing employment. Russia has already begun to take an active interest in developing the oil resources in the Arctic region, and the UK and Argentina are in dispute over the Falkland Islands and its off-shore potential oil resources.

Failed states such as Somalia pose international problems as havens for international terrorism and piracy to the whole global community. A failed nuclear state poses the greatest threat to global stability, particularly with the threat of nuclear terrorism. However, any intervention by outside forces into a sovereign state can be justified only on humanitarian grounds when all other diplomatic efforts have been exhausted and can be sanctioned only by agreement of the UN General Assembly and with the full agreement of the Security Council in accordance with Article 21 of the UN Charter.

Summary

- Because of the need to access new markets, increasingly scarce resources and cheaper labour, to do business globally is now less a luxury and more a matter of competitive survival.
- The BRICs will become increasingly important global players and will challenge the economic leadership of the West. As the US share of global economic output continues to decline, a more balanced picture is developing among the industrialized countries. With the growing pace of globalization, there will be an increased need for international managers to operate effectively in the global marketplace, demonstrating a wide range of cross-cultural competencies. They will face increasing complex and uncertain environments, characterized by continuous change.
- However, cultural differences will remain important and will need to be taken into account in the production of new products, as 'glocalization' will be the trend for the future in order to gain competitive advantage and meet the individual requirements of a growing body of more affluent local consumers.
- Globalization will continue to be attacked as it is seen by its opponents to provide a cover for the failure of individual countries to deal with their social, economic and ethical problems. Protesters will continue to attempt to persuade governments to address these problems. The G8, the G20, the World Bank, the IMF, the OECD and the UN have all

acknowledged that poverty is the greatest challenge. Globalization will also continue to pose a perceived threat to diversity if people become purely consumers with little or no respect for their own cultural heritage. With the threat of continued financial crisis, there will be the risk of succumbing to the demands for protectionism.

- There has been an increased awareness of the corporate social responsibility of global companies towards their employees, particularly with regard to health and safety, working conditions and fair wages, the environment and their shareholders. This approach has, to an extent, counterbalanced some of the disadvantages and negative views on the effects of globalization on LDCs and local cultures.
- International business and diplomacy have both displayed increased interactivity, with more emphasis on wider networking and consultation across national boundaries, developing a 'coalition of the willing' to cooperate to find mutual solutions to global trade problems.
- Nevertheless, globalization will be seen to fail if it provides legitimization or an excuse for the inability of individual states to cope with their own social, economic, ethical and environmental problems through poor governance.
- Globalization will also be seen to fail if the G8, the G20, the World Bank, the IMF, the OECD and the UN do not work together to achieve the global targets originally set for 2015 to halve global poverty, reduce infant mortality and ensure that every child has the right to education.

References

Giddens, A. (1999) *Runaway World: How Globalisation is Reshaping Our Lives* (London: Profile Books).

Hill, C.W. (2005) *International Business: Competing in the Global Marketplace*, 5th edn (New York: McGraw-Hill).

Huntington, S. (1993) *The Clash of Civilizations* (New York: Free Press).

Levitt, T. (1983) 'The Globalization of Markets', *Harvard Business Review* 61(3): 92–102.

Mandelson, P. (2012) 'Foreword' to *Report on Globalization* (London: Institute of Public Policy Research).

Rugman, A.M. and Collinson, S. (2006) *International Business*, 4th edn (Harlow: Pearson Education).

Snyder, D.P. (2004) 'Five Meta Trends: Changing the World', *Futurist* 38(4): 22–7.

Stiglitz, J. (2002) *Globalization and its Discontents* (New York: Norton).

Stiglitz, J. (2007) *The Times*, 19 February.

Wild, J., Wild, K. and Han, J. (2006) *International Business: The Challenges of Globalisation* (Upper Saddle River, NJ: Prentice Hall).

Further reading

Bartlett, C. and Chosal, S. (1998) *Managing Across Borders: The Transnational System* (Boston, MA: Harvard Business School Press).

Brewster, C., Harries, H. and Sparrow, P. (2001) *Globalisation and Human Resources* (London: Chartered Institute of Personnel Development).

The Economist (2001) 'A Survey of Globalisation: Globalisation and its Critics', 29 September.

The Economist (2008) 'A Bigger World: Special Report on Globalisation', 20 September.

Forster, N. (2000) 'The Myth of the International Manager', *International Journal of Human Resource Management* 11(1): 126–42.

Hobsbawn, E. (2007) *Globalization, Democracy and Terrorism* (London: Little, Brown).

Rugman, A.M. (2003) 'Regional Strategy and the Demise of Globalisation', *Journal of International Management* 9: 409–17.

Rugman, A.M. (2005) *The Regional Multinationals* (Cambridge University Press).

Shaw, W, and Glennie, A. (2012) *Report on Globalization* (London: Institute of Public Policy Research).

Stevens, M. and Bird, A. (2004) 'On the Myth of Believing that Globalization is a Myth', *Journal of International Management* 10: 501–10.

Wolf, W. (2004) *The Case for the Global Market Economy* (New Haven, CT: Yale University Press).

12
Cultural Diplomacy and Nation Branding

Summary

Definitions
Aims of cultural diplomacy
'Soft power' – definitions and examples
New concept of 'smart power'
Instruments of cultural diplomacy
The concept of 'nation brand'
Nation brand management
Case study: the Beijing Olympics and the London Olympics

Introduction

This chapter covers the development of the role of cultural diplomacy in communicating national values, ideas and policies to the general public worldwide. It also includes the differences between 'hard' and 'soft' power. Examples are provided of the development of instruments for spreading cultural diplomacy through broadcast media, cultural missions and education, and the emergence of advertising concepts in the understanding of cultural diplomacy. It examines how nation brand management can be used to improve a nation's standing in the world. The chapter concludes with a short case study on the Beijing and London Olympic Games.

Cultural diplomacy

Cultural diplomacy is one of the means by which a country increases its visibility on the global stage and gains political and economic influence. A country does this by drawing attention to its culture, traditions, lifestyle and through export promotion in such a way as to make it attractive to other nations and regional groups. It achieves this by using cultural missions through education and training, emphasizing the arts, sport and the media.

Cultural diplomacy is a deliberate policy employed by both governments and institutions to increase influence and recognition abroad in the eyes of other countries. It involves the exchange of ideas, art and other cultural aspects, all aiming to foster cultural understanding between nations. However, the exchange of culture through special exhibitions, visits by ballet and theatre groups and others can have another effect: it can be used not only to improve the political and commercial aspects of the projecting country but also to improve its overall international standing. At its most effective, cultural diplomacy can create a cultural presence in the receiving country and help ensure that it more fully recognizes and understands the projecting nation; however, it can also encourage exports and even attract inward investment merely by its presence. As a former Director of the British Council said: 'A visit by Britain's Royal Ballet can be more valuable than a trade mission.' Cultural diplomacy can therefore be seen as the third pillar of foreign policy alongside political diplomacy and economic diplomacy.

The evolution of cultural diplomacy

Cultural diplomacy can be seen as part of the evolution of the diplomatic mission, whereby ambassadors and other diplomatic staff and their embassies have developed a way of maintaining contact and influence with foreign allies and their courts. The system first consisted of a plenipotentiary or government spokesperson represented at court with the sole intention of influencing the monarch or leader. As diplomatic missions grew, over time ambassadors related to each other as professional colleagues, friends and rivals, and a parallel communication channel of ambassador to ambassador opened up, with allies working together to influence the government of the country in which they resided.

In the twentieth century, this communication channel and cooperation was extended to international NGOs working in the country, such as international charities, educational organizations and international organizations like the UN. A major change was the development of communication between the embassy and a limited, wider non-diplomatic public, such as business leaders and opinion formers, including the press and other parts of the media. It was a natural progression for embassies to extend their mission to the development of cultural diplomacy, often through specialized agencies, closely linked to and often carrying diplomatic status. At this level, diplomatic missions became more involved with the general public through activities such as language and cultural training, and the promotion of cultural events and trade missions. They now have become engaged not only through radio and TV but through websites, emails and blogs. The final stage in this evolution has been the emergence of the embassies supporting trade missions and of the foreign ministry as the coordinator of trade initiatives. In addition, embassies have been involved in many countries, together with companies, politicians, celebrities and nationals living and working abroad, in raising the international profile of the country as a whole. This overall process of evolution can be represented as below:

- Ambassador to court.
- Ambassador to ambassador.
- Ambassador to opinion formers (outside the embassy).
- Ambassador to general public (through cultural diplomacy agencies).
- Nation to world (through all available channels).

In analysing this process, two stages in the progression are highlighted. The first is the development and implementation of cultural diplomacy, while the second is the recent development of nation branding to raise, enrich or update a country's international profile.

'Soft' power

In the nineteenth century, in his treatise *On War*, Carl Von Clausewitz, the great Prussian military general and theorist of war, recognized the relationship between war and coercion and politics and agreement. For him, war was part of politics. He wrote: 'War is not merely a political act, but also a real political institution, a continuation of political commerce, a carrying out of the same by other means.' In the late twentieth century, this was developed by many theorists, notably Joseph S. Nye, who contrasts the concepts of 'hard' power, that is, military, economic and other forms of coercion to influence opinion and get one's way, with that of 'soft' power, that is, persuasive action by non-military means. Nye sees soft power as a power of attraction which depends on the ability to influence the preference of others. He describes it as: 'A means of educating the general public and present and future decision-makers to think favourably about the country whose country offerings they are enjoying' (Nye, 2004: 4–5).

However, 'soft' power can have a harder edge in that it can actively leverage and positively energize diplomacy in such areas as human rights, disaster relief and other humanitarian issues, the protection of the environment and the potential dangers of climate change. It can also help to prepare the ground for wider diplomacy in foreign policy.

Earlier examples of the use of 'soft' power have been the use of 'panda diplomacy' exemplified in the first instance when the former Soviet Union was presented with pandas as a gift from China in 1957. President Nixon visited China in April 1972 and was given a gift of two pandas. In 1974, the former Prime Minister Edward Heath made the first visit to China by a British political leader and also received two pandas; two white rhinos were sent to China in return. In 2005, China, in an attempt to resume closer ties with Taiwan, offered a gift of a pair of pandas.

Writing in *The Times* on 30 April 2011, Lord Hall of Birkenhead, the CEO of the Royal Opera House in London, emphasized the importance of culture in the exercise of 'soft' power and called on the UK government to use it more often. In a debate on cultural diplomacy in the House of Lords, he said: 'When it works well, it helps to explain what lies behind conflict; to give understanding of different viewpoints and cultures; to find solutions to issues and conflicts that seem intractable; and to promote dialogue and deep and lasting relationships of mutual understanding.'

Nye argues that the use of diplomacy in promoting the culture of one group of people to another creates greater awareness and helps develop interaction between the two cultures through cultural activities. The important point is that this interaction must be a two-way process. 'Soft' power can also be used to help a country 'punch above its weight' and develop a stronger international identity. Examples include:

- advanced technology, particularly the export thereof;
- active concern for the environment on the global stage;
- overseas aid and development assistance (for example, the UK's current commitment to 0.7 per cent of GNI);
- membership of alliances and multilateral institutions (for example, the UN, NATO, the EU, the IMF and the WTO);
- a free media with worldwide reach (for example, the BBC World Service);
- well-developed educational services (for example, university exchanges, scholarships, English language teaching and the British Council);
- hosting major events (for example, the Summer Olympic Games, the football World Cup and heads of government meetings);
- evidence of social harmony and welfare provision in a democratic society.

Although the difference between cultural diplomacy and propaganda is subtle, it is still important. Propaganda persuades you to believe my point of view, often against your own will, whereas cultural diplomacy encourages you to identify with my views because you like the kind of views I represent. The element of choice is fundamentally important in distinguishing between the two. The other important point is that cultural diplomacy is not limited to states or governments, as NGOs and high-profile individuals often play an important part, whether sponsored by the state or not.

'Smart' power

The new concept of 'smart' power, a combination of 'hard' power (the power to coerce or threaten by using military or economic power) and 'soft' power (the power to convince and persuade through cultural diplomacy), has been introduced. The term 'smart' power was first coined after the invasion of Iraq as a more feasible alternative to the neo-conservatism of the Bush administration. According to Nye, America must 'learn to cooperate and listen if it is to become a "welcomed world leader"'. He defines 'smart' power as: 'The power to persuade other countries to do what the USA wants.' Examples can include the formation of NATO, the post-Second World War Marshall Plan and global free trade (Nye, 2009).

Instruments of cultural diplomacy

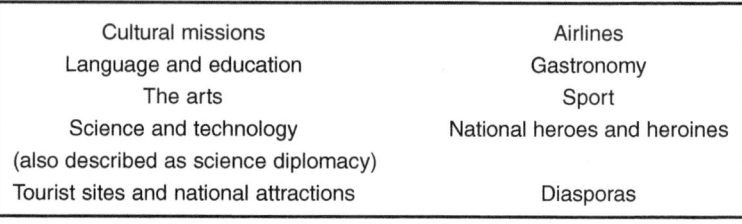

Figure 12.1   Instruments of cultural diplomacy

Cultural missions

Cultural missions are bodies specifically created for the purpose of cultural diplomacy. They are now taking on a wider role, especially in countries where diplomatic relations are not well established. Much of what is done in fostering cultural relations has long-term aims and benefits. Examples include the British Council, the Goethe Institut, the Cervantes Institute, Alliance Française, Culturesfrance and the Chinese Confucius Institute.

The British Council

The British Council operates in over 100 countries and is the overseas cultural arm of the UK government. It is sponsored by the Foreign and Commonwealth Office (FCO) by means of a grant-in-aid, but is operationally independent. It is responsible for building mutually beneficial relations with other countries and providing an up-to-date picture of life in the UK. The Council provides cultural exchanges, exhibitions, education, including English language courses and teaching material, scholarships, consultancy and the provision of teachers.

In recent years, the British Council has positioned itself as a cultural relations agency rather than as an agency of cultural diplomacy. In other words, it increasingly sees its role as bringing peoples together, mainly through the medium of English as an international language. By definition, it is a *mutual* activity involving cultural diplomacy and cooperation between governments, cultural agencies and corporations, and not a 'marketing Britain' activity designed solely to promote British culture and British business.

Culturesfrance

Culturesfrance was described by Philippe Douste-Blazy, the then French Foreign Minister, in 2006 as an attempt to give French culture 'a label, a signature, a trademark' in the eyes of the world. The agency aims to promote French literature, cinema, fashion and the arts abroad to restore 'le rayonnement', the radiating influence of the French language and culture. This is associated with investment to halt the decline of the influence of the French language when faced with the increasing spread of English as the main international language.

Language and education

As we saw in Chapter 4, English is recognized as the major language of global communication as well as a lingua franca. It has also spawned a major international industry in English language learning and in teacher training. Cultural diplomacy often takes the form of cultural exchanges and scholarships as well as the provision of English language teachers overseas. Very often, it is the cultural missions themselves that provide this role, but other actors such as university courses both at home and abroad can achieve the same result. Other examples include the large number of short summer courses or 'learning holidays' that draw many young people from around the world to the projecting country. An example is the major effort being made by the Confucius Institute, which was set up to promote a wider understanding of Chinese language and culture. The Confucius Institute for Business has been opened in London, jointly established by Tsinghua University and the London School of Economics. Another example of the use of education in cultural diplomacy is the Fulbright Scholarship sponsored by the USA.

The arts

Culture is often associated with the arts, in particular with 'high art', which can include exhibitions of paintings and sculpture and the performing arts of theatre, film, classical opera and ballet. Even during the Cold War, visits were made to the UK and the USA by the Moscow State Circus and the Bolshoi Ballet. The Royal Ballet visited Cuba in 2009 and was given a very enthusiastic reception. The exhibition in 2011 of Afghanistan Art and Culture at the British Museum aimed to develop a better knowledge and understanding of Afghanistan. Another example is the cooperation between the Royal Opera House in London and the National Centre for the Performing Arts in Beijing. Although extremely influential, these 'high art' events are often targeted at a country's educational elite. However, equally important are more widely popular events such as film festivals, pop music and fashion. These are often closely associated with the international media, which can ensure they have an impact far beyond the immediate circle of those who attend.

Science and technology

Although relatively few agencies have invested in it, the widespread knowledge of a country's advanced level of science and technology can have a very positive impact on a country's image. A recent example was the British pavilion at the Shanghai Expo in 2010, a six-month trade fair on which China spent twice as much as it did on the Beijing Olympics. A total of 45,000 people a day visited the British pavilion, where over 140 trade and investment-related events were staged. The British Council also put on daily programmes of entertainment throughout the duration of the Expo.

Non-governmental organizations

An example of the use of NGOs in the furtherance of cultural diplomacy is Médecins sans Frontières, an international medical support NGO which was originally founded by a group of French doctors in 1971 after the Biafran War in Nigeria. It is now a completely international organization, but its very name gives influence to its founder, France. International technical aid given to LDCs by NGOs to help improve their harvest, irrigation, medical support and many charitable activities are other examples, as is the highly publicized collaboration between astronauts on Russian and US space missions.

Tourism

Tourism promotion is another area which helps to raise a country's profile. It is primarily aimed at increasing the number of people visiting the country. It can also contribute to the overall attraction of a country by presenting images such as its landscape, historic cities and culture, as well as its arts and its people. It is controlled by national agencies who are able to build the image of the projected country.

Below are some examples of slogans coined to encourage tourism in certain countries.

'Incredible India'
'Smile, you're in Spain'
'Malaysia, truly Asia'
'Island of Aphrodite' – Cyprus
'Tranquil land of smiles' – Thailand
'This is the heart of Africa' – Nigeria

Figure 12.2   Building national images

After the Cold War, the USA promoted 'Good Tourism' among its citizens to encourage them to visit the former Iron Curtain countries in order to establish an image of the friendly American.

Airlines

By 'flying the flag', a national airline can carry a nation's name and values around the world. However, a change in brand image can rebound on the airline concerned. For example, in 1997, British Airways tried to increase the internationalization of its image by redecorating the tail fins of its aircraft with international images rather than the red, white and blue of the national flag. This initiative was unsuccessful and the former Prime Minister, Margaret Thatcher, publicly criticized it by wrapping a handkerchief around the tailfin of a model BA airliner to hide the design. The then Head of British Airways, Rod Eddington, reversed the 'world images' branding. Airlines include in their branding everything from comfort, service, atmosphere and design to their security. Due to privatization and competition from other commercial airlines, national airlines are increasingly under pressure, but the larger ones such as Air France and Lufthansa and the recent merger of British Airways with the Spanish airline Iberia are still recognized as 'flag carriers'.

Gastronomy

The French have made gastronomy into an art form. French cuisine and French wines are well known and highly regarded throughout the world. Other countries have emulated the French with respect to wines, for example, Spain, Chile and South Africa. Culinary diplomacy is now a well-recognized form of 'soft power' and is actively promoted, for example, by the governments of Korea, Sweden and Mexico. Indian and Chinese restaurants, by contrast, appear in many countries as a result of private enterprise, rather than as any form of government policy.

Broadcasting

Broadcasting has a long history as a means of cultural diplomacy and, at times, blatant propaganda. During the Cold War, the Voice of America was set up specifically for the latter purpose. In Myanmar, Aung San Suu Kyi, the supporter of increased democracy, considered the BBC her lifeline during her long years of house arrest. Kofi Annan described the BBC as 'the UK's greatest gift to the world'. In 1992, Germany set up Deutsche Welle, broadcasting in 30 languages, including German.

The BBC World Service, founded in 1932 as the BBC Empire Service, is respected worldwide for its reputation for reliable and accurate news, supplemented by its educational programmes and its independent editorial policy. Originally funded by the FCO, but now financed by the licence fee rather than by direct government grant, the World Service and its Arabic and Persian TV channels cost £287 million in 2011. Despite recent cuts, it continues to broadcast language services in 28 languages and remains the world's largest international broadcaster, with an audience of 180 million on radio, TV and online.

Sport

As part of popular culture, hosting or achieving good results in high-profile international sports events have a major impact on national image, for example, the Olympic Games and the FIFA World Cup. However, the 1936 Olympic Games in Berlin was a blatant example of using sport for the propaganda of National Socialism.

National heroes and heroines

The use of sporting 'icons' and the cult of celebrities have been used to achieve cultural influence. An example was David Beckham in support of the UK's bid for the 2012 Olympics in Singapore. Negative instances, of course, can have an adverse effect, such as the exposure of drug cheats in, for example, athletics and cycling. The list of heroes and heroines, both past and present, could include Churchill and Nelson for the UK, Mahatma Gandhi for India and Nelson Mandela for South Africa.

Diasporas

A significant immigrant population can also influence the image of a country abroad by virtue of its skills and culture, which add value to the host country and reflect well on their country of origin. The Irish, Scottish and Indian diasporas, for example, have been notably effective in this respect. However, the image of diasporas can act as a disadvantage when the migrant community is seen as under-privileged. This has been the case, for example, with North African immigrants in France, particularly in the outer suburbs of Paris, Turkish migrants in Germany and Mexican immigrants, notably in the southern states of the USA.

Nation brand management

Anholt and Hildreth (2004) suggest that cultural diplomacy can be legitimately characterized as part of a 'nation brand', a term Anholt originally coined in 1998. It is an instrument through which other nations and their people can be influenced and has its roots in what has been called the 'country of origin effect'. The concept of nation branding is derived from the commercial notion of a brand. A brand is a set of rational and emotional benefits and experiences that enable a product to command a premium in its chosen market.

Another way of describing a brand is a name, term, sign or combination of these that is intended to identify the goods and services of one business or organisation and to differentiate it from those of its competitors. Only when this product or service kindles an emotional dialogue and connection with the consumer can this product truly qualify to be a brand.

Anholt maintains that nation branding is most likely to be successful when the brand is lived by the citizens: 'Country branding occurs when public speaks to public; when a substantial proportion of the population of the country – not just civil servants and paid figureheads – gets behind the strategy and lives it out in their everyday dealings with the outside world' (Anholt, 2003: 123).

Nation brand management is something that a nation uses to project its image, employing the instruments of cultural diplomacy. It aims to help a country raise its international profile through imaginative policies of promoting diplomatic, economic, entertainment and sporting prowess. These aims can be characterized as follows:

- creation of a positive, confident self-image of a country;
- achievement of greater political acceptability, respect and influence internationally;
- raising export potential;
- increasing attraction as a destination for inward investment;
- increasing tourism and tourism-generated income.

Effective nation branding can influence where foreign companies invest and market their goods or outsource their manufacturing. It may also be instrumental in persuading international sporting bodies, such as the International Olympic Committee, where major sporting events are to be held. The image of a country may also influence the decision as to where supranational bodies, such as the EU and NATO, establish their headquarters.

Anholt considers that his central conception of nation brand is to regard the image or reputation of a particular country as a whole, which would include all its international actors, those from the general population, its business companies, politicians, celebrities and the diaspora. It would also include its engagement in cultural and diplomatic relations, product and investment promotion, talent recruitment and, most importantly, its actions on the international stage. However, he strongly considers that it is completely impossible to simply 'brand' a nation in the commercial product sense.

Anholt has therefore distanced himself from the concept of 'branding' with its marketing implications. He maintains: 'On the one hand, "brand" is a perfect metaphor for the way places compete with each other in the global marketplace for products, services, events, ideas, visitors, talent, investment and influence. This is simply the reality of globalisation and it is inescapable. On the other hand, "branding" makes many people think of superficial marketing tricks, perhaps some cynical portrayal of the nation state and other human communities.' In his view, a country's reputation is defined by what it does, by what it makes and not by how it advertises itself. He maintains: 'A national reputation cannot be constructed; it can only be earned.'

Instruments of nation branding

A number of international political and sporting events and institutions can have an influence on how a country is seen overseas. These include the following:

- political – influence with other heads of state;
- economic – for example membership of the WTO;
- entertainment – the development of a national film industry with export potential, such as Bollywood in India, French and British cinema, and Hollywood in the USA;
- sport – hosting a leading international sporting event, such as the World Athletics Championships, the Wimbledon Tennis Championships and the Olympic Games.

Anholt has evolved the concept of the nation brand hexagon. A country's image is formed by a wide range of factors represented in the hexagon. These are six natural 'channels' through which countries typically convey their images to the world:

- tourism;
- exports;
- people;
- governance;
- culture and heritage;
- investment.

In another work, *Competitive Identity*, Anholt replaces the term 'national brand strategy' with 'competitive identity' as the core of the hexagon. He defines 'competitive identity' as: 'The synthesis of brand management with public diplomacy and with trade, investment, tourism and export promotion' (2007: 7). He makes the change in emphasis as the term 'brand' is misleading, since it can also have negative and emotive associations. His 'Competitive Identity Model' has been extended to cities and regions of countries, covering images, identities and the reputation of places. His more recent work, *Places* (2009), provides insight into how countries, regions and cities can begin to understand, measure and manage their international standing and identity. It focuses on examining in what ways it is actually possible to influence a national image.

Anholt's Nation Brands Index (2005) is an extensive social survey which has been used by many governments and other agencies. It is based on the premise that the way in which a country is perceived can make a critical difference to the success of its business, trade and tourism efforts, as well as its diplomatic and cultural relations with other nations. A similarly extensive survey is his City Brands Index, which covers how the world views its cities.

Nebenzahl (2001) considers that: 'Country image is not a static phenomenon but country images are long-lasting and difficult to change. That is why in order to improve a country's image it may be easier to create new positive associations rather than try to refute older ones.' This has been the aim of successive German governments since 1945 and has also been the case in Spain from 1975 onwards after the Franco regime. Another example of rebranding is that of the Lebanon after the 1975–1990 civil war. This consisted of the widespread use of the logo of the national flag, promoting the Lebanon as a desirable tourist location and as an important financial centre. Lebanese food and famous entertainment stars such as Shakira were also publicized.

The UK has a unique cultural identity based on its monarchy, traditions and pageantry. It also had an empire lasting 250 years, which made it one of the leading and most powerful countries in the world. The UK (and in particular London) is still seen as one of the leading global tourist destinations. London is also viewed as a major international financial centre. The value of the monarchy as a long-term, politically neutral guide to national strategy and purpose is of great importance. In 1999/2000, the British Council commissioned a survey of overseas attitudes to Britain entitled 'Through Other Eyes'. Broadly, it concluded that Britain was suffering from an identity crisis, bound by its past but uncertain of where its future lay. This perception implied that although Britain is one of the most open and progressive developed countries in the world, its image is too often associated with the past. It can be seen by some foreigners as a rather large theme park. In fact, its success has derived from fostering innovation with which to challenge the future.

The importance of the Olympic Games

The Summer Olympic Games have become one of the pre-eminent ways of focusing global attention on a city or a country, raising its profile, attracting foreign visitors and encouraging investment. The existing image is a major factor in the selection process of a candidate for the host city. There is a symbiotic relationship between the existing brand image of a candidate city and the new brand image created by hosting the Olympic Games. When considering the location for the Olympic Games, the International Olympic Committee takes into account factors such as the following:

- the population of the country must support the bid and be prepared to make it work;
- the country must have significant tourism potential;
- the country must have a foreign and domestic policy that is compliant with the Olympic ideal.

In any international sporting event, Anholt points out, national image or 'brand' can strongly influence the choice of host country for a wide range of business decisions, including major sporting and cultural events. As he writes: 'Using facts alone to pick the host country for an international sporting event is fine up to a point, but in the end it has to be a location that the television audience finds exciting and appealing. Athletes and spectators have to feel happy about travelling and staying there, and their perceptions and prejudices about the place can carry just as much weight as practical considerations such as cost and transport links' (Anholt and Hildreth, 2004).

Case study: the 2008 Beijing Olympics

China has actively engaged in ways to exercise the use of 'soft' power as an adjunct to public diplomacy. The Chinese government sees 'soft' power as a fundamental component of its projection of national, economic, military and political power. It helps guard China against international criticism and boosts the country's international standing. President Hu, in his report to the 17th Party Congress of the Chinese Communist Party on 15 October 2007, declared that 'soft' power was not only a major component of national power but was also an 'important source of national cohesion'.

The Beijing Olympic Games were branded by the Chinese as 'The Peoples' Olympics'. For China, hosting the 2008 Summer Olympics was a major opportunity to 'brand' itself to the world as a leading power. The design of the Olympic emblem combined the Olympic spirit with Chinese culture. The use of mascots represented the national characteristics of China's most popular animals, namely the fish, the panda, the Tibetan antelope and the swallow, along with the Olympic flame.

The build-up to the Games was preceded by cultural diplomacy on a large scale, which included the following events:

- 2002: the foundation of the Chinese Culture Centre in Paris.
- 2002–2004: the Chinese government sponsored a series of Chinese New Year celebrations in New York, Bangkok, Sydney and London. In London, 200,000 attended the Chinese New Year celebrations in Trafalgar Square.
- 2004: the Chinese Culture Year was celebrated in a number of European cities.
- 2004: a large Chinese culture tour covered 22 African countries. This was, in effect, a precursor for Chinese economic expansion in its search for raw materials.
- 2005: the Festival of China was held at the Kennedy Center in the USA.

In addition, China hosted the Sixth Asia Arts Festival and increased American awareness of the Chinese export market, including the need to overcome the residual negativity of 'made in China' and the perceived cultural imperialism of Starbucks, McDonald's and American pop music and films. In Moscow, a Year of China programme was established to promote Chinese culture.

The Chinese also emphasized that their Games were to be 'green' and 'high tech'. All the above events were very actively reported in the *China Daily*, an English newspaper, and by the state-owned Xinhua News Agency and China Radio International (CRI), which, after the BBC, had the second largest audience in the world. The Confucius Institutes overseas promoted the Chinese language and culture abroad. The image of Chinese sports heroes, for example, Yao Ming, the Chinese baseball star of the NBA Houston Rockets, was exploited, typifying the image of Chinese people as positive, active and endowed with team spirit. In addition, Chinese kung fu clubs were set up overseas and popular films such as *Crouching Tiger, Hidden Dragon* and film stars such as Bruce Lee and Jackie Chan were widely publicized. Furthermore, Chinese cultural values formed from their cultural past were extolled, including the idea that peace is precious, the spirit of order and discipline and the importance attached to education. All these were to counter negative perceptions, particularly in the West, of China posing an economic and potential military threat, the vexed question of human rights and restriction on ethnic minorities, problems in Tibet and the ongoing Taiwan question.

Case study: the 2012 London Olympics

Britain's bid for the 2012 Olympic Games to be held in London emphasized five aspects, all presenting the image of a modern, confident, innovative and caring Britain:

- Youth: the British bidding team included young people representing all main multicultural groups from the East End of London, where the Olympic Park would be constructed. The implicit message was to support Britain's youth, who represented the future of sport in the UK.
- Multiculturalism: London was presented as a multicultural society with over 25 per cent of its citizens coming from ethnic minorities. It would be the international host of all nations, whatever their colour, race or creed.
- Regeneration: the Olympic Games would provide London with the stimulus to regenerate a run-down eastern part of the capital and provide new sporting facilities, not just as a sports venue but also as an integral part of community life in London.
- British identity: the British values of tolerance, 'fair play' and sportsmanship, freedom of expression, civic sense of cohesion and voluntary work, individualism, social welfare, a strong sense of history, dislike of over-regulation and excessive centralized control were to be highlighted as indicative of British cultural values.

- Britain's position in the world: this would be emphasized through such means as British culture, art, support for LDCs through international aid, London's position as the major financial centre, world-renowned educational institutions, high-tech industries and welcoming deregulated financial markets and financial services attracting inward investment.

The International Olympic Committee meeting in Singapore made its decision to choose London on three sets of factors:

- The facilities to be provided, including the competitors' accommodation, the supporting infrastructure and security arrangements.
- The overall ambience – the welcome, the facilities for the teams and the pageantry.
- The enhancement of the values of the Olympic ideal and the legacy that the Games would leave behind, including the buildings and the infrastructure to provide a new, prosperous and sustainable environment for the local population.

In addition, the bid emphasized that London had the passion as well as the logistical and financial means to create an exciting and motivational environment. The bid was also helped by the personality and commitment of the British bid leader, the twice Olympic gold medallist Sebastian Coe, and the networking skills of the then Prime Minister, Tony Blair.

On 27 April 2007, Keith Khan, the Olympic Games Head of Culture, announced that the Games would offer Britain the opportunity to rebrand itself, emphasizing Britain's diversity, youth, fashion and technology. Using iPods and social networking sites, Khan wanted to create a youth atmosphere for the Games, with a Games World Festival of Youth Culture and an international exhibition programme.

David Ritterband, the Marketing Director for the Mayor of London's office and a former advertising executive at Saatchi & Saatchi, aimed to rebrand London and reinvent its identity through the Games: 'The 2012 Games gives us an opportunity to talk about ourselves differently and how we want to be seen in the world' (*The Times*, 27 March 2009). He aimed to enhance the perception of London as a pleasant place to live, shop, work and play, and the Games would offer the chance to showcase London's businesses.

The Opening Ceremony of the 2012 London Olympic Games aimed to create images of Britain that would remain in people's minds. These included the arts, the history of Britain's development from a rural society to an industrial power, the development of the welfare state, British inventions (including the World Wide Web), contemporary popular culture and its celebration of youth. The Games themselves emphasized the spirit of competition and friendship between nations. The large number of volunteer helpers, 'the Games Makers', with their friendly welcome and helpfulness throughout the period, was much appreciated and made a very positive impression on overseas visitors.

Summary

- Cultural diplomacy can play an important part in raising a country's profile and as the 'third pillar' of foreign policy. It can also increase influence in international affairs, stimulate exports and attract inward investment.
- The main instruments of cultural diplomacy include cultural missions, language and education, broadcasting, national airlines, the arts, science and technology, gastronomy, sport, national heroes and heroines and immigrant diasporas.
- Cultural diplomacy is now well established as an important tool in the work of diplomacy and international NGOs and will continue to be developed in creating good relationships between international actors.
- The concept of the 'country of origin effect' has had an impact on much more than simply a country's exported products. It also impacts on its people, culture, ideas and government policies, attracting tourists, talent and investors. This 360-degree expansion of the 'country of origin effect' is what Anholt calls 'nation brand'.
- The Summer Olympics in London in 2012 attracted worldwide publicity, fame and prestige, helping to increase tourism and raising the UK's international profile. It also provided the stimulus to develop the urban and national infrastructure and amenities. Both London in 2012 and Beijing in 2008 were impressive examples of the 'Olympic effect'.

References

Anholt, S. (2003) *Brand New Justice: The Upside of Global Branding* (London: Butterworth Heinemann).

Anholt, S. (2007) *Competitive Identity* (Basingstoke: Palgrave Macmillan).

Anholt, S. (2009) *Places* (Basingstoke: Palgrave Macmillan).

Anholt, S. and Hildreth, J. (2004) *Brand America: The Mother of All Brands* (London: Cyan Books).

Hall, Lord of Birkenhead (2011) *The Times*, 30 April.

Nebenzahl, D. (2001) *National Image and Competitive Advantage* (Copenhagen Business School Press).

Nye, J. (1990) *Bound to Lead: The Changing Nature of American Power* (New York: Basic Books).

Nye, J. (2004) *Soft Power: The Means to Success in World Politics* (New York: Public Affairs).

Nye, J. (2009) 'Soft Sell', *The Times*, 15 January.

Nye, J. (2011) *The Future of Power* (New York: Perseus Books).

Further reading

Anholt, S. (1999) *Another One Bites the Grass* (New York: John Wiley & Sons).

Barsamian, D. and Chomsky, N. (2001) *Propaganda and the Public Mind* (London: Pluto Press).

Berger, P. and Huntington, S. (2003) *Many Globalisations: Cultural Diplomacy in the Contemporary World* (Oxford University Press).

Chunovic, L. (2004) *Why Do People Love America?* (London: Sanctuary Publishing).

Dinnie, K. (2008) *Nation Branding: Concepts, Issues, Practice* (London: Butterworth Heinemann).

Edelman, M. (2001) *The Politics of Misinformation* (Cambridge University Press).

Furneaux-Harris, B. (2009) 'To Think and Fail', Brand Management Seminar, London November.

Golding, P. and Harris, P. (1997) *Beyond Cultural Imperialism: Globalisation, Communication and the New International Order* (London: Sage Publications).

Goldstein, A. (2005) *Rising to the Challenge: China's Grand Strategy and International Security* (Stanford University Press).

Held, D., McGrew, A., Goldblatt, D. and Perraton, J. (1999) *Global Transformations: Politics, Economics and Culture* (London: Polity Press).

Hobsbawm, E. (2007) *Globalisation, Democracy and Terrorism* (London: Little, Brown).

Huntington, S. (2002) *The Clash of Civilizations and the Remaking of World Order* (New York: Free Press).

Kagan, R. (2003) *Paradise and Power* (London: Atlantic Books).

Kolb, B. (2006) *Tourism Marketing for Cities and Towns* (London: Butterworth Heinemann).

Leonard, M. (2006) *Public Diplomacy* (London: Foreign Policy Centre).

Marshall, Sir P. (2004) *Positive Diplomacy* (Basingstoke: Macmillan).

Morgan, N., Pritchard, A. and Pride, R. (eds) (2004) *Destination Branding* (Oxford: Elsevier).

Olins, W. (2004) *On Brand* (London: Thames & Hudson).

O'Shaughnessy, N. (2004) *Politics and Propaganda: Weapons of Mass Seduction* (Manchester University Press).

Riordan, S. (2004) *The New Diplomacy* (London: Polity Press).

Robb, D. (2004) *Operation Hollywood* (Amherst, NY: Prometheus Books).

Schneider, C. (2003) *Diplomacy that Works: Best Practice in Cultural Diplomacy* (Princeton, NJ: Center for Arts and Culture).

Seabrook, J. (2004) *Consuming Cultures: Globalisation and Localities* (Oxford: New Internationalist Publications).

Snow, N. (1998) *Propaganda Inc.: Selling America's Culture to the World* (New York: Seven Stories Press).

Szondi, G. (2008) 'Public Diplomacy and Nation Branding. Conceptual Similarities and Differences', *Discussion Paper in Diplomacy No. 112* (Netherlands Institute of International Relations, Clingendael, October).

13
Transfer of Skills, Technology and Knowledge

Summary

Terminology
Technology transfer
The challenge
International aid
Profile of the effective aid adviser
Knowledge, turnkey arrangements and management contracts
Resistance to change
Barriers to transfer
Overcoming problem areas
International Joint Ventures
Case study
Effective transfer of skills and knowledge
Licensing and franchising

Introduction

This chapter is concerned with the rapid increase in technological advancement and its transfer across cultures. This is a vital area for the UK in its endeavours to seek competitive advantage in exporting in the face of fierce global competition. It is helped by the liberalization of cross-border movements, primarily in the EU, and the use of electronic communication, research and market intelligence.

Technology transfer

Technology transfer can be split into two main areas:

- *Trade in goods and services*: this consists of manufactured goods and services, for example, computer software and financial services. This can be achieved either by direct exporting, export sales teams or local agents, or by joint ventures, for example, BP/Amoco's liquefied natural gas project in Guandong, China. In some cases, financial assistance from the International Finance Corporation, a branch of the World Bank Group, may be made available for international projects such as infrastructure development that will improve a country's economy.

- *Trade in skills and knowledge*: this consists of direct selling technical know-how, licensing, franchising, knowledge agreements, management contracts and consultancy. This is an expanding area and with the comparative decline in UK manufacturing, it is becoming of increasing importance in the UK's export drive. Examples include HSBC introducing personal banking systems in China and PricewaterhouseCoopers and KPMG providing advice to Eastern European cultures on accounting systems.

In both cases, understanding of the impact of culture on assisting in the winning of export orders is often of vital importance, particularly in the transfer of skills and knowledge to other cultures.

'Information exchange is an integral, often overlooked, aspect of globalization' (International Monetary Fund, 2000). Foreign direct investment brings technical innovation, including knowledge about production methods and management techniques that represent a highly valuable resource for developing countries.

The advantages of technology transfer are that the receiver country or company gains the benefit of advanced technology as a result of the development that has already been carried out by the other company. In certain countries, the transfer of technology, skills and knowledge is a precondition for allowing foreign companies to set up operations. The supplier may obtain the advantage of access to low-cost labour and materials, a future market in the local environment and first-hand knowledge of the local culture's sensitivities and preferences, as well as the goodwill that the new technology has generated and the granting of possible tax concessions to encourage investment. In addition, there is the benefit of new jobs being created and increasing the skills base of the local workforce. Disadvantages can include the squeezing out of similar projects in the domestic market and the difficulty in repatriation of income accrued in the receiver country back to the provider's home base.

The transfer of skills and knowledge is not confined to developed countries; indeed, it applies increasingly to joint ventures in many parts of the world. It is also an important role for expatriates working overseas as, for example, project managers, members of trade missions, staff in embassies and High Commissions, particularly commercial attachés, aid workers in government agencies and NGOs, and teachers working overseas. This transfer is a complex process involving much planning, including market research, product design, recruitment of local staff and their training, as well as complying with the regulations of the receiving country. In many situations, the transfer involves elements of management of change with the emphasis on building trust, the need for shared objectives, realistic expectations and the identification of key change agents, including, where appropriate, government officials, managers and supervisors.

In the UK, with the decline in manufacturing, there is an increase in selling the skills and knowledge rather than the product itself and in providing long-term consultancy in such areas as engineering, construction, accountancy, educational systems and financial services. Many of these are part of foreign direct investment (FDI). Essentially, the process involves 'translating' knowledge and skills from the cultural context of the provider to that of the receiving culture.

Research carried out by the Canadian International Development Agency (CIDA) in the early 1990s (Kerley, 1990) shows that although high technological standards were a prerequisite for eventual success in transfer, much depended on the communication skills adopted during the transfer process and on achieving congruence with the local culture. This was echoed by Michael Heseltine during his time as Deputy Prime Minister in 1995 in charge of revitalizing UK exports, when he said: 'It's no good being able to design good, new products or new services, if you can't communicate their value to customers in a language and manner they understand.'

The challenge

The transfer of skills and knowledge is a very demanding task requiring energy, patience, perseverance and commitment to overcome a variety of cultural, social, economic and political obstacles. The main areas which may prove problematic are the local cultural values and sensitivities, the interpersonal skills required to establish a climate of trust and mutual respect, the amount of training required both in the providing culture and the recipient culture, and establishing criteria against which progress can be assessed. Above all, there is a need for shared objectives for the project, with clear and realistic expectations of the benefits to both parties in the agreement which will contribute to their long-term business association.

Trade missions

Trade missions act as a focal point for exporting and external trade relations. They help to promote trade between nations and increase a country's exports as well as coordinating import and export procedures. Embassies and High Commissions abroad provide valuable support for trade missions from the home country. Today's diplomats receive considerable training in business matters, often being seconded to multinational companies for a period to gain real experience. Those working in trade commissions may require a detailed briefing on the cultural background of potential recipients as well as on their business practices. An example of a very effective trade mission was the British representation at the Shanghai Expo in 2010.

The Department for International Development

Formerly known as the Overseas Development Agency (ODA), the Department for International Development (DfID) is responsible for implementing the government's allocation of overseas aid. It also provides a number of advisers and project managers to give technical and professional help to overseas governments. Much of this aid goes to LDCs, mainly in Africa and Asia, on such projects as famine relief, assistance in areas of drought, disease eradication and the welfare of refugees caught up in internal conflicts.

Advisers usually receive a detailed briefing on the culture, economy and politics of the area in which they will be operating before their departure. They are selected because of their professional and technical expertise in the area of the aid project, as well as because of their ability to work in remote areas, to be self-reliant and to have empathy with the host culture. At times, they may have to operate in dangerous areas where there is the risk of becoming involved in local conflicts, civil war or, in extreme cases, being taken hostage.

These advisers have to work closely with their local counterparts and need to understand how they themselves are perceived by the local people. Inevitably, there can be situations where the stereotypical view of the Western aid adviser is that of somebody who is comparatively rich, an expert and mainly concerned with upholding the views of the donor country. As a result, they may encounter some hostility. Foreign advisers may also encounter some resentment from host country nationals because of the length of time they stay in the country before handing over responsibility for the project to local managers and the local workforce.

In such situations, much tact is required, as well as the ability to stand back and delegate responsibility, acting more as a facilitator or as a 'coach' as the project develops. People often learn best 'by doing', by real experience. They also need to be able to evaluate progress and report back to their headquarters in case adjustments have to be made.

Profile of the effective aid adviser

The following skills listed in Figure 13.1 are required in addition to being professionally qualified with the appropriate education, training and experience.

Realistic pre-departure expectations: aware of the constraints and barriers to effective performance, but confident as a result of good pre-departure briefing that these can be overcome
Flexible approach to ideas and points of view; adopting a non-judgmental perspective
Acknowledging and respecting input from representatives of the receiving culture
Good, patient listening skills
The ability to perceive the needs of others
The ability to build relationships and work in a team
Sensitivity to and respect for local social and cultural values
The ability to show initiative and propose solutions to unexpected problems that may arise
Confidence in his or her professional expertise and ability to inspire others

Figure 13.1   Profile of the effective aid adviser

Analysis of risks

The transfer of technology to overseas companies or governments, whether as part of international aid, FDI or setting up IJVs, always carries certain risks. These can be minimized by preparatory risk analysis involving detailed market research, evaluating the existing competition in the chosen market and an assessment of the political and economic stability of the country in which such investment is considered. The analysis would also include an assessment of the projected spending power of the population, the stability of its currency, existing business and labour regulations, the bureaucratic pressure of government agencies and the general security of the area. Although this chapter is more concerned with the cultural aspects that are part of the overall risk analysis, in order to be successful, the following factors should be reviewed when drawing up a technology transfer programme:

- the availability of an educated and trained local labour force;
- the cultural appropriateness of the technology for the intended recipients;
- local government policies on licensing restrictions, equity ownership and local asset ownership by foreigners;
- local taxation laws and restrictions on the repatriation of payments back to the supplier country;
- the effectiveness of legal protection in the local market;
- the risk of national expropriation if there is a change of government.

One of the most important areas where there can be cultural dissonance is in relation to corporate culture, particularly if one culture is very dominant and wishes to exercise overall control over the venture. In the case of certain IJVs, the local government may insist on a partnership with the provider but will retain overall control. In Saudi Arabia, for example, foreign oil companies are expected to hire and train Saudi petroleum engineers.

Knowledge agreements

Selling knowledge abroad is an increasing trend. An obvious attraction is that the actual investment in the foreign operation can be relatively small, although there is a risk that the knowledge can be used in a competitive product or system unless stringent legal safeguards covering copyright, patents and trademarks are enforced. Another area that may cause problems is the need to ensure consistent quality control. In certain cases, the provider may be involved in an ongoing consultancy capacity.

Turnkey arrangements

A turnkey arrangement is a contract under which one company agrees to design, build and install the necessary equipment for a new plant and then hand the plant over to the purchaser to manage completely when it is up and running. The arrangements can often include the continued training of staff after the facility is fully operational. Such projects can comprise, for example, nuclear power plants, airports, oil refineries and major infrastructure projects as well as defence sales, such as BAE Systems' contract for the provision of arms for Saudi Arabia. An example of a large construction company involved in a turnkey project is the US engineering giant Bechtel, which completed the new Hong Kong International Airport in 1998.

The contracts may require expertise in hiring and motivating local workers and can be in remote areas, with the resultant requirement for accommodation, appropriate infrastructure and a number of expatriate workers. There is also a need for detailed contracts to cover when the project is to be completed to the required handover standard, how long the training will continue after the handover date and when final payment is to be made. There is also the risk that a supplier may be awarded the project by the receiving government for mainly political reasons, such as to enhance the reputation and prestige of that government and not for the technology advantages for the local community.

Management contracts

Management contracts usually involve a company providing management expertise and personnel to assist a foreign company for a fee for an agreed period, for example, the provision and/or training of specialist key management personnel. The advantage is that the providing company receives income without much capital investment. An example of this is the managing by the British Airport Authority (BAA) of airports in Indianapolis, Naples and Melbourne (Daniels, Radebaugh and Sullivan, 2007: 500). Other examples include international hotel operations and large computer systems.

In a management contract, the local company will most likely hold all of the equity, but in some instances the provider may also hold a small amount. This allows the provider to negotiate other terms if required. Management contracts are often operated in publicly owned industries, in particular, transport, utilities, service industries such as hotels and hospitals, food processing and in the petrochemical industry (Brooke, 1996: 89).

Possible barriers to the transfer of skills and knowledge

The most likely barriers to the transfer of skills and knowledge are cultural differences and resistance to change and training requirements, but could include many of the following points listed in Figure 13.2.

Local cultural sensitivities	Government interference
Different value systems	Excessive bureaucracy
Poor project definition	Communication problems
Language difficulties	Inappropriate technology
Training requirements	Lack of specialist skills
Health and safety regulations	Environmental concerns/pollution
Resistance to change	Security problems
Unrealistic expectations	

Figure 13.2   Barriers to the transfer of skills and knowledge

Local cultural sensitivities

Local cultural sensitivities can include different views of the cultural importance of time. As discussed earlier, there are often problems in adjustment between basically monochronic and polychronic cultures. In addition, attitudes towards authority and seniority can cause problems, as can different methods of gaining consensus at meetings. At a local level, cultural differences can include religious practices, holidays, festivals, prayer times and fasting. All these require sensitive adjustment to different cultures and work practices.

When Nissan, Toyota and Honda were encouraged by the British government to set up car plants in the UK, the Japanese companies prepared by first learning about the trade unions in the existing plants and the British management style. There were some initial problems in establishing Japanese-style working practices, for example, just-in-time, 'lean production' and worker involvement in increasing quality. Training was introduced to explain these and employee commitment to the new working practices was achieved by detailed consultation and the successful promotion of synergy between the two cultures.

In the years shortly after the collapse of communism in Eastern Europe, both Hungary and Poland offered tax and other financial incentives to entice Western firms such as General Electric and General Motors to build factories in their countries to help speed up the transition from a command economy to a market economy. A lack of cultural sensitivity and cultural awareness was at first a major barrier for companies seeking to invest in the Czech Republic. This was seen in the initial stages of the merger of Skoda/Volkswagen because of the lack of understanding as how to manage the Czech workforce, which at first did not fully understand the changes in its working practices.

When transferring skills and technology, it is important to consider the pressure for local responsiveness, such as the following:

- differences in consumer tastes and preferences (for example, North American families like to purchase pick-up trucks, whereas in Europe, these are viewed as utility vehicles for firms);
- differences in electrical systems (for example, in North America, electrical systems are based on 110 volts, whereas in Europe, it is 240 volts);
- host government demands (for example, health care systems differ between countries regarding the distribution of pharmaceutical products).

Different value systems

These may include possible different standards regarding health and safety regulations at work, concern for the immediate environment, prevention of pollution, transparency of accounting and possible corrupt practices. There may also be different concepts or complete lack of knowledge regarding quality control procedures and commercial confidentiality. Some countries do not have the same standards regarding human rights, religious tolerance and respect for minority groups. Other concerns include different labour practices, trade union activity and equality of opportunity.

Language difficulties

The choice of the main negotiating language can cause problems, particularly if English is the chosen language and the receiving culture requires interpreters and translators. If that is the case, interpreters will require specific technical knowledge so that technical details can be accurately translated. If, however, there is a requirement for the expatriate staff to gain fluency in the local language, it will be necessary to allocate time for language training well in advance of the implementation stage. Between 40 and 50 per cent of UK exports go to non-English-speaking countries and few of the new markets have close cultural or linguistic ties with the UK. Trainers should be skilled in the use of techniques for checking understanding and should possess good presentational skills. There are potential problems when other cultures have to deal for the first time with Western business concepts such as quality control, staff performance appraisal and performance targets. After years of operating in a business culture which has been highly centralized and state-controlled, with limited opportunity for personal initiative, excessive overstaffing and protection from any form of external competition, there is significant room for misunderstanding and the need for retraining.

Poor project definition

Considerable preparation is essential to ensure that there is agreement between the parties from the outset as regards technical detail, the timescale for completion, the share of the cost of investment and expectations relating to output and production schedules. In addition, both the supplier and the receiver should have a proven capacity to deal with large-scale projects and the motivation and commitment to instigate early planning for both the human and management aspects.

Training requirements

Background briefing may be necessary in advance of the commencement of the project in the provider's country on the cultural differences in the recipient country. Training of local staff will be a high priority and much will depend on local human resources, educational standards and the provision of trainers, teachers and supervisors. Once the change agents have been identified, the training programme should include:

- the most effective language in which to communicate in the target culture;
- the interpersonal skills required to establish a climate of trust and mutual respect;
- the identification of the local conditions which may influence the way in which skills are transferred (for example, the level of education and technical knowledge of the local staff);
- the expectations of the receiving culture in terms of the timeframe for the handover period, the need for ongoing support, the identification of culturally sensitive areas and the need for confidentiality regarding technical inventions and specialized systems.

The training and professional development of local managers, supervisors and trainers will reduce the future dependence on employing expatriates. The training for the technology transfer should include the production of detailed job descriptions, job specifications and standard operating procedures where there is a need to formalize and record a set of explicit instructions which must be carried out in certain specific situations, for example, safety checks and quality control and plant operating procedures.

Health and safety regulations

Health and safety standards may well be of a lower standard in the recipient culture. Working conditions, safety equipment and medical care will need to be investigated and shortcomings remedied, and specialist training in safety procedures will need to be given.

Resistance to change

Resistance to change is likely to be an important area, particularly the need to convince the local community of the benefits of the new technology and the local workforce of the requirement to adhere to stricter safety regulations, efficient working practices and quality inspection. The receiving culture may differ radically in its management approach to its workforce, operating an essentially top-down approach with little participation in decision making or consultation at lower levels. It is essential to try to identify key change agents and to achieve their early commitment to the project, in particular the full support of senior management and, where appropriate, representatives of the government. It may be necessary to buy in expertise from outside the participating parties in order to have the benefit of experience in similar situations.

The reaction of the host/receiving culture to foreign expertise can itself be a barrier to transfer. The transferring culture's senior staff can be seen as a potential threat, taking local jobs and arousing uncertainty as to how long they will stay. A more cynical view may include a perception that they are mainly interested in what they can get for themselves out of the project, be it financial gain or having as their main motive the spread of political and commercial influence of the country implementing the transfer. Such concerns may further exacerbate latent resentment and create the following problem areas:

- resistance to local reduction in the workforce once the new technology is in place;
- lack of understanding of the need for quality control;
- lack of initiative to promote further progress after years of under-performance, poor leadership and non-existent after-sales service, all compounded by inadequate financial control;
- lack of comprehensive job descriptions, staff appraisals and performance criteria;
- attempting to try to manage change from a command, centralized and controlled system to a more liberal one too swiftly in the progression to a market economy.

Overcoming resistance to change depends to a large extent on how the senior staff of both the provider and receiver of new technology take the appropriate steps to manage the changes involved. In order to achieve the required change, it is suggested that the following key planning stages be implemented:

- communicate to all concerned the vision of the future – how the new technology will be beneficial to the company and the population as a whole;
- identify the barriers to change that will need to be overcome;
- identify the key change agents and opinion leaders who will assist the process of accepting the changes – managers, supervisors and trainers;
- agree the necessary investment in skills and capital to bring about the acceptance of change.

Much of the resistance to change can be reduced by ensuring that both the supplier and the receiver agree in advance on common shared objectives, and design and implement the project whereby both benefit from long-term economic progress. Cooperation at all levels is essential to maximize cultural synergy and collaboration for the common good. In order for this to be successful, the supplier should, as soon as technologically feasible, stand back and provide opportunities for local managers to have 'hands-on' responsibility. Only as a result of this will local managers be seen to be taking real decisions in the process, thus enhancing their local credibility and respect within the community and their own self-esteem. Cultural synergy will be achieved only when cultural influences are recognized and cultural differences and similarities are used to create new organizational structures, management procedures and working relations.

Communication

There needs to be an established communication system, for example, by holding regular meetings to discuss day-to-day progress in the transfer system, with reports to senior management to ensure that problems are anticipated and solutions are found before they become a serious issue.

Government and bureaucratic interference

Some governments, such as those of China and Russia, retain the right to have the controlling interest in FDI or IJVs in what are considered key industries, such as telecommunications, defence, financial services, petroleum and chemicals. This is, in effect, a form of protectionism and runs counter to the concept of trade liberalization as encouraged by the WTO. Excessive bureaucracy may also pose problems, for example, in areas such as work permits, customs regulations, taxation and repatriation of funds.

Inappropriate technology

The proposed technology transfer may appear too complex and too expensive for the objectives of the project, which may be mainly acquired for prestige purposes in the recipient country. It is important to stress the expected benefits to the receiving culture, for example, more jobs, increases in the local skills base and economic benefits to the local economy. Eagerness to adopt the foreign technology may be tempered in some cases by the realization of the need to introduce technology which may be more culturally appropriate and thus avoid potential resistance by the labour force that the new foreign technology would have entailed.

Environmental concerns

The long-term effects of pollution, both to the atmosphere through excessive carbon emissions and to the local area (including water supply contamination), must be considered. Here the providing culture has a duty of care to keep any long-term damage to the local environment to a minimum.

Security problems

Security covers not only the personal security of staff working on the project but also the confidentiality of technical know-how, the protection of patents and intellectual copyright, including designs, trademarks and logos, and correctly drawn-up licensing agreements. These aspects are of particular importance as the legal requirements may differ from country to country.

It is also advisable to establish and specify realistic objectives in the technology transfer process against a feasible timeframe, with agreement as to how performance is to be measured, what standards, including safety, are required and how quality is to be maintained and controlled in the future.

Selection of staff

As in multinational teams, the selection of key personnel is crucial for success in ensuring the effective transfer of knowledge, skills and technology across cultures. Apart from the requirements of professional expertise, those selected should have a good tolerance for ambiguity and the ability to cope with situations involving frustration and, at times, even hostile resentment. They also need cultural empathy in the ability to see how things are seen from the receiver's point of view. Whenever possible, local managers should be involved in the transfer at an early stage and local workers should be employed in such areas as the construction of facilities and the development of supporting infrastructure. It is important to build up the confidence of local managers by giving them opportunities to show their capability.

International Joint Ventures

Another form of approach which involves the transfer of skills, knowledge and technology is to set up an IJV. This is an agreement that can often be classified as a strategic alliance between two or more independent partners, or, in certain cases, with national government involvement, to own and control an overseas business. It can be to set up a completely new business, in many cases with a management that is separate from the partner's own management structures. When two or more partners are involved, such a venture is often called a consortium. IJVs may be encouraged by governments to make it financially and economically attractive for foreign investors to join in a partnership with a local company. They are an expanding area in international business, particularly in Russia and China.

A good example of an IJV is the production of the European Airbus, involving Aérospatiale, British Aerospace, Daimler-Benz Aerospace and Spain's Constructiones and Aeronautica. Earlier examples, of course, include Anglo-French cooperation in the consortia to build Concorde and the Channel Tunnel.

In some countries, such as China, the government may insist that IJVs are the only way in which a foreign company can enter the market in certain sectors of the economy. Reasons for forming IJVs can involve the desire to create a greater market by combining resources, reducing the risks by sharing the cost of investment, production and marketing, and achieving economies of scale. Added incentives are to acquire advanced technology, share the cost of research and development, share management expertise and reduce labour and transportation costs, as well as avoiding tariffs and customs duties. Foreign companies may decide to set up Research and Development (R&D) centres in other countries to satisfy their governments' requirements for transferring technology to local partners in return for tax incentives.

There are considerable cultural benefits to be gained from working with a local partner who has detailed knowledge of the local tastes, preferences, market potential and contacts, particularly with the local government. This local knowledge should be maximized to produce as much synergy as possible.

There are, however, potential risks in setting up an IJV. These include the sharing of competitive knowledge and technology, and the risk of nationalization or other forms of local government pressure. Paragraph 8 of the UN Resolution 'Permanent Sovereignty over Natural Resources' (1962) provides that: 'Foreign investment agreements freely entered into, or by sovereign states, shall be observed in good faith.' However, the validity of taking over foreign assets in the national interest also implies an obligation to pay compensation under customary international law. In addition, disputes may arise over differing objectives, the locus of control, pricing and production policy, and the amount of capital to be allocated for expansion or for dividends to shareholders. Some of these potential problems can be avoided by one partner having a majority ownership, which allows it to exercise control, especially over its technology. Nevertheless, shared ownership arrangements can still lead to disagreements and battles for control due to conflicts of interest over strategy and objectives. This was particularly evident in the case of the large TNK-BP Anglo-Russian JV, which was intended to act as a major example of Russia/UK cooperation but which has been fraught with difficulty since its inception in 2003. The situation has been further complicated by the intention of the Russian government-controlled oil giant Rosneft to acquire 50 per cent of BP's stake in TNK-BP, thus creating the world's largest oil producer.

Case study: transfer of technology to a Chinese company

A British multinational chemical company wishes to set up a joint venture with a Chinese chemical company in China in order to establish an advanced petrochemical project to serve the domestic market. The British company will be supplying much of the high technology involved, together with specialist training for the Chinese workforce who will be constructing the complex and subsequently taking a major share in operating the system on completion. The British company has held preliminary negotiations in China and has met with a number of potential problem areas. Its negotiating team has reported back to the Board in the UK. The Board has asked for a full briefing before further progress can be made. The following are the likely problem areas to be overcome before transfer of the technology and related skills can be successfully carried out:

- management of change: a modern Western enterprise with a well-established market economy background is seeking to set up a joint venture in a developing quasi-market economy. The result will produce both cultural and economic problems in adjustment;
- the need to identify key change agents, ensuring top management commitment and support from the Chinese government;
- government 'interference' is likely as the project progresses, particularly the insistence on having a majority control in what is considered to be an economically strategic industry;
- bureaucracy over labour regulations, local taxation and planning regulations;
- language difficulties, which will require specialist interpreters and translators;
- different negotiating styles, differences in representation, status and decision making;
- a need for precise project definition at all stages;
- quality control, health and safety regulations and inspection;
- training requirements for the local workforce, including managers and supervisors, taking into account educational standards, working practices, defining training objectives and local wage rates;
- sharing competitive knowledge and technology, including legal confidentiality safeguards;
- a need for environmental safeguards to avoid pollution and contamination of the local environment.

Figure 13.3 below provides a suggested approach through the key planning stages of such a transfer of technology.

Preparation	– gain commitment to project – assemble expertise – background briefing on cultural and social differences in receiving culture, including culturally sensitive areas
	↓
Detailed discussion	– government/top management support – develop trust between adviser and receiver – training required/planned
	↓
Implementation of project	– training of local workforce – construction and installation of specialist plant
	↓
Project completion	– greater participation by recipient – training of local managers and supervisors completed
	↓
Evaluation of project	– report and necessary follow-up

Figure 13.3   Model of effective transfer

Licensing and franchising

Licensing and franchising are two other main methods whereby technology, skills and knowledge are less directly transferred.

Licensing

Licensing is the practice whereby an organization or company (the licensor) owns intangible property rights, for example, patents, trademarks, know-how and copyright, and agrees to sell to another organization/company (the licensee) the right to use these for a specified period of time in return for a fee/royalty. The agreement may be for an exclusive arrangement whereby no other organization or company is permitted to have such rights for a specified geographical region for a specified period of time. The licensor and the licensee rely on each other to maintain quality and to promote the brand's image.

Licensing is often a less risky method of international expansion for the licensor than other methods of entry into the marketplace. There are certain advantages in licensing as the main requirement of the licensor is to provide technical information and assistance, whereas the licensee is responsible for funding the start-up of operations and the costs of development. There is, however, the risk of the licensor's technology and know-how being illegally acquired by competitors; in addition, the licensee may attempt to expand operations within the existing territory of the licensor.

Franchising

Franchising is a specialized form of licensing whereby the franchisor sells to an independent party (the franchisee) the right to use a trademark that is fundamental to the franchisee's business in return for a percentage of the franchisee's profits. It differs from licensing in that it gives an organization/ company more control over the actual marketing of the product.

Franchising is commonly found in the fast food sector (for example, Domino's Pizza, Pizza Hut, Kentucky Fried Chicken, Burger King and McDonald's worldwide) as well as in the clothing industry (for example, Benetton, which relies on franchised stores to market its products). It is also found in the car hire industry (for example, Hertz Rentals), in hotel chains (for example, Holiday Inn) and in car dealerships, entertainment and business services. Franchising usually involves a longer commitment than licensing, and franchising contracts specify the terms and the conditions that the franchisee must follow in return for permission to use the franchisor's brand name and logo. The franchisor may provide assistance with training staff and sales promotion and may stipulate certain requirements to be followed, such as standards of customer care, quality and health and safety standards.

The franchisee has the major advantage of knowing the local culture's preferences and can, with permission, modify its products accordingly. This is the case, for example, in India, where McDonald's offer 'veggie burgers' and drink companies produce varieties of drinks acceptable to the local palate and religious sensitivities.

Summary

- Technology transfer across cultures is not always an easy process and often does not lend itself to quick solutions. It requires skills to oversee complex, and at times ambiguous and often stressful, management of change scenarios. The identification of the potential obstacles at an early stage in the process is essential.
- The effective transfer of skills and knowledge across cultures is a very demanding task requiring energy, commitment and considerable training skills. It also involves an understanding of cultural sensitivities and often much patience and a willingness to overcome a variety of interpersonal, social, economic and political obstacles. Much relies on the ability to establish a climate of trust and mutual respect between the two cultures involved and, where possible, to maximize cultural synergy.
- These skills are particularly relevant for those involved in joint ventures, working as project directors, aid advisers, members of NGOs working

with the international community and diplomatic staff involved in developing trade links and the promotion of their nation's business interests in potential export markets. There are advantages and disadvantages involved in taking part in IJVs; one of the most desirable benefits is the gaining of local knowledge.

- At the outset, there is a need for comprehensive briefing of both parties, including management and workers, on the culture and business style, and the differences need to be fully identified and explained. The establishment of agreed procedures which are accepted by all concerned is essential to the success of the endeavour. These include setting realistic goals with targets for achieving each stage in the transfer, as well as incorporating wherever possible cultural synergy and the development of effective multicultural joint teams to oversee the transfer at all stages of the process.

- Training of the workforce in the necessary culture should include the production of job descriptions and job specifications required to implement the new technology as part of a management of change programme. To ensure a smooth transfer, there should be ongoing consultation between both parties at all stages. In addition, local government policies should be clear on any licensing restrictions, restrictions on equity ownership and ownership by foreigners of local assets, as well as sound protection for intellectual property rights and legal protection in the local market.

- Licensing and franchising are other methods whereby technology, skills and knowledge can be transferred. These offer less risk in capital outlay for both the licensee and franchisee, but both will need to meet certain standards of performance and quality as stipulated by the owners of the intangible property rights.

References

Brooke, M. (1996) *International Management: A Review of Strategies and Operation* (Cheltenham: Stanley Thorne Publishing).

Daniels, J., Radebaugh, L. and Sullivan, D. (2007) *International Business: Environments and Operations* (Upper Saddle River, NJ: Prentice Hall).

International Monetary Fund (2000) 'Globalization: Threat or Opportunity?', available at www.imf.org/external/np/exr/ib/2000/041200to.htm (date accessed 22 December 2012).

Kerley, D. (1990) *Cross-Cultural Effectiveness: A Study of Canadian Technical Advisers Overseas* (Borden, Canada: Canadian International Development Agency).

Further reading

Bartlett, C. and Ghoshal, S. (1998) *Managing Across Borders: The Transnational Solution* (Cambridge, MA: Harvard Business School Press).

Griffin, R. and Pustay, M. (2005) *International Business* (Harlow: Pearson).

Hurn, B. (1996) 'International Transfer of Skills and Knowledge', *Cross-Cultural Management* 3(1): 33–6.

Kayes, A., Kayes, D. and Yamazuki, Y. (2005). 'Transferring Knowledge Across Cultures: A Learning Competencies Approach', *Performance Improvement Quarterly* 18: 87–100.

Kotter, J. and Cohen, D. (2002) *The Heart of Change* (Cambridge, MA: Harvard Business School Press).

Rugman, A. and Collinson, S. (2006) *International Business* (Harlow: Pearson).

Seurat, S. (1979) *Technology Transfer: A Realistic Approach* (Houston, TX: Gulf Publishing).

Torrington, D., Hall, L. and Taylor, S. (2008) *Human Resource Management* (Upper Saddle River, NJ: Prentice Hall).

14
Cultural Profiling and Classification

Summary
• Definition
• Resources available
• Key cultural indicators
• The ECOLE principle of how to build a country profile for comparison and analysis
• Cultural clusters
• Stereotypes and generalizations
• Cultural fault lines
• Personality testing – examples of profiling
• Cross-cultural application of personality testing
• Limitations of cultural profiling

Introduction

This chapter discusses approaches to cultural profiling, its value and limitations, and how cultural profiling can be used as a method to compare cultures and as an aid in education and training for those working at an international level or relocating to another country. It also analyses key areas of investigation in cultural profiling, such as country knowledge, psychological attunement and personality factors. In addition, it assesses the success of cultural profiling instruments in the identification, recruitment and training for international mobility, including computer-generated profiling, graphic profiling and animated profiling.

Definition

Cultural profiling is an assessment tool for identifying cultural styles and preferences. It is a variation on management profiling, a way of analysing what kind of manager an executive is likely to be. Whereas a management profile tries to identify strengths and potential challenges in an individual manager's personality and style, a cultural profile tries to match a person's management style against the demands of a particular cultural group he or she may be dealing with.

Cultural profiling is often used to identify potential problems in relocation, but is also of value in identifying possible difficulties between members of multicultural teams. It helps an organization and individuals to assess their own cultural style and compare it with the culture to which they are moving.

A cultural profile is a summary of the key salient cultural issues that diplomats and business people may have to consider when operating in a foreign culture. It enables the focus to be concentrated on key issues and provides a common basis for comparison. Such areas include:

- values and attitudes – motivation, time and space, cultural taboos;
- communication styles – direct, indirect, formal, informal;
- leadership and decision-making styles – top-down, bottom-up, consultative, directional;
- social and professional behaviour – respect for age, status, qualifications, social etiquette;
- factors influencing lifestyle – cost of living, taxation, health and medical services, security, bureaucracy;
- organizational characteristics – centralized, decentralized;
- religious influences – state, secularism, ritual, freedom of expression;
- relations with other countries – trade, economics, membership of trade groups, defence;
- factual data – demographics, politics, language, minorities, climate, geography.

Cultural profiling may involve psychometric testing or simple comparison checking. Although it is sometimes used (not always appropriately) as a recruitment tool, it is much better suited to use as a guide to education and training needs. For example, if a member of staff is known to be more culturally attuned to working in the UK and is being posted to work in a foreign culture, it is helpful to identify the key differences in management style and what training may be needed to help that member of staff adapt more easily to the new environment.

Most executives and employees tend to be selected primarily on their ability and qualifications. Experience abroad and cultural awareness tend to be taken into account less often. This is why a degree of cross-cultural pre-departure training is important (as covered in Chapter 6) and why an assessment of cultural skills and aptitudes prior to training is helpful in identifying the training focus.

Resources available

The key to cultural profiling lies in the different methods used to identify cultural characteristics. A large number of tests, questionnaires and other instruments have been designed to help identify personality traits and the extent to which they are conducive to living and working successfully in a specified foreign culture. These can be broken down into three main categories, which are given in Figure 14.1 below.

Personality: psychometric testing tools of personality applied to different cultures and cultural clusters.

Management style: identification of key areas of difference in management style and their use in comparing one business culture with another.

Cultural style: a broader description of cultural traits, taking into account language, geographical background and history.

Figure 14.1 Types of cultural profiling

Personality and management studies are both employed in the recruitment and training of appropriate personnel. Resources in this area include the application of Cattell's 16 personality factors to cross-cultural interaction and the Myers-Briggs Type Indicator developed by the Myers & Briggs Foundation (the latter is discussed in Chapter 6). The specific application to management comes from management studies conducted by Richard Lewis Communications, the Chartered Institute of Personnel and Development in the UK and others.

The understanding of cultural style is a discipline much favoured in business schools, universities and other organizations. This approach involves a more holistic teaching method using pictures, films and interactive media to present a culture in all its aspects – traditions, folklore and lifestyle.

Key cultural indicators

The key cultural indicators that cultural profiling seeks to identify include the main background features which determine how a group of people approach life. Geography and vegetation are also key indicators, as are religion, kinship and relations with neighbours, including neighbouring communities. Much of this is encapsulated in the history of a community, which in turn will determine its core values along with its core fears, both of which are designed to ensure the survival of the group. Moreover, these will determine what they will resist and fight against. An awareness of these broad macro-features will help us to understand the expectations of a group from the outset. Although individuals may vary from this profile, knowledge of the broad indicators and how to react to them is a very helpful step in understanding another culture.

In addition, there are the micro-factors, the more detailed features that help us to understand a community's prevailing management style. Richard Lewis' *Lewis Model* identifies management features according to how they organize their use of time (see also Chapter 3). Following Lewis and others, Tomalin and Nicks (2010) have identified five factors which differentiate management styles and which can be studied comparatively. They have summarized these features by using the acronym 'ECOLE', which stands for expectations, communication, organization, leadership and etiquette. Within each category, they have identified a number of key differentiators, which are as follows:

- *Expectations (E)*: the core cultural values, the core cultural fears, the attitudes to space and to time and the motivation factors that characterize a business culture.
- *Communication (C)*: the key communication features, whether people are typically direct or indirect in their mode of speech, whether they prefer detailed explanation or general inference in giving instructions, whether they prefer to explain background context before saying what they want or the other way round, whether they are formal or informal in their style of address, whether they believe that emotions should be displayed or held in check, and, finally, whether their style of speech is fast or slow. Another important feature of communication is the understanding and the use of English as a world language. This was discussed in more detail in Chapter 4.
- *Organization (O)*: key features here include the business day and the business week, how people work in teams, how projects are organized and, above all, the attitude towards timely delivery of results.
- *Leadership (L)*: the predominant management style of a community is important in this category. How are decisions arrived at and communicated? Is responsibility held by the team or by individuals? What degree of delegation exists and what degree of responsibility exists within each level of delegation? The study of leadership can also cover gender issues, notably the position of women in leadership and the type of feedback and appraisal methods commonly in use.
- *Etiquette (E)*: although considered the most important factor because it is often the most evident feature in cross-cultural communication, etiquette is probably the least significant, simply because it is easier to change or adapt to. Nevertheless, there are three areas of etiquette that are seen to be of great importance. First is greetings and leave-taking. This can determine the first and last impressions. The second is gift-giving – knowing what to give and how much is acceptable, when to give and whether to wrap or unwrap in the presence of the giver. This can cause considerable embarrassment if done incorrectly. As regards hospitality, it is important to be aware of whether this is usually provided within the home or in

a public restaurant. It is also advisable to be aware of the conventions regarding arrival and departure, what and how much to eat and drink, where to sit and how the system of toasts works.

The function of ECOLE and other similar systems helps visitors (particularly business visitors) to identify quickly the key areas of potential difference and decide on the degree of appropriate adaptation. This may depend on seniority and culture, but also on the type of event. The main aim should be to focus on the differences and decide whether these are significant. If they are, the next step is to consider how best to react.

Cultural clusters

The use of cultural clusters is another way to classify and understand other cultures. Ronen and Shenkar (1985) carried out research by grouping countries into a number of clusters, each containing cultures which were deemed to be similar in a number of ways, with the proviso that there were some differences. One area where similarity prevailed was that of language. This was evident, for example, in the Latin American cluster, which contained Argentina, Chile, Colombia, Mexico, Peru and Venezuela, where Spanish influence was extensive, both in language and in many aspects of culture. Other cultural clusters included the Anglo, Nordic, Germanic, Latin European, Arab, Near Eastern and Far Eastern clusters. In addition, the research concluded that there were similarities within each of the clusters regarding work practices, work relations and job satisfaction.

Stereotypes and generalizations

As we have seen in Chapter 1, it is very easy to lapse into stereotypes and is equally important to try to avoid them. A stereotype is a statement which is considered to describe a whole country or culture and its people. It is fixed, does not allow for much variation and may have positive or negative connotations. It is often created out of historical prejudice and may have no relevance, if it ever did, to people today. Nevertheless, stereotypes such as the 'formal British', the 'inscrutable Chinese' and the 'brash American' still influence attitudes today.

In dealing with different cultures, the term 'generalization' may be preferable. A generalization is a statement about cultural behaviour which is recognized as being generally true of a large group of people in a country. Generalizations are a platform for further investigation, and although they state general trends, they do allow for some degree of deviation. As such, any generalization will be stated in the following terms: 'Most people' or 'a large number of people'. However, it is obvious that even generalizations about a national culture need to be treated with care. A number of factors will sub-differentiate national cultures and will need to be taken into account. These are as follows:

- *Regional differences*: the regions of a country may have many different styles and behaviours, and may contain people from different cultural backgrounds.
- *Professional differences*: professional experience will cause people's cultural behaviour to differ. One of the greatest differentiators is the difference between multinationals and locally based small and medium enterprises (SMEs). Multinationals often adopt the culture of the original head office or, more commonly, the international corporate culture based on US management approaches and methods. SMEs, which may in fact in some countries have a fairly large number of employees, are more likely to conform more closely to national business norms and conventions. There are also the social differences induced by family expectations and by issues of class, caste, attitudes to age and to multinationals in the workplace. Finally, and most importantly, is the personal experience of the people with whom you are dealing, their standard of education and whether they have travelled abroad, in which case also raising the issue of whether they are accustomed to fully understanding working methods that may be different from their own. When dealing with a new country, the key is to show interest and find out about it, especially its dominant organizational and leadership style. However, although it is natural to look at national styles first, it is important to use this as a platform for drilling down into the different levels of regional, professional, social and personal experience.

Cultural fault lines

In *The Clash of Civilizations* (1993), Huntingdon emphasizes that the differences between civilizations and cultures are at their most extreme on the 'cultural fault lines': 'The most important conflicts of the future will occur along the cultural fault lines separating seven or eight civilizations from one another.' Huntingdon considers that these are Western, Confucian, Japanese, Islamic, Hindu, Slavic-Orthodox, Latin American and possibly African. He highlights in particular the Arab/Israeli and Kashmir disputes as areas of potential cultural conflict.

We can apply the term 'cultural fault line' to any situation or relationship that can cause tension in a local community. If you recognize and are sensitive to the main cultural fault lines, you are less likely to cause offence or create embarrassment when dealing with people who are not from your community. The main cultural fault lines are likely to be as follows:

- *Language*: this occurs when two or more parts of the same national community speak different languages and have different cultures that are perceived to be in conflict with each other. Belgium's Flemish speakers (who are mostly based in Flanders) and the French-speaking communities in Wallonia and Brussels are one such example. In working with Belgians, it is helpful to be sensitive to the language community they represent.

- *Religion*: different parts of the community may be of different religions or belong to different sects within the same religion. Combined with class or economic divisions within a country, this can cause tension. Examples include the Roman Catholic/Protestant divide in Northern Ireland and the Shi'a/Sunni divide in the Middle East, for example, in Bahrain, Saudi Arabia and Iraq.
- *Race*: in some countries, different races living together can cause tension. An example of this is the White American/Black American divide, although this is now in a much weakened form as a result of the deseg-regation laws of the 1960s.
- *Economics*: some countries are divided into a rich region adjacent to a poor region. An example of this is Italy, where traditionally the Mezzogiorno, the area south of the capital, Rome, is traditionally considered to be much poorer than the more industrial north.
- *Politics*: in some countries, there are strong political rivalries or even sepa-ratist movements. An example is the recent Sudan/South Sudan conflict or China's uneasy relationship with Tibet.
- *History*: historical rivalry arouses sensitivity as it may have been the cause of wars and other conflicts. The relationship between the Turks and the Greeks over Cyprus is an example of this.

In all these areas, there are two main concerns. The first is the importance of acquiring knowledge to understand the historical background to these issues. The second is sensitivity to the views held by colleagues and contacts and the desire not to cause offence by raising potentially embarrassing topics.

The relationship between personality factors and cross-cultural traits

The main question for psychologists and for recruitment and HR managers has been whether research into personality factors and traits translates across cultures. In other words, if you are a Chinese manager intending to work in Nigeria or Brazil, are there certain personality traits that will allow you to adapt more easily and, if so, should these be a factor in deciding whether you are fit to do the job? In the selection and assessment of execu-tives for relocation, the key factors tend to be qualifications and experience rather than adaptability to a particular social or cultural environment. As discussed in Chapter 6, we have seen that failure to adapt to foreign customers and environments is a major cause of failure in overseas assign-ments and contracts. We should therefore try to compare key personality traits across cultures and, where appropriate, use this comparison as a tool in recruitment.

Personality testing

When attempting to understand a community or group you are dealing with, it is important that you begin by understanding yourself and your own prejudices. Understanding your own attitude and values is the first step in understanding others and dealing with them sensitively, not just in cross-cultural dealings but in business itself. This is why psychologists and business trainers have invested in developing tools for understanding personality and management styles. The first of these is personality testing.

Cattell's 16 personality factors

The 'father' of personality testing is the British psychologist Raymond Cattell, who made exhaustive studies of personality traits in the 1930s and 1940s. He produced a typology of 16 personality types based on his 16 PF (16 personality factors) questionnaire (Cattell, 1946). The questionnaire was released in 1949. In some form, this is still used today as a way of assessing suitability for particular jobs and as a tool in recruitment. Cattell's 16 personality factors, as they are known, have been translated and used throughout the world in assessment centres and by recruitment officers.

Cattell distinguished 16 primary personality factors: warmth, reasoning, emotional stability, dominance, liveliness, rule consciousness, social boldness, sensitivity, vigilance, abstractedness, privacy, apprehension, openness to change, self-reliance, perfectionism and tension. He also identified low-range and high-range descriptors for each characteristic. For example, if you take the first primary factor, warmth, a low-range descriptor would be impersonal, cool and reserved, whereas a high-range descriptor would be outgoing, attentive to others and people-centred.

The research into Cattell's 16 personality factors was replicated by W.T. Norman in 1963, who suggested that five key traits would be sufficient to form an effective personality assessment. Many researchers have debated how Cattell's 16 factors relate to the Norman's 'big five', with some arguing that 'dominance', for example, is spread across all five, with little specific influence on any one of them (Cattell and Mead, 2008).

Norman's five key traits are as follows:

- extroversion/introversion;
- high anxiety/low anxiety;
- tough-mindedness/receptivity;
- independence/accommodation;
- self-control/lack of restraint.

In his formulation, Norman matches his five traits to Cattell's personality characteristics. For example, in the first characteristic, extroversion/introversion, an extrovert personality is likely to be warm, lively, bold, forthright and self-reliant. An introverted personality is likely to be more reserved, serious, shy, private and group-oriented.

These 'big five' personality traits have become a standard frame of reference within recruitment and assessment.

The DISC profile

Another analysis of personality traits is the DISC profile. DISC is an acronym which stands for Dominance, Inducement, Submission and Compliance. However, this is often changed to:

D Drive
I Influence
S Steadiness
C Caution or Conscientiousness

The DISC profiling model is based on the psychological theories of William Moulton Martston and is explained in his book *The Emotions of Normal People* (1928). Its conclusions were also validated in comparison with Cattell's 16 personality traits by Professor Jim Morrison (1991).

DISC is based on the theory that behaviour can be characterized by the four personality types listed above. Everybody has elements of the four characteristics, but the extent of each one will vary between people. It is a tool which can be used to find ways of integrating people into the environment, harmonizing personal relations within a group (for example, the integration of staff in a new team or department) and developing effective intercultural relations. Assessment takes place through a word-associating questionnaire that identifies the key personality characteristics and their relative strengths.

The cross-cultural application of personality testing

All the widely used tools of personality testing claim to have a degree of cross-cultural relevance and have been applied in international profiling. These include the 'big five', (described above), the Myers-Briggs Type Indicator and the Mendenhall and Oddou model (see Chapter 6).

In addition to those already described, cross-cultural researchers have a range of cultural profiling tools that offer a more or less precise assessment of an individual's management, cultural style and potential for adaptation to other cultural environments. Specifically designed to help executives working internationally to define their own management styles and to identify which cultural groups they are best suited to work with, many of these tools use computerized testing as a means of assessment. We can divide these into three categories: computer-generated profiles, graphic profiling and animated profiling.

Computer-generated profiles

The first step in computer-generated profiling is to pose questions which are answered by ticking boxes or responding to yes/no alternatives, or by the use of multi-choice questions. A computer-generated report based on your profile is then produced.

An example of this method is the CULTURE ACTIVE profile provided by Richard Lewis Communications. This is accessed by a password given by the Richard Lewis GLOBAL Communications organization, and the user completes a questionnaire in three parts containing about 150 questions, statements and multiple-choice options. Some of the questions and statements contain contradictions, designed to identify the real personality and cultural style of the user and weed out discrepancies. A result of the programme is a detailed profile describing the user's management personality and style and recommending adaptability to particular cultural environments. More details are available at: www.crossculture.com.

Graphic profiling

A significant development in profiling has been the use of graphics to represent cultural differences. An interesting experiment was carried out by Professor Gilles Spony in his Spony Profiling Model (SPM). This approach uses a questionnaire to identify cultural and management style preferences. The system then takes your profile and matches it not against specific countries but against cultural clusters or continents. The profile then provides a map to show the area of the world where your cultural style would be most acceptable. It also offers a computer-generated report and finally a graphic which maps your style against key indicators. This allows people working internationally to see at a glance in which part of the world they would best fit and also how they might best work in a local organization. For example, a user with a strong independent and individual style might find it easier to fit into an SME in the USA or Western Europe, but harder to fit into an organization or country with a team-player mentality, such as East Asia or many multinationals. The value of profiling instruments like the SPM is that they offer a graphic illustration of a user's management style and personality, which can be both company and country-based (Spony, 2006).

Animated profiling

On a computer, the differences between the perception of one's own cultural style and the perception of another's can be shown visually and also mapped against the most appropriate cultural style.

One of the best examples of this is the *Aperian* model of world cultures, which is part of the Robert House GLOBE Project approach to leadership in world cultures. This offers a visual means of comparing cultural styles. The profile is based on a series of questionnaires, the results of which are used to provide visual profiles on a graph against a series of indicators. Users map their own management style against a number of indicators. Their 'map' is then automatically presented as a continuous line by the computer. At the click of a mouse or trackpad, the user can then call up the expert profile of any country he or she is dealing with and even that of other colleagues who have mapped their styles on the system and have given their permission for comparison. Details are available at: www.aperianglobal.com.

The framework approach

A simpler but similar approach is offered by the RADAR profile explained by Tomalin and Nicks (2010). In this case, users map their personal styles against ten paradigms.

Their style is then represented as a graph which can then be compared with the 'expert' view of other countries, using the same ten indicators. An example of the Tomalin and Nicks profile, comparing the UK and the USA, can be seen below in Figure 14.2. The USA is represented by a continuous line and the UK by a dotted line.

As we look at the two major theoretical approaches to the designing of profiling tools for assessing cultural appropriateness, we recognize two sources:

- psychological personality analyses applied to organizations and cultures;
- social and behavioural styles applied to national cultures.

What is common to both is the organization of information into frameworks that can be applied by specialists to the study of business behaviour, business organizations and national business cultures. The value of the framework approach is that it organizes psychological and social characteristics into an easily applicable form. The problem is that humanity rarely conforms to organizational convenience and that psychological and social characteristics may be in danger of being shoehorned into categories to fit the framework. Overall, however, our experience is that the psychological and social frameworks we have studied, if used sensitively, can act as an aid to supporting organizational and cross-cultural adaptation.

The RADAR profile

How do we then adapt the framework to the individual? In simple terms, we have the profile. What do we do with it? An example of use is the RADAR system, developed by Tomalin and Nicks, which describes a process for adapting personal styles to harmonize cultural differences. It is based on the 80/20 principle first described by the Italian economist Wilfredo Pareto in the nineteenth century. Pareto based his principle on the assertion that 20 per cent of a country's population contributed 80 per cent of its wealth.

US/UK cultural styles – a comparison

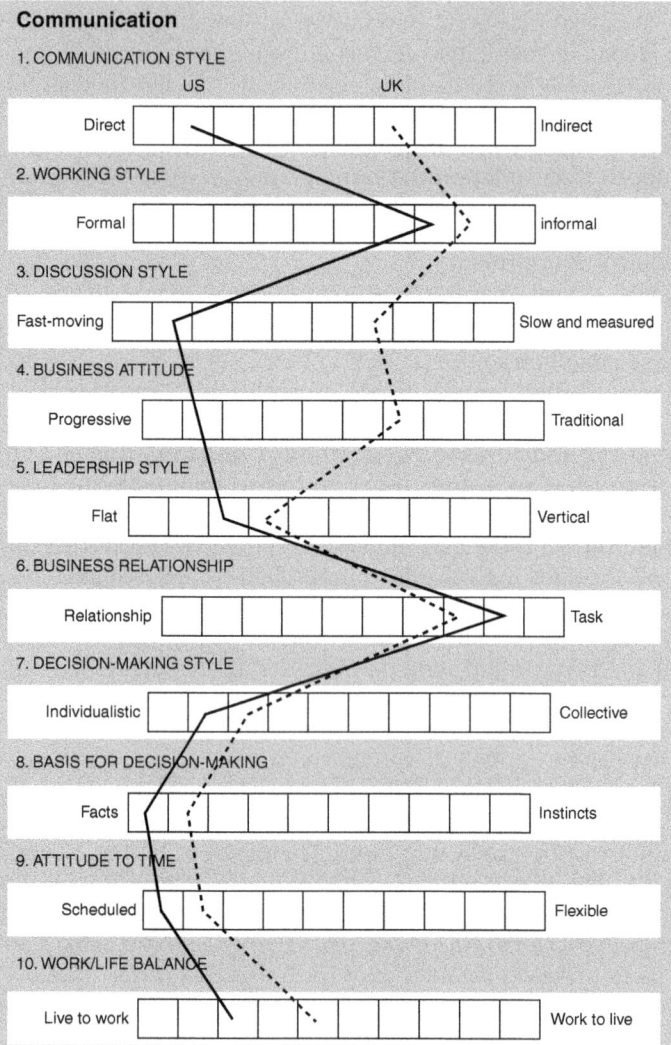

Figure 14.2   Framework analysis: UK/USA example (Tomalin and Nicks, 2010: 316)

In the twentieth century, this was applied to company profitability, with the similar assertion that 20 per cent of a company's clients provided 80 per cent of its profits.

In cultural terms, the hypothesis is behavioural. Tomalin and Nicks assert that a 20 per cent change in behaviour can achieve an 80 per cent change in attitude from others. The RADAR system uses this hypothesis to present a five-step process in promoting adaptation in cultural behaviour. RADAR is an acronym of five letters (Tomalin and Nicks, 2010: 70–1):

- *Recognize (R)*: the first step is to recognize that your misunderstanding or confusion is because you have a cultural communication problem, probably due to differences in behaviour.
- *Analyse (A)*: the second step is to analyse, using the framework, the source of the difference. This will reveal the gaps in perception between the two parties.
- *Decide (D)*: the third step is to decide how to close the gap, that is, deciding whether to change or adjust your behaviour or ask the other person to do so by about 20 per cent, depending on the situation. Tomalin and Nicks recommend doing this by using the 80/20 principle to decide what 20 per cent change should be made to balance the relationship.
- *Act (A)*: put what you have decided into action.
- *Review (R)*: finally, and most importantly, review the outcome to check whether your approach has been successful. If not, try another approach. Remember that success is about doing more of what works and less of what does not.

The principle behind the RADAR system is simple and reassuring. Huge changes are not necessary to achieve cultural compatibility. What are needed are small, incremental changes. Once those changes have been made, the other person in the adaptation process will often adapt more strongly to accommodate your willingness to change. This is a 'rule of thumb', validated by experience, but it is one of the simplest examples of how a framework can be applied to improve performance across cultures.

The limitations of cultural profiling

It is reasonable to question the scientific accuracy of the comparison as to whether the user's perception of his or her style is correct and whether the expert analysis is more than the collected views of a number of informed observers. If it is not, in the absence of scientifically verifiable evidence, mapping does allow the user to identify possible differences in attitude, communication style and management style, and promotes reflection on how to harmonize the perceived difference.

The understanding of culture is, as we have seen, ultimately an art, not a science. This kind of profiling is a way of indicating how to identify differences and how to adjust behaviour to optimize good relations with the other party, but it is not objectively verifiable. This is why it is a convenient tool for use in education and training and pre-departure briefing, but should not be used on its own as a definitive selection criterion.

The other problem with national cultural profiling is that the user's style may not match the default national style. For example, in Japan, one of the key principles in negotiation is 'nemawashi' (preparation for collective negotiation) and 'ringi-sho' (multiple-point formal sign-offs). The Japanese make decisions cautiously to ensure that everyone is fully supportive. Once this is achieved, negotiations can then move quickly forward. However, when the authors were analysing one company which was used to working with American organizations on a long-term basis, profiling revealed that the Japanese colleagues had adopted the practice of their American counterparts, with individual point decision making at an operational level and single sign-offs. In other words, they had become much more culturally flexible and no longer conformed to their national default style in what is seen as an essential feature of Japanese management practice.

Summary

- Cultural profiling is a useful tool to help identify cultural styles and preferences and potential difficulties when dealing with people of other cultures.
- The key factor in cross-cultural interaction is sensitivity to other cultures. Cultural 'fault lines' are introduced as indicators of possible areas where sensitivity might be needed, while emphasizing the need to avoid stereotyping.
- The comparison of key personality traits and the cross-cultural application of personality testing is carried out using various profile models, including the DISC profile and computer-generated, graphic and animated profiling models.
- It should be clear from the above discussion that cultural profiling in itself is not an assured criterion of adaptability to a particular environment, social or business milieu but a useful guide. However, there is considerable value in using cultural profiling as a guide to identifying areas of special support needed in pre-departure or pre-project education and training. It is also a useful tool in analysing and repairing communication and relationship breakdowns when projects or international assignments go wrong.
- Finally, cross-cultural profiling is probably more suitable as a pre-assignment or in-project education and training tool than being used by itself as a definitive recruitment assessment tool.

References

Cattell, H. and Mead, A. (2008) 'The Sixteen Personality Factor Questionnaire 16PF' in Boyle, G., Matthews, G. and Saklofske, D. (eds), *The SAGE Handbook of Personality Theory and Assessment in Personality Measurement and Testing*, vol. 2 (Los Angeles, CA: Sage Publications).

Cattell, R. (1946) *The Description and Measurement of Personality* (New York: World Books).

Huntington, S. (1993) *The Clash of Civilizations* (New York: Free Press).

Martston, W. (1928) *The Emotions of Normal People* (London: Paul, Trench and Trubner).

Morrison, T. (1991) *Kiss, Bow or Shake Hands* (New York: Abrams Media).

Ronen, S. and Shenkar, O. (1985) 'Clustering Countries in Attitudinal Dimensions: A Review and Synthesis', *Academy of Management Review* 10(3): 435–54.

Spony, G. (2006) *FUTURETOBE* www.futuretobe.net.

Tomalin, B and Nicks. M. (2010) *The World's Business Cultures and How to Unlock Them* (London: Thorogood Publishing).

Further reading

Conn, S., and Rieke, M. (1994). *The 16PF Fifth Edition Technical Manual* (Champaign, IL: Institute for Personality and Ability Testing, Inc.).

Fukuyama, F. (1992) *The End of History and the Last Man* (New York: Free Press).

Gesteland, R. (2001) *Cross-Cultural Business Behaviour* (Copenhagen Business School Press).

Gregory, R. (2011) *Psychological Testing: History, Principles, and Applications*, 6th edn (Boston, MA: Allyn & Bacon).

Mendenhall, M., Dunbar, E. and Oddou, G. (1987) 'Expatriate Selection Training and Career-Pathing: A Review and Critique' *Human Resource Management* 26(3): 331–45.

Wild, J., Wild, K. and Han, J. (2006) *International Business: The Challenge of Globalisation* (Harlow: Pearson).

15
Teaching Cross-Cultural Communication

Summary

Course design
Teaching methodology
Language training
Presentations across cultural boundaries
Country briefings
Case studies
Critical incident scenarios
Cultural capsules
Cultural assimilators
Simulation and role playing
Cultural proverbs
True/false exercises
Cultural values checklists
Business in a foreign culture checklist
Stereotype and perception exercises

Introduction

In this chapter, we draw upon our wide experience of teaching cultural awareness and cross-cultural communication to UK and international students at
both undergraduate and postgraduate level, and of running training courses
for business and diplomatic staff, briefing them for working and living
overseas. We aim to provide examples of good practice and to analyse the
effectiveness of different teaching methods, providing some of the tools we
have found to be of value in teaching this important subject. 'One of the goals
of cross-cultural training must therefore be to alert people to the fact that they
are constantly involved in a process of assigning meaning to the actions and
objects they observe' (Trompenaars and Hampden-Turner, 1997: 196).

Areas covered include the teaching of cross-cultural awareness, communication skills, specific country/regional briefings, business procedures, negotiating skills, building and sustaining multinational teams, and language training. All these aim to develop intercultural competence, which can be described as the ability to interact effectively across cultures. 'Learners cannot simply shake off their own cultural baggage, for their culture is a part of themselves, has formed them and created them as social beings' (Byram and Morgan, 1994).

Training aims to provide benefits in the following areas:

- breaking down cross-cultural barriers;
- building trust between cultures;
- developing self-awareness and learning about one's own strengths, weaknesses and prejudices;
- acquiring cognitive information, that is, facts about the target culture;
- developing an understanding of how one's own culture is seen by foreigners;
- opening up new cultural horizons;
- developing improved interpersonal skills and sensitivity towards those of another culture;
- developing awareness of conventional behaviour in situations in the target culture;
- stimulation of intellectual curiosity in and empathy towards the target culture;
- developing an understanding that we all exhibit culturally conditioned behaviour.

This chapter aims to bring together the theory and practice in the earlier chapters which we have found effective in our own work in this area, and to offer suggestions for those responsible for the design and delivery of courses relating to cross-cultural communication problems.

Teaching methodology

The training methodology used by those teaching cross-cultural communication skills should reflect the evolution from top-down learning of mainly cognitive knowledge to interactive learning with students encouraged to participate, challenge and discuss. Teaching should, wherever possible, be experiential, with students taking part in role playing, acting out short scenarios, practising appropriate non-verbal behaviour and learning by interaction with fellow international students. Teachers and trainers, when group size permits, should act more as facilitators than lecturers.

Feedback both from teachers and other members of the group is of great importance and can be assisted by video recording. Incorrect cultural responses to situations can thereby be more easily analysed and rectified. Learning should be encouraged using multimedia facilities, including film, video, CCTV and the Internet. Sessions can be enlivened by input from nationals of the target cultures and by those who have just returned from overseas with their anecdotes and practical examples. Recent returnees are particularly valuable in keeping the teaching material up to date.

In order to develop a well-structured cross-cultural communication programme, the following steps are suggested:

- identify the target audience;
- assess their needs and expectations by carrying out a needs analysis;
- detail the aims of the programme so as to meet the expectations;
- decide the contents of the programme within the agreed time allowed for the training;
- evaluate the effectiveness of the programme by feedback from course critiques;
- fine-tune any required amendments after consultation with end-users.

Training should be carefully planned where appropriate to include the families of those going to live and work in other cultures. It should be designed not only to protect the organization's investment and reputation in sending personnel overseas, but also to help those personnel find a level of personal fulfilment and satisfaction in their new environment.

Language training

There is a growing perception that English has become the international language. According to Eurostat (2009), English was studied as a foreign language by 94.6 per cent of EU secondary school pupils in 2009. In addition, there has been a large increase in the number of people studying English at different levels in Eastern Europe and, significantly, in China. In total, it is estimated that there are over 1.5 billion speakers of English as either their first or second language.

However, in recent years, there has been a reduction in foreign-language teaching in the UK, both in schools and universities, particularly in the case of German. In addition, a number of universities have stopped including the one-year overseas component as an integral part of a language degree. Nevertheless, there has been an increasing trend to include a foreign language as part of many business degrees.

If a high degree of fluency is required, a formal structured course should begin well before the departure date and the commencement of the foreign appointment. As such language training is expensive and time-consuming, it is essential to carry out a thorough needs analysis to identify the individual's requirements and expectations. If time is, of necessity, limited, the emphasis should initially be on teaching survival elements and building confidence to encourage further learning on arrival overseas. This initial approach is sometimes called 'guerilla linguistics', which involves learning some useful everyday phrases in the local language. Tuition should, whenever possible, be carried out by native speakers and, ideally, both the expatriate working partner and accompanying spouse should participate. Tonal languages, such as Chinese or Thai, are particularly difficult, and potential students should be given some form of language aptitude test before starting a course.

Presentations across cultural borders

The subject of presentations across cultural borders was covered briefly in Chapter 5. In this chapter, we concentrate on how teachers can advise students who are likely to be required to give such presentations. Giving a business presentation to people of other cultures can be quite daunting and is fraught with potential difficulties. It is therefore important to carry out some preparatory research in order to:

- establish the aim of the presentation and the expectations of the audience;
- ascertain the level of English of the audience;
- decide if the introduction will be in the foreign language;
- organize the presentation in a logical sequence;
- decide whether to use interpreters;
- decide on the length, remembering that the audience may have a limited concentration span if English is their second language;
- decide how much time should be devoted to questions;
- decide if translations of both handouts and presentation slides are required;
- ensure signposts are included in the presentation to assist understanding.

Students should be advised that it is important to pay attention to protocol by following the local cultural customs carefully. It may be good practice in the foreign culture to begin a presentation with a formal introduction. If this is the case, the students should ensure that they use the correct names and pronunciation, together with any necessary official titles, for example, doctor, professor or government officials' titles. It may be desirable to begin the short introduction in the language of the country they are visiting, but they should rehearse carefully and check both the pronunciation and the accuracy of the translation. If this is carried out well, they can then safely revert to using English or continue using skilled and trusted interpreters. In any case, they should use spoken rather than written language, which is too formal for the context.

Delivery should be slower than is normally used with an English audience, with relatively short sentences, avoiding complex grammatical structures, but taking care not to appear patronizing. The best guide is to watch the audience's reaction, remembering always to speak clearly and include pauses to give time for the audience to read the slides and assimilate what has been said. Too many facts and statistics should be avoided, as these can be best given as handouts. Students should refrain from using acronyms unless they are readily understood. They should also avoid the use of metaphors which are difficult to translate across cultures and should refrain from using slang or colloquial expressions.

Students should practise drafting presentations and rehearsing them, ideally in front of nationals of the foreign culture. They should master their scripted presentation well enough to rely only on key points on a prompt card and should, if possible, deliver any parts in the foreign language verbatim. Whenever possible, they should use bold, clear and uncluttered visual aids, but should avoid 'death by PowerPoint'.

Schneider and Barsoux recommend appropriate presentation styles for different nationalities. They advise, for example, that for a French audience, when making a business presentation: 'It is important to provide theory, history and context' (Schneider and Barsoux, 2003: 38). Americans are advised that their own approach of starting with an executive summary or conclusions is not deemed appropriate for other cultures, who may consider such an approach too aggressive or even arrogant.

In summary, students should be advised to take into account the following points when preparing presentations across cultural boundaries:

- Double-check preparation (venue, seating, lighting, use of equipment) in advance.
- Begin if possible with the language of the host country.
- Pay attention to protocol as outlined above.
- Use appropriate body language – stand up straight, but not too stiff, with suitable eye contact.
- Use humour with care as the meaning may well become lost in translation or the subject matter may be deemed inappropriate for the particular culture.
- Summarize key points on the screen, ideally in both languages, and leave sufficient time for the audience to read and digest them.
- Leave sufficient time for questions and discussion.
- At the end, ensure that written summaries are provided.

Above all, it is important to allow sufficient time for a dress rehearsal or 'dry run', practising both delivery and keeping to the agreed time allowed.

Country briefings

Country briefings are often the most indepth part of any cross-cultural and pre-departure training and should be provided before moving overseas.

These briefings are built around mainly factual input and should contain up-to-date information on a country's geography, history, politics, economics, climate, foreign relationships, infrastructure, communications, working environment and living conditions. Insight should be provided, if time allows, into local customs, business practices, social conventions and, where appropriate, conflict between local and Western values. Courses can be organized within a company or in a neutral venue by a professional training establishment specializing in this area, such as the Centre for International Briefing at Farnham Castle in the UK. If possible, the teaching should include input by nationals with recent experience of the country and there should be ample opportunity to question and explore the cultural differences.

Taking China as an example, a typical briefing could cover:

Country focus:	Geography
	Overview of main milestones in history
	Economic development post-Mao
	Government system and politics
	Hong Kong since 1997
	Foreign policy
People and society:	Traditions and customs
	Confucianism and Buddhism
	Demographics
	Social structure
	Attitude towards Westerners
Living in a particular city:	Cost of living
	Climate
	Accommodation, transport, driving
	Gas, electricity, telephone, water
	Health and hygiene
	Children's education facilities
	Leisure and recreation facilities
	Social etiquette – entertaining, gift-giving
	Security, crime, dealing with the local police
Business practices:	Business etiquette
	Dealing with bureaucracy
	Ethics and corruption
	Negotiating style
	Organizing meetings
	Employment conditions
	Business services

The above is essentially cognitive training, emphasizing factual information about the host culture. It should be built into a cultural training programme that gives practical advice on appropriate behaviour in the areas listed, so that those going overseas may successfully interact with Chinese nationals and empathize with their customs and practices.

Case studies

Case studies have been described by Yin (1994) as: 'An empirical enquiry concerned with contemporary phenomena in a real-life context.' Essentially, a case study involves the indepth study of one or more examples of a particular phenomenon, such as the management development strategy in a company or the training of entrants to the foreign service of a particular country.

Case studies tend to be appropriate for 'how' and 'why' types of questions, where the emphasis is on acquiring a fuller understanding of the nature of a relationship. They have the advantage of allowing events to be examined over time. Students are required to collect data from a number of sources in order to develop a more complete understanding of the sequence of events and their outcomes. They can use a variety of data collection methods, including questionnaires, interviews, observation and archival data. The use of such multiple sources of data should increase the validity of their findings.

Case studies may be current or retrospective. If the case is actually 'in progress', that is, ongoing, students may have little control over the time needed to conduct the study. If the study is retrospective, the recall memory of respondents may be inaccurate or incomplete, so unless considerable reliable archival data is readily available, it may be better to stick to 'the recent past'.

An advantage of the case study as a teaching method is that generalization from the specifics may be possible, although care must be taken to see that there are sufficient points of similarity to ensure an acceptable degree of validity. As with role playing, case studies are particularly useful in experiential teaching. Teachers and trainers should operate mainly as facilitators and avoid too directional an approach.

Critical incident scenarios

Critical incident scenarios involve the description of typical cultural incidents in which students are required to decide on the correct cultural behaviour response. They are relatively simple to design and do not require much time for students to consider. The incidents should be based on practical situations which the students are likely to encounter. Responses can be given individually or in group work and can either be oral or written. In some cases, students can be required to role play their proposed solutions which can be video recorded and discussed at a later stage. If possible, the student answers should be compared with the solutions presented by native members of the target culture.

The following areas lend themselves to the development of scenarios which can be introduced into cultural training to involve students directly in the learning process. These could include:

- on arrival: immigration, settling into accommodation, obtaining a driving licence, taking a taxi, going shopping, going to the bank, interviewing domestic servants;
- socializing: invitations, greetings, going to a restaurant, hospitality etiquette, giving and receiving gifts, interaction with local people;
- the workplace: attitude towards time, punctuality, status, seniority, work practices, decision making, ethical values, bureaucracy, networking and organizing meetings.

A variation is to use 'mini dramas', which can consist of three to five incidents of misunderstanding that can occur due to poor cultural communication. This approach can be further developed whereby additional information is made available with each episode, but the precise fundamental cause of the misunderstanding does not become fully apparent until the last scene of an episode.

Example of a critical incident

You are in Beijing as the Sales Manager of your company. You are accompanied by your assistant and you are trying to complete a deal to sell tractors to the Chinese. Negotiations have been going on for three days and you are beginning to feel confident of a satisfactory outcome. You therefore decide to fly back to London on the Wednesday and you tell your assistant to stay in order to put the final touches to the plans, reminding him of the need to agree the formal contract on the Friday and telling him that any minor technical details can be clarified later.

Comment

The Chinese usually request considerable technical detail before they will make a formal agreement. It is therefore essential to provide as much information as possible and give them time to study it. The Chinese are generally monochronic, but have a flexible attitude to time. They do not like being rushed and value time for reflection and further consideration. This can be both difficult and frustrating. In negotiations with the Chinese, it takes a lot of time with no final agreement possible until close relations have been established. The decision for the Sales Manager to return to London before the conclusion of the final agreement is considered premature and the Chinese would expect the Sales Manager himself to stay and not just leave his assistant to oversee matters. This shows disrespect as the Chinese place great store on hierarchy and seniority.

Culture capsules

The use of culture capsules is another way of teaching cultural differences. These consist of an explanation of a particular cultural difference between a situation in a foreign culture and what would occur in the home culture, for example, friends greeting each other. Students are asked to point out the differences. Culture capsules can also be used to great advantage in language teaching. Further examples could include the exchange of business cards, contrasting the Japanese ritualistic presentation of the 'meishi' with the more informal manner of most Western cultures.

The cultural assimilator

The cultural assimilator was originally defined by Fiedler, Mitchell and Triandis (1971) as: 'A programme learning technique that is designed to expose members of one culture to some of the basic concepts, attitudes, role perceptions, customs and values of another culture.' Scenarios include situations where people from one culture are required to interact with those of another culture where a clash of cultures might occur, for example, in taking part in a meeting, in negotiations, in the use of body language or in giving a presentation. The use of the cultural assimilator is a more developed method than the cultural capsule. Usually two different cultures can be compared and contrasted – for example the British and the Italian styles of communication, the contrasting use of body language, tempo and display of emotion.

The incident should, whenever possible, be first piloted with those who have relevant and recent experience of the culture to ensure its accuracy and suitability. Those taking part are presented with a number of alternative choices and are required to select what they consider to be the most appropriate cultural response to the situation. If a correct solution is given, the student can move on to the next situation. If an incorrect solution is proposed, the student is then requested to reconsider and make another choice from the alternatives. The incorrect answers must be sufficiently plausible alternatives so as not to be quickly rejected.

An example is given below.

This may happen to you!

You are a businessman with an appointment in one of the Gulf states for 10.00 am with Mr Al-Saeedi, your business counterpart. You have arranged the meeting to discuss your business proposal in more detail. You are concerned to arrive on time and you play safe by arriving at 09.55 am. You are greeted by his personal assistant and told that he will arrive shortly. You accept a cup of coffee in the ante-room to his office. Your next appointment is not until 11.30 in the same building, so you are not yet particularly concerned.

At 10.25 am, Mr Al-Saeedi arrives and apologizes, and you are ushered into his office and offered more coffee. After exchanging a few social pleasantries, you anticipate being able to get down to business. However, his personal assistant enters and he and Mr Al-Saeedi discuss something of apparent importance in Arabic. Mr Al-Saeedi again apologizes and enters into a long telephone conversation, again in Arabic.

At 10.40 am, you resume your conversation with Mr Al-Saeedi, who seems more interested in talking about your family, the weather in the UK and his son, who is studying in London.

At 10.50 am, his personal assistant again enters, this time with correspondence to be signed.

At 10.55 am, there is another telephone call, this time from his brother in Riyadh. You are now beginning to feel annoyed and anxious, and keep looking at your watch. You remind Mr Al-Saeedi gently that you have another meeting scheduled for 11.30 am. He smiles and tells his personal assistant to phone to say you will be arriving soon. You continue your meeting, which is very amicable, but you do not seem to have made any agreement yet to do business. Mr Al-Saeedi insists that he takes you to dinner at a top restaurant that evening.

You eventually move on to your next appointment, realizing that the Arab concept of time is very different from yours. In the event, the fact that you have been invited to dinner is a very encouraging sign that you are building a good personal relationship with Mr Al-Saeedi, which bodes well for future successful business.

This scenario can be discussed with the group and the attitude towards time in the two cultures (monchronic and polychronic can be emphasized). It also says much about schedules and punctuality, and the fact that Mr Al-Saeedi has a more relaxed approach to business meetings, which for him in the initial stages are more concerned with building trust and personal relationships.

Simulation and role playing

Simulation, including the use of role playing, can be a very effective means of teaching cross-cultural awareness and cross-cultural communication. However, simulations require time and expertise to implement. Their use in business training is well established, but is somewhat less so in cultural training. Simulation exercises have the advantage of involving a group of students who can be divided into teams. The students are required to act out a particular situation over a period of time. They should be given considerable freedom to develop their assigned roles from the initial briefing so that they feel they have 'ownership' of the parts they are expected to play.

Role-playing exercises require carefully scripted settings with detailed background briefing as well as sufficient time for the players to study their roles and prepare to enact them during the exercise. The teaching staff should act mainly as facilitators and should inject additional input to test the players further by putting them under pressure. Role playing can often engender passion among the students if they have fully read themselves into their respective roles. This form of learning is mainly experiential and therefore more memorable as it brings to life much of the theory that the students have previously learned.

Simulation exercises can be used, for example, involving students in a boardroom meeting in which policy decisions have to be made, and the student players representing different board members being required to justify their positions. Finally, a consensus has to be agreed on the way ahead. Such a simulation should replicate the real tensions, disagreements and challenges which occur in a real-life situation. In addition, team-building and decision-making skills can be practised. The exercise can incorporate CCTV input (for example, newsflashes), input by the directing staff and the injection of periods of real-time pressure play to test the players' reactions in a crisis, their time-management skills and the consequences of cultural misunderstandings and poor intercultural communication skills. It is advisable, whenever possible, to video record the whole simulation exercise so that the teaching staff can review the proceedings with the students and discuss the lessons to be learned in detail.

The learning outcomes from role playing are considerable and are listed in Figure 15.1 below.

Importance of preparation before speaking
Practice in speaking in public
Practice in the need to follow accepted protocol and be aware of national and cultural sensitivities
The awareness of the problems that can arise during translation and interpreting
The need to use the correct communication style for the target culture

---

Figure 15.1   Learning outcomes

Some students may find experiential techniques to be unfamiliar and even daunting, as they may have been used to more prescriptive teaching methods in their home country. They may be unfamiliar with open discussion, both with their fellow students and with their teachers. They may find, in particular, the encouragement and the opportunity to challenge their teachers very difficult to deal with. Therefore, they may require help to develop their confidence and their powers of expression before they can contribute fully in group exercises and simulations. The teachers themselves in such circumstances should make an effort to be aware of the educational background of their students and their learning methods, and adapt their methodology accordingly.

Proverbs and cultural values

This exercise can be used to explore cultural assumptions and values by examining proverbs which often express values that are broadly accepted within a cultural group. Proverbs are often paradoxical or metaphorical. We can also examine them for their exaggeration of attitudes commonly held by a cultural group. Each has a quality of permanence in the culture and recurs in its folklore. Proverbs, like metaphors, can provide valuable insight into a culture, with vivid imagery and material for discussion. They must, however, be used with caution, as, like metaphors, they do not always apply to every individual or even every sub-group within a society. Nevertheless, they do highlight national differences in an easily understandable way and provide a rich vocabulary for discussion. Figure 15.2 provides some British examples.

Example	Values
Cleanliness is next to godliness	Cleanliness
Time is money	Value of time
Birds of a feather flock together	Guilt through association
Waste not, want not	Frugality
Early to bed, early to rise	Diligence
God helps those who help themselves	Initiative
A man's home is his castle	Privacy, property
No rest for the wicked	Guilt, work ethos

Figure 15.2   British proverbs

An example of a proverb exercise

Below is a list of proverbs from different cultures. Next to each proverb, students should write the cultural value they think the proverb teaches and indicate the country/countries where similar proverbs are used. Some may apply to several countries/cultures. Where possible, students should be asked to write in the version they would use in their own country and give the English translation.

Proverb	Meaning
A penny saved is a penny earned	Thrift (for example, France, Germany and the UK, who all use a similar metaphor)
There is no time like the present	Opportunism (for example, France, Germany, Italy and the UK)
When in Rome, do as the Romans do	Adaptation (for example, France, Germany, Slovakia and the UK)
Every cloud has a silver lining	Optimism (for example, France, Germany and the UK)
Children are a staircase to paradise	Children are a gift of god (for example, Arab cultures)
A house without an elderly person is like an orchard without a well	Reverence for the elderly in a family (for example, Arab cultures)
The eye is an organ of aggression	Eye contact may be hostile (for example, in Zulu culture)

Students can also be asked to draw up a list of well-known proverbs from their own culture and ask the other nationalities in the group to compare them with similar proverbs in their own culture. It is also interesting to see if the translations into different languages match the English words or whether different words are used to express the same meaning.

True/false exercises

True/false exercises are a straightforward but effective way of checking levels of knowledge of other cultures either at the beginning of a course or as quick revision exercises. The alternatives (true or false) are selected by the students. A typical example is given below, which could, of course, be further expanded.

German culture

It is unusual for Germans to use first names early in a business relationship	T/F
It is usual for Germans to shake hands when first meeting	T/F
It is usual for Germans to interrupt and 'talk over' in a conversation	T/F
Germans begin a business meeting presentation with jokes and humour	T/F
Germans are good listeners	T/F

Japanese culture

White flowers in Japan are given at funerals	T/F
Number four is considered lucky in Japan	T/F
Japanese attach more importance to written contracts than verbal agreements	T/F
Japanese often send money to bereaved friends as an expression of sympathy	T/F
The typical Japanese company regards market share as more important than profit	T/F

Cultural values checklists

Cultural values checklists can be used to advantage when asking students to mark their responses as to how they see their own culture and, using a separate form of marking, how they see the foreign culture. A further exercise can be for them to compare their answers to the same checklist after they have been living and working in the foreign culture for a short period of time to see whether they have changed or modified their original replies. Tomalin and Nicks (2010) suggest a ten-point checklist (see Figure 14.2).

The simple exercise below consists of 15 cultural values. Students are required to circle the ones they select from the range of the nine points, with marking in the middle showing no particular preference for either.

1. STATUS, TITLE
   Important for reasons other than merit   Earned by merit
   (i.e. hereditary)

   * * * * * * * * *

2. ATTITUDE TO TIME
   Mañana attitude   Every moment counts

   * * * * * * * * *

3. CHILD REARING
   Strict reliance on control,   Permissive, reliance
   rewards and punishments   on child responsibility

   * * * * * * * * *

4. PROBLEM SOLVING
   Rational, logical approach   Instinctive, impulsive

   * * * * * * * * *

5. INDIVIDUALISM/COLLECTIVISM
   Very individual   Group-minded

   * * * * * * * * *

6. FAMILY
Strong, first loyalty   Other relationships are as
                                              important

   * * * * * * * * *

7. PRIVACY
   Highly valued, wide personal space   Less important, prefer a crowd

   * * * * * * * * *

8. WOMEN
Inferior to men in status in society   Superior to men in status in society

* * * * * * * *

9. WORK
Work to live   Live to work

* * * * * * * *

10. MATERIAL OBJECTS
Of great value   Of less value

* * * * * * * *

11. RELATIONSHIP WITH ELDERS
Honour, respect, deference   Of less importance, disregarded

* * * * * * * *

12. THE ENVIRONMENT
Can be controlled by man   Beyond man's control

* * * * * * * *

13. COMMUNICATION STYLE
Polite, indirect   Frank, open, direct

* * * * * * * *

14. TIME
Mainly monochronic   Mainly polychronic

* * * * * * * *

15. RELIGION
An essential part of life   Less important

* * * * * * * *

Doing business in a foreign culture

Another student exercise that the authors have used to good effect is to issue business people who are about to go to work in another culture for the first time with a short questionnaire aiming to highlight the key cultural differentiators between their culture and the one in which they are going to work. Many of their answers will be their perceptions, which may be incorrect, and these can be discussed further with their tutors. An example of such a questionnaire follows.

Question	My culture	Their culture
1. Is English widely understood in business?		
2. Do people use first names or last names in greeting and general conversation?		
3. Can humour be used in meetings and presentations?		
4. Do people proceed direct to business at meetings or do they first use 'ice-breakers'?		
5. Is it essential to build good personal relationships before doing business?		
6. How important are socializing and hospitality?		
7. How important is punctuality? Do things always keep to schedules?		
8. Do decisions have to be unanimous or do they depend on consensus?		
9. What importance is given to status and hierarchy?		
10. Is an agreed agenda issued before a meeting?		

The next step is to summarize the key differences for both your culture and the foreign culture, and discuss the reasons for the differences.

Exercise on stereotypes

As we have seen earlier, stereotypes are quick, simplistic ways of classifying people into categories. They are useful as we try to sort people into categories and therefore become handy pigeon holes. They are relatively harmless if used only as a rule of thumb, but can be dangerous if they are taken as the whole truth about other people, for example, in relation to race, gender, class and religion. Unfortunately, most stereotypes contain value judgments. Our own group loyalty tends to encourage us to believe our group is more important or better than other groups. Although national barriers are disappearing, national stereotypes may take longer to remove. The danger lies in the speed and intensity of the assumptions, perceptions and predictions about other people on very thin information and evidence, and our attribution of the supposed characteristics of a whole group to its individual members. Stereotypes can take two different forms:

- traits that we admire – ambition, cleverness, boldness, industry, modesty;
- traits that we deplore – laziness, stupidity, untrustworthiness.

Students should be aware of their stereotypical views of people from other cultures. By using a simple exercise, 'What do you know about people from these cultures?', they can list separately the characteristics they perceive as 'positive' from the 'negative' ones. Trainers can then discuss any ascribed stereotypes and question whether such generalizations are in any way valid. This short exercise could be used, for example, by a businessman instructed at very short notice to go to the 'Baltic States' to ascertain the market for a particular IT system. He has no previous experience of the area.

'What do we think we know about them already?'

For each of the following three nationalities, write a maximum of six words or phrases which describe how you perceive people of these countries:

Estonians

....

....

Latvians

....

....

Lithuanians

....

....

Comment

It is very likely that the businessman's answers will reveal some generalizations and stereotypical views. In addition, he will probably not have considered the three nationalities as being very distinct, as he has been conditioned to refer to them as the 'Baltic States', that is, as one group.

In discussion, students should realize that stereotyping is very often inaccurate, but, nevertheless, it can retain a very forcible and suggestive power. If the points made, whether true or false, are repeated enough times, there is a strong tendency for them to be believed.

Perception exercises

There are a number of simple exercises to help explain perception to students. These include a famous perceptual illusion in which the brain switches between seeing a young girl and an old woman. For many years, the creator of this figure was considered to be the British cartoonist W. Hill, who published it in 1915 in *Puck*, a humour magazine in America, inspired by the British magazine *Punch*. Hill almost certainly adapted it from an original concept widely popular on trading and puzzle cards. This is represented below in Figure 15.3.

Figure 15.3 The 'young lady/old lady' (http://mathworld.wolfram.com/YoungGirl-OldWomanIllusion.html, date accessed 17 December 2012)

This exercise shows that our perception is our reality, at least until we know better. In our daily life, perception involves checking data for validity. In dealing with perception, it is important to impress upon students that:

- perception is selective and is very often culture-driven;
- perception works on differences more than similarities;
- perceived differences lead to various reactions depending on the level of culture affected;
- our perception of another culture is relative, very often in comparison to our own set of values.

Summary

- The methodology of teaching cross-cultural communication can involve cultural awareness training, country-specific briefings, case studies, critical incident scenarios, simulation and role playing, and cultural values exercises. In addition, there may be a need for language training.
- The choice of methods depends greatly on the time and resources available.

- Whenever possible, teaching should be experiential, encouraging students to make choices, and sufficient time for discussion should be allowed as required. Simulation, role playing and case studies can be used to advantage.
- Whenever possible, nationals of the foreign culture should be involved. If appropriate and if time permits, members of the family as well as the working partner should be involved in at least part of the pre-departure cultural training.
- All teaching should use up-to-date scenarios, based on relevant experience in the target culture, involving nationals of the destination culture if possible.
- The benefits of intercultural competence and cultural awareness training should be emphasized to all students – in particular, that such training enhances their people skills and future employment opportunities.

References

Byram, M. and Morgan, C. (1994) *Teaching and Learning, Language and Culture* (Clevedon: Multilingual Matters Ltd.).

Fiedler, F., Mitchell, T. and Triandis, H. (1971) 'The Cultural Assimilator: An Approach to Cross-Cultural Training', *Journal of Applied Psychology* 55: 95–102.

Schneider, S. and Barsoux, J-L. (2003) *Managing Across Cultures*, 2nd edn (Upper Saddle River, NJ: Prentice Hall).

Trompenaars, F. and Hampden-Turner, C. (1997) *Riding the Waves of Culture* (London: Nicholas Brealey Publications).

Yin, R. (1994) *Case Study Research: Design and Methods* (London: Sage Publications).

Further reading

Bennett, R., Aston, A. and Colquhoun, T. (2001) 'Cross-Cultural Training: A Critical Step in Ensuring the Success of International Assignments', *Human Resource Management* 39(2): 239–50.

Brislin, R. (1981) *Cross-Cultural Encounters* (New York: Pergamon Press).

Brislin, R. and Yoshida, T. (1994) *Intercultural Communication Training: An Introduction* (London: Sage Publications).

Brown, D. (2000) *Principles of Language Learning and Teaching*, 4th edn (New York: Longman).

Byram, M. (ed.) (2001) *Developing Intercultural Competence in Practice* (Bristol: Multilingual Matters Ltd.).

Eurostat (2009) *Eurostat Yearbook – Education*.

Fowler, S. (2005) 'Training Across Cultures: What Cultures Bring to Diversity Training', *International Journal of Cultural Relations* 30(2): 401–11.

Geber, G. (1991) 'Virtual Teams', *Training* (April): 36–40.

Gesteland, R. (1999) *Cross-Cultural Business Behaviour* (Copenhagen Business School Press).

Graf, F. (2004) 'Assessing Intercultural Training', *Journal of Industrial Training* 4(2): 199–214.

Hadley, A. (2000) *Teaching Language in Context*, 3rd edn (Independence, KY: Heinle).

Holliday, A., Hyde, M. and Kullman, J. (2004) *Intercultural Communication: An Advanced Resource Book* (London: Routledge).

Hurn, B. (2011) 'Simulation Training Methods to Develop Cultural Awareness', *Industrial and Commercial Training* 43(4): 199–206.

Kramsch, C. (1998) *Context and Culture in Language Teaching* (Oxford University Press).

Landis, P., Bennett, J. and Bennett, M. (2003) *Handbook of Intercultural Training* (Thousand Oaks, CA: Sage Publications).

O'Sullivan, K. (1994) *Understanding Ways: Communication Between Cultures* (Sydney: Hale and Iremonger).

Seelye, H. (1993) *Teaching Culture: Strategies for Intercultural Communication* (Lincolnwood, IL: National Textbook Company).

Storti, C. (1999) *Figuring Foreigners Out: A Practical Guide* (Yarmouth, ME: Intercultural Press).

Tomalin, B. (2009) 'Instruments for Intercultural Business Training', in A. Feng, M. Byram and M. Fleming (eds), *Becoming Interculturally Competent through Education and Training* (Bristol: Multilingual Matters).

Tung, R. (1981) 'Selection and Training of Personnel for Overseas', *Columbia Journal of World Business* 16(1): 68–78.

Wild, J., Wild, K. and Han, J. (2006) *International Business: The Challenge of Globalisation* (Harlow: Pearson).

Index

Abercrombie, D. 89
accent 80, 83
Accenture International Women's Day
    Survey 134
acceptance stage 59–60
access to markets 212
achievement/ascription cultures 50–1
acknowledgement 87
action chain 26
Action-Centred Leadership 127
active listening 86–7
Adair, J. 127
adaptation stage 60, 88
adjustment stage 115–16
Adler, N. 111, 118, 172
Aérospatiale 259
affective versus neutral 49–50
affection 146
affirmative action 194–5
Africa/Africans 9, 25, 33, 41, 56, 69
    communication skills 82, 90
    globalization 215, 221
    multiculturalism and diversity 201
    negotiations 165
    teamworking 151
    technology transfer 244
agendas 151–2, 171–2
agents and mediators 171
agreement in meetings 155
aid advisers 244–5, **245**
airlines 231
Akhihito, Emperor 92
alienation 119
Alliance Française 228
ambiguity 14, 16, 113
American English 71–2, **72**
Amsterdam Treaty 1999 197
Anglophone cultures 32–3, 35–6, 41, 63
Anholt, S. 232–4, 236
animated profiling 268–9
Annan, Kofi 171, 231
anthropology 3
anti-corruption laws 168
'any other business' 173

APEC 209
Aperian model 268–9
Apollo Syndrome 145
Apple 217
apologies 167
appearance 93
Arab Spring 209
Arab countries/Arabs 22, 25, 31, 33,
    35–6, 56, 58
    communication skills 90–1, 93–4
    negotiations 166, 168, 171, 186–8
    teamworking 150–3
Arctic region 221
Argentina 221
arigata meiwaku viii
Armstrong, A. 129
artificial languages 68–9
arts 225, 229
ascriptive cultures 51
Ashridge Business School 100
Asia/Asians 7, 9, 25–7, 31–3, 36, 38,
    39, 49, 56
    communication skills 79, 81–3, 92
    leadership 138
    multiculturalism and diversity 205
    negotiations 169
    teamworking 146, 148, 152–3
    technology transfer 244
    see also individual regions/countries
assessment centres 103–4
assimilation of immigrants 194, 202
assumption of similarities 13
asylum seekers 204
attendance of meetings 153
audience expectations 82–3
Aung San Suu Kyi 191, 231
Australia/Australians 9, 22, 25, 31, 33,
    69, 71, 194–5, 203–4
authority issues 51, 130
    see also seniority

back-up team-roles 143
bad language 80
BAE Systems 246

Barakat, H. 90
barriers to communication 10–12,
    11–12, 17
barriers to listening 85–6
barriers to transfer of skills and
    knowledge 247
Barry, B. 192
Barsoux, J. 102, 127–8, 130, 278
Basic English 68
BBC World Service 66, 231
Bechtel 246
Beckham, David 232
Beech, N. 138
Beijing Olympics 230, 236–7
Belbin, Meredith 141, 143, 145
Belgium 4, 133, 154, 203, 265
Bennett, Milton 58–60
best practice 96
Bhaskar-Shrinivas, P. 112
bias 37–8, 42–4, 103
bilingualism 73
Binyon, Michael 166
Blair, Tony 9, 216, 238
BMW 210
Boas, Franz 3
body language 89
Bollywood 70, 234
Bond, Michael 37–8, 39, 43
Borge, Victor 148
Boroditsky, Lena 3
borrowings from English 67
borrowings into English 62–3, **63**
bowing 92
BP 213
BP/Amoco 242
Brahm Levey, G. 192
Brake, T. 137
Brazil 72, 93, 112
brevity 81
BRIC nations 72, 208–9, 211, 213, 216
British *see* UK/British
British Aerospace 253
British Airport Authority 246–7
British Airways 231
British Council 64, 66, 225, 228, 235
British languages 65
broadcasting 231
Brooke, M. 247
Buddhism 184–5
Bulgaria 91

Burger King 256
burqa ban 203
Bush, George Sr. 91
Bush, George W. 9, 165
business-specific training 110–11
Byers, Roger 210
Byram, Michael 136, 275

Cadbury's 210
Café Direct 220
call centres 80
Camp David 165, 171
Canada/Canadians 9, 22, 32–3, 194–5,
    199–200
Canadian International Development
    Agency (CIDA) 104, 115, 243
can-do culture 174
Cantonese 71
Cardon, P. 169, 185
Caribbean 69
CARICOM 209
Carter, Jimmy 200
Cartesian tradition 175
case studies 280
caste system 179
categorization 13–14
Cattell, H. 266
Cattell, R. 261, 267
Cattell's 16 personality factors 266–7
celebrities 232
Central Europeans 36, 43
Centre for International Briefing 108, 279
Centre for Humanitarian Dialogue 171
Cervantes Institute 228
chairpersons 153–4
change management 254
Channel Tunnel 253
charismatic leadership 131
charities 209
Chartered Institute of Personnel and
    Development, UK 261
Chatelaine, General 171
cheap labour 209, 214–15
Chevron 213
Chile 231
China/Chinese 15, 22, 25–6, 32, 37,
    39–40, 42, 45, 49, 56, 58
  communication skills 87, 90
  cultural diplomacy and nation
    branding 226–7, 230–1, 236–7

China/Chinese – *continued*
  cultural profiling   265
  globalization   211–15, 221
  language issues   66, 70–2
  leadership   134, 138
  negotiations   168–9, 183–6
  teaching cross-cultural
    communication   276, 279, 281–2
  teamworking   150
  technology transfer   242, 251, 253–5
China National   213
China Radio International   237
Chinese Communist Party   236
Chinese Confucius Institute   228, 229,
  237
Chinese language   72, 229
Chinese Value Survey (CVS)   37–8, 43,
  184
Chirac, Jacques   66
Chomsky, Noam   3
chromatics   95
Churchill, Winston   15, 87, 178, 232
cinema   234, 237
citizenship tests/training   194, 198–204
Civil Rights Movement   200
clarification   87
clear objectives for meetings   150–1
climate change   220
Clingendael Institute   108
clothing   93
CNN (Cable News Network)   217
coaching   130, 244
Coca-Cola   210
codes of conduct   6, 164
coding/transmission/decoding/feedback
  process   10–11
Coe, Sebastian   238
cognitive training   279
Cohen, R.   163–4, 166, 168
Cold War   229, 231
collectivism   33–6, 49, 53, 132, 138,
  146, 178
Collinson, S.   129, 209, 214, 217
colloquialisms   66, 70
colours   95
committees   173
communication styles   6–7, **7**, 260, 262
communication systems   251
competencies   100–1, 129, 136–7, 172
competitive advantage   212

competitive identity   234
competitive listening   85
computer-generated profiles   268
computerized testing   267–8
conceptual fluency   18
concise/expressive communication
  paradigm   8
Concorde   253
Confucianism   38–9, **39**, 182–4, **184**,
  185
  dynamism values   39
Constructiones and Aeronautica   253
consultative processes   33–4
consumer tastes   248
containerization   220
contextualization   12
continuum approach   47, 53
control   146
convergence   43
conversational overlap   80
coping strategies   xi, xiii, 116–17, 121
corporate culture   6, 30, 44, 109, 147,
  245
corporate power   217
Costa   220
costs   99, 107
country of origin effect   232
country-specific briefings   109, 278–80
courtesy   81
Cox, T.   142
Cranfield University   145
creole   69, 71
crisis stage   114
criteria for overseas personnel   101
critical incident scenarios   188, 280–2
criticism, direct/indirect   15
cross-cultural learning process   59
cross-cultural traits   267–72
cross-national advertising   138
'crusade'   166
Crystal, David   63, 65
culinary diplomacy   231
cultural assimilator   282–3
cultural awareness development   **101**
cultural convergence   217
cultural determinism   44–5
cultural divergence   218
cultural diplomacy   xiii, 224–5
  evolution of   225–6
  instruments of   **228**, 228–32

smart power 227–8
soft power 226–7
cultural diversity xii, xiii, 13, 48, 142, 145
  definition 191
cultural imperialism 216–17, 237
cultural missions 228–9
cultural pluralism 193–4
cultural profiling
  clusters 263
  definition 259–60
  fault lines 264–5
  key indicators 261–3
  limitations 271–2
  personality factors/cross-cultural traits 265–72
  resources 261
  types of **261**
cultural values 42, 44–5, 52–3, 237, 260, 285–9
culture
  definitions **4**, 4–5, 48
  explicit 5
  invisible 5
  and language 58
  manifestations of 41–2
CULTURE ACTIVE profile 268
culture capsules 282
culture gap 95
culture shock viii, xiii, 59, 105, 111–12
  cycle **122**
  responses to 113–14
  stages of 114–16
  symptoms 113
culture-distance concept 112
culture-rich approach 142
Culturesfrance 229
cyclic time 58
Cyprus 265
Czech Republic 49, 248

Daimler-Benz Aerospace 253
Daniels, J. 247
Davies, G. 142
Davos meetings 209
Dayton Peace Accords 171
decision making 182
deductive/inductive approaches 175
defence stage 59
democracy 227

democratic leadership 130
denial stage 59
Denmark 36, 129
Department for International Development 244
details and suggestions communicators 7–8, 83
Deutsche Welle 231
developing countries 50
Developmental Model of Intercultural Sensitivity 58–9
diasporas 232
difference, accepting 16, 88
diffuse versus specific 50
diplomacy 163, 167
direct/indirect communicators 7
disappearing languages 64–5
DISC profile 267
distance 94
distortion 11
Diverse Europe at Work Project 205
diversity 195–6
diversity team roles 143
Doha Conference 214
Domino's Pizza 256
Douste-Blazy, Philippe 229
Dowling, P. 142
dual career problem 107, 134
Dutch *see* The Netherlands

East Asia 146
Eastern Europeans 33, 43, 66, 73, 242, 248, 276
ECOLE approach 262–3
economic factors 234, 265
economic imperialism 221
The Economist 102, 134
Eddington, Rod 231
educational issues 134, 137, 175, 227, 260, 271
Edwards, T. 137
Egypt 95
electronic communication 81
emails 81–2
emotional/neutral communicators 9, 49–50
emotive words 85
empathy 87–8
English 'borrowings' from other languages 63

English as an international language   72
English language   62–5, 212, 217, 229, 276
   advantages/disadvantages   65–8, 166
   varieties of   69–72
entertainment   26, 234
environmental issues   220, 227, 252, 254
equality   195–7
Equality and Human Rights Commission   197
Esperanto   68
Estuary English   72
ethnicities   43, 196, **196**
ethnocentrism   12–13, 58–9, 195–6
ethnorelativism   59–60
etiquette   164, 168, 180, 182, 260, 262–3
EU Charter of Fundamental Rights 1989   197
Euromanagers   102
Europanto   68–9
European Airbus   253
European Survey on Language Competence   74
European Union (EU)   66–7, 73–4, 132, 163, 166, 196, 205, 209, 212, 233
Europeans   8, 21, 145
Eurostat Yearbook – Education   276
Eurozone   209
   crisis   219
evaluation   85
expatriate failure   104–7, 116
expectations   151, 262
experiential learning   284–5
exploitation   216
extroversion/introversion   267
Exxon Mobil   213
eye contact   91, 146

FACE approach   87
Facebook   81, 209
face-saving   138, 148, 167, 169, 182, 185
face-to-face communication   11, 157
facial expressions   91
facilitation   130, 244, 280, 284
factual information   279
failed states   209
failure   104–7, 116
Fairtrade Foundation   219–20

Falkland Islands   221
false friends/'faux amis'   **67**, 80
family issues   100, 106–7, 119–20, 165
fast/slow communicators   9–10, 79
fear and anxiety   12
Feather, Vic   169
feedback   11–12, 18, 87, 275
Female FTSE 100 Board Report   133
femininity   34–6, 132
feng shui   186
Fernandez-Armesto, Felipe   191
Fiedler, F.   282
FIFA World Cup   232
financial climate   219
Finland/Finns   49, 56, 87
first-order factors   135
Fisher, R.   163, 169
focus   87
follow-up   155
foreign assignment interest groups   **99**
Foreign and Commonwealth Office   228
foreign culture questionnaires   288–9
foreign direct investment (FDI)   243, 245, 251
formal/informal communicators   8–9, 81–2, 150, 165, 174
Forster, E.M.   ix
Fortune Global 500   **213**
Fortuyn, Pim   202
Foseco case study   149
four dimensions (Hofstede)   30–1, **31**
framework approach   269, **270**
France/French   26–8, 35, 52
   communication skills   90–1, 93–5
   cultural diplomacy and nation branding   231–2
   language issues   70
   leadership   131, 133
   multiculturalism and diversity   192, 194, 201–2
   negotiations   168, 175–6
   selection/preparation process   103
   teaching cross-cultural communication   278
   teamworking   144–5, 148, 150–2, 154–5
   technology transfer   253
franchising   256
'franglais'   67, **67**, 68
French language   66–8, 74, 79, 229

Fulbright Scholarship   229
future-oriented cultures   27, 52

G8/G20   211, 213
Gaelic   65
Gamble, A.   192
Gandhi, Mahatma   232
Gap   209
gastronomy   231
Gates, Bill   64
GATT   211
Gazprom   213
gender   34–6, 133–5, 174, 179–80, 183,
    195
General Electric   248
General Motors   220, 248
generalizations   43, 263–4
German language   73–4
Germany/Germans   7, 10, 22, 24–5, 28,
    32–3, 35–6, 49–51, 56, 58
    communication skills   82–3, 94
    cultural diplomacy and nation
        branding   231–2, 235
    language issues   70
    leadership   131
    negotiations   176–8
    teamworking   144, 146, 148–55
gestures   90–1
Gibb, Nick   74
Giddens, A.   208
gift-giving   168, 178, 183, 188
give-and-take relationships   146, 174
glass ceiling   134, 174
global corporations   213–14
global media   227, 231
global village   210
globalization   39, 43, 53, 56, 126, 129,
    157, 208–9
    components   210–11
    cultural convergence   217–18
    cultural divergence   218–19
    definition   209–10
    driving forces   211, 211–12
    future trends   219–21
    as a myth   214
    opposition to   214–17
Global Leadership and Organizational
    Behaviour Effectiveness (GLOBE)
    project   45, 135, 268–9
Globish   69

glocalization   218, **219**
Goethe Institut   228
'Good Tourism' promotion   230
government interventions   251, 254
Graham, J.   175
graphic profiling   268
graphology   103
Greece/Greeks   56, 91, 95, 154
group leadership   54
'guanxi'   186
Guéant, Claude   202
guerilla linguistics   277
Guirdham, M.   115
Gulf states   282–3
Guy, V.   69

Hall, Edward T.   4, 7–8, 10, 20–9, 50
Hall, Mildred R.   4, 10, 20–9, 50
Hall of Birkenhead, Lord   227
Hampden-Turner, C.   47, 274
Han, J.   217
handshakes   92–4
haptics   93
'haragei'   181
harmony   146, 184, 186
Harvard Program on Negotiation   163
Havel, Vaclav   219
head-hunters   138
health and safety   250, 254, 256
Heath, Edward   226
heaven/hell definitions   **15**
Heller, J.   128
Henley Management College   143
Herberger Jr., R.   175
Heseltine, Michael   243
Heywood, A.   192
hierarchies   31–3, 82, 175, 178–9
high/low-context communicators   21–3,
    23, 28–9, **29**, 50, 82, 155, 165, 187
hijab ban   201–2
Hildreth, J.   232, 236
Hill, C. W.   210
Hill, W.   291
Hindi   10, 70, 73, 79
Hinglish   **70**, 179
historical factors   265
Hofstede, Geert   4, 5, 7–8, 20, 25,
    29–46, 49, 53, 111, 114, 132, 184
    research reviewed   42–5
    sixth dimension   40–1

Hofstede, Gert Jan   30, 39
Hokkien   70
Hollywood   234
homogenization   217
Honda   210, 247
honeymoon stage   114
Hong Kong   40, 71
Hong Kong International Airport   246
hospitality   168, 176, 183
hosting events   227
House, Robert   45, 135, 268
HSBC   94, 103, 242
Hu, President   236
hugging   92
human resource management   100,
   107, 134
humanitarian issues   226
humour   4, 82, 148–9, 165–6, 173–4,
   177, 182
Hungary   49, 248
Huntington, Samuel   73, 216, 218, 264
Hurn, B.   102, 133, 149
Hussein, Saddam   92, 166

Iberia   231
IBM   29–30, 44
iceberg analogy   5–6
ice-breakers   88, 148, 165
ignorance   12, 16
IKEA   217
illegal immigration   204
immigration   **198**, 204–5, 232
implicit/explicit culture   5–6
inappropriate locations   86
inappropriate technology   251
inattentiveness   86
INCA Project   136
inclusion   146
India/Indians   27, 39–40, 45
   communication skills   79–80, 91, 94–5
   cultural diplomacy and nation
      branding   231–2
   globalization   213, 215
   language issues   63, 69–70, 72–3
   negotiations   179–80
Indian Oil   213
indigenous minorities   203
individual leadership   54
individualism   31, 33–6, **34**, 41, 49, 53,
   132, 146

Indulgence versus Restraint (IVR)   31,
   40–1, **41**, 44
industrial psychology   29
Industrial Training Research Unit   143
inequalities   31–3, 214–17
inner/outer-directed people   52
insecurity   14, 16
'Inshallah'   188
insiders and outsiders   22
inspirational leadership   131
institutional globalization   210–11
insularity   74
intangible property rights   255
integration   59–60, 119, 194, 201–3
interactive learning   275–6
intercultural skills   205
interdependence   208–9, 220
international aid   227, 230, 244–5,
   245
international communities   99
International Finance Corporation   242
international graduate
   programmes   138
International House, London   108
International Joint Ventures (IJVs)   48,
   141, 245, 251–4
international management   102, **126**,
   126–7, **128**, 128–9
International Monetary Fund
   (IMF)   209, 210, 211, 242
international negotiation
   see negotiation
International Olympic Committee   235,
   238
international organizations   225, 227
internationalization   142
Internet recruitment   138
interpersonal skills   243, 249
interpretations   85
interpreters   148, 152–3, 167–8, 248
interruptions   10, 85, 153, 187
intonation   79
Iran   209
Iraq War   228
Israelis   33
IT developments   212
Italy/Italians   22, 29, 51, 56, 58
   communication skills   90–1, 93–4
   cultural profiling   265
   language issues   70

leadership   131, 133
 negotiations   168
 teamworking   145, 149–50, 154, 156

Jackson Personality Inventory   103
Japan/Japanese   7–8, 15, 17, 22–3, 25–6,
   28, 31, 33–7, 40, 49, 51–2, 56
   communication skills   79–81, 87,
   90–5
   cultural profiling   271
   globalization   212–13, 220
   leadership   132, 134, 138
   negotiations   167–70, 180–3
   teamworking   146, 149–50, 152–4
   technology transfer   247
Japan Post Holdings   213
Jenkins, N.   149
'jikoshokai'   182
Joynt, P.   138

Kachru, Braj   69–70
KcKenna, E.   138
Kennedy, John F.   195
Kentucky Fried Chicken   256
Kenya   171
Kerley, D.   243
Khan, Keith   238
kissing   94
knowledge agreements   246
knowledge transfer   110, 242, 254
   barriers   247, 247–52
Korea/Koreans   22, 36, 56, 95, 231
   North   209
   South   15, 40, 91, 134, 138
KPMG   110, 242
Kraft   210
Krio language   69

Lagarde, Christine   211
'laïcité'   201
laissez-faire leadership   130
language issues   3–4, 58, 78–80, 82–3,
   147, 152–3, 166–7, 181, 197–8,
   248–9, 254, 264–5
   see also individual languages
language teaching/training   73–4, 109,
   148, 189, 229, 248–9, 276–7
Latin America/Americans   9, 25, 31–6,
   41, 49–50, 58, 66, 73, 82, 90–4, 146,
   263

Latin cultures   26, 32, 81, 83, 92, 134,
   151
Latin language   64–5
layers of culture   52–3
layout of meetings   151
laziness   12
leadership   54–5, 154, 260, 262
   across cultures   126–9
   criteria for success   128–9
   cross-cultural implications   133
   definition   125
   development for women   133
   and gender   133–5
   global leadership training   135–7
   styles   129–33
learning outcomes   **284**
learning styles   275–6, 284–5
Lebanon   235
legislation   193, 196–7
less developed countries (LDCs)   214–16,
   219–20, 230, 244
Levin, A.   127
Levitt, Theodore   217
Lewicki, R.   171
Lewis, Richard D.   9–10, 21, 25, 44,
   56–8, 83, 130, 133, 268
Lewis Cultural Model   **57**, 262
licensing   255–6
lifestyle factors   260
linear-active cultures   56, 58, 130
lingua franca   **64**, 64–5, 73, 78–9, 229
linguistics   2–3
listening skills   17, 83–7, 170–1
Livable Rotterdam Party   202
local knowledge   247–8, 253
London Olympics   237–9
London terrorist attacks 2005   192
long-term orientation (LTO)   31, 37–40,
   39, 40, 43–4, 181
loyalty   51
Lufthansa   231

'Ma fi mushkilleh'   188
Major, John   72
Malaysia   49, 100
management
   change   254
   contracts   246
   cultures   32–3
   Euromanagers   102

management – *continued*
    international   102, **126**, 126–7, **128**,
        128–9
    leadership   125
    multi-active/reactive   131
    participative   130
    performance   138, 250
    styles   48
Mandarin Chinese   73
Mandela, Nelson   232
Mandelson, Peter   216
manifestations of culture   41–2, 52
map, culture as   5, **55**, 55–6
Marani, Diego   68
marginal listeners   85
maritime trade   220
market forces   210, 215, 250
markets, access to   212
Marks & Spencer   209
Marshall Plan   228
Martston, William Moulton   267
Marx, E.   129
masculinity/femininity index   34–6, **35**,
        40–1, 132
mass communication   216
Mason, Philip   ix
Master of Business Administration
        (MBA)   134
Mattock, J.   69
Maugham, Somerset   120
McDonald's   6, 210, 256
McKinsey   134
Mead, A.   266
Mead, R.   185
Médecins sans Frontières   209, 230
Mediterranean cultures   9, 22, 49–50,
        93–4
meetings   149–55, **150**, 155, 174, 176,
        187
Mehrabian, Albert   89
'meishi'   182
melting pot approach   174, 200
Mendenhall and Oddou model   103,
        267
mental programming   5, 30
Mexico/Mexicans   50, 95, 201, 231
Microsoft   64
Middle East   82, 91–4, 134, 146, 165,
        265
migration   191

Min Zhu   211
mini dramas   281
minimization stage   59
Minkov, Michael   30, 34, 40, 44
misunderstandings   10–12, 166, 188
Mitchell, George   171
Mitchell, T.   282
Mitford, Nancy   15
Mitterrand, Francois   166
mobile phones   82
mobility lubricants   105
Mole, John   44, 54–6
Mole Map   55
monochronic/polychronic cultures
        23–8, **27**, 51, 56, 247, 281, 283
monoculturalism   195–6
Morgan, C.   275
Morrison, Jim   267
Morton, B.   138
mosaic approach   200, 203–4
motivation   132, 143
MTV   217
Mullins, L.   129–30
multi-active cultures/managers   56, 58,
        131
multicultural executives   133
multicultural teams   110, 126, 141–2
multiculturalism   43–4, 192–3, 237
multiculturalism and diversity, national
        policies
    Australia   203–4
    Belgium   203
    Canada   199–200
    France   201–2
    The Netherlands   202–3
    Switzerland   199
    UK   197–9
    USA   200–1
Multilingual Capital survey   197–8
multinationals   6, 100–1, 103, 209, 214,
        218
Muslim cultures   41, 83, 93, 134, 171,
        186, 188, 201–3
Myanmar   231
Myers-Briggs Type Indicator
        (MBTI)   103, 261, 267

Nakata, Cheryl   44
names and titles   185, 277
'naniwabushi'   182

nation branding   226, **230**, 232–5
Nation Brands Index   234
national cultures   30, 43
national heroes/heroines   42, 232
national identity   198
national policies   197–204
Native Americans   3–4
NATO   228, 231, 233
natural disasters   220
natural resources   221
nature   52
Nebenzahl, D.   235
needs focus   127
negotiating styles   164, 254
   American   174–5
   Arab   186–8
   British   172–4
   Chinese   183–6
   French   175–6
   German   176–8
   Indian   179–80
   Japanese   180–3
   Russian   178–9
negotiation   162–3, **164**, 164–5
   agents and mediators   171
   assessment of cultural influences   **170**
   definitions   163–4
   'face'   169
   fundamentals   **172**
   gifts and hospitality   168
   ice-breakers   164–6
   interpreters/translators   167–8
   language issues   166–7
   negotiating styles   172–88
   skills   110, 170–1
   training   188–9
Nelson, Horatio   232
Nerriere, Jean-Paul   69
The Netherlands/Dutch   4, 7, 22, 25,
   33, 35–6, 58, 131, 133, 149, 153–5
   Biafran War   230
   national policies   202–3
networking   87–8, 150, 187
neutrality   49–50
New Zealand/New Zealanders   9, 25, 33
news coverage   237
Nicks, M.   7–8, 16, 262, 269–71
Nissan   247
Nixon, Richard   226
Nokia   217

non-governmental organizations
   (NGOs)   99, 133, 163, 209, 225,
   227, 230, 239, 242, 256
non-verbal communication (NVC)
   89–95, **90**, **95**
Nordic cultures   33, 35–6, 41
Norman, W. T.   266–7
norms and values   52–3
North America/Americans   7–8, 25,
   32–3, 35, 56, 58, 73, 83, 92, 130
   see also Canada; USA
North American Free Trade Agreement
   (NAFTA)   62, 209, 212
Northern Europeans   9, 33, 90, 94, 133,
   155
Northern Ireland   265
Norway   133
Norwegian Government Training
   Scheme (NORAID)   108
note-taking   86
Nye, Joseph S.   226–8

Obama, Barack   92, 214
Oberg, Kalvero viii, 5–6, 59, 112–13, 122
occupational psychology   102–3
Occupy movement   215
offence   7
office spaces   28
off-shore English   69, 147, 153
olfactics   94–5
Olympic Games   230, 232–3, 235–9
one child policy (China)   40
online recruitment   138
open door policy   25
ordnung   177
organic organizations   54
organization   262
Organization of the Petroleum
   Exporting Countries (OPEC)   62
organizational theory   47, 54–5
Orwell, George   ix
outsourcing   209–10, 214, 216–17
Overseas Assignment Inventory   102

Panama Canal   220
panda diplomacy   226–7
Papua New Guinea   69
paralinguistics   95
paraphrasing   86
Pareto, Wilfredo   269

participation style in meetings   155
participative management   130
particularism   48–9, 53
Pascal, Blaise   15
passive listening   85
past-oriented cultures   27, 51
patois   69
perception   14–18
perception distance   145
perception exercises   290–1, **291**
performance management   138, 250
Perham, Marjorie   ix
'Permanent Sovereignty over Natural
    Resources' UN Resolution   253
Permex   213
personal issues   100
personal relationships   146, 179, 186–7
personal space   28, 94, 151
personality factors   265–72
personality testing   266
Petrobus   213
Phillips, Trevor   198
phonetic/non-phonetic spelling   66, 71
ping-pong/bowling communicators   9–10
Pinker, Steven   3
piracy   220–1
Pizza Hut   256
Plain English Campaign   68
Poland   86, 248
political elements   43, 220, 226, 234,
    265
pollution   217
polychronic cultures *see* monochronic/
    polychronic cultures
popular art   229
population control   40
Portugal   35, 49, 154
posture   92
poverty   215–16
power distance index (PDI)   8, 31–3,
    32, 129, 132, 184
PowerPoint   83
pragmatic approach   173
prayers   187
pre-departure training   108
prejudice   16, 85, 145–6
preliminaries   25
preparation   150, 162, 165, 176
preparatory training   100, 102, 106–8,
    110

presentations   82–4, 277
present-oriented cultures   27, 51
PricewaterhouseCoopers   106, 242
primary leadership dimensions   135
primary team-roles   143
production globalization   210
professional differences   264
progress   250
project definition   249, 251, 254
promotion systems   51
protectionism   214, 217
protest   215
protocol   154, 164, 277
proverbs   **285**, 285–6
proxemics   94
psychological assessments   103–4
public/private spheres   50, 88
punctuality   152, 180
Putin, Vladimir   165

quality control   250, 254, 256
questions, ability to ask   88
quotas for minorities/women   133,
    194–5

race issues   265
RADAR profile   269–71
Radebaugh, L.   247
rationalism   54, 175
Ravitch, D.   192, 194
reactive cultures/managers   56–7, 131
Received Pronunciation   72
receiving   85
recession   204
recognition of difference   142
recovery stage   114–15
recruitment   137, 260, 265–6
Rees, C.   137
reflecting   87, 89
refusals   180, 185
regeneration   237
regional differences   264
regionalization   214
relationship orientations   48–51
relationship with nature   52
relationship with time   51
relativism   42
religious sensitivity   80, 93, 152, 187–8,
    201, 247, 260, 265
remembering   85

repatriation 117–22
repeating 86
Research and Development 253
resistance to change 250–1
respect 82
responding 85
responsibility 16, 138
restraint 40–1
reverse culture shock 117–19
reversion 119
Richard Lewis Communications 261,
 268
Rieth, Lord 231
right response/right message 10
'ringi-sho' 271
risk 36–7, 175, 212, 245–6, 253
Ritterband, David 238
rituals 42, 279
role playing 283–5, **284**
Ronen, S. 263
Roosevelt, Theodore 200
Rosneft 254
Rugman, A. 129, 209, 214, 217
Russia/Russians 42, 72, 93, 131, 165,
 171, 178–9, 221, 229, 251, 253–4
Russian language 73

Saatchi & Saatchi 238
Sainsbury's 209
salad bowl approach 194
Sapir, Edward 3
Sapir-Whorf Hypothesis 3
Sarkozy, Nicolas 202
Saudi Arabia 246
Saussure, Ferdinand de 2
Scandinavian countries 7, 22, 25, 29,
 32–3, 35, 50, 83
Schein, Edgar 125
Schengen Agreement 197
Schneider, S. 102, 127–8, 130, 278
Schutz, W. 146
science 230
Scott, J. 169, 185
screening methods 102–4
secularism 201
security concerns 157, 252
selection process 100, 102–4, 137–8,
 143, 145, 252, 265, 271
selective listening 85
self-awareness training 156

Self-Perception Inventory Analysis 143
semiotics 2–3
seniority 82, 154, 164, 168, 181–2, 247
Shanghai Expo 2010 230, 244
shared experiences 164–5, 187
Shaw, George Bernard 71
Shell 6, 103, 105–6, 213
 Expatriate Survey 105
Shenkar, O. 263
short-term orientation (STO) 31,
 37–40, **39**, 44
Shuler, R. 142
Sierra Leone 69
signposting, signalling, summarizing
 approach 83–4
silence 79–80, 87, 95, 152, 170, 181,
 187
simulation 283–5, **284**
Singapore 69, 232
Singlish 70–1
Sinopec Group 213
situational leadership 127–8
skills transfer 110, 242, **247**, 247–52
Skoda/Volkswagen 248
Skype 82
slogans (tourism) **230**
small talk 25, 165, 185
smart power 227–8
'smart sanctions' 166
smells 94–5
smiling 91
Snyder, D.P. 210
social media 82
social responsibility 6
socialization 4
socializing 155, 174, 187
soft power 216, 226–7, 236
Somalia 221
Sony 217
South Africa 231–2
Southeast Asians 9, 39, 41, 152, 171
Southern Europeans 25, 49, 146
Soviet Union 226
space 28–9
Spain/Spanish 50, 70, 79, 90, 94, 129,
 131, 133, 150, 154, 231, 235, 253
Spanish language 10, 72–3, 79
Speak Good English Movement 70
specialization 175
specific/diffuse cultures 50

speed of speech   79
spoken language   78–80, 277–8
Spony, Gilles   268
Spony Profiling Model   268
sport   230, 232–9
Standard English   72
STAR approach   16–17, **17**
Starbucks   220
State Grid   213
status   50–1
Stelzer, Cita   87
stereotypes exercise   289–90
stereotyping   13–14, 145–6, 195, 263–4
Stiglitz, Joseph   215–16
Stockman, N.   184
Storti, C.   116, 121
Strait of Hormuz   220
Strauss-Kahn, Dominique   211
stress in speech   79
stress of change   112
stressors   **112**, 112–13
Strine   **71**
structured approach   177
subjective well-being   41
subsidies   220
Suez Canal   220
Sullivan, D.   247
summarizing   147
survey approaches   44, 53
swearing   80
Swedes   32, 56, 131, 133, 144, 231
Switzerland/Swiss   24, 56, 152, 199–200
symbiotic language-thought   4
symbols   41
symptoms of culture shock   113
synergy   147, 200, 251, 253
systematic organizations   54
Szaly, L.   166

taboo subjects   88, 165, 265
Taiwan/Taiwanese   40, 227
Taoism   184–5
Tata Group   213
tax evasion   217
teaching cultural awareness   274
  case studies   280
  country-specific briefings   278–80
  critical incident scenarios   280–2
  cultural assimilator   282–3
  cultural values   285–9

culture capsules   282
  foreign culture questionnaires   288–9
  methodology   275–6
  perception exercises   290–1, **291**
  presentations   277–8
  proverbs   285–6
  simulation and role playing   283–5, **284**
  stereotypes exercise   289–90
  true/false exercises   286
team building   141
  cultural synergy   147
  main issues   147–9
  meetings   149–55
  requirement and challenge   142–3
  roles   143–5, **144**
  training   149
  training methodology   156, 275
  trust   145–6
technology   7, 44, 81–2, 150, 157, 178, 212, 227, 230, 248
  inappropriate   251–2
technology transfer   241–3, **255**, 256–7
  barriers   **247**, 247–52
  case study   254–5
  knowledge agreements   246
  management contracts   246–7
  risk   245–6
  turnkey arrangements   246
temporal elements   23–8, 51–2, 57–8, 247, 281, 283
territoriality   28–9
terrorism   157, 192, 219–21
texting   82
Thailand/Thais   58, 91–2, 94, 169
Thatcher, Margaret   166, 231
thought and language   3–4
Tibet   265
The Times   227
timing in speech   79–80
timing of meetings   152
TNK-BP   253–4
Toffler, Alvin   viii
Tomalin, B.   7–8, 16, 83, 157–8, 262, 269–71
tonal languages   277
Torbiorn, I.   115
Toubon, Jacques   67
touching   93
tourism   230, 235

Toyota   6, 213, 247
trade barriers decline   212
trade in goods and services   241–2
trade missions   243–4
trade unions   247
Trades Union Congress   169
training   254, 260, 271
  business-specific   110–11
  citizenship   194, 198–204
  cognitive   279
  courses   109–10, 137, 143
  language   73–4, 109, 148, 189, 229,
    248–9, 276–7
  leadership   135–7
  methodology   111, 156, 275
  negotiation   188–9
  preparatory   100, 102, 106–8, 110
  requirements   249
  self-awareness   156
  team building   149, 156
transfer of skills and knowledge   242
transformational leadership   131
translators   148, 167–8
Triandis, H.   282
Trompenaars, Fons   4, 7, 25, 44, 47–53,
  181, 274
true/false exercises   286
trust   34, 145–6, 165
Tung, R.   105, 118, 129
Turner, Charles Hampden   47
turnkey arrangements   246
turn-taking   80
Twin Towers attack (9/11)   157
Twitter   81–2, 209

UK/British   9–10, 17, 22–5, 27–9, 32–4,
  37, 49, 52, 58
  communication skills   81–2, 90–1, 93–5
  cultural diplomacy and nation
    branding   230, 232, 235, 237–9
  cultural profiling   269
  globalization   221
  leadership   131, 133
  multiculturalism and diversity   192,
    194–9, 204
  negotiations   164, 172–4
  selection/preparation process   103
  teamworking   145, 148–51, 153–6
  technology transfer   242–3, 246–8,
    253–5

UN Charter   163
uncertainty avoidance index (UAI)
  36–7, **37**, 39, 53, 132, 175
unemployment   250
UN Resolution: Permanent Sovereignty
  over National Resources   253
Uniting Europe through Cultures
  (UNEC) project   88
universal grammar   3
universalism   48–9, 53
updating of analyses   42–3
urbanization   216
Ury. W.   163, 169
USA/Americans   9–10, 21–2, 27–8, 31,
  33, 49–52
  communication skills   81, 94–5
  cultural diplomacy and nation
    branding   228, 230, 232
  cultural profiling   265, 269
  globalization   213–14, 220
  language issues   69, 71, 73
  leadership   132
  multiculturalism and diversity   194–5,
    200–1
  negotiations   165–6, 171, 174–5
  teamworking   144, 146, 148–9, 151,
    154–5
  technology transfer   246

value judgments   14, 16–17
value systems   4, 30, 248
values   42, 44–5, 52–3, 237, 260, 285–9
verbal communication   78–80
Victor, D.   167
virtual meetings   157–8
Voice of America   231
volume   79
Von Clausewitz, Carl   226

Wal-Mart   210, 213
Watson, C.   193
Welch, D.   142
Welsh   65
Western Europe   130, 133, 146, 153–4,
  214
Wharton Business School   47
what/why – why/what
  communicators   8
white Australia policy   203
Whorf, Benjamin-Lee   3

Wild, J.   217
Wild, K.   217
wine production   231
Women in Diplomatic Service
    Group   135
Women's Global Leadership
    Forum   134–5
Women's Matters Global Survey   134
word-association   267
work-life balance   50
World Bank   211, 215, 242

World Trade Organization (WTO)   163,
    209, 210, 211, 251
written communications   22, 80–1, 173
'wu lun'   184

Xinhua News Agency   237

Yao Ming   237
Yin, R.   280
'young lady/old lady' image   291
youth   237

Printed and bound in Great Britain by
CPI Antony Rowe, Chippenham and Eastbourne